HISTORY *of* CURTIS LAND
1635–1683

WITH

EXCERPT ON FRANCIS LAND

Compiled by

Betty Jewell Durbin Carson

DAR Member #832584

HERITAGE BOOKS

2014

HERITAGE BOOKS
AN IMPRINT OF HERITAGE BOOKS, INC.

Books, CDs, and more—Worldwide

For our listing of thousands of titles see our website
at
www.HeritageBooks.com

Published 2014 by
HERITAGE BOOKS, INC.
Publishing Division
5810 Ruatan Street
Berwyn Heights, Md. 20740

Heritage Books by the author:

The Brice Family Who Settled in Fairfield County, South Carolina, about 1785 and Related Families

Durbin and Logsdon Genealogy with Related Families, 1626–1991

The Durbin and Logsdon Genealogy with Related Families, 1626–1991, Volume 2

Durbin and Logsdon Genealogy with Related Families, 1626–1994

Durbin and Logsdon Genealogy with Related Families, 1626–1998

Durbin-Logsdon Genealogy and Related Families from Maryland to Kentucky, Volumes 1–2

CD: The Durbin and Logsdon Genealogy with Related Families, 1626–2000, 3rd Revised Edition

History of Curtis Land, 1635–1683; with Excerpt on Francis Land

Our Ewing Heritage, with Related Families, Part One and Two, Revised Edition
Betty Jewell Durbin Carson and Doris M. Durbin Wooley

CD: Our Ewing Heritage, with Related Families, Revised Edition
Betty Jewell Durbin Carson and Doris M. Durbin Wooley

International Standard Book Numbers
Paperbound: 978-0-7884-5580-3
Clothbound: 978-0-7884-6058-6

LAND SURNAME

The surname of **LAND** was a locational name "the dweller at the launde" from residence to beside an open wood. The name also is spelled LAWN, LANDT, Van den LAND, LANDH, LANDELL, LE LAND, and LANDBERG, to name but a few.

Surnames before the Norman Conquest of 1066 were rare in England having been brought by the Normans when William the Conqueror invaded the shores. The practice spread to Scotland and Ireland by the 12th century, and in Wales they appeared as late as the 16th century.

Most surnames can be traced to one of four sources: location at from the occupation of the original bearer, nicknames or simply font names based on the first name of the parent being given as the second or surname to their child.

Early records of the name mention William de la Lande, who was recorded in the year 1273 in County Oxford. William atte Lande of Yorkshire, was listed in the Yorkshire Poll Tax of 1379. Edward Lande was documented in County Lancaster in the year 1400, and Thomas Land appears in Lancashire in 1453. Later instance of the name mention Richard Land and Elizabeth Fuller who were married at St. James, Clerkenwelt London in the year 1570. Hugh Jeanes and Susan Land were married at St. Peters, Cornhilt London in 1651.

Most of the European surnames in countries such as England, Scotland, and France were formed in the 13th and 14th centuries. The process had started somewhat earlier and had continued in some places into the 19th century, but the norm is that in the 10th and 11th centuries, people did not have surnames, whereas by the 15th century, most of the population had acquired one. The associated arms are recorded in Sir Bernard Burkes *General Armory, Ulster King of Arms in 1884.*

Descendants of Curtis Land: 1635-1683

Generation No. 1

1. CURTIS[1] LAND was born 1635 in Devon County, England, and died April 20, 1683 in Charles City, Charles City Co., Virginia. He married MARY HODGES 1662. She was born 1638. He was a son of William Land, mother unknown. There was a William Curtis Land b. 1600 in Middlesex, England.

Children of CURTIS LAND and MARY HODGES are:
i. WILLIAM[2] LAND, b. Abt. 1665.
2. ii. CURTIS LAND, b. 1668, Charles City, VA; d. March 18, 1727/28, Surrey Co. VA.

Generation No. 2

2. CURTIS[2] LAND *(CURTIS[1])*[1,2,3] was born 1668 in Charles City, VA[4,5], and died March 18, 1727/28 in Surrey Co. VA[6,7]. He married (1) MARY WILLIAMSON[8] WFT Est. 1678-1720[8]. She was born WFT Est. 1660-1683[8], and died WFT Est. 1705-1771[8].
Notes for CURTIS LAND:
1. Curtis1 Land was born Abt. 1635 in England - Possibly Devon County, and died April 20, 1683 in Charles City, VA. He married Mary Hodges Abt. 1662. She was born Abt. 1638.
Children of Curtis Land and Mary Hodges are:
+2 i. William2 Land, born Abt. 1665 in Charles City, VA; died Aft. 1713 in Surrey Co ., VA.
+ 3 ii. Curtis Land, born Abt. 1668 in Charles City, VA; died March 18, 1727/28 in Surry Co., VA.
3. Curtis2 Land (Curtis1) was born Abt. 1668 in Charles City, VA, and died March 18, 1727/28 in Surrey Co., VA. He married Mary Williamson Abt. 1691. She was born Abt. 1670, and died September 11, 1740.
Children of Curtis Land and Mary Williamson are:
+ 3 i. John3 Land, born Abt. 1690; died Aft. December 15, 1729 in Albemarle Co. VA.
ii. Rebecka Land, born Abt. 1695; died Aft. December 15, 1729.
+4 iii. Curtis Land, born 1702; died May 15, 1783 in Sussex, VA.
+5 iv. William Land, born Abt. 1693; died Aft. November 15, 1781.
v. Robert Land, born Abt. 1700; died Abt. 1740 in Albemarle Co., VA.
vi. Thomas Land, born 1705; died September 25, 1740 in Albemarle Co., VA.
(Research): Curtis Land of Albemarle Parish Virginia
1660: CURTIS LAND sworn in as Constable Hog Island?
1667: CURTIS LAND patented land near Williamsburg. He later settled in Surry Co., across the James River.
CHARLES CITY COUNTY VIRGINIA 1676-1679, pp 17, 18, 30, 73.
ORDER BK p 207: ordered that MARMADUKE BROWN pay CURTIS LAND for 3 days as witness.
ORDER BK p 208: 14 SEP 1677: MAJOR JNO STITH & CURTIS LAND were ordered to Value the boat of MR. RICH MOSBY which had been damaged. Boat Valued at 300 lbs tobacco. ALLEN JENKINS, aged about 40 yrs, explained the extent of damage.
ORDER BK p 246: CURTIS LAND asks guardianship of the orphans of JOHN BURNETT, granted. The overseers of BURNETT'S will and MR. RICH MOSLEY are ordered to give CURTIS LAND the orphan s estate and he to give account with security.
CURTIS LAND presents ANN BURNETT to the court and is by the court and consent of said orphan apprenticed to LAND.
SURRY CO: 20 MAR 1 711/20 JUN 1715 (BK6 p64) WILLIAM HUNT-Will Wit: CURTIS LAND
SURRY CO: 17 M AY 1721 (BK 7)EDWARD BRADDY, Est signed by CURTIS LAND
SURRY CO WILLS & ADM (1671-1750) Davis pg 109
CURTIS LAND - Will 15 DEC 1729/18 MAR 1729, Wife MARY (Executor)
sons:
I. CURTIS LAND - plantation 150 acres I bought from ROBERT INMAN
II. THOMAS LAND - plantation I now live on

III. WILLIAM LAND - mare and colt
IV. JOHN LAND - 2 horses, 2 cows
V. ROBERT LAND - 2 horses, 2 cows
dtr:
VI. REBECKAH LAND - 2 horses, 2 cows
(Research): Curtis Land of Albemarle Parish Virginia

Children of CURTIS LAND and MARY WILLIAMSON are:

3. i. JOHN[3] LAND, b. Abt. 1690; d. Aft. December 15, 1729, Albemarle County, Virginia.
ii. REBECCAH LAND[15], b. 1695[15].
4. iii. CURTIS[3] LAND[24], b. 1702[24]; d. May 15, 1783, Sussex, Virginia, USA[24]; m. PRISCILLA BIRD[24], 1732[24]; b. 1716[24]; d. 1771, Sussex, Virginia, USA[24].
5. iv. WILLIAM[3] LAND, b. 1693; d. Aft. November 15, 1781.
v. ROBERT LAND[14], b. Abt. 1700[14]; d. Abt. 1740, Albemarle County, Virginia[14].
. vi. THOMAS LAND[18,19], b. 1705[20,21]; d. September 25, 1740, Albemarle County, Virginia[22].

Generation No. 3

3. JOHN[3] LAND *(CURTIS[2], CURTIS[1])*[26] was born Abt. 1690[26], and died Aft. December 15, 1729 in Albemarle County, Virginia[26]. He married MRS. JOHN LAND UNKNOWN[26].

Child of JOHN LAND and MRS. UNKNOWN is:

9. i. THOMAS[4] LAND, b. Abt. 1712, Orange County, Virginia; d. October 17, 1788, Chester County, South Carolina.

4. CURTIS[3] LAND *(CURTIS[2], CURTIS[1])*[26] was born 1702[26], and died May 15, 1783 in Sussex, Virginia[26]. He married PRISCILLA BIRD[26] Abt. 1732 in Sussex, Virginia[26]. She was born 1716, and died Aft. 1771 in Sussex Co VA.

Notes for CURTIS LAND:
1783 Will of Curtis Land Sussex Co, VA Will Book D page 153
In the name of God Amen. I Curtis Land the Elder of Sussex County being sick and weak but of a sound and perfect mind and memory thanks be to Almighty God for the same knowing the certainty of Death and the uncertainty of the time thereof do make constitute and appoint this to be my last will and testament in manner and form following.
Item I give and bequeath unto my son Bird Land one hundred acres of land by estimation be the same more or less it being the land he now lives on with all the appurtances thereunto belonging or in any wise appertaining and all other things that I have presented him with to him and his heirs and assigns forever.
Item I give and bequeath unto my son Curtis Land one hundred acres of land it being the land I now live on with all the appurtenances thereunto belonging or in any wise appertaining to him the said Curtis Land and his heirs and assigns forever.
Item I give and bequeath unto my son Curtis Land one gray horse saddle and bridle that he now possesseth one feather bed and furniture thereunto belonging it being the bed he now lieth on three cows and my gun to him his heirs and assigns forever.
Item I give and bequeath unto my son William Land one bay horse saddle and bridle one feather bed and furniture thereunto belonging one cow and one blew sow to him his heirs and assigns forever.
Item I give and bequeath unto my son Charles Land one cow and one spotted sow and piggs one feather bed and furniture thereunto belonging.
Item I give and bequeath unto my daughter Elizabeth Joiner five shillings to her and her heirs forever.
Item I give and bequeath unto my daughter Rebeckah Champbells five shillings to her and her heirs and assigns forever.
Item I give and bequeath unto my daughter Winnefred Houchings five shillings to her and her heirs forever.
Item I give and bequeath unto my daughter Mildred Land one feather bed and furniture thereunto belonging it being the bed that is called her own to her and her heirs and assigns forever.
Item I give and bequeath unto my daughter Priscilla Land five shillings to her and her heirs and assigns forever.
Item I give and bequeath unto my daugher Ruth Land five shillings to her and her heirs forever.

Item My will is that my son Charles Land should go for himself at the age of eighteen years and have his estate delivered to him at that age and to live with his brother Curtis Land.
Item My will is that my wife Priscilla Land should keep my hole estate during her life time or widdowhood.
Item I give and bequeath unto my three sons to with Curtis Land William Land and Charles Land all the rest and remainder of my estate to be equally divided between my three sons Viz Curtis Land William Land and Charles Land to them their heirs and assigns forever.
Item My will is that my estate should be inventoried but not appraised.
Item I nominate and appoint my son Curtis Land my hole and sole Executor of this my last will and testament revoking and disanulling and making voice all former wills heretofore made by me.
As witness whereof I have hereunto set my hand and affixed my seal this seventeenth day of November 1771.
Curtis Land (Seal)
Witnesses
Joseph Penn?
Webb Land (X his mark)
Henry Freeman, Junr
At a court held for Sussex County the 15th day of May 1783 the last will and testament of Curtis Land decd was exhibited in court by Curtis Land the Executor therein named proved by the oaths of Webb Land and Henry Freeman Junr witnesses thereto and ordered to be recorded and on the motion of the said Executor who made oath thereto according to law and with William Loften? his security entered into and acknowledged their bond in the penalty of five hundred pounds conditioned as the law directs Certificate is granted him for obtaining a probate thereof in due.

Children of CURTIS LAND and PRISCILLA BIRD are:

10. i. CURTIS[4] LAND, b. December 01, 1733, Sussex, Virginia; d. December 01, 1817, Sussex, Virginia.
11. ii. ELIZABETH LAND, b. 1735; d. Aft. 1771.
12. iii. BIRD[4] LAND[27], b. 1737[27]; d. WFT Est. 1769-1828[27]; m. REBEKAH ??[27], WFT Est. 1757-1787[27]; b. Abt. 1744[27]; d. WFT Est. 1769-1838[27].
13. iv. REBECCA LAND, b. February 02, 1738/39, Albemarle County, Virginia; d. Aft. 1771.
14. v. WINIFRED LAND, b. February 28, 1740/41, Albemarle, Virginia; d. Aft. 1771.
vi. MILDRED LAND[26], b. August 10, 1747, Albemarle, Virginia[26]; d. Aft. 1771[26].
vii. WILLIAM LAND[26], b. November 02, 1749, Albemarle County, Virginia[26]; d. Aft. 1810, Sussex, Virginia[26]; m. ELIZABETH ARMSTRONG[26], December 23, 1772[26]; b. Bef. 1765[26].
viii. PRISCILLA LAND[26], b. March 03, 1750/51, Albemarle County, Virginia[26]; d. Aft. 1796[26]; m. EDWARD KAYS[26], December 14, 1796, Princess Anne County, Virginia[26].
ix. RUTH LAND[26], b. February 02, 1755, Albemarle County, Virginia[26]; d. Aft. 1787, Sussex, Virginia[26]; m. CARY MAGEE[26], December 20, 1787, Sussex, Virginia[26].
15. x. CHARLES LAND, b. March 02, 1760, Albemarle County, Virginia; d. May 23, 1838, Edgecombe County, North Carolina.

Curtis Land by 1708 VA- 15 May 1783 Sussex Co VA md by ? Priscilla (d aft 17 71 Sussex Co VA).
SUSSEX CO: 17 Nov 1771/15 May 1783. Bk D p 153. Will of Curtis Land, Sr.
Wife: Priscilla
Will named sons: Bird, Curtis, William, Charles.
Dau's: Elizabeth Joiner, Rebecca Campbell, Winifred Hutchins, Mely (Mily?) Land, Priscilla Land, Ruth Land.
Wit: Joseph Renn, Webb Land, Henry Free man
Jr. Exec: son Curtis Land

5. WILLIAM[3] LAND *(CURTIS[2], CURTIS[1])*[28,29] was born 1693[29], and died Aft. November 15, 1781[30]. He married ELIZABETH L. LEWIS[30] Abt. 1718 in Southampton, Virginia[30]. She was born Bet. 1707 - 1742.

Children of WILLIAM LAND and ELIZABETH LEWIS are:

16. i. JOHN[4] LAND, b. 1718; d. January 19, 1781, Surry County, Virginia.
17. ii. ROBERT LAND, b. 1720; d. Bef. February 11, 1797, Sussex, Virginia.
18. iii. WILLIAM LAND, b. 1722.
19. iv. JOHN LAND, b. 1730.
20. ii. BIRD LAND, b. Bef. 1739, Sussex Co VA; d. August 22, 1794, Southampton Co VA.
21. iii. CHARLES LAND, b. March 02, 1760, Albemarle Co, VA.

8. CURTIS[3] LAND *(CURTIS[2], CURTIS[1])*[35] was born December 01, 1702 in VA[35], and died May 15, 1783 in Sussex Co VA[35]. He married PRISCILLA BIRD[35] 1732 in Sussex Co VA[35]. She was born 1716[35], and died Aft. 1771 in Sussex Co VA[35].

Children of CURTIS LAND and PRISCILLA BIRD are:
23. i. CURTIS[4] LAND, b. December 01, 1733, Sussex, VA.
24. ii. BIRD LAND, b. Bef. 1739, Sussex Co VA; d. August 22, 1794, Southampton Co VA.
25. iii. CHARLES LAND, b. March 02, 1760, Albemarle Co, VA.

Generation No. 4

9. THOMAS[4] LAND *(JOHN[3], CURTIS[2], CURTIS[1])*[36] was born Abt. 1712 in Orange County, Virginia[36], and died October 17, 1788 in Chester County, South Carolina[36]. He married ELEANOR MCCLANAHAN[36] Abt. 1732 in Augusta County, Virginia[36]. She was born Abt. 1715 in Augusta County, Virginia[36].

Notes for THOMAS LAND:
Some researchers report that this Thomas Land was the son of Robert Land, son of Edward Land, who is named in his father's will. But he **did not** name any sons Renatus, Robert, or Edward which would be expected.
Abstract of Renatus Land's will 1 October 1680:
Lynn Haven Parish, Lower Norfold County, Virginia
"RENATRIS LAND of Linhaven pish, Lower Norfolk County in Virginia . . .
Book 4f, 96: dated 1 Oct 1680. Proved 10 May 1681 by Geo. Walker.
. . . to my eldest sonne Ronatus Land ye rest of my plantation, that Is now In the occupation of David Whitford att ye age of Nineteene years . . . a gould ring wth a signe of a deaths head upon it
. . . unto my second sone Edward Land and my third son Robt Land, my plantation I now live upon . . . a payre of silver Cod piste buttons, and a sett of Silver buttons for shirt collar & wrist . . .
. . . unto my sonne Robert Land . . . a Silver hatt band . . .
. . . unto my Eldest daughter Elizabeth Land . . . a Small diamond ring . . .
. . . unto my daughter Ann Land . . . .
. . . unto my wife frances land . . .
. . . my sonne Renatris Land, and my brother Francis Land my Execuetors . . .
witnesses Wm Webb
Geo. Walker
Renatres Land and Seale

Abstract of the will of Renatus Land to his wife Frances and children Renatus, Edward, Robert, Elizabeth, and Ann as it appears in the book: Brief Abstract of Lower Norfolk County Wills, 1637-1710, Charles Fleming McIntosh, Dames of America 1914.

Children of THOMAS LAND and ELEANOR MCCLANAHAN are:
i. WILLIAM HENRY[5] LAND[36], b. Abt. 1730, Augusta County, Virginia[36].
26. ii. EPHRAIM LAND, b. Abt. 1732, Orange County, Virginia; d. 1836, Stokes County, Virginia.
27. iii. THOMAS LAND, b. Abt. 1734, Augusta, Virginia; d. 1832, Wilkes County, North Carolina.
28. iv. JOHN LAND, b. Abt. 1734, Orange County, Virginia; d. March 23, 1781, Chester County, South Carolina.

10. CURTIS[4] LAND *(CURTIS[3], CURTIS[2], CURTIS[1])*[36] was born December 01, 1733 in Sussex, Virginia[36], and died December 01, 1817 in Sussex, Virginia[36]. He married MRS. CURTIS LAND UNKNOWN[36].

Child of CURTIS LAND and MRS. UNKNOWN is:
i. JOHN[5] LAND[36], b. Bet. 1760 - 1789; d. Aft. December 01, 1817, Wilkes County, North Carolina[36].

11. ELIZABETH[4] LAND *(CURTIS[3], CURTIS[2], CURTIS[1])*[36] was born 1735[36], and died Aft. 1771[36]. She married JOHN JOINER[36].

Children of ELIZABETH LAND and JOHN JOINER are:
- i. JOHN[5] JOINER[36], d. Aft. February 22, 1821, Laurens, Georgia[36].
- ii. CURTIS JOINER[36], d. Aft. February 22, 1821, Laurens, Georgia[36].
- iii. ELIZABETH JOINER[36], m. UNKNOWN LANGLEY[36].

12. BIRD[4] LAND *(CURTIS[3], CURTIS[2], CURTIS[1])* [36]was born 1737 [36], and died December 11, 1794 in South Hampton, Virginia[36]. He married REBEKAH LEWELLIN[37,38] Abt. 1760[38]. She was born Abt. 1744 [38]. Buried South Hampton, Virginia.

Children of BIRD LAND and REBEKAH LEWELLIN are:
- i. LUCAS[5] LAND[40], b. September 21, 1761, Albemarle County, Virginia[40]; d. Bef. 1787[40].
- ii. LEWELLEN LAND[40], b. October 21, 1767, Albemarle County, Virginia[40]; d. Aft. 1810, Sussex, Virginia[40]; m. MARY JONES[40], April 30, 1792, Sussex, Virginia[40]; b. 1765[40].
- iii. LUCRETIA LAND[40], b. December 23, 1770, Albemarle,Virginia[40]; d. Aft. 1794[40]; m. BRITTON BOWERS[40].

13. REBECCA[4] LAND *(CURTIS[3], CURTIS[2], CURTIS[1])* [40]was born February 02, 1738/39 in Albemarle County, Virginia [40], and died Aft. 1771[40]. She married BERSHEBA CAMPBELL [40].

Child of REBECCA LAND and BERSHEBA CAMPBELL is:
- i. BERSHEBA[5] CAMPBELL[40], d July 02, 1821, Washington, North Carolina[40]; m. UNKNOWN MILLER[40].

14. WINIFRED[4] LAND *(CURTIS[3], CURTIS[2], CURTIS[1])* [40]was born February 28, 1740/41 in Albemarle, Virginia [40], and died Aft. 1771[40]. She married LEWIS HUTCHENS [40] Abt. 1762 [40].

Children of WINIFRED LAND and LEWIS HUTCHENS are:
- i. PRESSILLIAN[5] HUTCHENS[40], b. June 02, 1763[40].
- ii. BETTY HUTCHENS[40], b. February 24, 1765[40].
- iii. ROBERT HUTCHENS[40], b. April 29, 1769[40].

15. CHARLES[4] LAND *(CURTIS[3], CURTIS[2], CURTIS[1])*[40,41] was born March 02, 1760 in Albemarle County, Virginia [42], and died May 23, 1838 in Edgecombe County, North Carolina[42]. He married (1) MARY ANN COOPER[42] November 08, 1786 in Southampton, Virginia[42]. She was born 1773[43], and died 1838 in Edgecombe, North Carolina, USA[43].

Children of CHARLES LAND and MARY COOPER are:

29. i. HENRY[5] LAND, b. 1788, Virginia.
30. ii. CHARLES LAND, b. 1794, North Carolina; d. Aft. 1860, Edgecombe County, North Carolina.
    iii. JOHN LAND[44], b. 1798, Edgecombe County, North Carolina[44]; m. REBECCA TAYLOR[44], May 15, 1825[44]; b. 1800, North Carolina[44].
31. iv. JESSE LAND, b. 1803; d. Aft. 1850, Triggs County, Georgia.
    v. FANNIE LAND[44], b. Abt. 1805[44]; m. MATTHEW WHITEHEAD[44].
32. vi. SUSAN (SOPHY) LAND, b. Abt. 1809.

Child of CHARLES LAND and MARY COOPER is:
- vii. CHARLES[5] LAND[45], b. 1794[43]; d. 1860, Edgecombe, North Carolina, USA[45]; m. PATSY DAWS[46,47,48], November 06, 1822[49]; b. Abt. 1790[50]; d. 1850, Edgecombe, North Carolina, USA[51,52].

16. JOHN[4] LAND *(WILLIAM[3], CURTIS[2], CURTIS[1])* [53]was born 1718 [53], and died January 19, 1781 in Surry County, Virginia[53]. He married (1) JANE H. L. PENNINGTON [53] May 24, 1752 [53]. He married (2) SARAH HOLT RAWLINGS [53] Aft. March 16, 1769[53].

Child of JOHN LAND and JANE PENNINGTON is:
- i. CHARLOTTE[5] LAND[53], b. May 24, 1752[53].

17. ROBERT[4] LAND *(WILLIAM[3], CURTIS[2], CURTIS[1])* [53]was born 1720 [53], and died Bef. February 11, 1797 in Sussex, Virginia[53]. He married (1) AGNES UNKNOWN [53]. She was born December 16, 1763 in Lunenburg, Virginia [53]. He married (2) MARY ANNE WEBB CARTER[53] 1741 in Isle of Wright, Virginia[53]. She was born 1723[53].

Children of ROBERT LAND and MARY CARTER are:

i. SUSANNA (SUCKEY)[5] LAND[53], b. June 20, 1742, Albemarle County, Virginia[53].
33. ii. JOHN LAND, b. Abt. February 19, 1743/44, Albemarle County, Virginia; d. Abt. 1814, Prince Edward Co., Virginia.
iii. ROBERT LAND[53], b. November 13, 1747, Albemarle County, Virginia[53]; d. November 02, 1797, Virginia; m. MARTHA CHAPPELL, April 16, 1786, Virginia; b. Bet. 1743 - 1769; d. Bet. 1791 - 1857.
iv. WEBB LAND[53], b. Abt. March 04, 1748/49, Albemarle County, Virginia[53].
v. MARY LAND[53], b. July 14, 1752, Albemarle County, Virginia[53].
vi. BETTY LAND[53], b. October 26, 1755, Albemarle County, Virginia[53].
vii. BENJAMIN LAND[53], b. June 21, 1758, Albemarle County, Virginia[53].
viii. NATHANIEL LAND[53], b. September 07, 1760, Albemarle County, Virginia[53].
ix. LEVINA LAND[53], b. December 15, 1767, Albemarle County, Virginia[53].
x. ISHAM LAND[53], b. November 13, 1771, Albemarle County, Virginia[53].

18. WILLIAM[4] LAND *(WILLIAM[3], CURTIS[2], CURTIS[1])*[53] was born 1722[53]. He married ELIZABETH VAUGHN [53]Bef. 1756[53].

Child of WILLIAM LAND and ELIZABETH VAUGHN is:

i. HENRY[5] LAND[53], b. 1735[53].

19. JOHN[4] LAND *(WILLIAM[3], CURTIS[2], CURTIS[1])* [53]was born 1730 [53]. He married (1) ELIZABETH ELLIDGE [53]. She was born Abt. 1735[53]. He married (2) ELIZABETH ELLIDGE.

Notes for ELIZABETH ELLIDGE:
5/10/1764: Lee, John, Memorial for 150 acres on Rocky Creek, Craven County, summarizing a chain of title to a grant to Isaac Ellidge of Dec. 20, 1762. Names indexed: Ellidge, Ann; Ellidge, Isaac; Lee, John.

1776c. or later: Ellidge, Joseph, account audited (File No. 2198) of claims growing out of the American Revolution.

12/20/1837: List of managers of elections and polls for Laurens and Chesterfield Districts, and St. Thomas and St. Denis Parish: includes Ellidge, Jacob, Jr.

South Carolina History and Archives.

Children of JOHN LAND and ELIZABETH ELLIDGE are:

34. i. FRANCES ELLIDGE[5] LAND, b. Bef. October 20, 1750; d. Aft. 1830, Roane, Tennessee.
ii. JAMES SMITH LAND[53], b. Abt. 1776[53]; d. Aft. 1811, Virginia[53]; m. ELIZABETH HART[53], November 09, 1797, Surrey, Virginia[53].

Child of JOHN LAND and ELIZABETH ELLIDGE is:

35. iii. FRANCES[5] LAND, JR., b. July 01, 1779.

20. BIRD[4] LAND *(CURTIS[3], CURTIS[2], CURTIS[1])* was born Bef. 1739 in Sussex Co VA, and died August 22, 1794 in Southampton Co VA. He married REBEKAH LEWELLIN[54,55] 1760. She was born Abt. 1744[55].

Notes for BIRD LAND:
(Research):ALBEMARLE PARISH REGISTER OF BIRTHS & SPONSORS
Birth Date

Child's Name
God Parents/Sponsors
BIRD & REBECCA LAND
21 Jun 1761 Christening date Lucas Abner Sturdivant, John Rowland, Winefred Land
28 Dec 1765 Lewis Jesse Rodgers, Eliz Rodgers, Amy Cocke
21 Oct 1767 Lewellen James Cocke, Abel Mabrey, Mary Land
23 Dec 1770 Lucretia John Land, Curtis Land, Sarah Flood
BIRD LAND (b bef 1739 and d 22 Aug 1794 to 11 Dec 1794 Southampton Co VA) md by 1760, REBEKAH (d bef 22 Aug 1794)
Will wit by Matthew Garnder Jr, Wm Fowler, Edwin (his X mark) Beal

Children of BIRD LAND and REBEKAH LEWELLIN are:

i. LUCAS[5] LAND, b. September 21, 1761, Albemarle, Virginia.
ii. LEWELLEN LAND, b. October 21, 1767, Albemarle Co, VA.
iii. LUCRETIA LAND, b. December 23, 1770, Albemarle County, Virginia.
36. iv. LITTLEBERRY LAND, b. Abt. 1772; d. December 20, 1827, Edgecombe Co. NC.

21. CHARLES[4] LAND *(CURTIS[3], CURTIS[2], CURTIS[1])* was born March 02, 1760 in Albemarle Co, VA. He married MARY ANN COOPER[57] November 09, 1785 in Southampton, VA. She was born 1773.

Child of CHARLES LAND and MARY COOPER is:

37. i. CHARLES[5] LAND, b. 1794, NC; d. Aft. 1860, Edgecombe Co. NC.

22. CHARLES[4] LAND *(CURTIS[3], CURTIS[2], CURTIS[1])* [58] was born March 02, 1760 [58], and died May 23, 1838 in Edgecombe, North Carolina, USA[58]. He married MARY ANN COOPER[58] November 09, 1786 in Southampton, Virginia[58]. She was born 1773[58], and died 1838 in Edgecombe, North Carolina, USA[58].

Child of CHARLES LAND and MARY COOPER is:

i. CHARLES[5] LAND[58], b. 1794[58]; d. 1860, Edgecombe, North Carolina, USA[58]; m. PATSY DAWS[59,60,61], November 06, 1822[61]; b. Abt. 1790[62]; d. 1850, Edgecombe, North Carolina, USA[63,64].

23. CURTIS[4] LAND *(CURTIS[3], CURTIS[2], CURTIS[1])* [65] was born December 01, 1733 in Sussex, VA [65]. He married UNKNOWN[66].

Child of CURTIS LAND and UNKNOWN is:

i. JOHN[5] LAND, d. Aft. December 01, 1817, Wilkes Co., North Carolina.

24. BIRD[4] LAND *(CURTIS[3], CURTIS[2], CURTIS[1])* [67] was born Bef. 1739 in Sussex Co VA [67], and died August 22, 1794 in Southampton Co VA[67]. He married REBEKAH LEWELLIN[67,68] 1760[69]. She was born Abt. 1744 [70].

Children of BIRD LAND and REBEKAH LEWELLIN are:

38. i. LEWIS[5] LAND, b. Albemarle Co, VA; d. July 28, 1854, Greenville, South Carolina.
ii. LUCAS LAND[71], b. September 21, 1761, Albemarle, Virginia[71].
iii. LEWELLEN LAND[71], b. October 21, 1767, Albemarle Co, VA[71].
iv. LUCRETIA LAND[71], b. December 23, 1770, Albemarle County, Virginia[71].

25. CHARLES[4] LAND *(CURTIS[3], CURTIS[2], CURTIS[1])* [71] was born March 02, 1760 in Albemarle Co, VA [71]. He married MARY ANN COOPER[71] November 09, 1786 in Southampton, VA[71]. She was born 1773[71].

Child of CHARLES LAND and MARY COOPER is:

i. CHARLES[5] LAND[71], b. 1794, NC[71]; d. Aft. 1860, Edgecombe Co. NC[71].

Generation No. 5

26. EPHRAIM[5] LAND *(THOMAS[4], JOHN[3], CURTIS[2], CURTIS[1])* [72] was born Abt. 1732 in Orange County, Virginia [72], and died 1836 in Stokes County, Virginia[72]. He married (1) UNKNOWN [72]. He married (2) POLLY BOLLIN [72].

Notes for EPHRAIM LAND:
LAND, EPHRAIM, Stokes County P.&W.S. Ct. September Term 1821 State of North Carolina, Court of Pleas and Quarter Sessions) On the 13th day of September 1821 personally appeared in open court, being a Court of record proceeding according to the common Law, with Jurisdiction unlimited in amount and having the power of fines and imprissonments, Ephraim Land aged eighty years on the fifteenth day of October resident in Stokes County in said State who being first duly sworn according to law, on his Oath declares that he served in the Revolutionary War as follows, that he enlisted in the year 1775 after the commencement of the war in Amelia County in Virginia, in Capt. Chas. Woodson's Company, Colonel Abraham Bluford's Regiment in the Virginia line, that he served from that time as a private Soldier for six years and three months and was discharged about nine months before the close of the war, in Consequence of being disabled by a wound in the hand at the Reedy fork in Guilford in 1781, that he was in Col. Washington's defeat at the Santee, and at Col. Bluford's defeat at the Hanging Rock, and was wounded in the hand at a skirmish at the Reedy fork in the spring of 1782 by a Musket ball, he has never before attempted to obtain a pension.

I, Ephraim Land, do solemnly swear that I was a resident of the United States on the 18th of March 1818, and that I have not since that time by gift; sale or in any manner, disposed of my property, or any part thereof, with intent thereby so to diminish it as to bring myself within the provisions of an act of Congress entitled "An Act to provide for certain persons engaged in the Land and Naval services of the United States in the Revoutioat War passed on the 18th day of March 1818 and that I have not nor has any person in trust for me, any property or securitiess Contracts debts due to me, nor do i have any income other than what is contained in the schedule hereto annexed and by me subscribed.

1 Bed 6 pewter plates 1 Dish 1 Basin A spinning wheel and Cards 7 or 8 lbs cotton 1 Hoe 1 Axe
I live with my wife aged Sixty, and a little Granddaughter about nine, my children have all left me, I live by cultivating a little patch of ground, which when able I dig up with my hands with difficulty being lame, I am very old infirm and poor, have always been crippled and disabled in my hand since my would and stand in need of the assistance of my Country for support.

Ephraim (X) Land

The Court adjudge that the property contained in the schedule is worth about twenty Dollars & that the facts stated in the declaration are true.
Sworn to and declared in open Court this thirteenth September 1821.

[Stokes County Superior Court April Court 1826 State of North Carolina, Stokes County.] At a Superior Court of Law holden for the County of Stokes aforesaid this 18th day of April AD 1826 the same being a Court of Record Ephraim Land aged ninety five years resident in the County of Stokes & State of North Carolina who being first duly Sworn according to Law in order to obtain the provisions made by the Act of Congress of the 18th March 1818 and 1st of May 1820 doth on his oath make the following declaration that he the said Ephraim Land Enlisted in the year 1775 after the Commencement of the Revolutionary War in Amelia County Virginia in Capt. Oba. Woodson's Company Colo. Abraham Blufords Redgement in the line of the State of Virginia the precise day not Recollected, first for the Term of Eighteen Months and before that time was quite out he Enlisted as a private Solder for Six years & three months and was discharged in consequence of a wound in the hand which disabled him, which wound was done by accident. That he was at Col. Blufords defeat at the Hanging Rock & that he was in Colo. Washingtons defeat at the Santee that when he was discharged his commander whose name he does not know Recollect told him that it was not necessary to have a written discharge as his wound which was done by accident while in the Service would be a Sufficient discharge he has no other Evidence now in his power than his own oath old age & poverty have now Reached him & he is now dependant on the cheraty of the County & a Pauper And in persuance of the Act of the 1st of May 1820 I Ephraim Land do Solemly Swer that I was a Resident Citizen of the United States on the 18th March 1818 that I have not since that time by Gift sale or otherwise disposed of my property or any part thereof with intent to thereby so to diminish it as to bring myself within the provisions of an act of Congress entitled "An Act to provide for certain persons engaged in the Land and Naval services of the United States in the Revolutionary War passed on the 18th day of March 1818 and that I have not nor has any person in trust for me, any property or securitiess Contracts debts due to me, nor do i have any income other than what is contained in the schedule hereto annexed and by me subscribed.

1 Bed 6 pewter plates 1 Dish 1 Basin A spinning wheel and Cards 7 or 8 lbs cotton 1 Hoe 1 Axe

I live with my wife aged Sixty who is very infirm, I have a little Granddaughter living with me Whom I have raised about nine, my children have all left me and Add nothing to my Support. I live by cultivating a little patch of ground, which when able I dig up with my hands with difficulty being lame, I am very old infirm and poor, have always been crippled and disabled in my hand since my wound and stand in need of the assistance of my Country for support.
Ephraim [X] Land
Sworn to & Subscribed in open Court [signed] Thos. Armstrong Clk.

Child of EPHRAIM LAND and UNKNOWN is:
39. i. MESCHACK[6] LAND, b. Abt. 1780.

Children of EPHRAIM LAND and POLLY BOLLIN are:
ii. ZACHARIAH[6] LAND[72], b. 1793[72].
iii. UNITY LAND[72], b. 1795[72]; m. WILLIAM FRANCE[72].

27. THOMAS[5] LAND *(THOMAS[4], JOHN[3], CURTIS[2], CURTIS[1])* [72]was born Abt. 1734 in Augusta, Virginia [72], and died 1832 in Wilkes County, North Carolina[72]. He married ANNE SUMTER[72] 1755 in Louisa County, Virginia[72]. She was born Aft. 1740 in Hanover County, Virginia[72].

Notes for THOMAS LAND:
5th Great-Grandfather, Thomas Land
1790 (1st Census of the United States.) | Wilkes County , North Carolina

Thomas Land, along with his son, Jonathan (my 4th great- grandfather) both appear in the 1st census of the United States in 1790 in Wilkes County, North Carolina. Thomas was born in Augusta County, Virginia about 1734. He married in 1754 to Annie Sumter (or Sumpter) sister of famed Revolutionary War General and one of South Carolina's founding fathers, General Thomas Sumter. Fort Sumter in Charleston Harbor , South Carolina, where the first shots of the Civil War were fired was named for the General. Thomas Land died the same year as his famous brother-in-law in 1832 in Wilkes County, North Carolina The first mention of the Sumter name occurs in 1763, when William Sumter bought from Thomas Land one hundred acres on Priddy's Creek, which had been patented in 1739 by Major John Henry, the orator's (Patrick Henry) father, and which Land had purchased from his son, William Henry. Sumter's next purchase was made in 1770 on the north fork of the Rivanna, at the south end of Piney Mountain. This land was conveyed by John Poindexter, who obtained the grant of it in 1738, and from whom the mountain was originally called Poindexter's Mountain, and the creek running through it (no doubt Herring's Creek at present), Poindexter's Creek. William Sumter continued his purchases, till he owned between six and seven hundred acres. In 1776 he and his wife Judith sold off all his property. One of the sales was made to John Sumter, probably a brother, and the land John then bought he and his wife Catharine conveyed in 1779 to Charles Bush. In all probability they sold to go elsewhere.
1787 Wilkes CO, NC State Census: Isbells District State or Colonial Census
Thomas Land, Sr.
2m -21/+60 (-1727/1766-87) = Thomas 1725 and probably son, Thomas, Jr. born abt 1766
3 females = Anna + daughter-in-law, Nancy McGee,+ grand daughter, Frances. Their daughter, Nancy had married in Wilkes County on 29,March 1782 to Benjamin Tilley. She would die young and her sister, Franka would marry Benjamin in March 1801 after the death of her 1st husband, Daniel Isbell. Franka married Daniel 18,May 1783 in Wilkes County. They were married by a Reverend John Barlow. Daniel was a veteran of the American Revolution serving under a Captain Isaiah Moody as a " fife Major in the Virginia line " Daniel was killed in 1797 " on the Kentucky River " according to Franka's pension. He was killed by a Thomas Lahorn. Benjamin and Franka lived out their days in Missouri. Ben died there15, March 1843. Thomas and Anna's daughter, Mary married Thomas Carlton about 1777 and would also die young. Granddaughters, Frances and later Susannah would marry brothers William and John Gray from Wilkes County and settle in Monroe County, Tennessee along with their brother, James Noah Land. Thomas and Anna's other sons were, John born 2,Dec.1755 in Virginia. He also served in the Revolution. John settled in Kentucky and fathered several children with two wives, Elizabeth Barlow and following

her death, Rebecca Renfroe. He lived out his years in the the Bluegrass region of Central Kentucky dying there abt 1804. Joseph,born in 1760 was reportedly one of the founding fathers of Carter County, Tennessee. He is listed as " Joseph Lands, Ranger " among the first officers of the county in a early history of Carter County, Tennessee. David,born abt 1770 there is little or no info on him. Jonathan ,born abt 1758 was my 4th gr, grandfather. He died after 1820 in Wilkes County, N.C. He married 27, Dec.1779 to Elizabeth Isbell, daughter of James Isbell and Frances Livingston. She was born 19,Oct 1762 in Orange County, Virginia and died in Wilkes County after 1820. (Glenn Land)

Notes for ANNE SUMTER:
Ann was the sister of Col. Sumter

Children of THOMAS LAND and ANNE SUMTER are:

	i.	DAVID[6] LAND[72].
40.	ii.	JOHN LAND, b. Abt. 1756, Virginia; d. 1804, Scott County, Kentucky.
41.	iii.	MARY LAND, b. May 03, 1756, Albemarle County, Virginia; d. 1796, Wilkes County, North Carolina.
42.	iv.	JONATHAN LAND, b. 1758, Albemarle County, Virginia; d. Aft. 1820, Wilkes County, North Carolina.
	v.	JOSEPH LAND[72], b. 1760[72]; d. Carter County, Tennessee[72].
43.	vi.	THOMAS LAND, b. Abt. 1766, Albemarle County, Virginia; d. 1798, Wilkes County, North Carolina.
	vii.	NANCY LAND[72], b. 1766[72]; d. Abt. 1790[72]; m. BENJAMIN TILLEY[72], March 29, 1782[72].
	viii.	FRANKA LAND[72], b. Abt. 1767, Virginia[72]; d. Aft. 1845, Wilkes County, North Carolina[72]; m. (1) BENJAMIN TILLEY[72]; m. (2) DANIEL ISBELL[72], May 18, 1873, Wilkes County, North Carolina[72].

Notes for FRANKA LAND:
Thomas Land, Sr.
2m -21/+60 (-1727/1766-87) = Thomas 1725 and probably son, Thomas, Jr. born abt 1766
3 females = Anna + daughter-in-law, Nancy McGee,+ grand daughter, Frances. Their daughter,Nancy had married in Wilkes County on 29,March 1782 to Benjamin Tilley. She would die young and her sister,Franka would marry Benjamin in March 1801 after the death of her 1st husband, Daniel Isbell. Franka married Daniel 18,May 1783 in Wilkes County. They were married by a Reverend John Barlow. Daniel was a veteran of the American Revolution serving under a Captain Isaiah Moody as a " fife Major in the Virginia line " Daniel was killed in 1797 " on the Kentucky River " according to Franka's pension. He was killed by a Thomas Lahorn. Benjamin and Franka lived out their days in Missouri. Ben died there15,March 1843. Thomas and Anna's daughter, Mary married Thomas Carlton about 1777 and would also die young. Granddaughters, Frances and later Susannah would marry brothers William and John Gray from Wilkes County and settle in Monroe County, Tennessee along with their brother, James Noah Land. Thomas and Anna's other sons were, John born 2,Dec.1755 in Virginia. He also served in the Revolution. John settled in Kentucky and fathered several children with two wives, Elizabeth Barlow and following her death, Rebecca Renfroe. He lived out his years in the the Bluegrass region of Central Kentucky dying there abt 1804. Joseph,born in 1760 was reportedly one of the founding fathers of Carter County, Tennessee. He is listed as " Joseph Lands, Ranger " among the first officers of the county in a early history of Carter County, Tennessee. David, born abt 1770 there is little or no info on him. Jonathan, born abt 1758 was my 4th gr ,grandfather. He died after 1820 in Wilkes County, N.C. He married 27,Dec.1779 to Elizabeth Isbell, daughter of James Isbell and Frances Livingston. She was born 19,Oct 1762 in Orange County, Virginia and died in Wilkes County after 1820. (Glen Land)

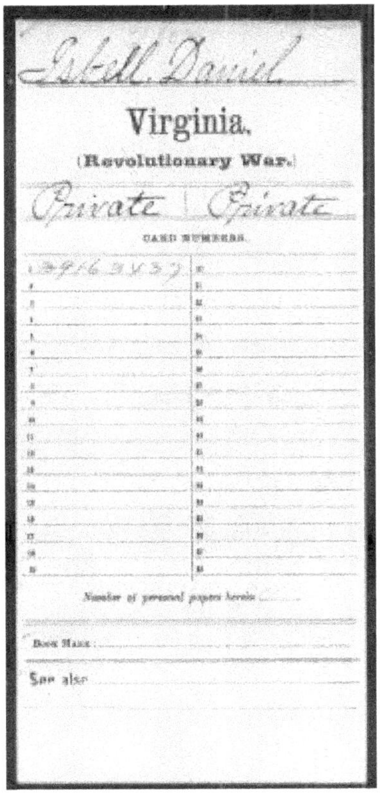

Estell, Daniel

Virginia.

(Revolutionary War.)

Private | Private

CARD NUMBERS.

Number of personal papers herein

Book Mark:

See also

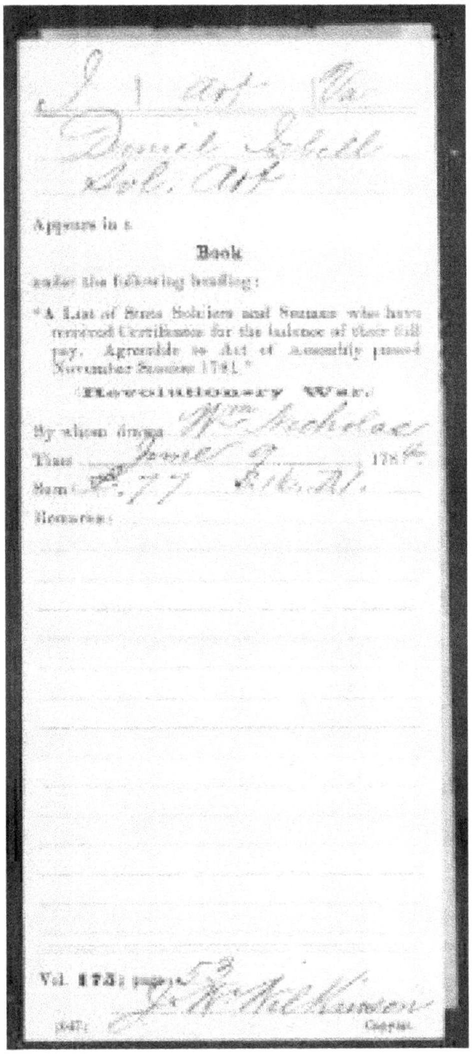

E | Art. | Va.

Daniel Estell

Sol. Art

Appears in a

Book

under the following heading:

"A List of State Soldiers and Seamen who have received Certificates for the balance of their full pay. Agreeable to Act of Assembly passed November Session 1781."

(Revolutionary War.)

By whom drawn Wm Nicholas

Time June 9, 1784

Sum £77

Remarks:

Vol. 173; page 53

J. W. Wilkinson

Copyist.

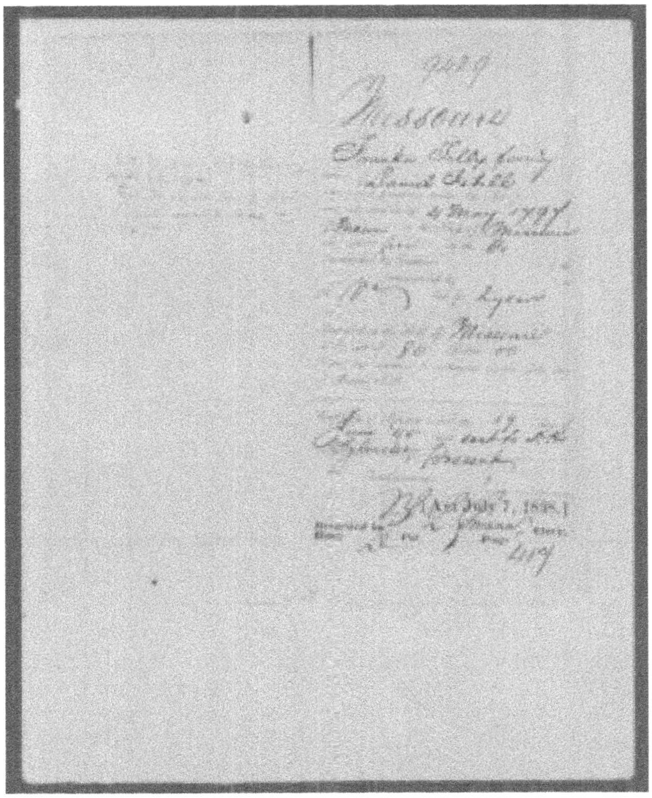

Missouri

(Act July 7, 1898.)

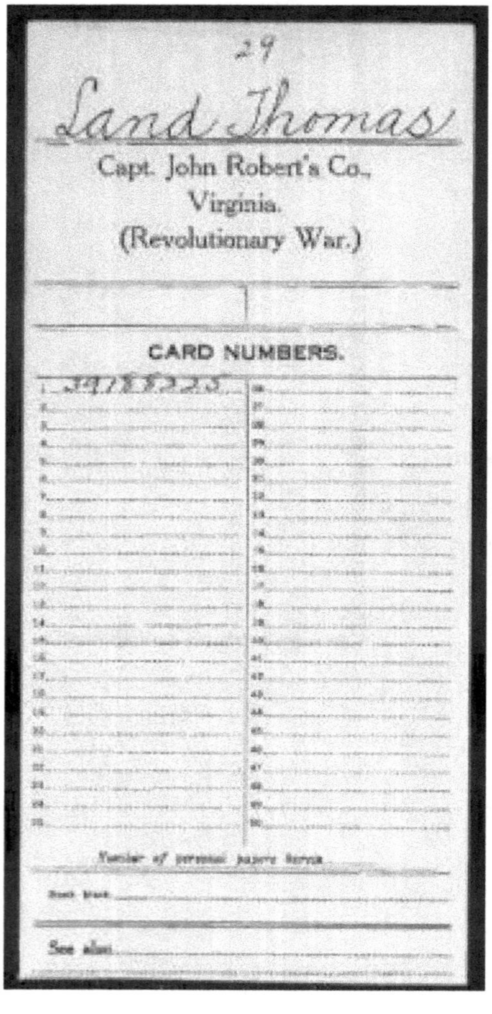

29

Land Thomas

Capt. John Robert's Co.,
Virginia.
(Revolutionary War.)

CARD NUMBERS.

1. 34785223

Number of personal papers herein

Book Mark

See also

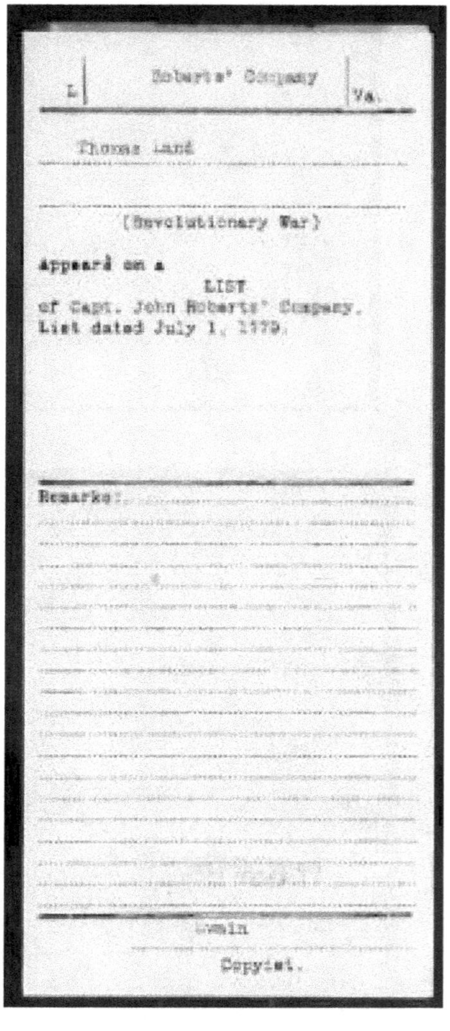

L | Roberts' Company | Va.

Thomas Land

(Revolutionary War)

Appeared on a

LIST

of Capt. John Roberts' Company.
List dated July 1, 1779.

Remarks:

Copyist.

Captain Joseph Gray, Union Confederate Soldier

Notes for JONATHAN LAND:

John Land Jr. sponsored his Baptismal in Albemarle Parish, Surry CO, VA.

28. JOHN[5] LAND *(THOMAS[4], JOHN[3], CURTIS[2], CURTIS[1])*[72] was born Abt. 1734 in Orange County, Virginia[72], and died March 23, 1781 in Chester County, South Carolina[72]. He married MARY SUMTER[72] Abt. 1764[72]. She was born Abt. 1745[72].

Children of JOHN LAND and MARY SUMTER are:

i. ELEANOR[6] LAND[72], b. Abt. 1764[72]; m. SILAS GLADDEN[72].

44. ii. JOHN LAND, b. Abt. 1768, South Carolina; d. Bef. 1830, Madison County, Alabama.

45. iii. SUMTER LAND, b. Abt. 1770.

iv. SARAH SOPHIA LAND[72], b. Abt. 1772[72]; m. EDMOND STRANGE[72].

v. CHARLOTTE LAND[72], b. Abt. 1781[72]; m. SHANNON THOMPSON[72].

John Land Muster Roll, Revolutionary War

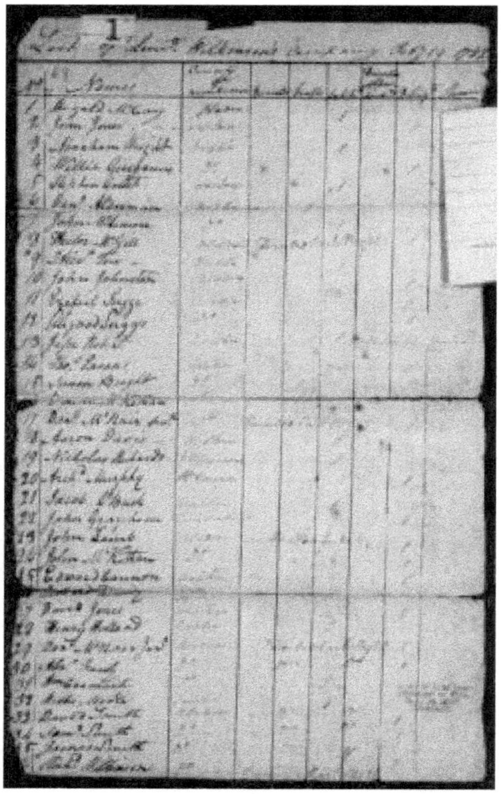

29. HENRY[5] LAND *(CHARLES[4], CURTIS[3], CURTIS[2], CURTIS[1])* [72]was born 1788 in Virginia [72]. He married PIETY WEAVER[72]. She was born 1790 in Edgecombe County, North Carolina[72].

Child of HENRY LAND and PIETY WEAVER is:

i. NANCY[6] LAND[72], b. 1828[72]; d Randolph, Georgia[72]; m. SIMON GREEN[72].

30. CHARLES[5] LAND *(CHARLES[4], CURTIS[3], CURTIS[2], CURTIS[1])* [72]was born 1794 in North Carolina [72], and died Aft. 1860 in Edgecombe County, North Carolina[72]. He married PATSY DAWS [72,73,74] November 06, 1822 in Edgecombe, North Carolina[75]. She was born Abt. 1790[75], and died 1850 in Edgecombe, North Carolina, USA[76,77]

Children of CHARLES LAND and PATSY DAWS are:

i. CATHERINE[6] LAND[78], b. 1830, North Carolina[78]; d. Aft. 1850, Edgecombe County, North Carolina[78]; m. HENRY CRUMPLEY[78]; b. 1828, North Carolina[78].

46. ii. MARY LAND, b. 1830, Edgecombe County, North Carolina; d. Aft. 1870, Wilson, North Carolina.

47. iii. JOHN HENRY LAND, b. May 22, 1831, Edgecombe County, North Carolina; d. January 17, 1927, Marion, South Carolina.

48. iv. CETH SMITH LAND, b. December 09, 1833, Edgecombe County, North Carolina; d. December 26, 1889, South Carolina.

31. JESSE[5] LAND *(CHARLES[4], CURTIS[3], CURTIS[2], CURTIS[1])*[78] was born 1803[78], and died Aft. 1850 in Twiggs County, Georgia[78]. He married (1) TABITHA DARBY [78]September 28, 1826 in Twiggs, Georgia [78]. She was born Abt. 1800 [78]. He married (2) FRANCES YEARTY [78]February 21, 1844 in Bibb County, Georgia [78]. She was born 1815[78].

Children of JESSE LAND and TABITHA DARBY are:

49. i. WILLIAM[6] LAND, b. 1827, Georgia; d. Aft. 1860, Twiggs, Georgia.

50. ii. JOHN LAND, b. 1830, Georgia; d. Aft. 1860, Twiggs, Georgia.

iii. ELIZABETH LAND[78], b. 1833[78].

iv. EMELINE LAND[78], b. 1837[78].

v. MARY LAND[78], b. 1839[78].

vi. DAVID YEARTY LAND[78], b. 1841[78].

Children of JESSE LAND and FRANCES YEARTY are:

51. vii. JESSE[6] LAND, b. 1845, Georgia; d. Aft. 1900, Twiggs, Georgia.

52. viii. CHARLES LAND, b. 1848, Georgia; d. Abt. 1900, Bibb, Georgia.

ix. GEORGE LAND[78], b. 1850, Georgia[78].

53. x. BENJAMIN FRANKLIN LAND, b. June 1852.

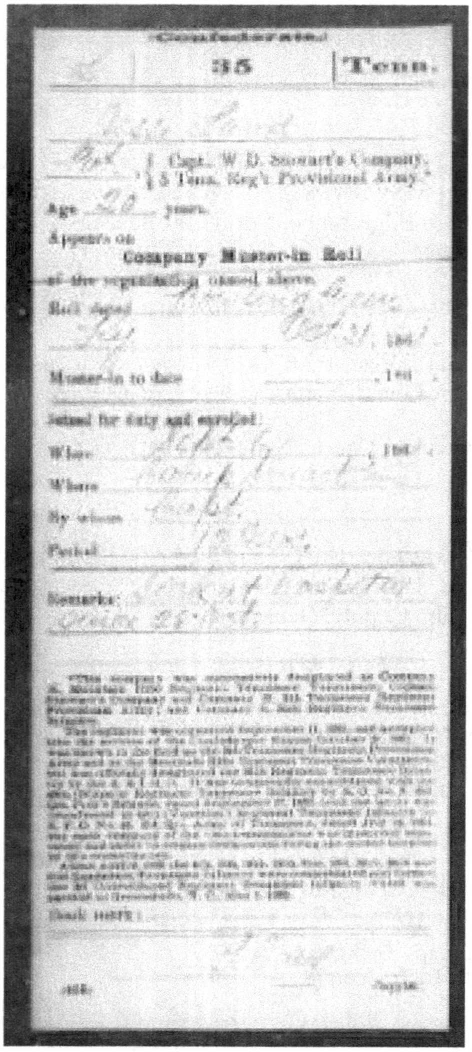
(Confederate.)

35 | Tenn.

Capt. W. D. Stewart's Company, 5 Tenn. Reg't Provisional Army.

Age 20 years.

Appears on

Company Muster-in Roll

of the organization named above.

Roll dated ..., 186

Muster-in to date ..., 186

Joined for duty and enrolled:

When ..., 186

Where

By whom

Period

Remarks:

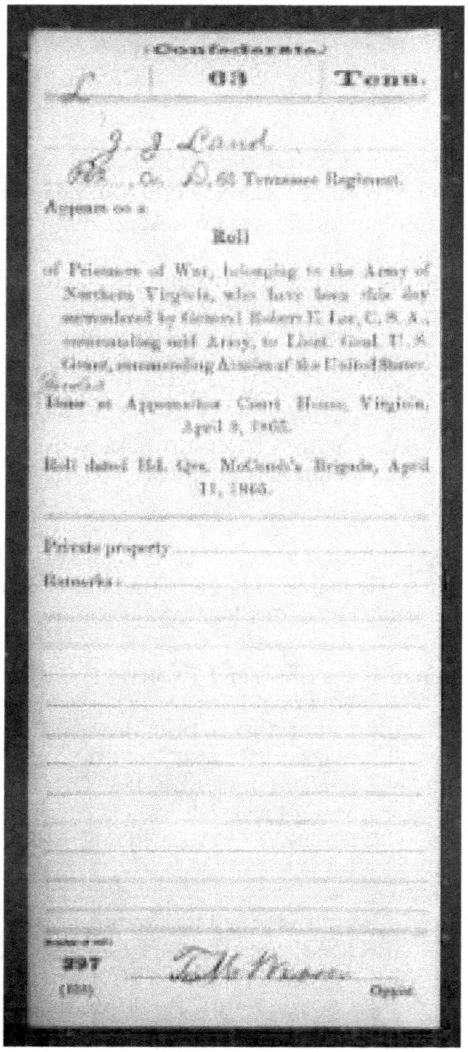
(Confederate.)

63 | Tenn.

J. J. Land

Co. D, 63 Tennessee Regiment.

Appears on a

Roll

of Prisoners of War, belonging to the Army of Northern Virginia, who have been this day surrendered by General Robert E. Lee, C. S. A., commanding said Army, to Lieut. Genl. U. S. Grant, commanding Armies of the United States.

Done at Appomattox Court House, Virginia, April 9, 1865.

Roll dated Hd. Qrs. McComb's Brigade, April 11, 1865.

Private property

Remarks:

297

32. SUSAN (SOPHY)[5] LAND *(CHARLES[4], CURTIS[3], CURTIS[2], CURTIS[1])* [78]was born Abt. 1809 [78]. She married ISAAC BRASWELL[78].

Child of SUSAN LAND and ISAAC BRASWELL is:

54. i. SOPHRONIA[6] BRASWELL, b. 1827, North Carolina.

33. JOHN[5] LAND *(ROBERT[4], WILLIAM[3], CURTIS[2], CURTIS[1])* [78]was born Abt. February 19, 1743/44 in Albemarle County, Virginia[78], and died Abt. 1814 in Prince Edward Co., Virginia. He married SUSANNA RAWLINGS Abt. 1774 in Prince Edward Co., Virginia. She was born August 17, 1756, and died Abt. 1813 in Prince Edward Co., Virginia.

Children of JOHN LAND and SUSANNA RAWLINGS are:

55. i. JOHN BRAXTON[6] LAND, b. Abt. 1771, Albemarle Co., Virginia; d. Abt. 1812, Buckingham Co., Virginia.

ii. ROBERT CARTER LAND, b. Abt. 1777, Cumberland Co., Virginia; d. October 13, 1844, Mecklenburg Co., Virginia.

iii. EDWIN LAND, b. Abt. 1780, Sussex Co., Virginia; d. 1849, Clinton Co., Kentucky.
iv. WILLIAMSON LAND, b. Abt 1789, Buckingham Co., Virginia; d. Bet. 1790 - 1879.

34. FRANCES ELLIDGE[5] LAND *(JOHN[4], WILLIAM[3], CURTIS[2], CURTIS[1])*[78] was born Bef. October 20, 1750[78], and died Aft. 1830 in Roane, Tennessee[78]. He married UNKNOWN[78].

Children of FRANCES LAND and UNKNOWN are:
56. i. FRANCES LAND[6] JR, b. July 01, 1779; d. October 10, 1854, Beaver Creek, Fairfield Co., South Carolina.
ii. HENRIETTA LAND[78], b. 1788[78].

35. FRANCES[5] LAND, JR. *(JOHN[4], WILLIAM[3], CURTIS[2], CURTIS[1])* was born July 01, 1779.

Children of FRANCES LAND, JR. are:
i. ELEDGE HALL[6] LAND.
57. ii. ELDRIDGE HALL LAND, b. 1819.

36. LITTLEBERRY[5] LAND *(BIRD[4], CURTIS[3], CURTIS[2], CURTIS[1])*[78,79] was born Abt. 1772[79], and died December 20, 1827 in Edgecombe Co. NC[79]. He married (1) MARY "MOLLY" MCLEMORE October 04, 1791 in Sout Hampton Co VA. She was born July 24, 1760 in Albemarle County, Virginia, and died 1827 in Edgecombe County, NC. He married (2) MARY MCLEMORE[80] October 04, 1791 in Southampton, Virginia[80]. She was born July 24, 1760 in Albemarle County, Virginia[80]. He married (3) MARY "MOLLY" MCLEMORE[81] October 04, 1791 in Sout Hampton Co VA[81]. She was born July 24, 1760 in Albemarle County, Virginia[81], and died 1827 in Edgecombe County, NC[81].

Notes for LITTLEBERRY LAND:
52. Littleberry5 Land (Bird4, Curtis3, Curtis2, Curtis1) was born 1771, and died December 20, 1827. He married Mary McLemore October 04, 1791 in Southampton, VA. She was born July 24, 1760 in Albemarle Co., VA.
Children of Littleberry Land and Mary McLemore are:
+ 93 i. Daniel Land, born 1793 in North Carolina; died September 12, 1857 in Wilson Co., NC.
+ 94 ii. Burrell Land, born 1794 in Tar River, NC; died Bef. 1840 in Noxubee Co., Ms.
+ 95 iii . Bird Land, born Abt. 1800 in Edgecombe Co., NC died Bef. 1850 in Noxubee Co., Ms.
+ 96 iv. Sally Land, born Abt. 1800.
+ 97 v. Amy Land, born Abt. 1802 in North Carolina.
+ 98 vi. Mary Polly Land, born Abt. 1803 in North Carolina; died 1860 in Edgecombe Co., NC.
Littleberry b abt 1772? d abt 20 Dec 1827 Edgecombe NC md abt ? Oct 1791, Southampton Co VA to Mary McLemore.
22 Aug 1794: named executor of his father Bird's, will
22 Aug 1794: heired 2 negro girls, Bet & Ginna, "now in his possession"
20 Dec 1827: Will of Littleberry named sons: Daniel, Burrell, Bird and dtrs: Polly Lancaster. Amy Joyner and Sally Hargrove.
1800 Edgecombe Co NC
1 m 26/45 (1755/74) = Littleberry
1f 26/45 (1755/74) = Mary
2m 0/10 (1790/1800) = Daniel and Burrell?
1810?
1820 Edgecombe Co NC
1m 45 (bef 1775) = Littleberry
1f 45+ (be f 1775) = Mary
2f 16/26 (1794/1804) = Amy & Sally or Polly
Children of Littleberry Land and Mary McLemore
1. Daniel b abt 1793 d 12 Sep 1857 md Martha Bullock, d/o Joel and Lucy Bullock Daniel was a Primitive Baptist Minister in Tarborough, Conetoe Church
2. Burrell b? d? md ? Seleter
3. Bird b? d? did he go to Mississippi by 1840?
4. Sally md Duncan Hargrove
5. Polly md Joseph Lancaster
6. Amy md 10 Sep 1827 Edgecombe Co NC, Thomas Joyner
(Research):EDGECOMBE CO NC DEED ABSTRACTS

1781: Samuel Sands/Lands from Wm Morgan Deed E-9
1784: Samuel Sands/Lands from Uriah S. Smith Deed 4-141
27 Nov 1790: Robert Lancaster of Edgecombe Co NC to Lewis Land of Southampton Co VA for 15 pds 100acres lying on both sides of Town Creek adj Jourdain Willifort, Edward Cobb and Robert Lancaster, Jr., being part of a larger tract granted to Robert Lancaster by the State on 28 Oct 1782.
Wit: Stephen Proctor (DB8-605)
(Is this Lewis who died 1854 Greenville, SC?)
26 Aug 1795 Abraham Bolton and Stephen Proctor of Edgecombe Co NC to Charles Land of Sussex Co VA for 185 silver dollars - a tract of 200a adj Daniel Stringer and Wm. Proctor, it being part of a tract granted to Thomas Roberds dated 1783. Wit: Jacob White, Morris Proctor (DB8:359)
(This is Revolutionary Soldier Charles m Mary Ann Cooper)
22 May 1799: Elisha Battle of Edgecombe Co NC toLewellen Land of same, for 40 pounds VA currency. 120a north bank of Tyancokey, adj James Ricks. Wit : Thos Deaver, Richard Powell (DB8-750)
1800: Lewellen Land to Jeremiah Hil liard (DB9-374) (Lewellen appears on the 1810 Sussex Co VA census)
22 Jan 1 798: Benjamin Williams of Edgecombe Co NC, wheelwright, to Littleberry Land of same, planter for 32 pds, 100acres, both sides of George Gardners Mill Bran ch, adj Jacob Robbins, Mathew Cole, ? Whitehead, and both of the above parties. Wit: John Weaver, Drury X Williams (DB 8-850).
1 Feb 1798: James Merritt of Edgecombe Co NC to Littleberry Land of same, for 16.13.4 current money, 100 acres south side of Tyancokey Swamp, part of tract granted to said James Merritt 28 Oct 1782. Wit: Benjamin Williams, William Robbins (DB8-909).

Children of LITTLEBERRY LAND and MARY MCLEMORE are:
58. i. BIRD[6] LAND, b. Abt. 1800, Edgecombe County, North Carolina; d. Bef. 1850, Noxubee County, Mississippi.
59. ii. SALLY LAND, b. 1800, Edgecombe Co. NC.
60. iii. AMY LAND, b. Abt. 1802, Edgecombe County, NC of Nash Co., NC.
61. iv. MARY "POLLY" LAND, b. Abt. 1803, Edgecombe Co. NC; d. 1860, Edgecombe Co. NC.
62. v. DANIEL[6] LAND, b. 1793, North Carolina; d. September 12, 1857, Wilson County, North Carolina.
63. vi. BURRELL LAND, b. 1794, Tar River, North Carolina; d. Bef. 1840, Noxubee County, Mississippi.
64. vii. MARY POLLY LAND, b. Abt. 1803, North Carolina; d. 1860, Edgecombe County, North Carolina.

37. CHARLES[5] LAND *(CHARLES[4], CURTIS[3], CURTIS[2], CURTIS[1])* was born 1794 in NC, and died Aft. 1860 in Edgecombe Co. NC. He married PATSY DAWS[82,83,84] November 06, 1822 in Edgecombe, North Carolina. She was born Abt. 1790[85], and died 1850 in Edgecombe, North Carolina, USA[86,87].

Child of CHARLES LAND and PATSY DAWS is:
65. i. JOHN[6] LAND.

38. LEWIS[5] LAND *(BIRD[4], CURTIS[3], CURTIS[2], CURTIS[1])*[88,89,90] was born in Albemarle Co, VA[91], and died July 28, 1854 in Greenville, South Carolina[91,92]. He married (2) ELEANOR UNKNOWN[93] Abt. 1782. He married (3) ELEANOR UNKNOWN[93] Abt. 1782[93]. He married (5) ELIZABETH MARTHA ???[94] WFT Est. 1782-1815[94]. She was born WFT Est. 1761-1781[94], and died WFT Est. 1788-1865[94]. He married (7) ELIZABETH MARTHA UNKNOWN[95] Abt. 1805 in South Carolina[95]. He married (8) OBEDIENCE BIDDY WEST[95] August 27, 1842[95]. She was born Abt. 1775 in Greenville, South Carolina[95].

Children of LEWIS LAND and ELEANOR UNKNOWN are:
i. MOSES[6] LAND[97,98], b. 1782[99,100]; d. Abt. 1860, Butler County, Kentucky[101].
ii. ANNA LAND[103,104], b. 1785[105,106]; m. UNKNOWN BARNETT[107].
iii. LITTLEBERRY LAND[109,110], b. 1788[111,112]; d. 1860, Georgia[113].
iv. FANNIE LAND[115,116], b. 1790[117,118]; d. Aft. 1834[119]; m. UNKNOWN BRANNON[119].
v. ELLANDER LAND[121,122], b. 1792[123,124]; d. Aft. 1834[125]; m. UNKNOWN WRIGHT[125].

Children of LEWIS LAND and ELIZABETH UNKNOWN are:
vii. ISAIAH[6] LAND[127], b. June 16, 1806, Greenville, South Carolina[127]; d. Aft. 1891, Greenville, South Carolina[127]; m. ANNA UNKNOWN[127], Abt. 1825[127]; b. Abt. 1803[127].
67. viii. STEPHEN LAND, b. May 22, 1808, Greenville, South Carolina; d. March 18, 1870, Paulding County, Georgia.
68. ix. ELIZABETH LAND, b. Abt. 1810, Greenville, South Carolina; d. Jefferson County, Tennessee abt 1880.
69. x. KINSON LAND, b. 1813, South Carolina; d. Abt. 1898, Randolph County, Arkansas.
xi. JANE LAND[127], b. 1815[127].

xii. JORDON LAND[127], b. 1819[127].

Generation No. 6

39. MESCHACK[6] LAND *(EPHRAIM[5], THOMAS[4], JOHN[3], CURTIS[2], CURTIS[1])* [127] was born Abt. 1780[127]. He married MARY BETH MURRY[127].

Children of MESCHACK LAND and MARY MURRY are:

i. WILLIAM[7] LAND[127].
ii. HENRY LAND[127], b. June 17, 1823[127]; d. 1841[127].

40. JOHN[6] LAND *(THOMAS[5], THOMAS[4], JOHN[3], CURTIS[2], CURTIS[1])* [127] was born Abt. 1756 in Virginia[127], and died 1804 in Scott County, Kentucky[127]. He married (1) ELIZABETH BARLOW[127]. She was born Abt. 1775 in Virginia[127], and died Aft. 1810 in Wilkes County, North Carolina[127]. He married (2) REBECCA NARCISSUS RENFROE[127] April 1802 in Madison County, Kentucky[127]. She was born January 24, 1775[127], and died September 06, 1863 in Macoupin County, Illinois[127]. Buried Land Cemetery, Scottville Twp., Macoupin County, Illinois[127]

Children of JOHN LAND and ELIZABETH BARLOW are:

70. i. MILDRED[7] LAND, b. December 27, 1782.
ii. THOMAS LAND[127], b. March 26, 1783[127]; m. VIRGINIA JANE MILLER[127], February 14, 1814, Madison County, Kentucky[127].
71. iii. HENRY LAND, b. December 25, 1784.
72. iv. JOHN FISHER LAND, b. December 02, 1786; d. 1849.
73. v. JUDITH LAND, b. October 22, 1788, Madison County, Kentucky.
74. vi. WILLIAM LAND, b. December 07, 1790, Kentucky; d. 1815.
vii. JAMES LAND[127], b. October 14, 1792, Jessamine, Kentucky[127]; d. July 24, 1866, Sullivan County, Indiana[127]; m. (1) EDITH LIVINGSTON[127]; b. Abt. 1790[127]; m. (2) JANE WILLIS[127], March 12, 1817, Jessamine County, Kentucky[127]; m. (3) PERMELIA HELMS[127], September 16, 1830[127]; b. Abt. 1805[127].
75. viii. NANCY LAND, b. October 02, 1794, Scott County, Kentucky.
76. ix. ELIZABETH LAND, b. January 01, 1796, Scott County, Kentucky; d. April 09, 1880, Adams Township, Decatur, Indiana.

Children of JOHN LAND and REBECCA RENFROE are:

77. x. FOUNTAIN[7] LAND, b. February 07, 1803, Madison County, Kentucky; d. 1876.
xi. CECILA LAND[127], b. December 15, 1804, Madison County, Kentucky[127]; m. GARLAND PARRISH[127], Maury County, Tennessee[127].

41. MARY[6] LAND *(THOMAS[5], THOMAS[4], JOHN[3], CURTIS[2], CURTIS[1])* [127] was born May 03, 1756 in Albemarle County, Virginia[127], and died 1796 in Wilkes County, North Carolina[127]. She married THOMAS CARLTON [127] 1777 in Albemarle County, Virginia[127]. He was born May 03, 1756 in Wilkes County, North Carolina[127], and died May 1845 in Wilkes County, North Carolina[127].

Children of MARY LAND and THOMAS CARLTON are:

78. i. JOHN[7] CARLTON, b. July 29, 1778, Wilkes County, North Carolina; d. March 01, 1855, Beaver Creek, Wilkes County, North Carolina.
ii. CYNTHIA CARLTON[127], b. Abt. 1784[127].
79. iii. HENRY CARLTON, b. Abt. 1786, Wilkes County, North Carolina; d. Aft. 1837, Jackson County, Alabama.
80. iv. NANCY CARLTON, b. Abt. 1788, Wilkes County, North Carolina; d. Aft. 1860, Jackson County, Alabama.
81. v. THOMAS CARLTON, b. January 22, 1790, Wilkes County, North Carolina; d. January 14, 1877, Wilkes County, North Carolina.
82. vi. CELIA CARLTON, b. Abt. 1791, Wilkes County, North Carolina; d. Aft. 1880, Jackson County, Alabama.
vii. LEWIS CARLTON[127], b. Abt. 1792[127].
83. viii. JANE CARLTON, b. April 15, 1793, Wilkes County, North Carolina; d. March 15, 1865.
84. ix. MARY CARLTON, b. December 24, 1795, Wilkes County, North Carolina; d. October 05, 1860, Acton, Hood County, Texas.

42. JONATHAN[6] LAND *(THOMAS[5], THOMAS[4], JOHN[3], CURTIS[2], CURTIS[1])* [127] was born 1758 in Albemarle County, Virginia[127], and died Aft. 1820 in Wilkes County, North Carolina[127]. He married ELIZABETH ISBELL[127] December 27, 1779 in Wilkes County, North Carolina[127]. She was born October 19, 1762 in Albemarle County, Virginia[127], and died Aft. 1820 in Wilkes County, North Carolina[127].

Notes for JONATHAN LAND:
John Land Jr. sponsored his Baptismal in Albemarle Parish, Surry CO, VA.

1790 Wilkes CO, NC census
1 free white male of 16 and upward including head of families (JONATHAN)
3 free white male under 16 years (JOHN, JAMES LINVILLE SR. and WILLIAM THOMAS LAND.)
5 free white female including head of family. (ELIZABETH and daughters, FRANCES, NANCY and MARY, and probably a daughter that didn't survive childhood. The next daughter listed in genealogy records, ANN wasn't born until 1794.) Jonathan & Elizabeth's oldest, James Linville Land Sr. was my 3rd great-grandfather. He was born abt 1779. On 6,Jan.1807 he married Edith Livingston. She was a daughter of John Orrell Livingston and Lucy Martin. James died abt 1844 while Edith lived into the 1870's. The children and grandchildren of James and his siblings would experience the scourge of Civil War in the 1860's. (see related page " Tar-heel Confederates in my family tree ") John Land, born abt 1780 married Nancy Earp. They reportedly migrated to Tennessee in the 1820's. Frances or " Franky " Isbell Land married Joel Dodson (Dotson) and died in Texas abt 1852. Joel Dodson was born about 1779 in either North Carolina or Virginia. His father died when he was a child and he was reared by his widowed mother, Martha (Patty) Dodson. They lived in the Beaver Creek area of Western Wilkes Co., NC. Joel married Frances Isbell Land in Wilkes Co. about 18 Oct 1806. Aaron Parks, possibly a kinsman, was bondsman. Frances Isbell Land was born during the 1780's, daughter of Jonathan and Elizabeth Isbell Land.
On 1 May 1805, Joel was granted 100 acres of land on Beaver Creek adjoining land purchased by his mother in 1794, being part of the John Cook Survey. On 20 Sep 1808, Joel and his mother sold their land to Thomas Birch and shortly therafter moved to the Stewart Creek area south of Lincoln Co. in 1809. Joel remained in Lincoln Co. until 1834 when he sold his land there to his brother, Joshua Dodson, and moved to Benton [now Calhoun] Co., AL where he received a certificate for land on 12 Oct 1835.
Joel died in Talladega Co., AL [w.d. 4 Sep 1846; w.p. 24 Sep 1846; Talladega WB D-85/6]. Frances died between 1846 and 1850 in Talladega Co. According to a great granddaughter, born in 1877, the family graveyard was located in the Chenneby community in northeastern Talladega Co., but the family tombstones were no longer in existence in the 1960's.
Joel and Frances Land Dodson apparently had seven children:
Elijah Dodson *
[Son] Dodson
Constant Dodson *
Mahala Dodson *
William Riley Dodson *
Joel Dodson Jr. *
Nancy Dodson.

Children of JONATHAN LAND and ELIZABETH ISBELL are:

- i. FRANCES ISABELL[7] LAND[127], b. 1782[127]; d. 1852[127].
- 85. ii. JAMES LAND, b. 1784, Wilkes County, North Carolina; d. May 1844, Wilkes County, North Carolina.
- iii. NANCY LAND[127], b. 1787[127]; m. WILLIAM MALTBA[127], May 30, 1809, Wilkes County, North Carolina[127].
- 86. iv. WILLIAM THOMAS LAND, b. September 13, 1788, Wilkes County, North Carolina; d. July 09, 1871.
- v. SUSANNAH "SUSAN" LAND[127], b. 1789[127].
- vi. JR. JOHN LAND[127], b. Abt. 1790, Wilkes County, North Carolina[127]; m. NANCY EARP[127], March 20, 1817[127]; b. 1793, Pittsylvania Co. VA[127].

  More About JR. JOHN LAND:
  Travel: May have moved to Tennessee in the 1820's[127]

- 87. vii. MARY LAND, b. Aft. 1791, Wilkes County, North Carolina; d. 1828.
- 88. viii. ANN LAND, b. 1794, Wilkes County, North Carolina; d. Bef. 1850, Wilkes County, North Carolina.
- 89. ix. ELIZABETH LAND, b. Abt. 1795, Wilkes County, North Carolina; d. Abt. 1835, Wilkes County, North Carolina.

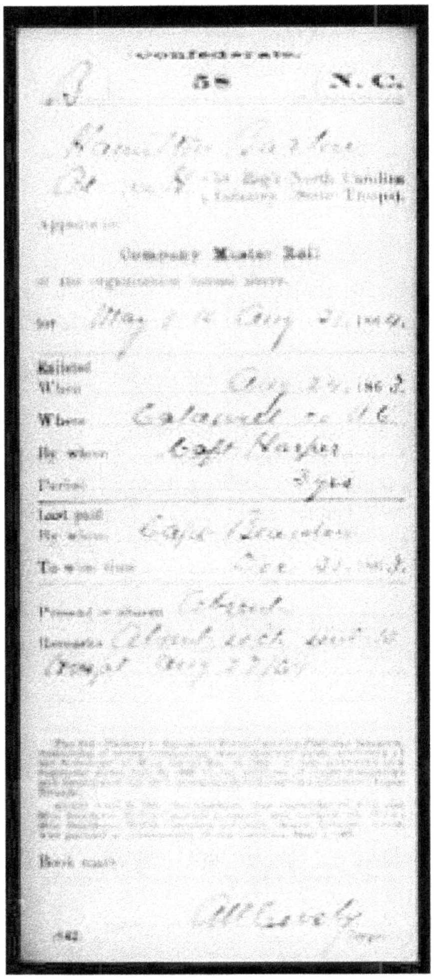
Confederate.

58 N.C.

Reg't North Carolina Infantry State Troops.

Appears on

Company Muster Roll

of the organization named above,

for May 1 to Aug 31, 1864.

Enlisted
When Aug 24, 1863.
Where
By whom Capt Harper
Period 3 yrs
Last paid
By whom
To what time Dec 31, 1863.

Present or absent Absent

Remarks

Book mark:

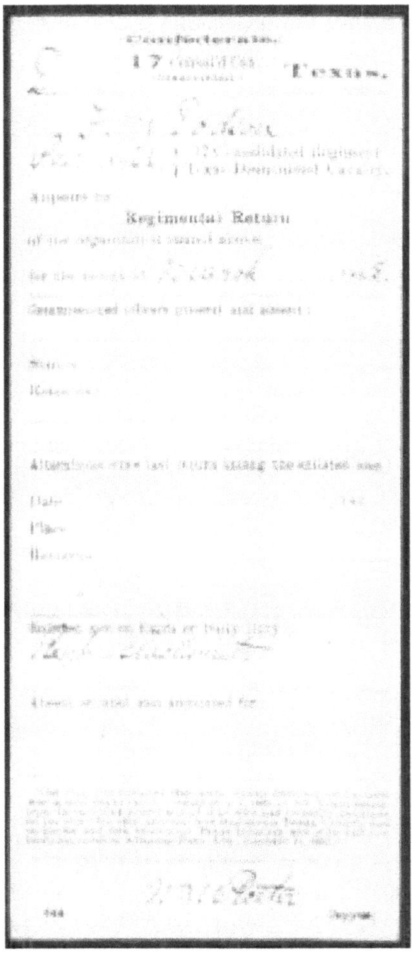
Confederate.

17 Consolidated Texas.

Appears on

Regimental Return

of the organization named above,

Commissioned officers present and absent:

Station

Remarks

Alterations since last return among the enlisted men:

Date

Place

Remarks

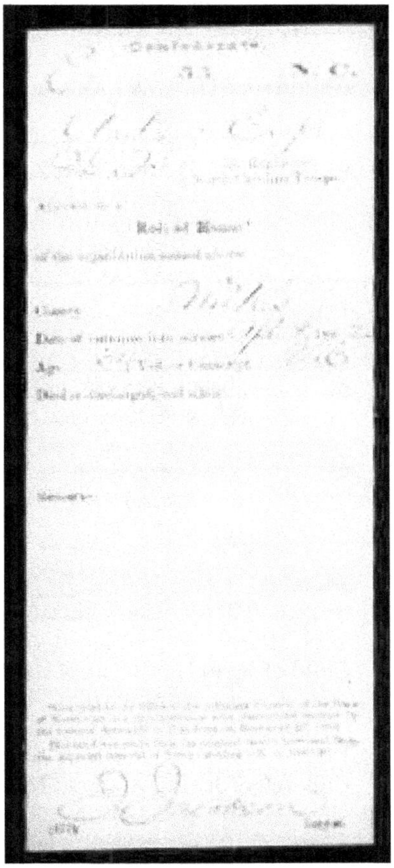
Confederate.

N.C.

Appears on a

Roll of Honor

of the organization named above.

Casualty

Date of entrance into service

Age

Died or discharged

Remarks

Confederate Soldiers: Barlow, Dodson and Earp

90. x. LETTICE LAND, b. 1796; d. July 1842, Lawrence County, Indiana.
91. xi. JR. JONATHON LAND, b. 1798, Wilkes County, North Carolina; d. Abt. 1865, Wilkes County, North Carolina.
xii. MAHALA LAND[127], b. 1804[127]; m. REUBEN KNIGHT[127], 1829, Wilkes County, NC.[127].
92. xiii. MILLIE LAND, b. 1806.

43. THOMAS[6] LAND *(THOMAS[5], THOMAS[4], JOHN[3], CURTIS[2], CURTIS[1])*[127] was born Abt. 1766 in Albemarle County, Virginia[127], and died 1798 in Wilkes County, North Carolina[127]. He married (1) ELIZABETH MORGAN[127]. He married (2) ANNA NANCY MCGEE[127] Abt. 1787 in Wilkes County, North Carolina[127]. She was born 1765[127].

Children of THOMAS LAND and ELIZABETH MORGAN are:
i. MARY[7] LAND[127], b. 1786[127]; d. 1867[127]; m. THOMAS WILSON[127].
ii. CHARLES LAND[127], b. 1793[127]; d. Limestone County, Alabama[127]; m. SARAH BASS THOMPSON[127].
93. iii. THOMAS LAND, b. 1795; d. 1867.
iv. ELIZABETH LAND[127], b. 1800[127]; d. 1821[127]; m. NATHAN BAKER[127].
v. SARAH LAND[127], b. 1803[127]; d. October 11, 1843[127]; m. SILAS WHERRY[127].
vi. CAROLINE LAND[127], b. 1805[127]; m. (1) JOSEPH C. MCBEE[127]; m. (2) WILLIAM JOHNSON[127].
vii. JOHN LAND[127], b. 1807[127].

Children of THOMAS LAND and ANNA MCGEE are:
94. viii. FRANCES[7] LAND, b. Abt. 1785, Wilkes County, North Carolina; d. Bef. 1850, Monroe County, Tennessee.
ix. SUSANNAH LAND[127], b. Abt. 1789, Wilkes County, North Carolina[127]; d. Bef. 1850, Monroe County, Tennessee[127]; m. JOHN GRAY[127], January 31, 1811, Wilkes County, North Carolina[127]; b. 1788[127]; d. 1850[127].
95. x. JAMES NOAH LAND, b. Abt. 1793, Wilkes County, North Carolina; d. Abt. 1893, Tennessee.
xi. ANNA LAND[127], b. Abt. 1795[127].

44. JOHN[6] LAND *(JOHN[5], THOMAS[4], JOHN[3], CURTIS[2], CURTIS[1])*[127] was born Abt. 1768 in South Carolina[127], and died Bef. 1830 in Madison County, Alabama[127]. He married (1) MARY DYE[127]. He married (2) MARY TYLER[127].

Child of JOHN LAND and MARY DYE is:
i. JOHN[7] LAND[127], b. Abt. 1788[127].

Children of JOHN LAND and MARY TYLER are:
ii. WILLIAM TYLER[7] LAND[127], b. Abt. 1805, Holmes County, Mississippi[127]; d. January 1850, Holmes County, Mississippi[127]; m. MAHULDA RAMSAY[127], July 26, 1827[127].
iii. ELIZA LAND[127], b. Abt. 1809[127]; m. JAMES SCOTT[127], July 05, 1827[127].
iv. ELIHU LAND[127], b. Abt. 1811[127]; m. MARGARETE WHERRY[127], July 21, 1833[127].
96. v. DELILAH LAND, b. 1812, Madison County, Alabama; d. Abt. 1870, Phelps County, Missouri.
vi. DAUGHTER LAND[127], b. 1814[127].
vii. JEREMIAH LAND[127], b. Abt. 1815[127].
viii. ENOS LAND[127], b. Abt. 1818[127].
ix. MARY ANN LAND[127], b. Abt. 1820[127]; m. AARON BURT[127], January 13, 1836[127].

45. SUMTER[6] LAND *(JOHN[5], THOMAS[4], JOHN[3], CURTIS[2], CURTIS[1])*[127] was born Abt. 1770[127]. He married (1) OBEDIENCE FEATHERSTONE[127]. He married (2) SARAH MAUDE RICHARDS[127].

Child of SUMTER LAND and OBEDIENCE FEATHERSTONE is:
i. RICHARD[7] LAND[127], b. Abt. 1800[127].

46. MARY[6] LAND *(CHARLES[5], CHARLES[4], CURTIS[3], CURTIS[2], CURTIS[1])*[127] was born 1830 in Edgecombe County, North Carolina[127], and died Aft. 1870 in Wilson, North Carolina[127]. She married ETHELRED JORDON[127] January 05, 1853 in Edgecombe, North Carolina[127]. He was born Abt. 1820[127].

Children of MARY LAND and ETHELRED JORDON are:
i. SMITH[7] JORDON[127], b. 1855[127].

ii. HENRY JORDON[127], b. 1857[127].
iii. CHARLES JORDON[127], b. 1859[127].
iv. MARTHA JORDON[127], b. 1861[127].
v. CATHERINE JORDON[127], b. 1866[127].
vi. JOHN JORDON[127], b. 1869[127].

47. JOHN HENRY[6] LAND *(CHARLES[5], CHARLES[4], CURTIS[3], CURTIS[2], CURTIS[1])*[127,128,129] was born May 22, 1831 in Edgecombe County, North Carolina[130], and died January 17, 1927 in Marion, South Carolina[130]. He married (1) SARA SUGGS[130]. She was born September 25, 1843 in Darlington, South Carolina [130]. He married (2) CAROLINE CRUMPLEY ODOM[130]. She was born Abt. 1830[130]. He married (3) CAROLINE CRUMPLY ODOM[131,132] December 23, 1850[132,133]. She was born 1830[133,134], and died 1860[135,136].

Children of JOHN LAND and SARA SUGGS are:
i. DELLA[7] LAND[137], m. (1) MCPHERSON; m. (2) J. C. WINSTEAD.
ii. SUSAN LAND[137], m. FURMAN MORTIMER, Aft. 1860, Darlington Co., South Carolina.

Children of JOHN LAND and CAROLINE ODOM are:
iii. HENRIETTA[7] LAND[137], m. CADE DAVIS[137].
97. iv. WILLIAM JEFFERSON LAND, b. October 11, 1851; d. February 24, 1929, Reeves Allen, Louisiana.
v. HENRITTA[7] LAND[138,139], b. WFT Est. 1849-1860[140,141]; d. WFT Est. 1853-1950[142,143].

48. CETH SMITH[6] LAND *(CHARLES[5], CHARLES[4], CURTIS[3], CURTIS[2], CURTIS[1])*[144] was born December 09, 1833 in Edgecombe County, North Carolina[144], and died December 26, 1889 in South Carolina[144]. He married MARY JANE THIGPEN[144] September 19, 1860[144]. She was born December 12, 1837 [144].

Children of CETH LAND and MARY THIGPEN are:
98. i. JOHN CALHOUN[7] LAND, b. June 25, 1862; d. July 25, 1943.
ii. DORA ADA LAND[144], b. December 07, 1866[144]; d. August 07, 1944[144].
iii. CHARLES HUGH LAND[144], b. April 28, 1872[144]; d. November 10, 1873[144].
iv. MARY JANE LAND[144], b. 1874[144]; d. 1893[144].
99. v. CETH SMITH LAND, b. March 05, 1876; d. December 27, 1924.

49. WILLIAM[6] LAND *(JESSE[5], CHARLES[4], CURTIS[3], CURTIS[2], CURTIS[1])*[144] was born 1827 in Georgia[144], and died Aft. 1860 in Twiggs, Georgia[144]. He married MOLLY UNKNOWN [144] 1857[144]. She was born 1840 [144].

Child of WILLIAM LAND and MOLLY UNKNOWN is:
100. i. JOHN T.[7] LAND, b. April 1858, Georgia; d. Aft. 1900, Randolph, Georgia.

50. JOHN[6] LAND *(JESSE[5], CHARLES[4], CURTIS[3], CURTIS[2], CURTIS[1])*[144] was born 1830 in Georgia[144], and died Aft. 1860 in Twiggs, Georgia[144]. He married ELIZABETH UNKNOWN [144]. She was born Abt. 1832 [144].

Children of JOHN LAND and ELIZABETH UNKNOWN are:
i. ELIZA E.[7] LAND[144], b. 1855[144].
ii. MARTHA J. LAND[144], b. 1857[144].
iii. MARY E. LAND[144], b. 1858[144].
iv. RHODY A. T. LAND[144], b. 1859[144].

51. JESSE[6] LAND *(JESSE[5], CHARLES[4], CURTIS[3], CURTIS[2], CURTIS[1])*[144] was born 1845 in Georgia[144], and died Aft. 1900 in Twiggs, Georgia[144]. He married LOUISA MITT [144]. She was born 1858 [144].

Children of JESSE LAND and LOUISA MITT are:
i. SARAH E.[7] LAND[144], b. 1872[144].
ii. GEORGE LAND[144], b. July 1875[144].

iii. JESSEY LAND[144], b. September 1876[144].
iv. JINNIE LAND[144], b. January 1889[144].

52. CHARLES[6] LAND *(JESSE[5], CHARLES[4], CURTIS[3], CURTIS[2], CURTIS[1])*[144] was born 1848 in Georgia[144], and died Abt. 1900 in Bibb, Georgia[144]. He married NANCY UNKNOWN[144]. She was born 1858 in Georgia[144].

Child of CHARLES LAND and NANCY UNKNOWN is:
101. i. WILLIAM[7] LAND, b. January 1876; d. Aft. 1910, Bibb, Georgia.

53. BENJAMIN FRANKLIN[6] LAND *(JESSE[5], CHARLES[4], CURTIS[3], CURTIS[2], CURTIS[1])*[144] was born June 1852[144]. He married MATILDA UNKNOWN[144]. She was born February 1857[144].

Children of BENJAMIN LAND and MATILDA UNKNOWN are:
i. MARY[7] LAND[144], b. 1875, Georgia[144].
ii. JAMES R. LAND[144], b. July 1883, Georgia[144].
iii. NANCY LAND[144], b. August 1885[144].

54. SOPHRONIA[6] BRASWELL *(SUSAN (SOPHY)[5] LAND, CHARLES[4], CURTIS[3], CURTIS[2], CURTIS[1])* was born 1827 in North Carolina. She married WILLIE DOUTRIDGE November 03, 1847 in Nash, North Carolina. He was born 1827 in North Carolina, and died Aft. 1860 in Nash, North Carolina.

Children of SOPHRONIA BRASWELL and WILLIE DOUTRIDGE are:
i. SUSAN[7] DOUTRIDGE, b. 1850.
ii. CHARITY DOUTRIDGE, b. 1852.

55. JOHN BRAXTON[6] LAND *(JOHN[5], ROBERT[4], WILLIAM[3], CURTIS[2], CURTIS[1])* was born Abt. 1771 in Albemarle Co., Virginia, and died Abt. 1812 in Buckingham Co., Virginia. He married FRANCES B. NICHOLSON Abt. 1797 in Buckingham Co., Virginia. She was born Bef. 1775 in Virginia, and died Abt. 1839 in Lexington, Saline Co., Missouri.

Children of JOHN LAND and FRANCES NICHOLSON are:
i. ELIJAH R.[7] LAND, b. Abt. 1798, Buckingham Co., Virginia; d. December 1823, Shelby Co., Kentucky; m. ELIZABETH H. ELLIS, January 24, 1820, Shelby Co., Kentucky.
ii. MARY LAND, b. Abt. 1799, Buckingham Co., Virginia; d. Abt. 1851, Jefferson Co., Missouri; m. STEPHEN GARROTT, April 05, 1821, Buckingham Co., Virginia.
iii. JANE K. LAND, b. Abt. 1800.
iv. ROBERT CARTER LAND, b. December 20, 1801, Buckingham Co., Virginia; d. July 28, 1882, Cambridge, Saline Co., Missouri; m. AMERICA UNKNOWN, Bet. 1818 - 1851.
v. CHARLOTTE LAND, b. June 03, 1804, Buckingham Co., Virginia; d. February 22, 1885, Cambridge, Saline Co., Missouri.
vi. NICHOLAS RUFUS LAND, b. Abt. 1809, Buckingham Co., Virginia; d. April 22, 1885, Corn Hill, Williamson Co., Texas; m. (1) MARGARET A. WILSON; m. (2) ELIZABETH A. GILES; m. (3) JUDITH SAUNDERS, December 23, 1834, Prince Edward Co., Virginia.
vii. FRANCES HATCHER LAND, b. March 25, 1811, Buchanan, Botetourt Co., Virginia; d. July 23, 1887, Granger, Williamson Co., TX.

56. FRANCES LAND[6] JR *(FRANCES ELLIDGE[5] LAND, JOHN[4], WILLIAM[3], CURTIS[2], CURTIS[1])*[144] was born July 01, 1779[144], and died October 10, 1854 in Beaver Creek, Fairfield Co., South Carolina. He married ELIZABETH LITTLETON Abt. 1802. She was born 1783 in South Carolina, and died October 18, 1871 in Beaver Creek, Fairfield Co., South Carolina. Burial: Beaver Creek Baptist Church, Fairfield Co., South Carolina. Another source gives her name as Elizabeth Halsell. Burial: Beaver Creek Baptist Church, Fairfield Co., South Carolina

Children of FRANCES JR and ELIZABETH LITTLETON are:
i. JOHN LAND[7] JR.

ii. ELEDGE HALL LAND, b. 1819, South Carolina; d. Aft. 1872; m. (1) NANCY JANE THOMAS; m. (2) MARY ANN ARNETT, Bef. 1845; b. October 12, 1829, Chester Co., South Carolina; d. December 20, 1848.

Notes for ELEDGE HALL LAND:
His name was also spelled Eldridge Hall Land.
Eldridge's children are listed with their grandfather, Francis Land, in the 1850 and 1860 Chester County, SC census lists. 1850: Land, Francis 72, $7680; Elizabeth, 67; Henrietta, 61; Eliza H., 31; Frances H., 29; Francis, 5; Sarah J., 3.
1860: Land, Elizabeth, 78; $9578; Francis 14; Sarah J. 13; Henrietta 75 (Halsilville PO).
Mr. Castles wrote a letter, dated October 17, 1959, to Mrs. Crowder and stated: "You made a good try of the Land name. It is Ellege Land. He was a prize bum. I have written proof of that. Think he died in the Chester County Poor House. His family would have nothing to do with him and with good cause.

Ellege H. Land was the son of Francis and Elizabeth (Halsell) Land. This is the Elizabeth Land buried in Beaver Creek Cemetery. Father says she was a Halsell or Halsey, as it was often spelled. That is the reason for my interest in the family. So far no proof of Elizabeth being a Halsey. The Halsellville section was full of them before the War. Alabama, Mississippi, Arkansas, and Texas have them all now.
The "next friend" was Francis Hicks Land, brother of Ellege. I think the "H" in Ellege's name stands for Halsell. Not sure of course."

A copy of Mr. Castles' letter was given by Cynthia Snider in 2000.

****
From the research of William F. Roberts (emailto:bill@wfroberts.com]
webpage: http://www.wfroberts.com/

INITIAL CHARGE
(NOTE: This document was hand written)
South Carolina
CHESTER DISTRICT
Whereas Elarey H. Land makes complaints on oath unto me, Wm. Thomas, Magistrate, that on the night of the fourth of May inst William Roberts Snor (Senior) did by (buy) corn from a Negro man contrary to the laws of South Carolina. Sworn before me the 5th day of May 1846.
Signed E.H. Land and by Wm. Thomas Magistrate

(The prosecutor was E.H. Land (Eledge H. Land) son of Francis Land and Elizabeth Littleton)

THE WARRANT FOR WILLIAM'S ARREST
Hand written
To Cephas Bolick Special Constable, these are therefore in the name of the State to command you forthwith to apprehend the said William Roberts and bring him before me to be dealt with according to the law in that case. Given under my hand and seal the fifth day of May one thousand eight hundred and forty six.
Wm. Thomas Magistrate

THE FORMAL CHARGE
Recorded by hand on a pre-printed form titled in the upper right corner
Indictment for Negro Trading - Morgan's Pt. Columbia>

STATE OF South Carolina
Chester District
At a court of General Session, begun and holden in and for the district of Chester in the State of South Carolina at Chester Court House in the District and state aforesaid, on the first Monday after the fourth Monday of October in the year of our Lord one thousand eight hundred and forty six.
The jurors of and for the District of Chester in the State of South Carolina aforesaid, that is to say upon their oaths, present, that William Roberts, Senior late of Chester district, laborer, in the District of Chester on the fourth day of May in the year of our Lord one thousand eight hundred and forty six with force and arms at Chester Court House in the District of Chester aforesaid, did buy and purchase for and from a certain slave of Francis Land named Joe a quantity of corn of the value of fifty cents the said slave then and there not having a permit so to sell, from or under the hand of the said F. Land or from and under the hand of any person having the care and management of said slave; against the form of the Act of General Assembly, in such case made and provided, and against the peace and dignity of the same State aforesaid. and the Jurors aforesaid, on their oaths aforesaid, do further present, that the said William Roberts on the Forth day of May in the same year aforesaid,

with force and arms at Chester Court House in the district of Chester aforesaid, did deal, trade and traffic with a certain slave of Francis Land named Joe by buying and purchasing from said slave a quantity of Indian corn and selling to said slave one pair of shoes the said slave then and there not having a permit so to deal , trade or traffic, from or under the hand of the said F. Land or from and under the hand of any person having the care and management of the said Slave, against the form of the Act of the General Assembly in such case made and provided, and against the peace and dignity of the said state aforesaid.
Signature (Appears to be Dawekins Lola)

Summary of Document
On June 6, 1846

Cephas Bolick, Special Constable was commissioned to bring the following before the court to provide testimony in the case against William Roberts.
Wm. Hedgepath, Cephas Bolick, Charles Parrott, Samuel Brice, John Thompson, (scratched through name. I could not read it.), Jesse Simpson, John Halsell, F.H. Land.

William Roberts was found guilty November 3 1846. He appeared to have been fined $93.15

From: wfroberts [bill@wfroberts.com]
Sent: Thursday, April 27, 2006 7:04 AM
To: Linda Hull
Subject: Re: Land
I'm coNCerned your couldn't get onto the web site. Did you try ww.wfroberts.com?
Regardless here is the limited information I have there. I will be changing Elizabeth Littleton to Elizabeth Halsell. That only makes this story more interesting because the son of the William Roberts, who traded with Francis Land's slave, was also named William Roberts and he married Jane Halsell (daughter of Peter Halsell and Sarah Combest)

Trading with a Negro

A William Roberts was arrested 9 May 1846 for trading with a Negro. Since there were a number of William Roberts, three of whom are my direct ancestors, the first question is which William Roberts are we talking about. I believe "Dogwood Bill" was dead by 1846. That would leave William Roberts, known as "Bill Sprout', and his son William Roberts, known as "Little Bill Sprout." The court papers repeatedly refer to William Roberts, Senior. The use of Senior or Junior in old court records was used to distinguish between people with the same name. It does not always imply a relationship. Since the legal documents made such an effort to distinguish between more than one William Roberts, there is little doubt that Bill Sprout was our relative who got in trouble with the law by trading with the slave.

William traded shoes with Joe, a slave belonging to Mr. Francis Land. John Halsell and Samuel Brice posted bond for William. John Halsell must have been John H. Halsell, Jane Halsell's brother. Jane Halsell had recently married William's son "Little Bill Sprout."

Following are transcripts of the court documents:

INITIAL CHARGE
(NOTE: This document was hand written)
South Carolina
CHESTER DISTRICT
Whereas Elarey H. Land makes complaints on oath unto me, Wm. Thomas, Magistrate, that on the night of the fourth of May inst William Roberts Snor(Senior) did by (buy) corn from a Negro man contrary to the laws of South Carolina. Sworn before me the 5th day of May 1846.
Signed E.H. Land and by Wm. Thomas Magistrate

(The prosecutor was E.H. Land (Eledge H. Land) son of Francis Land and Elizabeth Littleton)

THE WARRANT FOR WILLIAM'S ARREST
Hand written
To Cephas Bolick Special Constable, these are therefore in the name of the State to command you forthwith to apprehend the said William Roberts and bring him before me to be dealt with according to the law in that case. Given under my hand and seal the fifth day of May one thousand eight hundred and forty six.
Wm. Thomas Magistrate

THE FORMAL CHARGE
Recorded by hand on a pre-printed form titled in the upper right corner
Indictment for Negro Trading - Morgan's Pt. Columbia>

STATE OF South Carolina
Chester District
At a court of General Session, begun and holden in and for the district of Chester in the State of South Carolina at Chester Court House in the District and state aforesaid, on the first Monday after the fourth Monday of October in the year of our Lord one thousand eight hundred and forty six.
The jurors of and for the District of Chester in the State of South Carolina aforesaid, that is to say upon their oaths, present, that William Roberts, Senior late of Chester district, laborer, in the District of Chester on the fourth day of May in the year of our Lord one thousand eight hundred and forty six with force and arms at Chester Court House in the District of Chester aforesaid, did buy and purchase for and from a certain slave of Francis Land named Joe a quantity of corn of the Value of fifty cents the said slave then and there not having a permit so to sell, from or under the hand of the said F. Land or from and under the hand of any person having the care and management of said slave; against the form of the Act of General Assembly, in such case made and provided, and against the peace and dignity of the same State aforesaid. and the Jurors aforesaid, on their oaths aforesaid, do further present, that the said William Roberts on the Forth day of May in the same year aforesaid, with force and arms at Chester Court House in the district of Chester aforesaid, did deal, trade and traffic with a certain slave of Francis Land named Joe by buying and purchasing from said slave a quantity of Indian corn and selling to said slave one pair of shoes the said slave then and there not having a permit so to deal , trade or traffic, from or under the hand of the said F. Land or from and under the hand of any person having the care and management of the said Slave, against the form of the Act of the General Assembly in such case made and provided, and against the peace and dignity of the said state aforesaid.

Signature (Appears to be Dawekins

****

Notes for Mary Ann Arnett:

Mary Ann's father, John Q. Arnett lists her in his will as his "oldest daughter who wedded to Eldridge H. Land leaving at her death two infant children viz Francis Land and Sarah Land my grandchildren." Will received April 28, 2003, from Bobby Ray Rawls" @ brrawls@crcom.net

Marriage Notes for Eldridge Land and Mary Arnett:
Marriage listed in Fairfield County Marriages 1775-1879 Implied in Fairfield County South Carolina Probate Records, by Barbara R. Langdon.

Generation No. 2

2. Francis Land, born 21 Jul 17703; died 10 Oct 1854 in Chester County, South Carolina3 He married 3. Elizabeth Halsell.

3. Elizabeth Halsell, born Abt. 1783; died 18 Oct 18713.

Notes for Francis Land:
Francis purchased land in August, 1798 per Deed Book F, page 227, 223, & 234, and in November, 1804 per Deed Book K, page 251.

On July 22, 1850, Francis made his will with a codicil recorded on October 27, 1854, in Chester Co., SC per Probate Records 97-1627, A-118, B-406 and in Deed Book 152, page 880. He left the following bequests:
To his sister Hannah, the house she lives in and she was to be supported out of his estate.
To his daughter Dorcas Castles, the west end of the tract known as the Wright Place.
To the children of Elige Land, Francis and Sarah Land, part of the Wright tract with rents to go to the use of his grandchildren.
To his son, Francis H. Land, negros after wife's decease and also the home place after the wife's decease.
To his son, Littleton Land, land.
To his daughter, Nancy Land, he left land and notes owed by John Peas and Elledge Land ($55.00) and Jesse Castles ($500).
To his wife, Elizabeth, 345 acres of land, slaves Baccus, Joe, and Charity, and Charity's four children, Tom, Mielly, Ben, and Sarah during her lifetime.
******

In 1854, his will added $1,300 in Confederate Bonds to go to his wife. Purchases from his estate sale were John Brice, W. Land, Jesse Castles, F. N. Land, Robert Halsell, J. Chapman, R. F. Castles, W. H. Castles, and C. P. Shurley.

--This information was supplied by Cynthia Synder.

-17-

WILL OF

JOHN Q. ARNETT

STATE OF SOUTH CAROLINA

FAIRFIELD DISTRICT

I John Q. Arnett being of sound mind and Boddy do this day make and declare, this my last will and Testament being in Posefsion of someproperty and haveing been married the Second time haveing also Raised or Partly Two sets of children as follows Mary Ann Arnett my oldest Daughter who weded to Eldredge H. Land leavein g at her Death Two infant children viz Frances Land & Sarah Land. my grand children my second Daughter the wife of Hereudon Chalk, the abouve children I did directly and indirectly given in the whole sum Two Thousand Dollars from various Souces by Reference to deed &c in the Clerks and Commissioners offices of Chester Distric in this State, to Explain more fully I did at the time of dividing divide nearly Equal at that time since that time by my Prudence and industry together with various Legaces from my last wifes grand Fathers the Feasters and Colemans have collected the Pooperty I am now attempting to dispose off, and hopeing that the authorities to whoom this may come will in behalf of my Respected Family Sustain this my last will is as follows my children by my Present wife ElizaT. Arnett shall Receive Two Thousand dollars Each as they arrive at the age of Twenty One years of age to give there mother a Receipt for the same and then she shall Remain in full Pofsession of all my Estate after my Just Debts is Paid, Sell or but and her acts shall be good that is Remain in full Possession of all as though I was living and she Dead that she may not be subject to her children, at her Death then the Ballance of what she may leave if any shall be Equally Divided by all my children the first or Two shares to my Diseased Daughters children if they be Liveing if not

WILL OF JOHN Q. ARNETT

viz John Feaster Arnett, Beny Ann Arnett these are appointed as I before said to carry out my Will and they shall Receive for the same one Hundred Dollars Each for Settling up and closeing the / Estate my wife, to make no distinction in giveing One of her children more that the other Except in Contract to attend and afsist her in carrying out her wishes my next youngest children is Susan Rebecca Arnett & Robert Samuel Arnett all of which I hope will be properly understood and Sustained in my Every Prayr Amen

3d is that I have Two illegitamate children in the District of/ Chester and State of S. C. and now liveing on 50 acres of Land the Same I give and bequeath to them at my Death viz Thos Robberts and Perlina Robberts children of Luci Roberts and that Dr Saml W. B. McClarkin is hereby appointed there Trustee to cary out the same in witnefs whereof I have hereunto set my hand and Seal this 12th day of November 1855

John Q. Arnett (L S)

Jacob Feaster Jr

Julia A Feaster

John C Feaster

Proven--Date not found

Recorded in Will Book # 19

Pages 460-462

Recorded Aug. 26, 1856

Apt. 106 File 537

1820 Chester Co., SC Census

L530 CHESTER CO, SC LAND Francis M-033 120 047 - 220010 20110

1850 Chester Co., SC Census
97B/1536 Land, Francis 72, $7680, Elizabeth 67, Henrietta 62, Eliza H. 31, Frances H. 29, Francis 5, Sarah J. 3

1860 Chester Co., SC Census
28B/423 Land, Elizabeth 789, $9578, Francis 14, Sarah J. 13, Henrietta 75 (Halsilville PO)

More About Francis Land:
Burial Place: Beaver Creek Baptist Cemetery, Fairfield Co., SC3

Notes for Elizabeth Halsell:
Family Search Records retrieved June, 2006, by Linda Hull from
http://www.familysearch.org/Eng/search/frameset_search.asp?PAGE=ancestorsearchresults.asp

FamilySearch™ International Genealogical Index v5.0 North America
Family Group Record

Husband
Francis Land

Birth: About 1752 , Chester, South Carolina
Christening:
Marriage: About 1785 , Chester, South Carolina
Death: 27 OCT 1854 , Chester, South Carolina
Burial:

Wife
Elizabeth Halsell

Birth: , Chester, South Carolina
Christening:
Marriage: About 1785 , Chester, South Carolina
Death:
Burial:

Children

----

1. Dorcas Land
Female

Birth: 25 JUN 1812 , Chester, South Carolina
Christening:
Death:
Burial:

----

2. Littleberry Land
Male

Birth: About 1796 , Chester, South Carolina
Christening:
Death: SEP 1885 , Chester, South Carolina
Burial:

----

3. Elledge H. Land
Male

Birth: About 1798 , Chester, South Carolina
Christening:
Death: After 1866
Burial:

****

More About Elizabeth Halsell:
Burial Place: Beaver Creek Baptist Cemetery, Fairfield Co., SC3

Children of Francis Land and Elizabeth Halsell are:
i. Dorcas Land, married Jesse Castles.

Notes for Dorcas Land:
Chester, SC 1860 Federal Census
ftp://ftp.us-census.org/pub/usgenweb/census/sc/chester/1860/
(File 4 of 11)

This Census was transcribed by Ray Beam and proofread by Jo Beam
for the USGenWeb Census Project, http://www.us-census.org/

Census_Year 1860
Microfilm # M653-1217
State SC
County Chester

--------------------Begin Actual Transcription---------------------------------

CENSUS YR: 1860 STATE or TERRITORY: SC COUNTY: Chester REEL NO: M653-1217 PAGE NO: 52
REFERENCE: 7 July 1860 - Chester Post Office

LN	HN	FN	LAST NAME	FIRST NAME	AGE	SEX	RACE	OCCUP.	REAL VAL.	PERS VAL.	BIRTHPLACE	MRD.	SCH.	R/W	DDB	REMARKS
23	462	424	Cassels	Jesse	44	M	W	farming	8,775	6,339	S. Carolina	.	.	.	.	.
24	462	424	Cassels	Dorcas	48	F	W	.	.	.	S. Carolina	.	.	.	.	.
25	462	424	Cassels	Wm	22	M	W	.	.	.	S. Carolina	.	.	.	.	.
26	462	424	Cassels	Robert F.	15	M	W	.	.	.	S. Carolina	.	.	.	.	.

27	463	425	Cassels	John	20	M	W	farming	.	1,075	S. Carolina	. . . . . .
28	463	425	Cassels	Ellen	20	F	W	.	.	.	S. Carolina	. . . . . .
29	463	425	Cassels	Elizabeth	11/12	F	W	.	.	.	S. Carolina	. . . . . .

1 ii. Eldridge Hall Land, died Aft. 1872; married (1) Nancy Jane Thomas; married (2) Mary Ann Arnett Bef. 1845.

iii. Nancy Land

iv. Littleton Land4, born 11 May 1807 in Chester Co., South Carolina; died 27 Sep 1885 in Chester Co., South Carolina5; married Sarah Wilkes; born 20 Jan 1807 in Baton Rouge, Chester Co., South Carolina6; died 19 Dec 1890 in Chester Co., South Carolina6.

Notes for Littleton Land:
Littleton is buried in Calvary Baptist Church Cemetery. Calvary Baptist Church was established in 1838. Census records list Littleton in Chester County in 1840, 1850, & 1860.

Story from the book, "A Goodly Heritage", page 152 says:

"The Broad River area of Chester County made national headlines in 1937 in an incident that read like an Arabian Nights tale.

Tradition, based on some known facts, was that a large land owner and blacksmith, Littleton Land, amassed a fortune and converted it into gold coins. When Sherman and his Union army headed toward Chester, it was rumored he brought three buckets of gold coins and buried them on his Broad River plantation. A servant, Zed Land, who cared for his master for many years reportedly told of helping to bury the money under the anvil block of the blacksmith shop.

Littleton Land, whose son was killed in the Civil War and whose daughter died young and unmarried, himself died of cancer around 1885, leaving no heirs. He deeded a portion of land to his faithful servant, Zed. The three buckets of gold over a period of years became no more than a tradition and a good topic of conversation and speculation.

On Easter Sunday, 1937, Tobin Crank, a young Negro truck and descendant of Zed Land, was chopping wood in the front yard of his home on the former Land farm. His axe went into the ground and struck a pile of gold coins in a rotting bucket.

Tobin Crank, 24, had struck it rich. A count of the money made by Mrs. Hattie Y. Harden, Probate Judge of Chester County, revealed there was $6,900 worth of gold coins, most of them in $20 gold pieces. Crank's wild excitement spread to his family and over the entire surrounding area, and the curious beat a path to his door. Rumor goes there was considerable diggin in those parts, also. The remaining two buckets of gold have not yet been found."

CENSUS YR: 1850 STATE or TERRITORY: SC COUNTY: Chester REEL NO: M432-851 PAGE NO: 186
REFERENCE: Enumerated 13 Nov 1850

93B/1464 Land, Littleton 42, $7126, Sarah 42, Lydia 16, Richard 14

1860 Census, Chester Co., SC

21A/316 Land, Littleton 53, $35710, Sallie 53, Lydia 27, Richard 25 (Baton Rouge PO)

1870 Census, Chester Co., SC

Page 72, House 50
Land, Littleton, 63, Sarah 83, Lydia 39

More About Littleton Land:
Burial Place: Calvary Baptist Church Cemetery, Chester County, SC7

Notes for Sarah Wilkes:

Article on Sarah Wilkes Land taken from page 275 of the Heritage History of Chester County, South Carolina, 1982 by Anne Collins:

Sarah Wilkes, daughter of William and Lydia (Clark) Wilkes was born near Baton Rouge, Chester County, South Carolina on 20 January 1807. She died on 19 December 1890 and was buried in the cemetery of Calvary Baptist Church. It is important to note that she gave South Carolina as the place of birth of her parents in the 1880 census of the United States. She married Littleton Land (1807-1885), son of Francis Land, Sr.

Littleton Land was the owner of more than a thousand acres of land that he farmed near Leeds, Chester County. He also owned several slaves. He is said to have been quite a miser and usually objected to his wife attending church, however, on one particular day he urged her to go to church. When she returned she missed a pot of gold and her husband would not tell her where it was.

He and his wife and their children died without ever having brought the pot of gold to light. Some years ago the old place was sold to a descendant of one of Littleton Land's slaves, and one day while plowing where Land's shop had been he uncovered a hoard of gold that amounted to about $6,000. It had been buried under the anvil block.

There was quite a stir about the find. Relatives claimed the money, but the court decided that it belonged to the new owner of the land. Some people of the neighborhood think that this was not the only money hidden by Littleton Land.

Children born to Mr. and Mrs. Land were Lydia born 25 December 1831, died 8 July 1883, and Richard Land born 1835, killed in the War Between the States in January 1862." -copy in possession of Linda Hull

More About Sarah Wilkes:
Burial Place: Calvary Baptist Church Cemetery, Chester County, SC

v. Francis Hicks Land, born 18218; married Julia E.; born Abt. 18338.

Notes for Francis Hicks Land:
F.H. Land is listed on a list of Election Managers for 1849:

To: SCCHEST2-L@rootsweb.com
Subject: [SCCHEST2] 1849 List of Election Managers

CHESTER LIST OF ELECTION MANAGERS 1849:

Court House: JOHN S. WILSON, JOHN J. McLURE , W.TAYLOR GILMORE.-

Fishing Creek Church: DR. R.A. CRAWFORD, GEORGE H. NEELY, JONAS RAIDER.

Republican: JAMES LEE, WM. E. KELSEY, W.P. BROACH.-

Cherry's Store: R.H. FUDGE, A.J. RODDY, R. CHERRY.-

McCreary and Gaston's Store: PETER HARDEN, A.B. BROWN, JAS. R. MORGAN.-

Rich Hill: J.B. MAGILL, HENRY MOFFUTT, JOHN G. BACKSTROM.-

Rossville : D.R. STEPHENSON, ABM. GIBSON, JNO. WESTBROOK.-

Boyd's : JESSE SIMPSON, F.H. LAND, NATH'L B. HOLLY.-

McAlilly's Mill : COLEMAN CROSBY, ANDERSON MAYS, T.R. COLVIN.-

Sander's : JAMES MEEK, SMITH SANDERS, ANDREW SANDERS.-

Wm. Cladwell's : WM. WYLIE, WM. G. BARBER, JOHN HOOD.-

Lowry's Old Academy : ROBERT HOPE, ALEX SMITH, WM. C. BECKHUM.-

Minter's : JAS.S. TURNER, CHAS. JOHNSEY, EVANDER MINTER.

The polls to be kept open two days at the Court House and only on Tuesday at the other places.-

{Source; 1849 edition of Reports and Resolutions for S.C.}
Free Post- nancie
--- Nancie O'Sullivan
--- drayton5@earthlink.net

Census_Year 1850
Microfilm # M432-851
State SC
County Chester

CENSUS YR: 1850 STATE or TERRITORY: SC COUNTY: Chester REEL NO: M432-851 PAGE NO: 194
REFERENCE: Enumerated 16 Nov 1850

28	1536	1536	Land	Francis	72	M	W	farmer	7,680	S. Carolina	.	.	.	.	.	.
29	1536	1536	Land	Elizabeth	67	F	W	.	.	S. Carolina	.	.	.	.	.	
30	1536	1536	Land	Henrietta	62	F	W	.	.	S. Carolina	.	.	.	.	.	
31	1536	1536	Land	Eliza H.	31	F	W	.	.	S. Carolina	.	.	.	.	.	
32	1536	1536	Land	Francis H.	29	M	W	farmer	.	S. Carolina	.	.	.	.	.	
33	1536	1536	Land	Francis	5	M	W	.	.	S. Carolina	.	.	.	.	.	
34	1536	1536	Land	Sarah J.	3	F	W	.	.	S. Carolina	.	.	.	.	.	

Chester, SC 1860 Federal Census
ftp://ftp.us-census.org/pub/usgenweb/census/sc/chester/1860/
(File 4 of 11)

This Census was transcribed by Ray Beam and proofread by Jo Beam for the USGenWeb Census Project, http://www.us-census.org/

Census_Year 1860
Microfilm # M653-1217
State SC
County Chester

CENSUS YR: 1860 STATE or TERRITORY: SC COUNTY: Chester REEL NO: M653-1217 PAGE NO: 56
REFERENCE: 11 July 1860 - Halselville Post Office

12	460	422	Land	Francis H.	39	M	W	farming	800	7,204	S. Carolina	.	.	.	.	.	.
13	460	422	Land	Julia E.	27	F	W	.	.	.	S. Carolina	.	.	.	.	.	
14	460	422	Land	Charles	8	M	W	.	.	.	S. Carolina	.	X	.	.		

15	460	422	Land	Richard G.	7	M	W	.	.	.	S. Carolina	. X . . .
16	460	422	Land	Rhoda E.	5	F	W	.	.	.	S. Carolina	. . . . .
17	460	422	Land	Frances	1	F	W	.	.	.	S. Carolina	. . . . .
18	460	422	Land	Harriet	4	F	W	.	.	.	S. Carolina	. . . . .
19	461	423	Land	Elizabeth	78	F	W	farming	4,400	9,578	S. Carolina	. . . . .
20	461	423	Land	Francis	14	M	W	.	.	.	S. Carolina	. . . . .
21	461	423	Land	Sarah J.	13	F	W	.	.	.	S. Carolina	. X . . .
22	461	423	Land	Henrietta	75	F	W	.	.	.	S. Carolina	. . .

vi. Jane Land9, born 25 Aug 1826; died 16 Jun 1849 in Fairfield County, South Carolina; married William Stevenson Jr..

Notes for Jane Land:
Obituary Notice from Associate Reformed Presbyterian Death & Marriage Notices, 1843-1863, From the Christian Magazine of the South, the Erskine Miscellany, and the Due West Telescope

Departed this life in Fairfield District, June 16th, 1849, Mrs. Jane Stevenson, wife of William Stevenson, Jr. and daughter of Francis and Elizabeth Land, aged twenty three years, nine months and twenty one days...(left) a husband...and infant son about three weeks old, which soon followed her to the grave. She had been a member of the Baptist Church.

____

Endnotes

1. Dept. of Commerce, Bureau of Census, Washington D.C., Census Records, (Dated June 21, 1937).
2. Barbara R. Langdon, Fairfield County Marriages 1775-1879 Implied in Fairfield Co. Probate Records.
3. Beaver Creek Baptist Church Cemetery Listing.
4. Anne Collins, Heritage History of Chester County, page 275.
5. Copied by Jean C. Apee, T. J. Caldwell, and J. E. Hart Jr. from tombstones, Calvary Baptist Churchyard Listing, Chester Co., SC, (November 8 & 9, 1982).
6. Anne Collins, Article titled Sarah Wilkes Land, (Heritage History of Chester County, South Carolina, 1982, 118 Saluda St. Chester, SC 29706).
7. Copied by Jean C. Apee, T. J. Caldwell, and J. E. Hart Jr. from tombstones, Calvary Baptist Churchyard Listing, Chester Co., SC, (November 8 & 9, 1982).
8. 1860 Chester County SC Census.
9. Associate Reformed Presbyterian Death & Marriage Notices 1843-1863, (Christian Magazine of the South, The Erskine Miscellany, The Due West Telescope, 1843-1863).

1880 Choctaw, Alabama Census: E. H. Land listed age 61, farmer. Eleye T. Land, born Alabama, age 13.

iii. FRANCES H. LAND.
iv. MARY LAND.
v. DORCAS LAND.
vi. NANCY LAND.
vii. LITTLETON LAND, b. 1805; d. 1883.
viii. LITTLEBERRY LAND, b. 1807; d. 1840.

57. ELDRIDGE HALL[6] LAND *(FRANCES[5], JOHN[4], WILLIAM[3], CURTIS[2], CURTIS[1])* was born 1819. He married NANCY JANE THOMAS.

Child of ELDRIDGE LAND and NANCY THOMAS is:
102. i. JOHN THOMAS[7] LAND, b. 1874, South Carolina.

58. BIRD[6] LAND *(LITTLEBERRY[5], BIRD[4], CURTIS[3], CURTIS[2], CURTIS[1])* [144,145] was born Abt. 1800 in Edgecombe County, North Carolina[146,147], and died Bef. 1850 in Noxubee County, Mississippi[148,149]. He married UNKNOWN SLEETER[150] 1824 in North Carolina[150]. She was born 1800 in North Carolina[150].

Children of BIRD LAND and UNKNOWN SLEETER are:

103. i. JOHN G.[7] LAND, b. 1825, North Carolina; d. Aft. 1880, Harrison County, Mississippi.
ii. ELISIA EVALINE LAND[152], b. 1828, Edgecombe County, North Carolina[152]; m. WILLIAM ENOCH[152], October 11, 1857, Rankin County, Mississippi[152].
104. iii. NANCY LAND, b. December 06, 1829, Edgecombe County, North Carolina; d. September 20, 1911, Dallas, Texas.
iv. MARY LAND[152], b. 1833, Edgecombe County, North Carolina[152]; m. DAVID WHITE[152], March 31, 1856, Rankin County, Mississippi[152].
105. v. ELMIRA SHERMAN LAND, b. 1836, Edgecombe County, North Carolina; d. 1870, Rankin County, Mississippi.
vi. MALE LAND[152], b. Abt. 1838, Edgecombe County, North Carolina[152]; d. Aft. 1870, Rankin County, Mississippi[152].
vii. SARAH G. LAND[152], b. 1838, Edgecombe County, North Carolina[152]; d. Aft. 1870, Rankin County, Mississippi[152].

59. SALLY[6] LAND *(LITTLEBERRY[5], BIRD[4], CURTIS[3], CURTIS[2], CURTIS[1])* [152,153] was born 1800 in Edgecombe Co. NC[153]. She married (1) DUNCAN HARGROVE[153] January 15, 1823[153]. He was born March 04, 1794 in Edgecombe Co. NC[153], and died 1871 in Edgecombe Co. NC[153]. She married (2) DUNCAN HARGROVE[154] January 15, 1823 in Edgecombe, North Carolina[154]. He was born 1792 in North Carolina[154].

Notes for SALLY LAND:
(Research): 96. Sally6 Land (Littleberry5, Bird4, Curtis3, Curtis2, Curtis1) was born Abt. 1800.
She married Duncan Hargrove January 15, 1823 in Edgecombe , NC. He was born 1792 in North Carolina.
Children of Sally Land and Duncan Hargrove are:
206 i. Delta7 Hargrove, born 1837.
207 ii. Edward L. Har grove, born 1841.
208 iii. Sarah Hargrove, born 1842.
209 iv. Annie Har grove, born 1844.
210 v. Malvina Hargrove, born 1848.

Notes for DUNCAN HARGROVE:
Cause of Death: Shot to death
"Duncan and Sally lived in a two story white house on a plantation on the old Tarborough to Raleigh Road. It is now a part of the city of Rocky Mount and the road is now called Cokey Road. He lived in the same area as his mother and grandfather.
The eldest son, Samuel , who married Lucinda Killibrew, bible records were in Vol. 3, No. 1, page 12 . It is interesting to note that two of Duncan's daughters married brothers. Martha married Robert Stringer Braswell and Mary married Benjamin S. Braswell. The Braswells are a very prominent family in Edgecombe and Nash Counties . I have not traced their line, nor any of the other children.
The relatives that I know living in Rocky Mount today are : Mrs. S. L. Daughtridge (Lucy Cummings) and William Hadden, both of Rocky Mount and Mrs. William F. Clay,
Greensboro, NC. Her father was son of Robert Gray, son of Samuel."
---Mae Kider Hargrove Pope
Duncan was 6' 4".
He was shot down on the town hall steps by a slave. The slave was hanged. (as told by Sally Hargrove Bailey)
The 1860 Census shows the following on Duncan:
He had the following slaves:
70 female, 30 f, 20 m, 18 m, 19 f, 17 f, 17 m, 15 m, 12 f, 14 m, and 3 slave houses.
15,000 real property and 12,000 in personal property.
(Research):Wills--Edgecombe Courthouse--Williams & Griffin "Records Early Edgecombe"--Mr. & Mrs. J. W. Watson "Tombstones & Census Records, Edgecombe County"--Early Marriage Edgecombe County 1733-1868.
Edgecombe County Will Abstracts 1858-1910. Pg 59 (272):
DUNCAN (X) HAREGROVE 26 July 1865 Oct Ct. 1871 O G/368

Eldest daughter LOUISANA JANE MOORE (widow of JOSEPH MOORE)
--five dollars, together with property I advanced her at the time of her marriage.
Eldest son SAMUEL HENRY HAREGROVE-
-five dollars, in addition to what I have already give him
. Son GRAY LEMON HAREGROVE--five dollars, in addition to what I have already give him.
Daughter MARY ELIZABETH BRASWELL (Wife of BENJAMIN G. BRASWELL)-- five dollars, in addition to what I have already give her.
Son THOMAS DANIEL HAREGROVE--five dollars, in addition to what I have already give him. Daughter-in-law AMIA HAREGROVE (wife of my son JAME S BURREL HAREGROVE)--one dollars, in addition to what I have already give them. Daughter MARTHA ANN CHARITY BRASWELL (widow of ROBERT S. BRASWELL)--five dollars, in addition to what I have already give her.
Daughters FRANCES DLLER HAREGROVE, SARA NINA HARE GROVE, FLORENCE ANNA HAREGROVE , MALVINA CATHRINE HAREGROVE and my son EDWARD S. HAREGROVE
--all my household and kitchen furniture, etc. Youngest son EDWARD and daughters FRANCES, SARA, FLORRENCE and MALVINA
--all the land where I now live while they are unmarried, with complete reversion to my son EDWARD.
1857 Aug. 17 - Edgecombe, N.C. deposition of Delilah SPICER going on 61 years. She is the widow of William SPICER'S brother, Moses SPICER. "My mother lived about two miles from William SPICER...." /S/ Delilah (her D mark) SPICER. - Deposition of Hartwell LONG past 60 years of age, not exceeding 63.... - Deposition of Newsom LONG about 58.... - Deposition of Gray ARMSTRONG, 70 to 75 years old,.... "SPICERS had in their possession a yellow or mulatto girl named Jenny who was not grown. At the age of about 18 or 19 I went to TN and settled in Sumner Co. where I remained about two years or long enough to make two crops. I came back in either 1805 or 1806. I married in this county (Edgecombe) after my return from TN in 1807. William SPICER was at my wedding and in the same year he removed to TN. I started to TN in Feb. and got there in March following and stopped on Station Camp Creek Sumner Co., TN.... I got back to N.C. near Christmas. ...William SPICER lived on the HARGROVE place which he had bought. SPICER sold the land to either John HILL or his two so ns, Peoples and Nathaniel HILL.... I have talked...

Children of SALLY LAND and DUNCAN HARGROVE are:

i. LOUISANA JANE[7] HARGROVE[155], m. JOSEPH MOORE[156,157], March 05, 1848[157]; b. , Pitt County, N. C[157].

ii. INA ELIZABETH HARGROVE[157], m. JACOB BRYANT[158].

106. iii. SAMUEL HENRY HARGROVE, b. April 22, 1825, Edgecombe Co. NC; d. December 17, 1873, Edgecombe Co. NC.

107. iv. GRAY LEMON HARGROVE, b. June 18, 1827, Edgecombe Co. NC; d. 1894, Edgecombe Co. NC.

v. MARY ELIZABETH HARGROVE[160,161], b. 1830[162,163]; m. (1) BENJAMIN S. BRASWELL[164]; m. (2) BENJAMIN GUILFORD BRASWELL[165], January 25, 1851; b. January 01, 1827, Halifax Co., NC[165].
Notes for BENJAMIN GUILFORD BRASWELL:
(Research):Enlisted for the war with Mexico, Jan. 5, 1847, Co. A, first North Carolina Regiment of foot volunteers.[2882706.ged]

vi. THOMAS DANIEL HARGROVE[166,167,168], b. 1832[169,170].
Notes for THOMAS DANIEL HARGROVE:
Confederate Soldier[2847174.ged]

vii. JAMES BURREL (BURWELL) HARGROVE[170], b. 1834, Edgecombe Co. NC[170]; d. October 27, 1864, Burgess' Mill, VA[170]; m. AMIA "ANNIE" WARREN[170], November 11, 1858[170].

Notes for JAMES BURREL (BURWELL) HARGROVE:
Bride: Amia Warren
Groom: James B Hargrove
Bond Date: 09 Nov 1858
County: Edgecombe
Record #: 01 082
Bondsman: Joseph Cobb
Witness: W A Jones, Clerk
Bond #: 000043821
Marriage Date: 11 Nov 1858
Performed By: John W Johnson, Justice of the Peace North Carolina Marr age Bonds, 1741-1868
Name: James Burwell Hargrove , Residence: Edgecombe County, North Carolina Enlistment Date: 16 July 1862
Distinguished Service: DISTINGUISHED SERVICE State Served: North Carolina Unit Numbers: 151 151
Service Record: Enlisted as a Private on 16 July 1862 at the age of 22

Enlisted in Company K, 44th Infantry Regiment North Carolina on 16 July 1862.
Transferred on 10 July 1863 from company K to company B absent on 25 November 1863
Sick on 30 January 1864 (Returned)
Killed Company K, 44th Infantry Regiment North Carolina on 27 October 1864 in Burgess' Mill, VA
Edgecombe County Wills and Abstracts 1858-1920
Page 59 (273)
James B. Hargrove of Beaufort Co. 8 April 1863 Nov Ct. 1864 O G/253 "...being a soldier in the Confederate States of America and stationed at a point near Washington in the County of Beaufort....." Entire estate to my wife Annie Hargrove.

Notes for AMIA "ANNIE" WARREN:
(Research): Edgecombe County Will Abstracts 1858-1910
Page 131 (603)
James A. Warren 14 May 1861 Feb Ct. 1863 O G/227
Sister Amy Hargraves (wife of J .B. Hargraves)--all my lands, consisting of a tract on the west side of Fishing Creek adj. James Savage, Henry O. Warren and Thomas Lawrence, and containing 26 acres. Balance of property to my brother George R. Warren.[2882706.ged]

viii. FRANCES DELLER "DELLA" HARGROVE[170], b. 1836[170].

108. ix. MARTHA ANN CHARITY HARGROVE, b. 1837, Edgecombe Co. NC; d. 1901.
x. EDWARD L HARGROVE[170], b. 1839[170].

Notes for EDWARD L HARGROVE:
Sources:
Abbrev: Reynolds Gray Bailey
Name: Edward S Hargrove , Residence: Edgecombe County, North Carolina Enlistment D ate: 15 August 1861 Distinguished Service: DISTINGUISHED SERVICE State Served : North Carolina Unit Numbers: 45 Service Record: Enlisted as a Corporal on 15 August 1861 at the age of 21
Enlisted in Company F, 3rd Light Artillery Regiment North Carolina on 15 August 1861.
POW on 26 April 1862 at Fort Macon , NC (And paroled)
Promoted to Full Sergeant on 30 January 1863 (Estimated day of Promo)
On rolls on 31 December 1864
Paroled on 26 May 1865 at Goldsboro , NC
Confederate soldier.
(Research):Served in Co. F, 40th Regiment, Heavy Artillery during the Civil War. He was in eight battles and fired the last three cannons at Fort Macon, North Carolina, before being taken a prisoner. He was exchanged and fought until the close of the war. He was with General Johnson when he surrendered. 1 Birth: 1841

More About EDWARD L HARGROVE:
Record Change: May 19, 2004[170]

xi. SARA NINA HARGROVE[170], b. 1842[170]; m. RICHARD HOLLAND[170]; b. 1750, Amelia County, VA[170].

109. xii. FLORENCE ANNA HARGROVE, b. March 27, 1844, Edgecombe Co. NC.
xiii. MALVINA CATHERINE HARGROVE[170], b. 1847[170].
xiv. MARTHA ANN CHARITY HARGROVE[170], b. 1837, Edgecombe Co. NC[170]; d. 1901[170]; m. ROBERT STRINGER BRASWELL[171,172], April 01, 1858[172]; b. March 08, 1836, Edgecombe Co. NC[172]; d. 1863[172].

Notes for ROBERT STRINGER BRASWELL:
(Research):There is a ROBERT S. BRASWELL listed as having served with the NC 17th Inf. (2nd Org.), Co. I (CSA).
Confederate soldier: Co.1, (Edgecombe Rebel s) 17th North Carolina infantry Regiment.
Groom: Robert S Braswell Bride: Martha Hargrove Bond Date: 30 Mar 1858 Bond #: 000042970 Marriage Date: 01 Apr 1858
Level Info: North Carolina Marriage Bonds, 1741-1868
Image Num: 003345 County: Edgecombe Record #: 01 024 Bondsman: J H Draughan Performed By: William F Mercer, Justice of the Peace[2882706.ged]

Children of SALLY LAND and DUNCAN HARGROVE are:
xv. LOUISIANA[7] HARGROVE[173], m. JOSEPH MOORE[173,174], March 05, 1848[175]; b. , Pitt County, N. C[176].

xvi. MARTHA ANN CHARITY HARGROVE[177], m. ROBERT STRINGER BRASWELL[177,178]; b. March 08, 1836, Edgecombe Co. NC[178]; d. 1863[178].

Notes for ROBERT STRINGER BRASWELL:
(Research):There is a ROBERT S. BRASWELL listed as having served with the NC 17th Inf. (2nd Org.), Co. I (CSA).
Confederate soldier: Co.1, (Edgecombe Rebel s) 17th North Carolina infantry Regiment.
Groom: Robert S Braswell Bride: Martha Hargrove Bond Date: 30 Mar 1858 Bond #: 000042970 Marriage Date: 01 Apr 1858
Level Info: North Carolina Marriage Bonds, 1741-1868
Image Num: 003345 County: Edgecombe Record #: 01 024 Bondsman: J H Draughan Performed By: William F Mercer, Justice of the Peace[2882706.ged]

xvii. SUSAN N. HARGROVE[179], m. RICHARD HOLLAND[179].
xviii. JAMES BUSNELL HARGROVE[180,181], b. 1834[181]; m. AMIA "ANNIE" WARREN[182], November 09, 1853[183].
Confederate Soldier

Notes for AMIA "ANNIE" WARREN:
(Research): Edgecombe County Will Abstracts 1858-1910
Page 131 (603)
James A. Warren 14 May 1861 Feb Ct. 1863 O G/227
Sister Amy Hargraves (wife of J .B. Hargraves)--all my lands, consisting of a tract on the west side of Fishing Creek adj. James Savage, Henry O. Warren and Thomas Lawrence, and containing 26 acres. Balance of property to my brother George R. Warren.[2882706.ged]

xix. DELTA HARGROVE[185], b. 1837[185].
xx. EDWARD L. HARGROVE[186,187], b. 1841[187].
Served in Co. F, 40th Regiment, Heavy Artillery during the Civil War. He was in eight battles and fired the last three cannons at Fort Macon, North Carolina, before being taken a prisoner. He was exchanged and fought until the close of the war. He was with General Johnson when he surrendered.

xxi. FLORENCE ANNA HARGROVE[187], b. 1841[187]; m. (1) LEWIS CROMWELL[187]; m. (2) BARNHILL[187].
xxii. SARAH HARGROVE[187], b. 1842[187].
xxiii. ANNIE HARGROVE[187], b. 1844[187].
xxiv. MELONIA HARGROVE[187], b. 1847[187].
xxv. MALVINA HARGROVE[187], b. 1848[187].

60. AMY^6 LAND *(LITTLEBERRY^5, BIRD^4, CURTIS^3, CURTIS^2, CURTIS^1)*[187,188] was born Abt. 1802 in Edgecombe County, NC of Nash Co., NC[188]. She married (1) NATHAN THOMAS "THOMAS" JOYNER[188] September 10, 1827 in Edgecombe County, NC[188]. He was born 1787 in St Mary's Parrish, Nash Co., North Carolina[188]. She married (2) THOMAS JOYNER[189] September 10, 1827 in Edgecombe, North Carolina[189]. He was born 1792 in North Carolina[189].

Children of AMY LAND and NATHAN JOYNER are:
i. NATHAN^7 JOYNER[190].
ii. LITTLEBERRY JOYNER[190], b 1828, Nash Co., NC[190].
110. iii. BURRELL HILDSMAN JOYNER, b. March 18, 1830, Nash Co., NC.
111. iv. IRA ELLIS JOYNER, b. November 1831, Nash Co., NC.
v. ELIZA JOYNER JOYNER[190], b. Abt. 1833, Nash Co., NC[190].
vi. JOHN DAVID "DAVID" JOYNER[190], b. 1838, Nash Co., NC[190].
112. vii. FRANCIS M. JOYNER, b. 1839, Nash Co., NC.
viii. JONAS A. JOYNER[191,192], b. January 01, 1840, Nash Co., NC[192].
113. ix. GEORGE W. JOYNER, b. 1845, Nash Co., NC.

Children of AMY LAND and THOMAS JOYNER are:
x. LITTLEBERRY^7 JOYNER[193], b. 1829[193].
xi. IRA E. JOYNER[193], b. 1832[193].
xii. ELIZA JOYNER[193], b. 1833[193].
114. xiii. NATHAN T. JOYNER, b. 1836, Nash, North Carolina; d. Aft. 1860, Nash, North Carolina.
xiv. DAVID D. JOYNER[193], b. 1838[193].

61. MARY "POLLY"[6] LAND *(LITTLEBERRY[5], BIRD[4], CURTIS[3], CURTIS[2], CURTIS[1])* [194] was born Abt. 1803 in Edgecombe Co. NC[194], and died 1860 in Edgecombe Co. NC[194]. She married JOSEPH LANCASTER[195,196] Bef. 1827.

Child of MARY LAND and JOSEPH LANCASTER is:
i. BIRD[7] LANCASTER[197,198].

62. DANIEL[6] LAND *(LITTLEBERRY[5], BIRD[4], CURTIS[3], CURTIS[2], CURTIS[1])* [199,200] was born 1793 in North Carolina[201], and died September 12, 1857 in Wilson County, North Carolina[201]. He married (1) MARTHA BULLOCH[201] Abt. 1813[201]. She was born 1794[201]. He married (2) MARY BULLOCH[202] Abt. 1813[202]. She was born 1794[202].

Children of DANIEL LAND and MARTHA BULLOCH are:
i. MALE[7] LAND[203], b. Aft. 1820[203].
ii. EMILY LAND[203,204], b. 1813[205,206]; d. November 07, 1890[207]; m. JAMES HENRY ARMSTRONG[207], December 21, 1831, Edgecombe, North Carolina[207].

115. iii. LUCRETIA LAND, b. November 26, 1822, North Carolina; d. May 27, 1894.

63. BURRELL[6] LAND *(LITTLEBERRY[5], BIRD[4], CURTIS[3], CURTIS[2], CURTIS[1])* [209,210] was born 1794 in Tar River, North Carolina[211], and died Bef. 1840 in Noxubee County, Mississippi[211,212]. He married LUCY MATILDA WILLIAMS [213,214] 1824 in Noxubee County, Mississippi[215,216]. She was born 1800 in NC[216].

Children of BURRELL LAND and LUCY WILLIAMS are:
116. i. LITTLEBERRY JOHN[7] LAND, b. 1827, North Carolina; d. Aft. 1870, Richland Parrish, Louisiana.
ii. MARY JANE LAND[217], b. 1833, North Carolina[217]; d. Aft. 1873, Noxubee County, Mississippi[217]; m. (1) CHARLIE ALEXANDER WOODS[217]; m. (2) HOSEA FLORA[217], November 21, 1875, Noxubee County, Mississippi[217].
iii. DAVID A. LAND[217,218], b. 1837, Mississippi[219,220]; d. December 1864, Camp Douglas, Ohio[221]; m. SARAH CAROLINE SMALL[221], Alabama[221].

117. iv. EVALINA LAND, b. March 15, 1838, Noxubee County, Mississippi; d. 1900, Louisiana.
118. v. HENRY GREY LAND, b. December 18, 1829, Edgecombe County, North Carolina; d. January 16, 1903, Noxubee County, Mississippi.
119. vi. MARY KATHERINE LAND, b. 1838, Noxubee County, Mississippi; d. 1864, Noxubee County, Mississippi.
120. vii. WILLIAM BURT LAND, b. 1831, Edgecombe County, North Carolina; d. November 08, 1898, Richland Parrish, Louisiana.
viii. JAMES D. LAND[222,223], b. 1825, NC[224]; d. Aft. 1860, Carroll Parrish, Louisiana[225].
ix. LITTLEBERRY JOHN LAND, b. 1827, NC.

64. MARY POLLY[6] LAND *(LITTLEBERRY[5], BIRD[4], CURTIS[3], CURTIS[2], CURTIS[1])* [227] was born Abt. 1803 in North Carolina[227], and died 1860 in Edgecombe County, North Carolina[227]. She married (1) JETHRO WEAVER[227]. She married (2) JOSEPH LANCASTER[227,228] Bef. 1827[229].

Children of MARY LAND and JETHRO WEAVER are:
i. ISAAC SOLOMAN[7] WEAVER[231].
ii. CHARLES WEAVER[231], b. February 24, 1831[231].
iii. JEREMIAH B. WEAVER[231], b. September 20, 1833[231].
iv. EASTER MORNING WEAVER[231], b. May 04, 1836[231].

65. JOHN[6] LAND *(CHARLES[5], CHARLES[4], CURTIS[3], CURTIS[2], CURTIS[1])*

Children of JOHN LAND are:
121. i. THOMAS C.[7] LAND.
122. ii. WILLIE G. LAND.

66. ELIZABETH[6] LAND *(LEWIS[5], BIRD[4], CURTIS[3], CURTIS[2], CURTIS[1])*[232] was born Abt. 1810 in Greenville, Sc.[232], and died Abt. 1880[232]. She married JOHN BAILEY[233,234] WFT Est. 1823-1855[234], son of BAILEY UNKNOWN and JEMIMA UNKNOWN. He was born Abt. 1804[235], and died WFT Est. 1837-1898[236].

Notes for JOHN BAILEY:
The Bailey family came to Arkansas from Alabama in 1865. It is said that the family split up after they got to Arkansas and some settled at Cabot. The others traveled about 100 miles north from Cabot, and settled west of what is now Ravenden Springs, Arkansas. John Bailey married Elizabeth, a sister to Kinson Land, and they settled near a large spring now known as Harper Spring located on Ferguson Creek. Randolph Co. History by Regina Cook, Project Director, 1992. John's occupation was listed on census as blacksmith.

Child of ELIZABETH LAND and JOHN BAILEY is:

123. i. WILLIAM W.[7] BAILEY, b. June 10, 1834, Georgia; d. September 24, 1909, Arkansas.

67. STEPHEN[6] LAND *(LEWIS[5], BIRD[4], CURTIS[3], CURTIS[2], CURTIS[1])*[237] was born May 22, 1808 in Greenville, South Carolina[237], and died March 18, 1870 in Paulding County, Georgia[237]. He married DIANNAH BAILEY[237] September 04, 1828[237]. She was born Abt. 1806 in South Carolina[237].

Children of STEPHEN LAND and DIANNAH BAILEY are:

i. ZEDEKIAH[7] LAND[237], b. 1829, Georgia[237]; d. 1909, Paulding County, Georgia[237]; m. MARY RAGSDALE[237], January 1850[237]; b. March 01, 1833, Coweta, Co., Ga[237].

ii. SYNTHIA CAROLINE LAND[237], b. June 06, 1831[237]; d. March 24, 1901, New Caanan, Georgia[237]; m. OLIVER POSEY PARRISH[237]; b. October 18, 1828, South Carolina[237].

124. iii. SUSANNAH LAND, b. November 06, 1837; d. 1906, Paulding County, Georgia.

125. iv. ELIZABETH JANE LAND, b. July 25, 1840, Henry County, Georgia; d. November 05, 1910, Paulding County, Georgia.

v. JEMIMA LAND[237], b. September 11, 1842, Georgia[237]; d. March 24, 1890[237]; m. JEREMIAH FREEMAN[237], February 24, 1861, Paulding County, Georgia[237].

vi. MARTHA ANN LAND[237], b. January 06, 1845, Georgia[237]; d. February 01, 1945, Paulding County, Georgia[237]; m. NATHAN CALVIN PARRIS[237]; b. December 15, 1842, Paulding County, Georgia[237].

vii. DAVID LAND[237], b. June 1848, Georgia[237]; d. July 15, 1929, Carroll County, Georgia[237]; m. SARAH JOSEPHINE[237], Abt. 1870[237]; b. October 07, 1849[237].

68. ELIZABETH[6] LAND *(LEWIS[5], BIRD[4], CURTIS[3], CURTIS[2], CURTIS[1])*[237] was born Abt. 1810 in Greenville, South Carolina[237], and died in Jefferson County, Tennessee[237]. She married JOHN BAILEY[237,238] Abt. 1833[239], son of BAILEY UNKNOWN and JEMIMA UNKNOWN. He was born Abt. 1804[239], and died WFT Est. 1837-1898[240].

Notes for JOHN BAILEY:
The Bailey family came to Arkansas from Alabama in 1865. It is said that the family split up after they got to Arkansas and some settled at Cabot. The others traveled about 100 miles north from Cabot, and settled west of what is now Ravenden Springs, Arkansas. John Bailey married Elizabeth, a sister to Kinson Land, and they settled near a large spring now known as Harper Spring located on Ferguson Creek. Randolph Co. History by Regina Cook, Project Director, 1992. John's occupation was listed on census as blacksmith.

Children of ELIZABETH LAND and JOHN BAILEY are:

i. JOHN[7] BAILEY, b. Abt. 1835.

126. ii. SARAH BAILEY, b. Abt. 1849.

69. KINSON[6] LAND *(LEWIS[5], BIRD[4], CURTIS[3], CURTIS[2], CURTIS[1])*[241] was born 1813 in South Carolina[241], and died Abt. 1898 in Randolph County, Arkansas[241]. He married (1) MARY UNKNOWN[241] Bef. 1837 in South Carolina[241]. She was born Abt. 1819 in Mississippi[241]. He married (2) HELEN HATSFIELD[241] Bet. 1863 - 1866 in Arkansas[241]. She was born 1836[241], and died Aft. 1910 in Randolph Co. Arkansas[242].

Children of KINSON LAND and MARY UNKNOWN are:

127. i. ELIZABETH J.[7] LAND, b. Abt. 1837, South Carolina; d. November 05, 1918, Oregon County, Missouri.

ii. DELILAH LUCRESA LAND[243], b. Abt. 1838, South Carolina[243]; m. ELISHA DODSON[243], September 12, 1871[243].
iii. PETER LAND[243], b. Abt. 1844, Georgia[243]; d. Bef. 1865[243].
128. iv. LEWIS LAND, b. Abt. 1848, Georgia.
129. v. JAMES B. LAND, b. June 18, 1852, Georgia; d. April 13, 1887, Randolph County, Arkansas.
130. vi. JORDON LAND, b. July 05, 1853, Georgia; d. January 03, 1922, Batesville, Independence County, Arkansas.
131. vii. MARY LAND, b. November 17, 1857, Alabama; d. April 03, 1922, Randolph County, Arkansas.

Children of KINSON LAND and HELEN HATSFIELD are:
132. viii. MARTHA MATILDA ROSETTA[7] LAND, b. August 07, 1872, Union TWP, Sharp Co. Ar.; d. February 11, 1952, Randolph Co. Arkansas.
133. ix. "DONA" FRANCIS CALDONIA LAND.

Generation No. 7

70. MILDRED[7] LAND *(JOHN[6], THOMAS[5], THOMAS[4], JOHN[3], CURTIS[2], CURTIS[1])* [243] was born December 27, 1782[243]. She married JOSEPH RENFROE[243] April 21, 1803[243].

Children of MILDRED LAND and JOSEPH RENFROE are:
i. THOMAS JEFFERSON[8] RENFROE[243], m. LOUISE STANLEY[243].
ii. JOHN RENFROE[243].
iii. RHODA RENFROE[243].
iv. JEMINA RENFROE[243].
v. NATHANIEL RENFROE[243].
vi. JOSEPH RENFROE[243].

71. HENRY[7] LAND *(JOHN[6], THOMAS[5], THOMAS[4], JOHN[3], CURTIS[2], CURTIS[1])* [243] was born December 25, 1784[243]. He married ELEANOR HOSSICK[243] January 18, 1809 in Madison County, Kentucky[243]. She was born September 30, 1789[243], and died February 28, 1863[243].

Children of HENRY LAND and ELEANOR HOSSICK are:
i. AMERICA[8] LAND[243], b. October 06, 1809[243]; d. August 23, 1855[243]; m. WILLIAM F. ROBERTS[243], December 23, 1829, Jessamine County, Kentucky[243]; b. February 20, 1808[243]; d. April 05, 1862[243].
ii. LUCINDA LAND[243], b. June 17, 1811[243]; m. JOHN ROBERTS[243], December 10, 1828[243].
iii. FOUNTAIN WILLIAM LAND[243], b. January 02, 1815, Scott County, Kentucky[243]; d. January 13, 1899, Jessamine, Kentucky[243]; m. MARTHA MORTON WILLIS[243], June 10, 1847[243]; b. September 22, 1819, Scott County, Kentucky[243].
iv. LEROY M. LAND[243], b. June 26, 1817[243]; d. January 27, 1893, Lexington, Kentucky[243]; m. SARAH J SPEARS[243], September 16, 1851, Kentucky[243]; b. Abt. 1825[243].
v. SOPHIA W. LAND[243], b. January 02, 1821, Jessamine, Kentucky[243]; d. September 13, 1876, Jessamine, Kentucky[243]; m. FRANKLIN TAYLOR[243].
vi. JOHN THOMAS LAND[243], b. June 17, 1828[243]; m. ELIZABETH H. WILLIS[243]; b. Abt. 1830[243].

72. JOHN FISHER[7] LAND *(JOHN[6], THOMAS[5], THOMAS[4], JOHN[3], CURTIS[2], CURTIS[1])*[243] was born December 02, 1786[243], and died 1849[243]. He married (1) REBECCA W. CROSBY[243] May 27, 1818 in Madison County, Kentucky[243]. She was born Abt. 1795[243]. He married (2) POLLY TAYLOR RENFROE[243] September 06, 1842[243]. She was born Abt. 1795[243].

Child of JOHN LAND and REBECCA CROSBY is:
134. i. ELIZABETH[8] LAND.

73. JUDITH[7] LAND *(JOHN[6], THOMAS[5], THOMAS[4], JOHN[3], CURTIS[2], CURTIS[1])* [243] was born October 22, 1788 in Madison County, Kentucky[243]. She married PETER RENFROE[243] December 29, 1812 in Madison County, Kentucky[243]. He was born Abt. 1785[243].

Children of JUDITH LAND and PETER RENFROE are:
i. REBECCA[8] RENFROE[243].
ii. EMILY MILDRED RENFROE[243], m. OSBORNE SANDERS[243].
iii. NANCY RENFROE[243], m. JAMES DUNCAN[243].
iv. AMANDA RENFROE[243], m. JAMES WALTERS[243].
v. JAMES M. RENFROE[243], m. MARY ROBERTS[243].

vi. MARY ANN RENFROE[243].

74. WILLIAM[7] LAND *(JOHN[6], THOMAS[5], THOMAS[4], JOHN[3], CURTIS[2], CURTIS[1])*[243] was born December 07, 1790 in Kentucky[243], and died 1815[243]. He married SUSANNAH WOOD[243]. She was born 1792 [243].

Child of WILLIAM LAND and SUSANNAH WOOD is:

i. WILLIAM[8] LAND[243], b. Aft. 1810[243].

75. NANCY[7] LAND *(JOHN[6], THOMAS[5], THOMAS[4], JOHN[3], CURTIS[2], CURTIS[1])*[243] was born October 02, 1794 in Scott County, Kentucky[243]. She married WILLIAM A. MASTIN[243] December 15, 1828[243]. He was born 1802 in Henry County, Virginia[243].

Children of NANCY LAND and WILLIAM MASTIN are:

i. ELLIE ANN[8] MASTIN[243].
ii. JOHN GABRIEL MASTIN[243], b. 1830[243].
iii. WILLIAM CONWAY MASTIN[243], b. 1839[243].

76. ELIZABETH[7] LAND *(JOHN[6], THOMAS[5], THOMAS[4], JOHN[3], CURTIS[2], CURTIS[1])*[243] was born January 01, 1796 in Scott County, Kentucky[243], and died April 09, 1880 in Adams Township, Decatur, Indiana[243]. She married WILLIS GULLEY[243] November 06, 1817 in Madison County, Kentucky[243]. He was born Abt. 1795 [243].

Children of ELIZABETH LAND and WILLIS GULLEY are:

i. THOMAS[8] GULLEY[243].
ii. AMANDA GULLEY[243], b. October 29, 1834[243]; d. May 20, 1927[243]; m. JOHN SACRA MASTERS[243]; b. July 19, 1830[243]; d. May 06, 1913[243].

77. FOUNTAIN[7] LAND *(JOHN[6], THOMAS[5], THOMAS[4], JOHN[3], CURTIS[2], CURTIS[1])*[243] was born February 07, 1803 in Madison County, Kentucky[243], and died 1876[243]. He married (1) EMILY RUYLE[243]. She was born in Sumner County, Tennessee[243]. He married (2) BARBARA SANDS[243] October 16, 1823[243]. She was born 1801 [243], and died 1831[243]. Burial: Scottville Twp., Macoupin County, Illinois[243]

Children of FOUNTAIN LAND and EMILY RUYLE are:

135. i. PHOEBE S.[8] LAND, b. October 19, 1831, Illinois.
ii. MARY LAND[243], b. Abt. 1832[243]; m. MORGAN WHITE[243], February 20, 1853, Macoupin County, Illinois[243].
iii. WILLIS LAND[243], b. 1835[243].

Children of FOUNTAIN LAND and BARBARA SANDS are:

iv. LUCETTA JANE[8] LAND[243], b. 1824, Tennessee[243].
136. v. HENDERSON P. LAND, b. 1827, Tennessee; d. 1903.
137. vi. REBECCA A. LAND, b. November 07, 1829, Illinois.
vii. WILLIAM LAND[243], b. 1830, Illinois[243]; m. ELIZABETH UNKNOWN[243].
138. viii. THOMAS LAND, b. 1831, Illinois.

78. JOHN[7] CARLTON *(MARY[6] LAND, THOMAS[5], THOMAS[4], JOHN[3], CURTIS[2], CURTIS[1])*[243] was born July 29, 1778 in Wilkes County, North Carolina[243], and died March 01, 1855 in Beaver Creek, Wilkes County, North Carolina[243]. He married (1) ELIZABETH BARLOW[243] August 14, 1802[243]. She was born Abt. 1775 in Virginia [243], and died Aft. 1810 in Wilkes County, North Carolina[243]. He married (2) SUSANNA SMYTH[243] April 30, 1813 in Wilkes County, North Carolina[243]. She was born March 06, 1781 in Caseberry Town, Cheshire England[243], and died January 12, 1848 in Wilkes County, North Carolina[243].

Children of JOHN CARLTON and ELIZABETH BARLOW are:

139. i. THOMAS[8] CARLTON, b. October 30, 1803, Wilkes County, North Carolina; d. August 03, 1873, Jackson, Alabama.
140. ii. LEWIS CARLTON, b. March 10, 1806, Wilkes County, North Carolina; d. 1853, Lawrence County, Indiana.

iii. MARY CARLTON[243], b. July 25, 1808, Wilkes County, North Carolina[243]; d. Aft. 1880, Procter, Camden County, Missouri[243]; m. ELI STORIE[243], October 01, 1828, Wilkes County, North Carolina[243].

Children of JOHN CARLTON and SUSANNA SMYTH are:

iv. REBECCA M[8] CARLTON[243], b. April 26, 1815[243].
v. HENRY E. CARLTON[243], b. February 21, 1817[243]; d. August 13, 1862, Shreveport, Louisiana[243]; m. MARY THOMAS EADS[243].
vi. CHARLES R. CARLTON[243], b. April 16, 1819[243]; m. SARAH CATHERINE SANER[243], November 15, 1841[243].
vii. ALBERT C. CARLTON[243], b. August 20, 1820[243]; d. November 30, 1906[243]; m. ELIZABETH POPE[243], Aft. 1850[243].
viii. JOHN SMITH CARLTON[243], b. June 22, 1823, Wilkes County, North Carolina[243]; d. Aft. 1865, Louisana[243].

79. HENRY[7] CARLTON *(MARY[6] LAND, THOMAS[5], THOMAS[4], JOHN[3], CURTIS[2], CURTIS[1])* [243] was born Abt. 1786 in Wilkes County, North Carolina[243], and died Aft. 1837 in Jackson County, Alabama[243]. He married PRUDENCE BROOKSHIRE[243] 1802 in Wilkes County, North Carolina[243].

Children of HENRY CARLTON and PRUDENCE BROOKSHIRE are:

i. LARKIN[8] CARLTON[243], b. 1807[243].
ii. THOMAS CARLTON[243], b. 1809[243].
iii. WILLIAM ELIAS CARLTON[243], b. 1811[243].
iv. DAUGHTER CARLTON[243], b. 1813[243].
v. DAUGHTER CARLTON[243], b. 1815[243].
vi. HENRY CARLTON[243], b. 1817[243].
vii. ALLEN CARLTON[243], b. 1819[243].
viii. JOHN WOOD CARLTON[243], b. 1821[243].

80. NANCY[7] CARLTON *(MARY[6] LAND, THOMAS[5], THOMAS[4], JOHN[3], CURTIS[2], CURTIS[1])* [243] was born Abt. 1788 in Wilkes County, North Carolina[243], and died Aft. 1860 in Jackson County, Alabama[243]. She married GEORGE CROUCH[243]. He was born Bef. 1788[243].

Children of NANCY CARLTON and GEORGE CROUCH are:

i. RUTHA[8] CROUCH[243], b. Abt. 1815[243].
ii. CAROLINE CROUCH[243], b. Abt. 1820[243].
iii. REBECCA CROUCH[243], b. Abt. 1823[243].

81. THOMAS[7] CARLTON *(MARY[6] LAND, THOMAS[5], THOMAS[4], JOHN[3], CURTIS[2], CURTIS[1])* [243] was born January 22, 1790 in Wilkes County, North Carolina[243], and died January 14, 1877 in Wilkes County, North Carolina[243]. He married (1) JANE MERRIMAN[243] March 26, 1813[243]. She was born February 28, 1796[243], and died April 10, 1821[243]. He married (2) RUTH BURCH[243] August 12, 1821[243]. She was born June 11, 1792[243]. He married (3) ELEANOR SWANSON[243] October 18, 1863[243].

Children of THOMAS CARLTON and JANE MERRIMAN are:

i. EVALINE[8] CARLTON[243], b. October 03, 1815[243].
ii. ALLEN BURTON CARLTON[243], b. March 05, 1818[243].

Children of THOMAS CARLTON and RUTH BURCH are:

iii. JOHN[8] CARLTON[243], b. August 23, 1822[243].
iv. DANIEL MILTON CARLTON[243], b. September 28, 1823[243].
v. HENRY CARLTON[243], b. October 28, 1825[243].
vi. JOEL ANDERSON CARLTON[243], b. October 16, 1827[243].
vii. MARTHA EADS CARLTON[243], b. August 15, 1830[243].
viii. MARY ANN CARLTON[243], b. August 15, 1830[243]; m. JAMES ELLER[243], October 24, 1849, Wilkes County, Nor3.[243].
ix. THOMAS CHEDLE CARLTON[243], b. October 31, 1833[243].

82. CELIA[7] CARLTON *(MARY[6] LAND, THOMAS[5], THOMAS[4], JOHN[3], CURTIS[2], CURTIS[1])* [243] was born Abt. 1791 in Wilkes County, North Carolina[243], and died Aft. 1880 in Jackson County, Alabama[243]. She married JOHN DAY[243] 1808[243]. He was born Bef. 1790 in Burke Co., NC[243], and died Abt. 1844 in Jackson Co., AL[243].

Children of CELIA CARLTON and JOHN DAY are:

- i. LOT[8] DAY[243], b. Abt. 1809[243].
- ii. WILEY DAY[243], b. Abt. 1812[243].
- iii. WYATT DAY[243], b. Abt. 1815[243].
- iv. ALLEN DAY[243], b. Abt. 1816[243].
- v. CALVIN DAY[243], b. 1822[243].
- vi. MILUS DAY[243], b. Abt. 1824[243].
- vii. HASTINGS DAY[243], b. Abt. 1827[243].
- viii. LARKIN DAY[243], b. Abt. 1829[243].
- ix. CLARISSA DAY[243], b. Abt. 1831[243].

83. JANE[7] CARLTON *(MARY[6] LAND, THOMAS[5], THOMAS[4], JOHN[3], CURTIS[2], CURTIS[1])* [243] was born April 15, 1793 in Wilkes County, North Carolina[243], and died March 15, 1865[243]. She married WILLIAM THOMAS LAND[243] November 22, 1814 in Wilkes County, North Carolina[243], son of JONATHAN LAND and ELIZABETH ISBELL. He was born September 13, 1788 in Wilkes County, North Carolina[243], and died July 09, 1871[243].

Notes for WILLIAM THOMAS LAND:
William Thomas Land, born 13,Sept 1788 and died 9, July 1871 in Wilkes County. William was a veteran of the War of 1812. He married 22,Nov 1814 to Jane Carlton, daughter of Thomas Carlton and Mary Land, (daughter of Thomas Land & Ann Sumter) Nancy Land, born abt 1789 married 30,May 1809 to William Maltba (Maltbey.) Mary Land, born abt 1790 was " murdered by her husband (Parrish Barlow) in a fit of insanity " in 1828 according to her grave stone. Ann Land, born abt 1794 married on Feb.19,1816 to Thomas Earp. Lettice Land,born abt 1796 married Lewis Carlton 23, Nov.1825. They reportedly lived out their days in Indiana. Jonathan Land Jr born abt 1798.married Margaret Mooney 23,Sept.1828. Elizabeth Land , born abt 1802 married another Carlton 23 Nov 1822. Mahala Land was born abt 1804. From the 1880 U.S. Census: District 91, Tarrant, Texas. The household of JONATHAN LAND DODSON son of Constant Dodson and Nancy Small, grandson of Joel Dodson and Franky Land. Great-grandson of Jonathan Land and Elizabeth Isbell.

More About WILLIAM THOMAS LAND:
Burial: Thomas Land Cemetery, Mount Zion Community, Wilkes County, North Carolina[243]

Children of JANE CARLTON and WILLIAM LAND are:

141. i. WILSON[8] LAND, b. October 27, 1815; d. September 08, 1847.
142. ii. NARCISSA LAND, b. November 08, 1817; d. December 1904.
iii. ELIZABETH LAND[243], b. April 22, 1820[243]; d. September 16, 1826[243].
143. iv. LINVILLE LAND, b. July 27, 1822; d. November 04, 1884.
v. MARY LAND[243], b. March 25, 1826[243]; d. April 11, 1906[243]; m. WILLIAM HALL[243], January 09, 1859[243]; b. Bef. 1825[243].
vi. THOMAS CHARLES LAND[243], b. March 18, 1828, Wilkes County, North Carolina[243]; d. November 30, 1912, Wilkes County, North Carolina[243]; m. JANE DULA THOMAS[243], 1878[243].

Notes for THOMAS CHARLES LAND:
THE " ROVER " THOMAS CHARLES LAND :
From Land researcher and descendent of William Thomas Land, Dudley Land : " Notes for Thomas Charles Land: It is said that T.C. Land fought in 65 Civil War battles. He achieved the rank of 2nd Lieutenant. In 1869 in company with David Wagner and his wife he emigrated to Jackson, Co. Oregon. After about two years they came to Coos County with John Hayes, Alfred Whidby, J.L. Wagner, and others. He settled in the Coos County area with the Wagner, Hayes, Wygan families. They named their settlement after their native North Carolina. About 1888 he returned to North Carolina. About 1891 he returned to Oregon (probably with great nephew, T.D. Land). About 1899 he returned to NC. It is no coincidence that his nickname was "the rover." From the Wilkes Historical Society, Wilkesboro, NC, written about 1900 before his death. "Thomas C Land is one of the landmarks of the county. He was born March 18,1828, and was raised on a farm, attending the old field schools a few weeks for a part of the winters. He attended old Beaver Creek Academy for a short time while Hugh Stokes was principal. At the outbreak of the Civil War he joined Col Sidney Stokes; company B 1st N.C.Inf. as a private..He was appointed commissary and later corporal. In the Seven Days Fight around Richmond he was wounded at the

battle of Malvern Hill. He was allowed to come home on furlough. During his absence from the army he was appointed 3rd Lt of Co .K the 53rd N.C .Regiment, which position he filled till July 1st,1863 at Gettysburg ,Pa. where he was promoted to 2nd Lt upon the death of his Captain and his nephew, William J .Miller. He was wounded at the battle of Winchester and a number of other times but not seriously. After the war, T.C. returned to Wilkes and engaged in teaching school and farming. In 1870 he went to Oregon and took up land and lived there until 1884 when he returned to Wilkes. In 1891 he again went to Oregon and lived there until 1898 when he returned to Wilkes and where he has lived since. While in the West he engaged in farming, teaching and mining . Col Land has considerable literary talent and is the author of the popular ballad, "The Death of Laura Foster" and a number of other poems. Col Land has been fond of hunting and while in the West he had quite a little experience in hunting deer, bear and elk. He has the horns of a large elk that he killed which he prizes very highly. Col Land is at present a member of the county Board of Education, the only office he ever held." More About Thomas Charles Land: Burial: Mt Zion Cemetery - Land Garden Nickname: Squire Occupation: Teacher Confederate Service in the Civil War : Thomas C. Land Residence Wilkes County NC; 33 years old. Enlisted on 5/31/1861 at Wake County, NC as a Corporal. On 5/31/1861 he mustered into "B" Co. NC 1st Infantry He was discharged for promotion on 8/2/1862 On 8/2/1862 he was commissioned into "K" Co. NC 53rd Infantry (date and method of discharge not given) He was listed as: * Wounded 7/1/1862 Malvern Hill, VA Promotions: * 2nd Lieut 8/2/1862 Soldier History Thomas C. Land Residence was not listed; Enlisted as a Corporal (date unknown). On 8/2/1862 he was commissioned into "K" Co. NC 53rd Infantry He Resigned on 4/1/1865 He was listed as: * Hospitalized 7/29/1863 Richmond, VA* Furloughed 8/3/1863 (place not stated) * Returned 9/30/1863 (place not stated) (Estimated day) * Wounded 9/19/1864 Winchester, VA* Returned 1/30/1865 (place not stated) (Estimated day) Promotions: * 3rd Lieut 8/2/1862 He also had service in: "B" Co. NC 1st Infantry Thomas in the 1880 census of Oregon : John HAYES Self M Male W 55 NC Farmer NC NC Susanna HAYES Wife M Female W 43 TN Keeping House TN TN Henry W. HAYES Son S Male W 20 TN Gold Miner NC TN James HAYES Son S Male W 23 TN Gold Miner NC TN Dolley C. HAYES Dau S Female W 18 TN At Home NC TN Julia A. HAYES Dau S Female W 16 TN At Home NC TN Lura R. C. HAYES Dau S Female W 14 NC At Home NC TN Joseph M. C. HAYES Son S Male W 12 NC Farm Hand NC TN John P. HAYES Son S Male W 10 NC Hand On Farm NC TN Jacob M. HAYES Son S Male W 8 NC NC TN Mary S. HAYES Dau S Female W 5 OR NC TN Thomas J. HAYES Son S Male W 10M OR NC TN Thomas C. LAND Other S Male W 52 NC Gold Mining NC NC.

More About THOMAS CHARLES LAND:
Burial: Mt Zion Cemetery - Land Garden[243]
Nickname: Squire[243]
Occupation: Teacher[243]

144. vii. NANCY LAND, b. November 24, 1830; d. April 30, 1903.
145. viii. MARTHA CAROLINE LAND, b. August 02, 1834, Wilkes County, North Carolina; d. August 20, 1904.
146. ix. JAMES CALVIN LAND, b. July 14, 1837, Wilkes County, North Carolina; d. April 23, 1925.

84. MARY[7] CARLTON *(MARY[6] LAND, THOMAS[5], THOMAS[4], JOHN[3], CURTIS[2], CURTIS[1])* [243] was born December 24, 1795 in Wilkes County, North Carolina[243], and died October 05, 1860 in Acton, Hood County, Texas[243]. She married JAMES LOWREY ALLISON[243]. He was born 1797[243].

Children of MARY CARLTON and JAMES ALLISON are:

i. LOWREY GILLESPIE[8] ALLISON[243], b. 1817[243].
ii. MALINDA LUCINDA ALLISON[243], b. 1819[243].
iii. ELIZA AMANDA ALLISON[243], b. 1820[243].
iv. JOHN H. ALLISON[243], b. 1823[243].
v. MARY EVALINA ALLISON[243], b. 1824[243].
vi. DRURY ALLISON[243], b. 1825[243].
vii. NANCY C. ALLISON[243], b. Abt. 1827[243].
viii. THOMAS N. ALLISON[243], b. 1830[243].
ix. CORNIELIA JANE ALLISON[243], b. 1832[243].
x. WILLIAM ALLISON[243], b. 1833[243].
xi. MARY ANN ALLISON[243], b. 1837[243].
xii. JAMES H. ALLISON[243], b. 1839[243].

85. JAMES[7] LAND *(JONATHAN[6], THOMAS[5], THOMAS[4], JOHN[3], CURTIS[2], CURTIS[1])* [243] was born 1784 in Wilkes County, North Carolina[243], and died May 1844 in Wilkes County, North Carolina[243]. He married EDITH LIVINGSTON [243] January 06, 1807[243]. She was born Abt. 1790[243].

Children of JAMES LAND and EDITH LIVINGSTON are:

147. i. HASTING[8] LAND, b. Abt. 1808; d. Aft. 1850.
148. ii. THOMAS LAND, b. 1809.
149. iii. JR. JAMES LAND, b. Abt. 1814; d. Abt. 1885, Alexander County, North Carolina.
150. iv. NIMROD LAND, b. August 31, 1821, Alexander County, North Carolina; d. September 28, 1883.
151. v. DAVID LAND, b. 1825, Wilkes County, North Carolina; d. 1900, Alexander County, North Carolina.

86. WILLIAM THOMAS[7] LAND *(JONATHAN[6], THOMAS[5], THOMAS[4], JOHN[3], CURTIS[2], CURTIS[1])*[243] was born September 13, 1788 in Wilkes County, North Carolina[243], and died July 09, 1871[243]. He married JANE CARLTON[243] November 22, 1814 in Wilkes County, North Carolina[243], daughter of THOMAS CARLTON and MARY LAND. She was born April 15, 1793 in Wilkes County, North Carolina[243], and died March 15, 1865[243].

Notes for WILLIAM THOMAS LAND:
William Thomas Land, born 13,Sept 1788 and died 9, July 1871 in Wilkes County. William was a veteran of the War of 1812. He married 22,Nov 1814 to Jane Carlton, daughter of Thomas Carlton and Mary Land, (daughter of Thomas Land & Ann Sumter) Nancy Land, born abt 1789 married 30,May 1809 to William Maltba (Maltbey.) Mary Land, born abt 1790 was " murdered by her husband (Parrish Barlow) in a fit of insanity " in 1828 according to her grave stone. Ann Land, born abt 1794 married on Feb.19,1816 to Thomas Earp. Lettice Land, born abt 1796 married Lewis Carlton 23,Nov.1825. They reportedly lived out their days in Indiana. Jonathan Land Jr born abt 1798.married Margaret Mooney 23,Sept.1828. Elizabeth Land, born abt 1802 married another Thomas Carlton 23,Nov 1822. Mahala Land was born abt 1804. From the 1880 U.S. Census : District 91, Tarrant, Texas. The household of JONATHAN LAND DODSON son of Constant Dodson and Nancy Small, grandson of Joel Dodson and Franky Land. Great-grandson of Jonathan Land and Elizabeth Isbell.

More About WILLIAM THOMAS LAND:
Burial: Thomas Land Cemetery, Mount Zion Community, Wilkes County, North Carolina[243]

Children are listed above under (83) Jane Carlton.

87. MARY[7] LAND *(JONATHAN[6], THOMAS[5], THOMAS[4], JOHN[3], CURTIS[2], CURTIS[1])*[244,245] was born Aft. 1791 in Wilkes County, North Carolina[245], and died 1828[245]. She married PARISH BARLOW[245]. He was born 1791[245], and died 1829[245]. Her husband Parish Barlow killed her "in a fit of insanity", so her grave at Kings Creek says.

Children of MARY LAND and PARISH BARLOW are:
i. CHARLOTTE[8] BARLOW[245], b. Abt. 1817[245]; m. JOHN HOLSCLAW[245].
ii. JULIA BARLOW[245], b. Abt. 1819, Wilkes County, North Carolina[245]; m. THOMAS PIPES[245].
iii. HAMILTON BARLOW[245], b. July 15, 1821[245]; d. November 13, 1882[245]; m. CYNTHIA FERGUSON[245].
iv. HORTON BARLOW[245], b. January 25, 1824[245]; d. January 10, 1887[245]; m. NANCY MALTBA[245]
v. DICEY BARLOW[245], b. 1826[245].
vi. EMILY BARLOW[245], b. 1828[245].

88. ANN[7] LAND *(JONATHAN[6], THOMAS[5], THOMAS[4], JOHN[3], CURTIS[2], CURTIS[1])*[245] was born 1794 in Wilkes County, North Carolina[245], and died Bef. 1850 in Wilkes County, North Carolina[245]. She married THOMAS EARP[245] February 19, 1816 in Wilkes County, North Carolina[245]. He was born Abt. 1794 in Pittsylvania Co. VA[245].

Children of ANN LAND and THOMAS EARP are:
i. ELIZABETH[8] EARP[245], b. Abt. 1818, Wilkes County, North Carolina[245]; d. Monroe County, Tennessee[245]; m. JOHN BIRCHFIELD[245].
ii. THOMAS S. EARP[245], b. April 08, 1822[245]; d. February 05, 1885[245]; m. ELEANOR NELLIE PEARSON[245].

More About THOMAS S. EARP:
Burial: Mt Zion Cemetery, North Carolina[245]

iii. WILLIAM MARTIN EARP[246,247], b. Abt. 1824[247]; d. Aft. 1880, Roane County, Tennessee[247]; m. ANNE HAMPTON[247].

William was a member of the 26th North Carolina Infantry Company I; one of those units was severely destroyed during Picket's Charge at Gettysburg, Pennsylvania.

William Thomas Land born 1785-1788

THOMAS LAND FAMILY

768

Little is known of the early migration of the Thomas Land family into Wilkes County. It is assumed they came from Ireland in the 1700's and had settled in Georgia or South Carolina, thence moving northwest to Wilkes County, N.C.

Thomas Land, of Mount Zion, married Jane Carlton of Wilkes 16 November 1814. They were the parents of nine children, all born at Mount Zion. (1) Wilson Land, married 22 October 1836 Rebecca Miller and had Mary L., born 1838. (2) Narcissa Land, married 10 October 1837 Henry Harrison Miller and had Wm. J. Miller, born 1838, Thomas Miller, born 1840 and Henry H. Miller, born 1842. (3) Mary Land, married 9 January 1859, William [illegible]. (4) Thomas C. Land was born 1830 and married in 1878 Jane Duke. He died after 1905. Thomas C. attended Beaver Creek Academy while Hugh Stokes was principal. He was a school teacher in Wilkes County and in Tennessee. He was also a poet. He wrote many verses about his extensive travels throughout the south and west. He farmed in Georgia, mined silver in the mountains of Nevada, worked on the railroad in Tennessee and Kentucky. He also wrote verses about Wilkes County and the "fair maidens thereof." (5) Lewis Land, married 4 August 1849 Rhoda [illegible]. They had Mary J., Wilson, William and Calvin.

(6) James Calvin Land was born in Wilkes County, N.C. at Mount Zion 14 July 1837, and was in his 88th year at the time of his death in 1925. He served in the war between the States [illegible]

dren, viz. Jacob, David, Joseph, Daniel, Mathias, John, Sarah, Susan, Roberta, Elizabeth, Nancy, Catharine and Martha. After their marriage, James Calvin and Nancy lived at Mount Zion on his father's farm. He was the youngest and took care of his father and mother. His brother, Thomas C. Land lived with them. They sold their property and made their home in Mount Pleasant, Tennessee at the home of their son, David Land. James Calvin and Nancy had four children.

Jane Catharine "Jennie" Land, daughter of James Calvin and Nancy, was born 6 June 1868, Mount Zion, Wilkes County, died 20 October 1943 at Boone, N.C., married 23 September 1891, Charles Calvin Wright (1862-1930). Jennie is buried in the family plot in Edgewood Baptist Church cemetery, Wilkes County. They had children Mary Dorris, David Ralph, James Thomas Carl, Clyde Robert and Charles Calvin, Jr.

William Thomas Land, 1st row

Thomas David Land, son of James Calvin and Nancy, was born 16 May 1870 at Mount Zion, died 10 June 1948 Mt. Pleasant, Tennessee, married Arline Robinett who died in 1979. Both are buried in Tennessee. They had children: Calvin, Thomas, Dudley, Charles and Mary Frances.

Sallie Caroline Land, daughter of James Calvin and Nancy, was born 25 December 1876, Mount Zion, died 28 July 1960 at Parsonsville, Wilkes County, married 15 November 1905 James Cicero Parsons, born 10 January 1871, died 1 December 1948. Both are buried at New Hope Baptist Churchyard, Wilkes County. They had children Mary Dorris, Nannie Elizabeth, Jennie Lucille, Mattie Land and Jessie Catherine.

Mary Elizabeth (Mollie) Land, daughter of James Calvin and Nancy, was born 10 March 1879 in Wilkes County, died 20 May 1912, Mt. Zion, Wilkes County, married R.C. [illegible]

"Nannie" Waggoner Land was a consistent member of Mount Zion Baptist Church and was well loved by all that knew her. She died in 1918, shortly after the move to Mount Pleasant, Tennessee and is buried there along with her husband, James Calvin.

(7) Martha Land, seventh child of Thomas and Jane Carlton Land, was born 3 September 1840, married 25 October 1865 L.J. Hendrix. (8) Nancy Land, eighth child of Thomas and Jane Carlton Land, was born in Wilkes County, died 6 December 1918, married 4 February 1851 A.B. West. (9) Betsy (Lizzie) Land, ninth child of Thomas and Jane Carlton Land, married 9 September 1856 Charles C. Miller.

Sources: Family records, personal knowledge, family Bible of Thomas Land.

— Jessie Parsons Rhyne

- iv. ANNIE EARP[247], b. Abt. 1826, Wilkes County, North Carolina[247]; d. Abt. 1870, Wilkes County, North Carolina[247]; m. WILLIAM ANDREW BROYHILL[247].
- v. ANDREW EARP[247], b. Abt. 1829, Watauga[247]; d. Abt. 1850, Monroe County, Tennessee[247].

89. ELIZABETH[7] LAND *(JONATHAN[6], THOMAS[5], THOMAS[4], JOHN[3], CURTIS[2], CURTIS[1])* [247] was born Abt. 1795 in Wilkes County, North Carolina[247], and died Abt. 1835 in Wilkes County, North Carolina[247]. She married THOMAS CARLTON[247] November 23, 1822 in Wilkes County, North Carolina[247], son of JOHN CARLTON and ELIZABETH BARLOW. He was born October 30, 1803 in Wilkes County, North Carolina[247], and died August 03, 1873 in Jackson, Alabama[247].

Children of ELIZABETH LAND and THOMAS CARLTON are:

- i. AMANDA[8] CARLTON[247], b. Abt. 1824[247]; d. August 1884, Jackson County, Alabama[247]; m. LEWIS A. ARMSTRONG[247].
- ii. JOHN WINSTON CARLTON[247], b. Abt. 1825, Watauga[247]; d. November 18, 1878, Jackson County, Alabama[247]; m. MARGARET HOLDER[247]
- iii. EUNICE NICEY CARLTON[247], b. October 18, 1829, Watauga[247]; d. January 22, 1889, Newton County, Missouri[247]; m. WILLIAM RUFUS KNIGHT[247], October 16, 1851, Jackson, Alabama[247]. Burial: Powers Cemetery[247]
- iv. LEWIS M. CARLTON[247], b. October 12, 1831, Watauga[247]; d. April 06, 1895, Lafayette County, Arkansas[247]; m. LOUISANA CAROLINE DOZIER[247].

90. LETTICE[7] LAND *(JONATHAN[6], THOMAS[5], THOMAS[4], JOHN[3], CURTIS[2], CURTIS[1])*[247] was born 1796[247], and died July 1842 in Lawrence County, Indiana[247]. She married LEWIS CARLTON[247] November 23, 1825 in Wilkes County, North Carolina[247], son of JOHN CARLTON and ELIZABETH BARLOW. He was born March 10, 1806 in Wilkes County, North Carolina[247], and died 1853 in Lawrence County, Indiana[247].

Children of LETTICE LAND and LEWIS CARLTON are:

i. MARY[8] CARLTON[247].
ii. ELIZABETH CARLTON[247], b. November 06, 1826, Wilkes County, North Carolina[247]; d. September 24, 1881, Lawrence County, Indiana[247]; m. JOHN P. FOSTER[247], January 07, 1845[247].
iii. NANCY CARLTON[247], b. Abt. 1828[247]; d. Lawrence County, Indiana[247]; m. F. FOUNTAIN FOSTER[247], April 13, 1847[247]. Burial: Carlton Cemeeary[247]
iv. JOHN JASPER CARLTON[247], b. December 14, 1830, Wilkes County, North Carolina[247]; d. March 16, 1863[247]; m. MARTHA KIMBLEY[247], March 17, 1854[247].
v. THOMAS B. CARLTON[247], b. Abt. 1833, Wilkes County, North Carolina[247]; d. August 03, 1841, Lawrence County, Indiana[247].
vi. LEWIS P. CARLTON[247], b. April 12, 1835, Wilkes County, North Carolina[247]; d. April 16, 1853, Lawrence County, Indiana[247].
vii. JAMES D. CARLTON[247], b. Abt. 1837[247]; m. MARY JANE CALDWELL[247], March 26, 1857[247].
viii. AMBROSE M. CARLTON[247], b. Abt. 1842, Lawrence County, Indiana[247]; d. Bef. 1852[247].

91. JR. JONATHON[7] LAND *(JONATHAN[6], THOMAS[5], THOMAS[4], JOHN[3], CURTIS[2], CURTIS[1])*[247] was born 1798 in Wilkes County, North Carolina[247], and died Abt. 1865 in Wilkes County, North Carolina[247]. He married MARGARET MOONEY[247] September 23, 1828[247].

Children of JONATHON LAND and MARGARET MOONEY are:

i. EMILY[8] LAND[247], b. March 06, 1826[247]; d. 1833[247].
ii. MINERVALAND[247].
iii. MARGARET ELIZABETH LAND[247], b. Abt. 1829[247].
152. iv. JOSEPH R. LAND, b. 1831.
153. v. ANN LAND, b. Abt. 1832, Wilkes Co. NC.
vi. MARY LAND[247], b. Abt. 1838[247].
vii. REBECCA LAND[247], b. Abt. 1840[247].

92. MILLIE[7] LAND *(JONATHAN[6], THOMAS[5], THOMAS[4], JOHN[3], CURTIS[2], CURTIS[1])*[247] was born 1806[247]. She married HARVEY MOONEY[247].

Children of MILLIE LAND and HARVEY MOONEY are:

i. WILLIAM[8] MOONEY[247], b. Abt. 1831[247].
ii. MARTHA MOONEY[247], b. Abt. 1835[247].
iii. HARRISON MOONEY[247], b. Abt. 1836[247].
iv. DELPHIA MOONEY[247], b. Abt. 1837[247].
v. FRANKLIN MOONEY[247], b. Abt. 1838[247].

93. THOMAS[7] LAND *(THOMAS[6], THOMAS[5], THOMAS[4], JOHN[3], CURTIS[2], CURTIS[1])*[247] was born 1795[247], and died 1867[247]. He married FRANCES GILLIUM[247].

Child of THOMAS LAND and FRANCES GILLIUM is:

i. THOMAS[8] LAND[247], b. December 07, 1815[247].

94. FRANCES[7] LAND *(THOMAS[6], THOMAS[5], THOMAS[4], JOHN[3], CURTIS[2], CURTIS[1])*[247] was born Abt. 1785 in Wilkes County, North Carolina[247], and died Bef. 1850 in Monroe County, Tennessee[247]. She married WILLIAM GRAY[247] December 13, 1802[247]. He was born 1774[247], and died March 12, 1855[247]. Burial: Mount Zion Cemetery[247]

Children of FRANCES LAND and WILLIAM GRAY are:

i. THOMAS[8] GRAY[247].
ii. CINTHIA GRAY[247].
iii. WILSON GRAY[247].
iv. NANCY GRAY[247].
v. MIRA GRAY[247].

vi. AMANDA GRAY[247].
vii. MARY ADALIANE GRAY[247].
viii. ANNA GRAY[247], b. 1803[247].
ix. FRANCES LOUISE GRAY[247], b. June 27, 1805[247].
x. RUTH GRAY[247], b. 1810[247].
xi. WARREN GRAY[247], b. February 05, 1822[247].
xii. WILLIAM GRAY[247], b. January 26, 1831[247].

95. JAMES NOAH[7] LAND *(THOMAS[6], THOMAS[5], THOMAS[4], JOHN[3], CURTIS[2], CURTIS[1])*[247] was born Abt. 1793 in Wilkes County, North Carolina[247], and died Abt. 1893 in Tennessee[247]. He married (1) RHODA PLEMMONS[247]. He married (2) NANCY ALLISON[247] 1820[247]. She was born in Haywood County, North Carolina[247].

Children of JAMES LAND and NANCY ALLISON are:

154. i. ALLISON[8] LAND, b. July 09, 1833, Monroe Co., TN; d. January 10, 1908, Monroe Co., Tn.
ii. WILLIAM LAND.
iii. ELLISON LAND.
iv. TILLMAN HOWARD LAND.

James Noah Land & Rhoda Plemmons

Notes for TILLMAN HOWARD LAND:
CIVIL WAR VETERAN TILLMAN HOWARD LAND was the youngest of 4 sons belonging to James Noah Land & Nancy Allison of Monroe County, Tennessee. His older brothers, William, Ellison, and James fought for the Confederacy in the Civil War. William in Company A of the 62nd Tenn. Ellison (or Allison which was his mother's maiden name) in the 39th Tenn. James in Company A of the 59th Tenn, while Tillman enlisted in Company B of the 59th.at Morristown, Tennessee April 27,1862. The last card in his rebel CMSR for the period of March-April,1863 says : " reported on last roll as absent without leave and since deserted and gone to Kentucky." Tillman's 3 brothers were captured and paroled at the surrender of the Confederate garrison at Vicksburg, Miss .July 4th 1863. Retuning to soon Union occupied East Tennessee and behind Yankee lines, the three probably never rejoined the rebel army. Tillman, on the other hand, on Sept 24,1864. enlisted in the UNION 7th Tenn Mtd Inf serving till the war's end and receiving a Federal pension in later years thus serving on both sides in the Civil War !!!!

96. DELILAH[7] LAND *(JOHN[6], JOHN[5], THOMAS[4], JOHN[3], CURTIS[2], CURTIS[1])*[247] was born 1812 in Madison County, Alabama[247], and died Abt. 1870 in Phelps County, Missouri[247]. She married BENJAMIN HUTCHINSON[247] Abt. 1830[247].

Children of DELILAH LAND and BENJAMIN HUTCHINSON are:

i. AMANDA[8] HUTCHINSON[247].
ii. MARTHA HUTCHINSON[247].
iii. SARAH M. HUTCHINSON[247].
iv. DAUGHTER HUTCHINSON[247].

v. CHILD HUTCHINSON[247].
vi. WILLIAM HUTCHINSON[247].
vii. JOHN D. HUTCHINSON[247].
viii. ELIZA ELLEN HUTCHINSON[247].
ix. BENJAMIN PERRY HUTCHINSON[247].

97. WILLIAM JEFFERSON[7] LAND *(JOHN HENRY[6], CHARLES[5], CHARLES[4], CURTIS[3], CURTIS[2], CURTIS[1])* [247,248,249] was born October 11, 1851[250,251], and died February 24, 1929 in Reeves Allen, Louisiana[252,253]. He married (1) VIRGINIA ESTELLE JONES[254] November 10, 1889[254]. She was born December 10, 1874[254]. He married (2) VIRGINIA ESTELE JONES[255,256] November 10, 1889[257,258]. She was born December 10, 1874[259,260], and died December 22, 1949 in Reeves Allen, Louisiana[261,262].

Children of WILLIAM LAND and VIRGINIA JONES are:
i. WILLIAM EBERT[8] LAND[263], m. LONA MAE DIVINE[263].
ii. DELLA MAE LAND[263], m. DEE WEIR[263].
iii. LIVING LAND[263], m. LIVING BANKESTER[263].
iv. MATTIE BELL LAND[263], b. August 08, 1891, Adel, Cook Co., Georgia[263]; d. March 23, 1969, Reeves Cal Casieu, Louisiana; m. MID DUNNEHOO.
v. GRACE LEE LAND[263], b. November 01, 1898, Florida[263]; d. December 27, 1974, Louisiana[263]; m. MINZO HARRISON[263].
155. vi. RAYMOND TIMOTHY LAND, b. December 31, 1900, Florida; d. January 18, 1965.
vii. NORA ESTELLE LAND[263], b. September 14, 1902, Florida[263]; d. March 16, 1969, Louisana[263]; m. OTTO HARRISON[263], 1918; b. November 28, 1898; d. December 12, 1961. Burial: Creel Cemetery
viii. CARLOS EUGENE LAND[263], b. April 18, 1905, Reeves Cal Casieu, Louisiana[263]; d. Aft. 1987[263]; m. ELIZABETH HUDSON[263].
ix. JAMES DEWITT LAND[263], b. December 07, 1909, Florida[263]; d. July 23, 1933, Louisiana[263].
x. THOMAS BYRON LAND[263], b. January 11, 1915, Reeves Cal Casieu, Louisiana[263]; d. November 09, 1986[263]; m. CLETA[263].
xi. JOHN CLYDE LAND, b. February 25, 1912, Reeves Cal Casieu, Louisiana; d. Aft. 1987; m. WARRENE AVIS BANKESTER, March 20, 1937; b. Aft. 1987.

98. JOHN CALHOUN[7] LAND *(CETH SMITH[6], CHARLES[5], CHARLES[4], CURTIS[3], CURTIS[2], CURTIS[1])* [263] was born June 25, 1862[263], and died July 25, 1943. He married MATTIE LEE OLIVER[263] September 20, 1885[263]. She was born February 27, 1866[263], and died December 22, 1920.

Children of JOHN LAND and MATTIE OLIVER are:
i. JANIE[8] LAND[263], m. HENRY AUBREY CLARK[263]; b. October 07, 1891[263]; d. August 17, 1954.
ii. GERTRUDE NESBITT LAND[263].
iii. BURNETT GUTHRIE LAND[263], b. July 07, 1886[263]; d. November 14, 1943[263]; m. EMMA LOUISE HARPER[263].
iv. MARY LOUISE LAND[263], b. February 03, 1888[263]; d. May 09, 1930[263]; m. SAM WILLIE HOGAN[263], December 14, 1908[263]; b. October 22, 1885; d. September 24, 1943.
v. FLORENCE LEE LAND[263], b. May 02, 1890[263]; d. March 19, 1904[263].
vi. VIRGINIA GERTRUDE LAND[263], b. April 11, 1892[263]; d. September 08, 1904[263].
vii. CETH SMITH LAND[263], b. February 28, 1894[263]; d. December 27, 1955[263]; m. (1) MARTHA COCKSREY PLOWDEN[263]; m. (2) ROSA LEE PLOWDEN[263].
viii. WARRINGTON OLIVER LAND[263], b. March 13, 1899[263]; d. July 25, 1964[263]; m. EDITH VIRGINIA GEIGER[263].
ix. JOHN CALHOUN LAND[263], b. September 28, 1901[263]; d. February 19, 1969[263]; m. ANNA ABBOT WIESIGERT[263].
x. CHARLES EDWARD LAND[263], b. November 23, 1904[263]; d. April 07, 1946[263]; m. ELVYN[263].
xi. MATTIE LEE LAND[263], b. January 07, 1907[263]; d. Aft. 1983[263]; m. CHARLES NEWTON DICKSON[263].

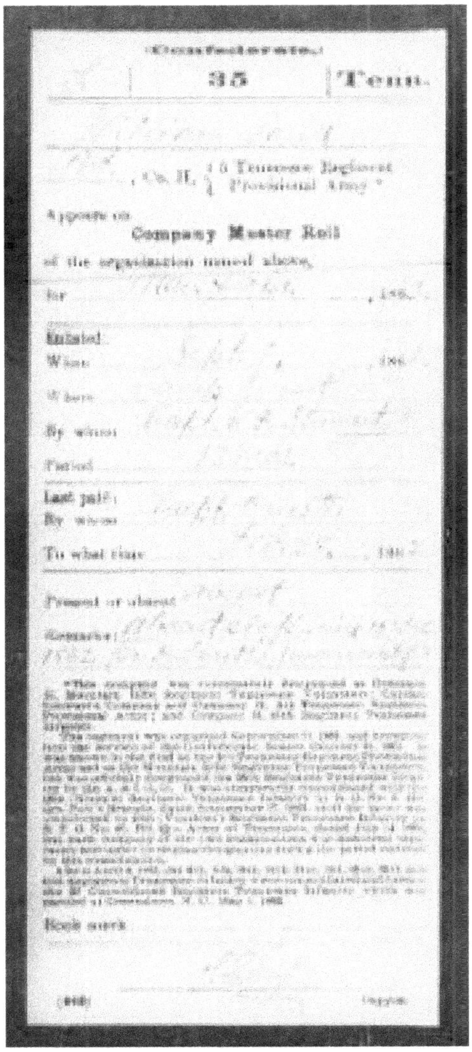

35 | Tenn.

, Co. H, 16 Tennessee Regiment
Provisional Army

Appears on

Company Muster Roll

of the organization named above,

for , 186

Enlisted:
When , 186
Where
By whom
Period

Last paid:
By whom
To what time , 186

Present or absent

Remarks:

Book mark

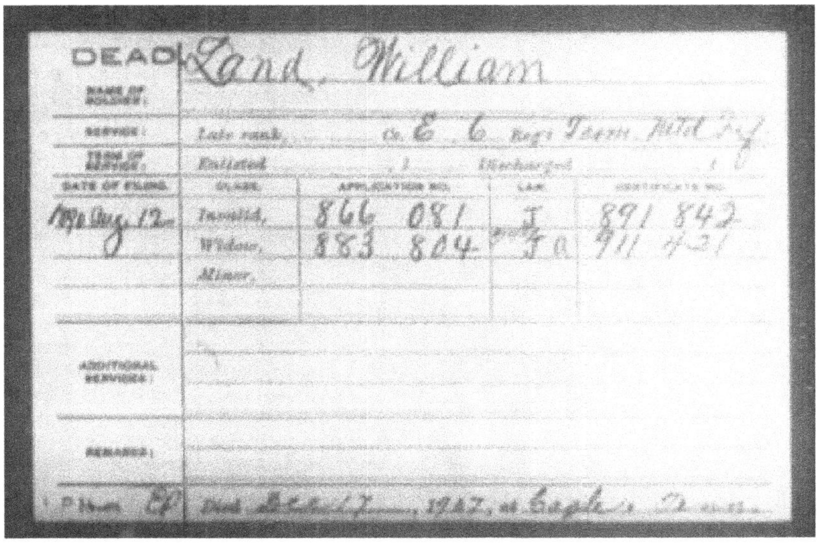

DEAD Land, William

NAME OF SOLDIER:	Land, William			
SERVICE:	Late rank, Co. E. 6 Reg't Tenn. Mtd. Inf.			
TERM OF SERVICE:	Enlisted , 1 Discharged , 1			
DATE OF FILING.	CLASS.	APPLICATION NO.	LAW.	CERTIFICATE NO.
Aug. 12	Invalid,	866 081	I	891 842
	Widow,	883 804	I A	911 421
	Minor,			
ADDITIONAL SERVICES:				
REMARKS:				

Died , 1917, at Eagle , Tenn.

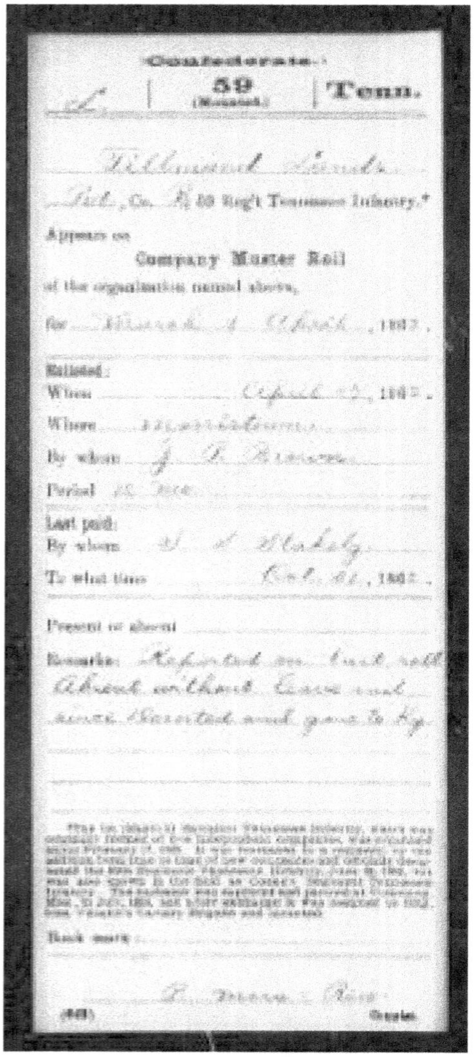

Confederate.

L | 59 (Mounted.) | Tenn.

Tillmand Lands

Pvt., Co. B, 59 Reg't Tennessee Infantry.*

Appears on

Company Muster Roll

of the organization named above,

for March & April, 1863.

Enlisted:

When April 23, 1862.

Where Morristown

By whom J. R. Brown

Period 12 mo

Last paid:

By whom [illegible] Blakely

To what time Oct. 31, 1862.

Present or absent

Remarks: Reported on last roll absent without leave and since deserted and gone to Ky.

[illegible]

Book mark:

[illegible]

(643) Copyist.

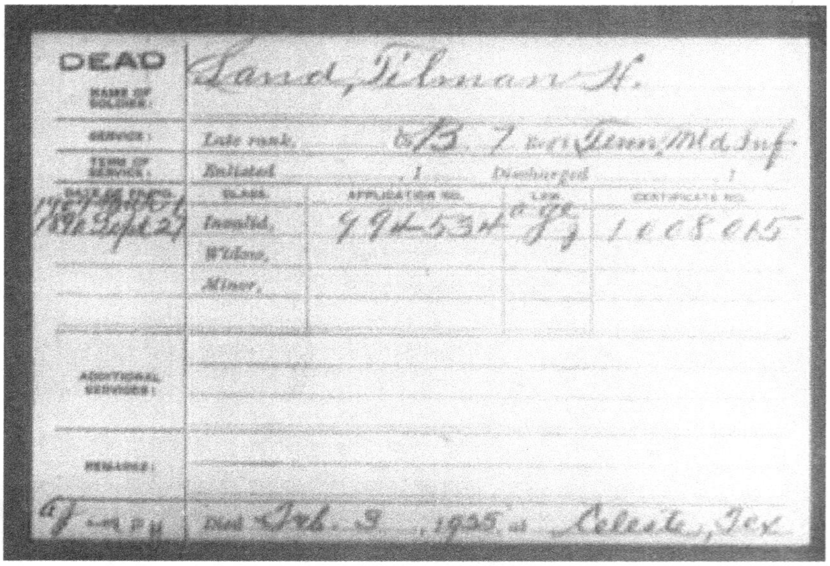

DEAD — NAME OF SOLDIER:	Land, Tilman H.
SERVICE:	Late rank, Co. B. 7 Reg't Tenn. Mtd. Inf.
TERM OF SERVICE:	Enlisted , 1 Discharged , 1

DATE OF FILING.	CLASS.	APPLICATION NO.	LAW.	CERTIFICATE NO.
1892 Sept 27	Invalid,	994534	[illegible]	1008015
	Widow,			
	Minor,			

ADDITIONAL SERVICES:

REMARKS:

[illegible] Died Feb. 3, 1935, at Celeste, Tex

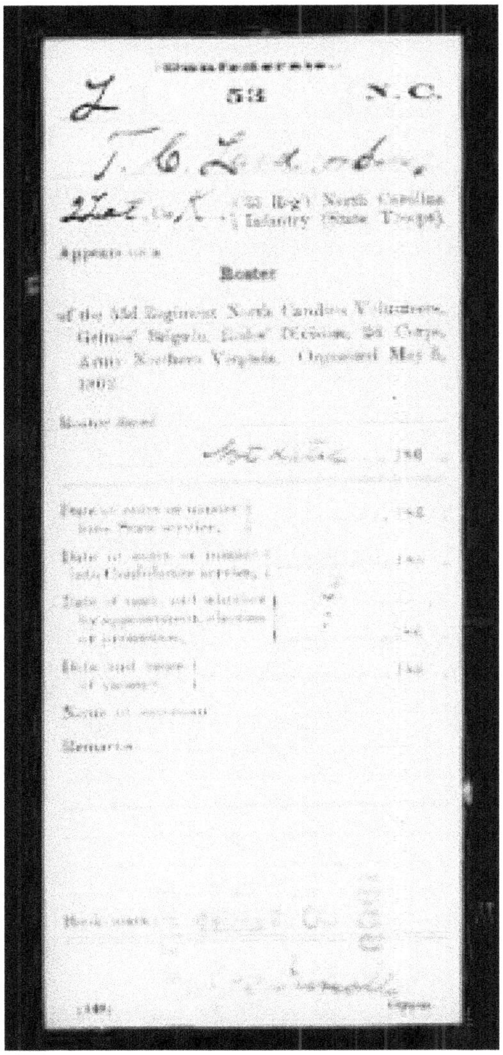

Confederate.

L 53 N.C.

T. C. Land

(53 Reg't) North Carolina Infantry (State Troops).

Appears on a

Roster

of the 53d Regiment North Carolina Volunteers, Grimes' Brigade, Rodes' Division, 2d Corps, Army Northern Virginia. Organized May 8, 1862.

Roster dated

Not dated, 186

Remarks:

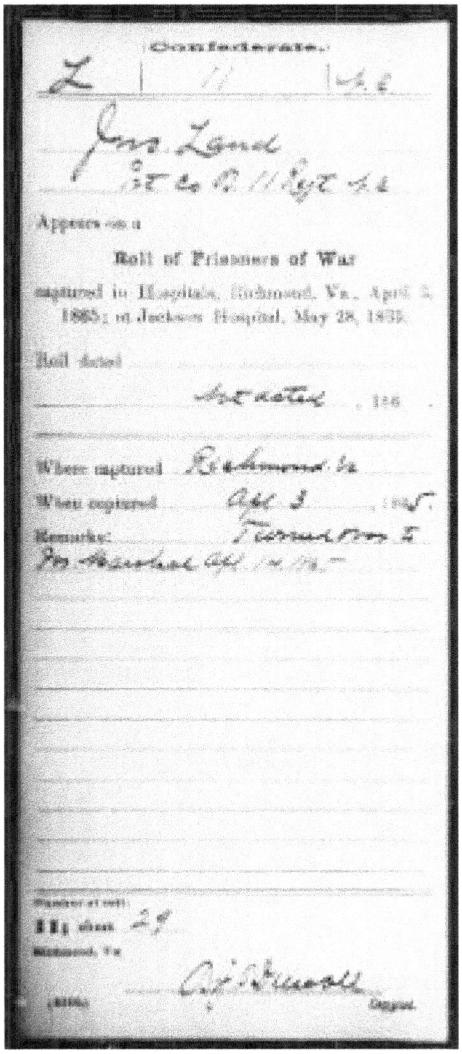

Confederate.

L | 11 | N.C.

Jno. Land

1st Co. B, 11 Reg't N.C.

Appears on a

Roll of Prisoners of War

captured in Hospitals, Richmond, Va., April 3, 1865; at Jackson Hospital, May 28, 1865.

Roll dated

Not dated, 186

Where captured Richmond Va.

When captured Apl. 3, 1865.

Remarks:

99. CETH SMITH[7] LAND *(CETH SMITH[6], CHARLES[5], CHARLES[4], CURTIS[3], CURTIS[2], CURTIS[1])*[263] was born March 05, 1876[263], and died December 27, 1924[263]. He married (1) VIRGINIA OLIVE CANTEY[263]. He married (2) FRANCES ELIZABETH JONES[263] January 02, 1910[263]. She was born 1886 in South Carolina[263].

Children of CETH LAND and VIRGINIA CANTEY are:

156. i. BENJAMIN SMITH[8] LAND, b. September 23, 1898; d. June 09, 1966.
ii. WILLIE LAND[263], b. February 01, 1901[263]; d. May 28, 1902[263].
157. iii. JOHN LAND, b. August 28, 1904; d. April 12, 1961.

Children of CETH LAND and FRANCES JONES are:

iv. DORA ANNIE[8] LAND[263], b. January 01, 1911[263]; d. September 04, 1968[263]; m. JOEL CHANDLER KENNEDY[263], April 02, 1930; b. May 08, 1910; d. December 20, 1951.
v. CHARLES LESTER LAND[263], b. July 05, 1916[263]; d. April 26, 1985, Pickens, South Carolina[263]; m. HATTIE CALVIN[263]; b. January 20, 1921; d. Aft. April 26, 1985.
vi. MARY FRANCES LAND[263], b. April 17, 1919[263]; d. April 05, 1985, Lexington, South Carolina[263]; m. MARION STROM JORDON[263].

100. JOHN T.[7] LAND *(WILLIAM[6], JESSE[5], CHARLES[4], CURTIS[3], CURTIS[2], CURTIS[1])*[263] was born April 1858 in Georgia[263], and died Aft. 1900 in Randolph, Georgia[263]. He married MARY E. UNKNOWN[263]. She was born May 1858 in Georgia[263], and died Aft. 1900 in Randolph, Georgia.

Children of JOHN LAND and MARY UNKNOWN are:

i. GEORGE W.[8] LAND[263].
ii. VIVIAN LAND[263].
158. iii. JOHN THOMAS LAND, b. May 04, 1873, Newberry County, SC.
iv. ANNIE M. LAND[263], b. May 1885[263].
v. LOTTIE LAND[263], b. February 1887[263].

101. WILLIAM[7] LAND *(CHARLES[6], JESSE[5], CHARLES[4], CURTIS[3], CURTIS[2], CURTIS[1])*[263] was born January 1876[263], and died Aft. 1910 in Bibb, Georgia[263]. He married MAMIE KING[263] 1910[263]. She was born 1885[263], and died Aft. 1910 in Bibb, Georgia.

Children of WILLIAM LAND and MAMIE KING are:

i. DAISY[8] LAND[263].
ii. LINNY LAND[263].
iii. TULLY LAND[263].
iv. JOSEPH LAND[263].
v. GREENE LAND[263].
vi. ANNIE LAND[263].

102. JOHN THOMAS[7] LAND *(ELDRIDGE HALL[6], FRANCES[5], JOHN[4], WILLIAM[3], CURTIS[2], CURTIS[1])* was born 1874 in South Carolina. He married EMMA SARAH QUINTON.

Children of JOHN LAND and EMMA QUINTON are:

i. MARY BEATRICE[8] LAND, b. 1911.
ii. JAMES MCCONNELL LAND, b. 1913.
iii. ELRIDGE HALL LAND, b. 1916; m. NANCY JANE THOMAS.
159. iv. JOSEPH LINDSEY LAND, b. June 25, 1918, Vaughn/Moore Co., NC; d. February 02, 1995, Clearwater/Pinellas, FL.

103. JOHN G.[7] LAND *(BIRD[6], LITTLEBERRY[5], BIRD[4], CURTIS[3], CURTIS[2], CURTIS[1])*[263] was born 1825 in North Carolina[263], and died Aft. 1880 in Harrison County, Mississippi[263]. He married SUE J. REEVES[263] November 21, 1866 in Rankin County, Mississippi[263]. She was born December 1844 in Harrison County, Mississippi[263].

Children of JOHN LAND and SUE REEVES are:

160. i. LUCY[8] LAND.
ii. EMILY LAND[263], b. 1871, Mississippi[263]; d. Aft. 1880, Harrison County, Mississippi[263].

104. NANCY[7] LAND *(BIRD[6], LITTLEBERRY[5], BIRD[4], CURTIS[3], CURTIS[2], CURTIS[1])* [263]was born December 06, 1829 in Edgecombe County, North Carolina[263], and died September 20, 1911 in Dallas, Texas[263]. She married SILAS BROWM PENRY[263] January 14, 1852 in Noxubee County, Mississippi [263]. He was born September 12, 1827 in Alabama[263]. Burial: Oak Cliff Cemetery[263]

Children of NANCY LAND and SILAS PENRY are:

- i. JACK E.[8] PENRY[263].
- ii. W.H. PENRY[263].
- iii. J. LEE PENRY[263], b. Abt. 1862[263].

161. iv. LOUIS CURL PENRY, b. October 24, 1864, Noxubee County, Mississippi.

105. ELMIRA SHERMAN[7] LAND *(BIRD[6], LITTLEBERRY[5], BIRD[4], CURTIS[3], CURTIS[2], CURTIS[1])* [263] was born 1836 in Edgecombe County, North Carolina[263], and died 1870 in Rankin County, Mississippi[263]. She married CHARLES WEILL[263] September 14, 1857 in Rankin County, Mississippi[263]. He was born 1822 in France [263].

Children of ELMIRA LAND and CHARLES WEILL are:

162. i. LEOPOLD[8] WEILL, b. 1859.

- ii. ALBERT WEILL[263], b. 1862[263].
- iii. ISIDORE WEILL[263], b. 1864[263].
- iv. JOHN WEILL[263], b. 1868[263].

106. SAMUEL HENRY[7] HARGROVE *(SALLY[6] LAND, LITTLEBERRY[5], BIRD[4], CURTIS[3], CURTIS[2], CURTIS[1])* [264] was born April 22, 1825 in Edgecombe Co. NC[264], and died December 17, 1873 in Edgecombe Co. NC[264]. He married LUCINDA KILLEBREW[264] February 13, 1851[264,265]. She was born January 12, 1824 in Edgecombe Co. NC [266], and died August 10, 1908 in Edgecombe Co. NC[266].

Notes for SAMUEL HENRY HARGROVE:
(Research):Bride: Lucinda Killibrew
Groom: Samuel H Hargrove
Bond Date: 22 Fe b 1851
County: Edgecombe
Record #: 01 082
Bondsman: Gray L Hargrove
Witness : John Norfleet
Bond #: 000043822
Marriage Date: 27 Feb 1851
Performed By: W illiam H Hines, Justice of the Peace North Carolina Marriage Bonds, 1741-1868
Edgecombe County Will Abstracts 1858-1910
Page 60 (275)
Samuel H. Hargrove 14 July 1873 Apr Ct. 1874 O G/444
Wife (unnamed)--all my land, stock, etc . for her lifetime with reversion to all my children.[2882706.ged]

(Research):Bride: Lucinda Killibrew
Groom: Samuel H Hargrove
Bond Date: 22 Fe b 1851
County: Edgecombe
Record #: 01 082
Bondsman: Gray L Hargrove
Witness : John Norfleet
Bond #: 000043822
Marriage Date: 27 Feb 1851
Performed By: William H Hines, Justice of the Peace North Carolina Marriage Bonds, 1741-1868
Edgecombe County Will Abstracts 1858-1910
Page 60 (275)
Samuel H. Hargrove 14 July 1873 Apr Ct. 1874 O G/444
Wife (unnamed)--all my land, stock, etc . for her lifetime with reversion to all my children.

Notes for LUCINDA KILLEBREW:
(Research):Edgecombe County Will Abstracts 1858-1910 P. 59 (274) Lucinda (X) Hargrove. 8 April 1907 Sept Ct 1908 O 1/246 Entire estate to my so n R. G. Hargrove.[2882706.ged]

Children of SAMUEL HARGROVE and LUCINDA KILLEBREW are:

163. i. MARY[8] HARGROVE, b. May 07, 1852, Edgecombe Co. NC; d. January 03, 1876, Edgecombe Co. NC.
ii. GEORGE S. HARGROVE[266], b. August 20, 1854, Edgecombe Co. NC[266]; d. June 30, 1855, Edgecombe Co. NC[266].
iii. WILLIAM H. HARGROVE[266], b. July 21, 1857, Edgecombe Co. NC[266]; d. December 24, 1873, Edgecombe Co. NC[266].
iv. LUCY HARGROVE[266], b. 1859, Edgecombe Co. NC[266].

164. v. LUCINDA HARGROVE, b. March 09, 1859, Edgecombe Co. NC.
vi. PRUDENCE HARGROVE[266], b. May 25, 1861, Edgecombe Co. NC[266]; d. November 07, 1906, Edgecombe Co. NC[266].
vii. SALLIE HARGROVE[266], b. September 20, 1867, Edgecombe Co. NC[266]; d. August 29, 1868, Edgecombe Co. NC[266].

165. viii. ROBERT GRAY HARGROVE, b. December 06, 1868, Edgecombe Co. NC; d. March 06, 1934, Edgecombe Co. NC.

107. GRAY LEMON[7] HARGROVE *(SALLY[6] LAND, LITTLEBERRY[5], BIRD[4], CURTIS[3], CURTIS[2], CURTIS[1])*[267,268] was born June 18, 1827 in Edgecombe Co. NC[268], and died 1894 in Edgecombe Co. NC[268]. He married (1) NANCY L. WORSLEY[269,270]. She was born February 1839[270], and died 1924[270]. He married (2) FELETIA LITTLE[271]. He married (3) MARTHA ANN FOXHALL[272] March 31, 1853 in Edgecombe Co. NC[272]. She was born 1815 in Edgecombe Co. NC[272], and died 1857 in Edgecombe Co. NC[272]. He married (4) MARTHA ANN FOXHALL GARDNER[273] March 31, 1853[273]. He married (5) FELICIA LITTLE[274] January 25, 1859[274]. She was born March 17, 1839[274], and died January 25, 1879[274].

Notes for LEMON HARGROVE:
"Gray Lemon (Lamon), the third child, left home at the age of 21 years with f ifty cents in his pocket to make his way in the world.
He became overseer fo r a young widow, Martha Ann Foxhall Gardner, who lived north of Tarborough. Later they were married and became the parents of two sons and one daughter. Shortly after the birth of the daughter, Martha Ann died. The child died three months later. Gray married twice more and was the father of 12 children by his second wife, Feletia Little.
Gray was a successful farmer and shrewd businessman, buying 17 more tracts of land to add to the existing farm. A strong believer in education, he hired a governess for his
children, and with the exception of one son, sent all of them who survived childhood away for higher education. Three of his sons completed medical schools.
Gray's son Peyton, at the age of 21 was stricken with hemorrhagic fever; another son, Charles, 27 years old, was called home from his medical practice in Norfolk,
Virginia to attend his brother. In two days Peyton was dead and five days later Charles died. They are buried in the Gray L. Hargrove Cemetery on the farm which is still owned by the family (Mae Krider Hargrove Pope).
The follow ing is the application from Mrs. A. C. Hughes (Hattie Hargrove) to the "United Daughters of the Confederacy" . I quote "Gray Lemon Hargrove, my father was a Lt. of The Home Guard. This company was sent over the state on guard duty to hunt deserters. He also gave several thousand dollars to the building of ships for the defense of our coast. . My uncle, Edward L. Hargrove, served in Co. F, 40th Regiment, Heavy Artillery. He was in eight battles some of them were as follows. A battle at Bentonsville, two at Kingston, N.C. one at Fort Johnson and around Wilmington. He fired the three last cannons at Fort Macon, NC before being taken prisoner, exchanged and fought until the close of the war. He was with General Johnson when he surrendered. Another uncle fought through the entire was and another was killed near Petersburg, Virginia." United Daughters of The Confederacy, NC Division, Lee County Chapter, N o. 1755. Date of admission Oct. 4, 1921. No 22 on Roll Book."
--Mae Krider Hargrove Pope
Mother has told me that Gray Lemon was a large man weighing over 300 lbs--RGB
(Research):Bride: Martha Ann Foxhall Gardner

Groom: Gray L Hargrove
Bond Date: 31 Mar 1853
County: Edgecombe
Record #: 01 082
Bondsman : D Williams
Witness: John Norfleet; David McDaniel
Bond #: 000043819
Marriage Date: 31 Mar 1853
Performed By: Jordan Thigpen, Justice of the Peace
North Carolina Marriage Bonds, 1741-1868
Bride: Felitia Little
Groom: Gray L Hargrove
Bond Date: 25 Jan 1859
County: Edgecombe
Record #: 01 082
Bondsman: Jordan Thigpen
Witness: W A Jones, Clerk
Bond #: 000043820
Marriage Date: 25 J an 1859
Performed By: David Cobb
North Carolina Marriage Bonds, 1741-1868
T he 1860 Census shows:
Slave Schedule: 70 year old female, 28 m, 14 m, 13 m, 7 f and 5 slave houses.
Real property 10,000 and personal property 8,000. The following people living in the household:
Lisha, 18
Robert Henry 5
John David 5
Thomas W. 6/12
(Note: Gray had been a widow for 3 years and Lisha could have been a live-in Governess with a 6 mo. old child, Thomas W.)
1880 Census:
Household:
Name Relation Marital Status Gender Race Age Birthplace Occupation Father's Birthplace Mother's Birthplace
Gray L. HARGROVE Self W Male W 53 NC Farmer NC NC
Alva G. HARGROVE Son S Mal e W 20 NC At Home NC NC
Edword T. HARGROVE Son S Male W 18 NC At Home NC NC
Willie F. HARGROVE Son S Male W 17 NC At Home NC NC
Lucy E. HARGROVE Dau S Female W 15 NC At School NC NC
Charley B. HARGROVE Son S Male W 13 NC At School NC NC
Sallie C. HARGROVE[2882706.ged]

Notes for NANCY L. WORSLEY:
(Research):1840 - Census - Edgecombe - (Nathan) Mayo Worsley - age 31, wife Nancy Worsley - age 40 to 49, son Ios A. W. Worsley - age 5 to 9, Edwin G. Worsley - age 5 to 9, daughter Carolin Worsley - age 10, daughter Nancy L. Worsley - age 1
1850 - Census - Edgecombe - (Nathan) Mayo Worsley [spelled here as "Wausley"]- age 41 Head of household consisting of Mary L. Worsley age 29 Mayo's second wife (Mary Louise Staton, daughter of Winfield Station and Julia Mayo), a daughter (by first wife) Caroline age 20, a son (by first wife) Edwin G. age 18, a son (by first wife) Ios A. age 16, a daughter (by first wife) Nancy L. age 10, a daughter Virginia E. age 8, a daughter Laura M. age 5, a daughter Aneliza age 2. Farmer with $3500 in real estate. All were born in NC
. (family 583)
1860 - Census - Edgecombe - (Nathan) Mayo Worsley - age 5
2 Head of household, $25,000 real, $55,000 personal prop. Mary L. Worsley - ag e 38 wife. Children: daughter Ida Worsley - age 7 months, daughter Francis Wo rsley - age 3, daughter Mary Worsley - age 5, son Nathan Worsley - age 7, son Franklin Worsley - age 9, son Thadeus Worsley - age 10, daughter Aneliza Worsley - age 12, daughter,

Laura M. Worsley - age 14, daughter Virginia Worsley - age 17, daughter Nancey L. Worsley - age 21.[2882706.ged]

Notes for MARTHA ANN FOXHALL:
Martha Ann first married Martin Gardner 1844--daughter William Ann Gardner. Second Marriage: Gray Lemon (Lamon) Hargrove 1853.
LAST WILL AND TESTAMENT OF GEORGE GARDNER WRITTEN ON 30 DECEMBER 1786 EDGECOMBE CO., NC. MAY COURT 17 89 EDGECOMBE CO., NC. (ABRIDGED VERSION) In the name of God, Amen, I, George Gardner, of Edgecombe County in the State of North Carolina, being in good health of body and of sound mind and memory, do make and ordain this my Last Will and Testament in manner and form following (to wit): My soul, I recommend unto the hands of God that gave it me and as touching my body, I recommend to the earth to be buried in a Christian and decent manner at the discretion of my Executors. An, as touching my worldly estate, I give and bequeath in manner and form following: In time (remainder of word is not legible), I will that my just debts and funeral charges be paid.
Item: I give and bequeath to my beloved son, Martin Gardner), ten shillings lawful money of this state to him and his heirs
Item: I give and bequeath to my daughter, Mary Seebery, five shillings lawful money of this state to her and her heirs.
Item: I give and bequeath to my daughter, Ann Pitman, five shillings, lawful money of this state to her and her heirs.
Item: I give and bequeath to my daughter, Zilphy Williford, five shillings lawful money of this state to her and her heirs .
Item: I give and bequeath to my daughter, Phereby Pitman, five shillings lawful money of this state to her and her heirs.
Item: I give and bequeath to my daughter, Phobe Proctor, five shillings lawful money of this state to her and her heirs.
Item: I lend to my beloved wife, Mary, the (next word is not legible) and profits of all my land and personal estate during of her natural life, or widowhood after my debts, charges, and legacies before given are paid of.
Item: I give and bequeath to my beloved son, William Gardner, the plantation that I now live on and all the land I hold on the east side of the Great Mill Branch that lieth (sic) below the mouth of the Little Mill Branch and so up the water courses(?) .... of the Little Mill Branch to the track line and so running the Liner Round to the Great Mill Branch and so up the water courses(?) of the Great Mill Branch to the first station, to him and his heirs forever.
Item: I give and bequeath to my beloved son, George Gardner, all the lands I hold on the west side of the Great Mill Branch and Little Mil l Branch beginning at the lower line on the west side of the Great Mill Branch running up the water courses(?) of the Great Mill Branch to the Little Mill Branch and up the Little Branch to the back line so running the courses(?) of the Liner Round to Martin Gardner line and from thence to the first station it being part of two surveys, to him and his heirs forever.
Item: My will and desire is that after the death or manage(?) of my beloved wife, Mary, a ll my personal estate be equally divided between my four youngest children, vis: William, George, Julian, and Lucrese Gardner and their heirs. And if either of them should die, vis: William or George, or Julian, or Lucrese, the surviving ones of them shall enjoy the deceased one's estate.
Item: I constitute and appoint my friend, Britton Brigers and Thomas Mercer, Executors of this my Last Will and Testament and revoking and disannuling (sic) all former wills and testaments by me heretofore made and published, and pronounce this and no other to be my Last Will and Testament, signed, sealed, published, and pronounced this Thirtieth day of December Anno Domino 1786. In the Present of } his George X Gardner mark Richard Strother Martha Mercer his James X Drauhan mark Gardner Will -
May Court 1789 - Recorded Edgecombe County by May Court 1789. The written will was duly proved in open court by the oaths of Richard Strother and James Drauhan. The Executors [2882706.ged]

Children of GRAY HARGROVE and MARTHA FOXHALL are:

i. WILLIAM ANN[8] GARDNER[274], b. Abt. 1850, Edgecombe Co. NC[274]; m. MALACH M. WILLIAMS[274].
166. ii. ROBERT HENRY HARGROVE, b. March 21, 1855; d. December 07, 1923.
167. iii. JOHN DAVID HARGROVE, b. March 24, 1856, Edgecombe Co. NC; d. February 23, 1932, Edgecombe Co. NC.
iv. MARTHA GRAY HARGROVE[274], b. March 22, 1857[274]; d. June 1857[274].

Children of GRAY HARGROVE and FELICIA LITTLE are:

v. ALPHONS "ALVA" GRAY[8] HARGROVE[274], b. December 28, 1859[274]; d. 1912[274]; m. WILLIAM ANN UNKNOWN[274]; b. 1857[274].

Notes for ALPHONS "ALVA" GRAY HARGROVE:
(Research):In the 1900 Census Alvin Hargrove is listed as a boarder with John Whitehurst. It is the next farm over from where he was born.
The 1910 Census shows Alvin now married to a William Ann ?. There are 3 boarders in the home.

vi. EDWIN THOMAS HARGROVE[274], b. December 11, 1861[274]; d. July 06, 1863[274].
vii. WILLIE FRANKLIN HARGROVE[274], b. January 14, 1863[274]; d. February 28, 1925, Kinston, NC[274].

Notes for WILLIE FRANKLIN HARGROVE:
Dr. Will Hargrove practiced medicine in Kinston, N.C. and never married.--RGB[2882706.ged]

168. viii. LUCY ELLA HARGROVE, b. September 07, 1864, Edgecombe Co. NC; d. Aft. April 11, 1930, Wake County, North Carolina.
ix. CHARLES BARDWOOD HARGROVE[274], b. August 05, 1866[274]; d. 1893[274].

169. x. SALLIE CAPITOLA HARGROVE, b. August 01, 1868.
xi. ELIZABETH "LIZZIE" GERALDINE HARGROVE[274], b. May 20, 1870[274]; d. July 28, 1871[274].
xii. PEYTON CLIFFORD HARGROVE[274], b. January 20, 1872[274]; d. 1893[274].
xiii. JOSEPH MARION HARGROVE[274], b. May 28, 1875[274]; d. 1878[274].

170. xiv. HATTIE IDORA HARGROVE, b. October 06, 1876, Edgecombe Co. NC.

108. MARTHA ANN CHARITY[7] HARGROVE *(SALLY[6] LAND, LITTLEBERRY[5], BIRD[4], CURTIS[3], CURTIS[2], CURTIS[1])* was born 1837 in Edgecombe Co. NC, and died 1901. She married ROBERT STRINGER BRASWELL[275,276] April 01, 1858. He was born March 08, 1836 in Edgecombe Co. NC[276], and died 1863[276].

Notes for ROBERT STRINGER BRASWELL:
(Research):There is a ROBERT S. BRASWELL listed as having served with the NC 17th Inf. (2nd Org.), Co. I (CSA).
Confederate soldier: Co.1, (Edgecombe Rebel s) 17th North Carolina infantry Regiment.
Groom: Robert S Braswell Bride: Martha Hargrove Bond Date: 30 Mar 1858 Bond #: 000042970 Marriage Date: 01 Apr 1858
Level Info: North Carolina Marriage Bonds, 1741-1868
Image Num: 003345 County: Edgecombe Record #: 01 024 Bondsman: J H Draughan Performed By: William F Mercer, Justice of the Peace[2882706.ged]

Children of MARTHA HARGROVE and ROBERT BRASWELL are:
i. CALLIE BERRY[8] BRASWELL[276].
ii. SARAH MARTHA BRASWELL[276], b. 1861[276]; d. 1906[276].

109. FLORENCE ANNA[7] HARGROVE *(SALLY[6] LAND, LITTLEBERRY[5], BIRD[4], CURTIS[3], CURTIS[2], CURTIS[1])*[276] was born March 27, 1844 in Edgecombe Co. NC[276]. She married JOHN R. BARNHILL[276] September 18, 1870. He was born March 03, 1838 in Edgecombe Co. NC[276], and died December 10, 1908[276].

Notes for JOHN R. BARNHILL:
(Research):A John J. Barnhill age 30 appears in Lower Fishing Creek in the 18 70 Edgecombe Census page 79
The North Carolina Veterans Grave Locations by Carere lists J.J. Barnhill but does not give his regiment. All the information the marriage and children of John J. came from Jesse Macon Lawrence , Jr. who posted his information on Rootsweb World Connect Project under Copeland, Harris, Lawrence , Neville, Pittman, Turner and Wheeler families[2882706.ged] Burial: Elmwood Cemetery, Enfield, Halifax County, North Carolina[276]

Children of FLORENCE HARGROVE and JOHN BARNHILL are:
i. EDGAR J.[8] BARNHILL[276], b. 1873, Edgecombe Co. NC[276].

ii. LULU BARNHILL[276], b. 1876, Edgecombe Co. NC[276]; d. October 27, 1960, Nash County, NC[276]; m. RICHARD TASWELL GRIFFIN[276], November 24, 1897; b. September 16, 1868[276]; d. January 02, 1951, Nash County, NC[276].
iii. LYCULUS "LUCIUS" BARNHILL[276], b. 1878, Edgecombe Co. NC[276].

171. iv. LOGAN JASPER BARNHILL, b. March 11, 1879, Edgecombe Co. NC; d. April 16, 1954, Enfield, Nash Co., NC.
v. WALTER BARNHILL[276], b. 1880, Edgecombe Co. NC[276]; d. June 24, 1961[276].

172. vi. DAVID W. BARNHILL, b. 1882, Edgecombe Co. NC; d. September 04, 1966.
vii. CARRIE D. BARNHILL[276], b. 1884, Edgecombe Co. NC[276]; d. April 1964[276]; m. JOHNNIE WARD[276]; b. Abt. 1884[276].
viii. CAROLINE VIRGINIA BARNHILL[276], b. 1884, Enfield, Nash Co., NC[276]; d. Nash County, NC[276]; m. JOHN ROBERT WARD[276]; b. 1886[276].

Notes for CAROLINE VIRGINIA BARNHILL:
Note: After locating the information about John J. Barnhill and his daughter Carie, I believe this is really Caroline Virginia Barnhill and that she was named after her aunt Caroline, John's sister. Upon interviewing a Mrs. Dorothy Skinner of the Red Oak area of Nash County, I was informed that Caroline Barnhill was born in Enfield, Halifax county and in Oct. 1911 she married John Robert Ward. Dorothy Ward (Skinner was born in July 1912 and she married Sam Skinner in May 1930. Photos of Caroline, John, Dorothy and her family appear on pages 34-35 of Rocky Mount and Nash County.
Father: John R. Barnhill b: 3 Mar 1838 in Edgecombe County, North Carolina Formed 1741 From Bertie County
Mother: Florence Annie Hargrove b: 27 Mar 1844
Marriage 1 John Robert Ward b: Abt 1886
Married: Oct 1911[2882706.ged]

110. BURRELL HILDSMAN[7] JOYNER *(AMY[6] LAND, LITTLEBERRY[5], BIRD[4], CURTIS[3], CURTIS[2], CURTIS[1])*[277,278] was born March 18, 1830 in Nash Co., NC[278].

Child of BURRELL HILDSMAN JOYNER is:
173. i. ORA[8] JOYNER, b. November 23, 1869, Edgecombe, North Carolina; d. April 18, 1907.

111. IRA ELLIS[7] JOYNER *(AMY[6] LAND, LITTLEBERRY[5], BIRD[4], CURTIS[3], CURTIS[2], CURTIS[1])*[278] was born November 1831 in Nash Co., NC[278]. He married NANCY B. BATCHELOR May 22, 1856 in Nash, North Carolina. She was born 1830 in Nash, North Carolina, and died Aft. 1870 in Nash, North Carolina.

Children of IRA JOYNER and NANCY BATCHELOR are:
i. ELLA[8] JOYNER, b. 1857; d. 1870, Nash, North Carolina.
ii. MADORA JOYNER, b. 1859; d. Aft. 1870, Nash, North Carolina.
iii. LUCY JOYNER, b. 1861; d. Aft. 1870, Nash, North Carolina.
iv. S. JOYNER, b. 1866; d. Aft. 1870, Nash, North Carolina.
v. FLORENCE JOYNER, b. 1868; d. 1879, Nash, North Carolina.

112. FRANCIS M.[7] JOYNER *(AMY[6] LAND, LITTLEBERRY[5], BIRD[4], CURTIS[3], CURTIS[2], CURTIS[1])*[278] was born 1839 in Nash Co., NC[278]. He married ELIZABETH "BETTY" EVANS[278] April 10, 1866 in Nash County, North Carolina. She was born 1839 in Nash Co., NC[278].

Children of FRANCIS JOYNER and ELIZABETH EVANS are:
i. GEORGE[8] JOYNER[278], b. 1867, Nash Co., NC[278].
ii. AMOS JOYNER[278], b. 1869, Nash Co., NC[278].
iii. JOHN A. JOYNER[278], b. 1875, Nash Co., NC[278].

113. GEORGE W.[7] JOYNER *(AMY[6] LAND, LITTLEBERRY[5], BIRD[4], CURTIS[3], CURTIS[2], CURTIS[1])*[279,280] was born 1845 in Nash Co., NC[280]. He married ZANEY ANN LINDSEY[280] January 09, 1865 in Nash Co., NC[280]. She was born 1837 in Nash Co., NC[280], and died in Cooper, Nash, North Carolina[280].

Children of GEORGE JOYNER and ZANEY LINDSEY are:
i. WILLIAM N.[8] JOYNER[280], b. 1866, Nash Co., NC[280].
ii. MATTHEW H. JOYNER[280], b. 1868, Nash Co., NC[280].
iii. MARY ANN JOYNER[280], b. 1870, Nash Co., NC[280].

iv. S. ANNA JOYNER[280], b. 1872, Nash Co., NC[280].
v. SUSAN A. JOYNER[280], b. 1874, Nash Co., NC[280].
vi. JOSIAH J. JOYNER[280], b. 1877, Nash Co., NC[280].

114. NATHAN T.[7] JOYNER *(AMY[6] LAND, LITTLEBERRY[5], BIRD[4], CURTIS[3], CURTIS[2], CURTIS[1])* [281] was born 1836 in Nash, North Carolina[281], and died Aft. 1860 in Nash, North Carolina. He married PENNY H. LINDSEY June 18, 1857 in Nash, North Carolina. She was born 1833 in Nash, North Carolina, and died Aft. 1860 in Nash, North Carolina.

Child of NATHAN JOYNER and PENNY LINDSEY is:
i. JOHN R.[8] JOYNER, b. 1858.

115. LUCRETIA[7] LAND *(DANIEL[6], LITTLEBERRY[5], BIRD[4], CURTIS[3], CURTIS[2], CURTIS[1])* [281,282] was born November 26, 1822 in North Carolina[283,284], and died May 27, 1894[285,286]. She married DAVID LANE[287,288] November 23, 1844 in Edgecombe, North Carolina[289,290]. He was born October 14, 1818 in NC[290].

Children of LUCRETIA LAND and DAVID LANE are:
i. LAWRENCE[8] LANE[291,292], b. 1849, NC[292].
ii. JOSEPH LANE[293,294], b. 1852, NC[294].

116. LITTLEBERRY JOHN[7] LAND *(BURRELL[6], LITTLEBERRY[5], BIRD[4], CURTIS[3], CURTIS[2], CURTIS[1])* [295] was born 1827 in North Carolina[295], and died Aft. 1870 in Richland Parrish, Louisiana[295]. He married (1) MARY UNKNOWN[295] 1859[295]. She was born Abt. 1819 in Mississippi[295]. He married (2) LAURA A. PERKINS [295] 1869[295]. She was born 1848 in Mississippi[295].

Notes for LITTLEBERRY JOHN LAND:
C.S.A.

Children of LITTLEBERRY LAND and MARY UNKNOWN are:
i. CHARLES[8] LAND[295], b. 1858, Carroll Parrish, Louisiana[295]; d. Aft. 1860, Carroll Parrish, Louisiana[295].
ii. OLIVALAND[295], b. 1860, Carroll Parrish, Louisiana[295]; d. Aft. 1950, Texas[295].

Child of LITTLEBERRY LAND and LAURA PERKINS is:
iii. ETHEL[8] LAND[295].

117. EVALINA[7] LAND *(BURRELL[6], LITTLEBERRY[5], BIRD[4], CURTIS[3], CURTIS[2], CURTIS[1])* [295,296] was born March 15, 1838 in Noxubee County, Mississippi[297,298], and died 1900 in Louisiana[299]. She married DAVID DEW [299] March 31, 1867 in Noxubee County, Mississippi[299].

Children of EVALINA LAND and DAVID DEW are:
i. JAMES WALTER[8] DEW[301], b. February 06, 1868[301].
ii. MARY DEW[301], b. Abt. 1869[301].
iii. LUCY ELIZABETH DEW[301], b. January 15, 1869[301].
iv. BERTA DEW[301], b. Abt. 1870[301].
v. BESSIE DEW[301], b. Abt. 1871[301].
vi. JETHRO THOMAS DEW[301], b. Abt. 1872[301].
vii. SUSAN CATHLEEN DEW[301], b. February 12, 1873[301].
viii. BURRELL THOMAS DEW[301], b. November 06, 1875[301].
ix. VIRGINIA MAE DEW[301], b. November 28, 1878[301].

118. HENRY GREY[7] LAND *(BURRELL[6], LITTLEBERRY[5], BIRD[4], CURTIS[3], CURTIS[2], CURTIS[1])* [301,302] was born December 18, 1829 in Edgecombe County, North Carolina[303,304], and died January 16, 1903 in Noxubee County, Mississippi[305]. He married MARY ANN SIBLEY[305] November 07, 1870[305]. She was born March 22, 1845 in Marengo County, Alabama[305].

Children of HENRY LAND and MARY SIBLEY are:

174. i. SAMUEL SIBLEY[8] LAND, b. December 01, 1871, Noxubee County, Mississippi; d. July 21, 1937, Noxubee County, Mississippi.
175. ii. SARAH BIRT LAND, b. November 29, 1875, Noxubee County, Mississippi; d. Noxubee County, Mississippi.
176. iii. DANIEL BURRELL LAND, b. November 29, 1875, Noxubee County, Mississippi; d. December 13, 1953, Noxubee County, Mississippi.
177. iv. HENRY GREY LAND, b. December 19, 1877, Noxubee County, Mississippi; d. July 24, 1955, Noxubee County, Mississippi.
178. v. MARY LUCY LAND, b. January 27, 1880, Noxubee County, Mississippi.
179. vi. ELIZABETH JANE LAND, b. February 18, 1882, Noxubee County, Mississippi.
180. vii. MILDRED JEFFERSON LAND, b. October 12, 1884, Noxubee County, Mississippi.

119. MARY KATHERINE[7] LAND *(BURRELL[6], LITTLEBERRY[5], BIRD[4], CURTIS[3], CURTIS[2], CURTIS[1])* [307,308] was born 1838 in Noxubee County, Mississippi[309,310], and died 1864 in Noxubee County, Mississippi[311]. She married DEMPSEY SPARKMAN[311] 1861[311].

Children of MARY LAND and DEMPSEY SPARKMAN are:

i. JEFFERSON D.[8] SPARKMAN[313], b. 1862, Mississippi[313].
ii. DAUGHTER SPARKMAN[313], b. Abt. 1863[313].

120. WILLIAM BURT[7] LAND *(BURRELL[6], LITTLEBERRY[5], BIRD[4], CURTIS[3], CURTIS[2], CURTIS[1])* [313,314] was born 1831 in Edgecombe County, North Carolina[315,316], and died November 08, 1898 in Richland Parrish, Louisiana[317]. He married (1) ANN ELIZABETH SMALL[317] 1858 in Mississippi[317]. She was born Abt. 1830[317]. He married (2) SARAH E. MCKINNEY[317] 1866[317]. She was born February 28, 1841[317].

Children of WILLIAM LAND and ANN SMALL are:

181. i. MARY MILDRED "MAGGIE"[8] LAND, b. 1852, Louisiana; d. April 18, 1885, Noxubee County, Mississippi.
182. ii. HENRY TAYLOR LAND, b. May 1861, Richland Parrish, Louisiana; d. 1928, Winston County, Mississippi.

Children of WILLIAM LAND and SARAH MCKINNEY are:

iii. MARY E.[8] LAND[319], b. 1868, Louisana[319]; d. Aft. 1880, Richland Parrish, Louisiana[319].
iv. WILLIAM RUFUS LAND[319], b. March 22, 1869, Illinois[319]; d. June 24, 1881, Richland Parrish, Louisiana[319].
v. ANNA ELIZA LAND[319], b. January 01, 1872, Louisana[319]; d. August 09, 1884, Richland Parrish, Louisiana[319].
vi. JOSEPH BIRT LAND[319], b. January 21, 1874, Richland Parrish, Louisiana[319]; d. October 06, 1882, Richland Parrish, Louisiana[319].
183. vii. LITTLEBERRY JOHN LAND, b. August 01, 1876, Louisiana; d. November 19, 1919, Richland Parrish, Louisiana.
viii. MARGARET LAND[319], b. September 03, 1880, Richland Parrish, Louisiana[319]; d. August 31, 1884[319].
ix. LAURAH GUSHEN LAND[319], b. April 30, 1883, Richland Parrish, Louisiana[319]; d. October 22, 1898, Richland Parrish, Louisiana[319].

121. THOMAS C.[7] LAND *(JOHN[6], CHARLES[5], CHARLES[4], CURTIS[3], CURTIS[2], CURTIS[1])*

Children of THOMAS C. LAND are:

184. i. SOLOMON R.[8] LAND, b. May 1868, NC; d. Aft. 1900, Wilson, NC.
185. ii. WILLIAM H. LAND, b. June 1870; d. Aft. 1900, Wilson, NC.
186. iii. JOSIAH JOSEPH B. LAND, b. 1879, NC; d. Aft. 1910, Edgecombe, North Carolina.

122. WILLIE G.[7] LAND *(JOHN[6], CHARLES[5], CHARLES[4], CURTIS[3], CURTIS[2], CURTIS[1])*

Child of WILLIE G. LAND is:

187. i. TURNER[8] LAND, b. 1837, NC.

123. WILLIAM W.[7] BAILEY *(ELIZABETH[6] LAND, LEWIS[5], BIRD[4], CURTIS[3], CURTIS[2], CURTIS[1])* [320] was born June 10, 1834 in Georgia[320], and died September 24, 1909 in Arkansas[320]. He married MARGARET GRIFFITH[320] WFT Est. 1852-1885[320]. She was born Abt. 1835 in Georgia[320], and died in Randolph Co., Arkansas[320].

Children of WILLIAM BAILEY and MARGARET GRIFFITH are:

188. i. RHODES[8] BAILEY, b. Abt. 1855; d. WFT Est. 1889-1965.
ii. JOHN W. B. BAILEY, b. 1856.
189. iii. GEORGE WASHINGTON BAILEY, b. January 25, 1857.
iv. SARAH BAILEY, b. Abt. 1860.
190. v. ALLEN A. BAILEY, b. Abt. 1864, Arkansas.
191. vi. MARTHA C. BAILEY, b. Abt. 1867.
192. vii. MOSES BAILEY, b. September 1869, Arkansas.
193. viii. SUSAN "SUSIE" BAILEY, b. Abt. 1872.
ix. JANEY BAILEY, b. Abt. 1874.
194. x. MARY ELIZABETH "MATILDA" BAILEY, b. Abt. 1876.

124. SUSANNAH[7] LAND *(STEPHEN[6], LEWIS[5], BIRD[4], CURTIS[3], CURTIS[2], CURTIS[1])*[321] was born November 06, 1837[321], and died 1906 in Paulding County, Georgia[321]. She married NOTEN DICKERSON PARRIS[321] 1853[321]. He was born September 14, 1831 in Spartanburg, SC[321].

Children of SUSANNAH LAND and NOTEN PARRIS are:

i. AMANDA[8] PARRIS[321], b. 1857[321].
ii. WILLIAM STEPHEN PARRIS[321], b. 1860[321].
iii. WILLIAM THOMAS PARRIS[321], b. January 09, 1862[321].
iv. MARY LOU PARRIS[321], b. 1863[321].
v. MARTHA ANN PARRIS[321], b. 1866[321].
vi. HENRY DILLARD PARRIS[321], b. May 03, 1867[321]; m. THEODOCIA LESTER.
195. vii. WARNER DAVID PARRIS, b. October 1871.
viii. ELBERT MELTON PARRIS[321], b. 1875[321].
ix. TRAVIE PARRIS[321], b. 1878[321].

Notes for TRAVIE PARRIS:
On a hot day Travie went running after a cow, got too hot, washed her face in the spring and died.

x. CINTHIA PARRIS[321], b. October 07, 1880[321].

125. ELIZABETH JANE[7] LAND *(STEPHEN[6], LEWIS[5], BIRD[4], CURTIS[3], CURTIS[2], CURTIS[1])*[321] was born July 25, 1840 in Henry County, Georgia[321], and died November 05, 1910 in Paulding County, Georgia[321]. She married NIMROD WELLS PARRIS[321] January 06, 1859 in Paulding County, Georgia[321]. He was born May 24, 1835 in Paulding County, Georgia[321].

Notes for NIMROD WELLS PARRIS:
Served in the 60th GA Infantry from May 10, 1862; Private May 10, 1862. Pension records show he was wounded through right arm and shoulder, resulting in permanent disability at Wilderness, VA May 6, 1864. Discharged.

Child of ELIZABETH LAND and NIMROD PARRIS is:

196. i. RONEY JEFFERSON[8] PARRIS.

126. SARAH[7] BAILEY *(ELIZABETH[6] LAND, LEWIS[5], BIRD[4], CURTIS[3], CURTIS[2], CURTIS[1])* was born Abt. 1849. She married MCCRURY.

Child of SARAH BAILEY and MCCRURY is:

i. GIBSON[8] MCCRURY.

127. ELIZABETH J.[7] LAND *(KINSON[6], LEWIS[5], BIRD[4], CURTIS[3], CURTIS[2], CURTIS[1])*[321] was born Abt. 1837 in South Carolina[321], and died November 05, 1918 in Oregon County, Missouri[321]. She married (1) E. J WILSON[321]. She married (2) JAMES HARVEY DODSON[321] in Marion County, Alabama[321].

Children of ELIZABETH LAND and E. WILSON are:

i. ELLEN[8] WILSON[321].
ii. MARGARET WILSON[321].

128. LEWIS[7] LAND *(KINSON[6], LEWIS[5], BIRD[4], CURTIS[3], CURTIS[2], CURTIS[1])*[321] was born Abt. 1848 in Georgia[321]. He married MARY UNKNOWN[321].

Child of LEWIS LAND and MARY UNKNOWN is:
- i. IDA[8] LAND[321], b. August 24, 1884[321]; d. December 11, 1884[321].

129. JAMES B.[7] LAND *(KINSON[6], LEWIS[5], BIRD[4], CURTIS[3], CURTIS[2], CURTIS[1])*[321] was born June 18, 1852 in Georgia[321], and died April 13, 1887 in Randolph County, Arkansas[321]. He married HELEN HATSFIELD[321] September 07, 1871 in Arkansas[321]. She was born Abt. 1851 in Alabama[321].

More About JAMES B. LAND:
Burial: Bly Cemetery, Randolph County, Arkansas[321]

Children of JAMES LAND and HELEN HATSFIELD are:
- i. ELIZABETH[8] LAND[321].
- ii. EVELINE LAND[321].
- 197. iii. JOEL CAMERON LAND.
- iv. MARTHA EMMA LAND[321].
- v. SARAH A. LAND[321].
- vi. ZILLUH EDNA LAND[321], b. Abt. 1862[321].

130. JORDON[7] LAND *(KINSON[6], LEWIS[5], BIRD[4], CURTIS[3], CURTIS[2], CURTIS[1])*[321] was born July 05, 1853 in Georgia[321], and died January 03, 1922 in Batesville, Independence County, Arkansas[321]. He married REBECCA TENNESSEE MOORE[321]. She was born December 22, 1852[321], and died August 10, 1910 in Batesville, Independence County, Arkansas[321].

More About JORDON LAND:
Burial: Oaklawn Cemetery, Batesville, Arkansas[321]

More About REBECCA TENNESSEE MOORE:
Burial: Oaklawn Cemetery, Batesville, Arkansas[321]

Children of JORDON LAND and REBECCA MOORE are:
- 198. i. REBECCA[8] LAND, b. December 06, 1874, Arkansas; d. January 15, 1930.
- 199. ii. LUCRETIA (LOU CRECY) JANE LAND, b. May 20, 1877, Pocahontas, Arkansas; d. September 15, 1957, Batesville, Independence County, Arkansas.

131. MARY[7] LAND *(KINSON[6], LEWIS[5], BIRD[4], CURTIS[3], CURTIS[2], CURTIS[1])*[321] was born November 17, 1857 in Alabama[321], and died April 03, 1922 in Randolph County, Arkansas[321]. She married ABRAHAM DECKER[321]. He was born March 20, 1846[321].

Children of MARY LAND and ABRAHAM DECKER are:
- i. EVALINE[8] DECKER[321].
- ii. WALTER DECKER[321].
- iii. HOMER DECKER[321].
- iv. CORBETT DECKER[321].
- v. JOE SHELBY DECKER[321], b. August 10, 1882[321].
- vi. FRANK CULAM DECKER[321], b. March 12, 1884[321].

132. MARTHA MATILDA ROSETTA[7] LAND *(KINSON[6], LEWIS[5], BIRD[4], CURTIS[3], CURTIS[2], CURTIS[1])*[322] was born August 07, 1872 in Union TWP, Sharp Co. Ar.[322], and died February 11, 1952 in Randolph Co. Arkansas[322]. She married BOOKER BESHEAR SHORE "DOC" TYLER[322] March 13, 1889 in Randolph Co., Arkansas[322]. He was born December 25, 1866 in Pocahontas, Randolph Co., Arkansas[322], and died March 29, 1914 in Randolph Co. Arkansas[322]. Burial: Brady Cemetery, Randolph Co. Arkansas

Children of MARTHA LAND and BOOKER TYLER are:

200. i. JOSEPH JAMES RUFUS[8] TYLER, b. February 24, 1890, Randolph Co. Arkansas; d. May 08, 1974, Pocahontas, Randolph Co., Arkansas.
201. ii. BERTHA DELIAH TYLER, b. 1891; d. WFT Est. 1918-1985.
202. iii. LUTHER EDWARD TYLER, b. April 02, 1895; d. December 21, 1980.
iv. IDA ARIZONA TYLER, b. 1897; d. 1914, Randolph Co. Arkansas.

More About IDA ARIZONA TYLER:
Burial: Brady Cemetery, Randolph Co. Arkansas

203. v. JAMES CURTIS TYLER, b. 1900.
204. vi. JOHN PARIS TYLER, b. 1901.
vii. WILLIAM SEWARD "BILL" TYLER, b. 1904.
viii. BETTY INEZ TYLER, b. 1906.
ix. TWIN TYLER, b. 1908; d. 1908.
x. GOMER EARNEST TYLER, b. 1912.

133. "DONA" FRANCIS CALDONIA[7] LAND *(KINSON[6], LEWIS[5], BIRD[4], CURTIS[3], CURTIS[2], CURTIS[1])* She married HUGHES.

Children of "DONA" LAND and HUGHES are:
205. i. JAMES EDGAR[8] HUGHES, b. May 1891; d. Yuma, AZ.
206. ii. MARTHA ANNA HUGHES, b. March 04, 1893; d. September 19, 1946.
207. iii. MARY EMMA HUGHES, b. December 1896, Randolph Co. Arkansas; d. May 15, 1979, Jacksboro, Texas.
208. iv. ROSY HUGHES, b. December 1899.
209. v. HENRY F. HUGHES, b. June 04, 1901, Randolph Co. Arkansas; d. November 06, 1989, Sulphur Rock, Independence Co., AR.
210. vi. BIRDIE HUGHES, b. 1904.
211. vii. THOMAS JEFFERSON HUGHES, b. January 20, 1906, Randolph Co. Arkansas; d. October 24, 1970, Randolph Co. Arkansas.

Generation No. 8

134. ELIZABETH[8] LAND *(JOHN FISHER[7], JOHN[6], THOMAS[5], THOMAS[4], JOHN[3], CURTIS[2], CURTIS[1])*[323]. She married RUBEN AGEE[323].

Children of ELIZABETH LAND and RUBEN AGEE are:
i. GEORGE WALFORD[9] AGEE[323].
ii. HOWARD AGEE[323].
iii. CHARLES AGEE[323].
iv. MARTHA AGEE[323].
v. ELIZA AGEE[323].
vi. HARRIETT AGEE[323].
vii. AMANDA AGEE[323].
viii. CALLIE AGEE[323].
ix. ALICE AGEE[323].
x. MARY JANE AGEE[323].
xi. SQUIRE AGEE[323].
xii. WILLIAM AGEE[323].

135. PHOEBE S.[8] LAND *(FOUNTAIN[7], JOHN[6], THOMAS[5], THOMAS[4], JOHN[3], CURTIS[2], CURTIS[1])*[323] was born October 19, 1831 in Illinois[323]. She married LEONARD JOSHUA THOMPSON[323] November 13, 1851[323]. He was born Abt. 1832[323].

Children of PHOEBE LAND and LEONARD THOMPSON are:
i. CAROLINE[9] THOMPSON[323], b. Abt. 1853[323].
ii. FOUNTAIN THOMPSON[323], b. Abt. 1855[323].
iii. REBECCA J. THOMPSON[323], b. May 25, 1857[323].
iv. SELINA B. THOMPSON[323], b. 1864[323].

136. HENDERSON P.[8] LAND *(FOUNTAIN[7], JOHN[6], THOMAS[5], THOMAS[4], JOHN[3], CURTIS[2], CURTIS[1])*[323] was born 1827 in Tennessee[323], and died 1903[323]. He married MAHALA ROBERTS[323] January 04, 1853 in Macoupin County, Illinois[323]. She was born 1830 in Tennessee[323], and died December 15, 1902[323].

More About HENDERSON P. LAND:
Burial: Land Cemetery, Scottville Twp., Macoupin County, Illinois[323]

More About MAHALA ROBERTS:
Burial: Land Cemetery, Scottville Twp., Macoupin County, Illinois[323]

Children of HENDERSON LAND and MAHALA ROBERTS are:
i. BARBARA[9] LAND[323], b. 1853[323].
212. ii. JAMES MONROE LAND, b. 1855.
213. iii. HENRY FOUNTAIN LAND, b. 1867; d. 1951.
iv. MARY LAND[323], b. 1867[323].

137. REBECCA A.[8] LAND *(FOUNTAIN[7], JOHN[6], THOMAS[5], THOMAS[4], JOHN[3], CURTIS[2], CURTIS[1])*[323] was born November 07, 1829 in Illinois[323]. She married HENRY C. WILEY[323] October 27, 1852 in Macoupin County, Illinois[323]. He was born July 27, 1829[323].

Children of REBECCA LAND and HENRY WILEY are:
i. NANCY ADDIE[9] WILEY[323], b. November 15, 1853[323].
ii. PHEBE WILEY[323], b. November 01, 1855[323].
iii. EMMA REBECCA WILEY[323], b. January 15, 1857[323].
iv. THEODORE F. WILEY[323], b. November 10, 1860[323].

138. THOMAS[8] LAND *(FOUNTAIN[7], JOHN[6], THOMAS[5], THOMAS[4], JOHN[3], CURTIS[2], CURTIS[1])*[323] was born 1831 in Illinois[323]. He married MARY ELLIOTT[323] April 05, 1846 in Macoupin County, Illinois[323]. She was born 1829 in Tennessee[323].

Child of THOMAS LAND and MARY ELLIOTT is:
i. SUSAN J.[9] LAND[323], b. 1849, Illinois[323].

139. THOMAS[8] CARLTON *(JOHN[7], MARY[6] LAND, THOMAS[5], THOMAS[4], JOHN[3], CURTIS[2], CURTIS[1])*[323] was born October 30, 1803 in Wilkes County, North Carolina[323], and died August 03, 1873 in Jackson, Alabama[323]. He married (1) SARAH A. HOLDER[323]. She was born Abt. 1836 in Jackson, Alabama[323], and died January 1880 in Jackson, Alabama[323]. He married (2) ELIZABETH LAND[323] November 23, 1822 in Wilkes County, North Carolina[323], daughter of JONATHAN LAND and ELIZABETH ISBELL. She was born Abt. 1795 in Wilkes County, North Carolina[323], and died Abt. 1835 in Wilkes County, North Carolina[323].

Children are listed above under (89) Elizabeth Land.

140. LEWIS[8] CARLTON *(JOHN[7], MARY[6] LAND, THOMAS[5], THOMAS[4], JOHN[3], CURTIS[2], CURTIS[1])*[323] was born March 10, 1806 in Wilkes County, North Carolina[323], and died 1853 in Lawrence County, Indiana[323]. He married (1) LETTICE LAND[323] November 23, 1825 in Wilkes County, North Carolina[323], daughter of JONATHAN LAND and ELIZABETH ISBELL. She was born 1796[323], and died July 1842 in Lawrence County, Indiana[323]. He married (2) ELIZABETH FOSTER[323] July 04, 1843[323]. She was born April 14, 1801[323], and died September 04, 1854[323].

Children are listed above under (90) Lettice Land.

141. WILSON[8] LAND *(WILLIAM THOMAS[7], JONATHAN[6], THOMAS[5], THOMAS[4], JOHN[3], CURTIS[2], CURTIS[1])*[323] was born October 27, 1815[323], and died September 08, 1847[323]. He married REBECCA MILLER[323] October 27, 1836 in Wilkes County, North Carolina[323]. She was born Abt. 1816 in North Carolina[323], and died Aft. 1860 in Wautauga County, North Carolina[323].

More About WILSON LAND:

Burial: Watauga[323]

Children of WILSON LAND and REBECCA MILLER are:

214. i. MARY LOUISE[9] LAND, b. May 28, 1838, Stoney Fork, Watauga County, North Carolina; d. October 25, 1901, Lenoir/ Caldwell County, North Carolina.
215. ii. MARTHA JANE LAND, b. September 03, 1840, Wilkes County, North Carolina; d. Texas.
216. iii. ELIZABETH LAND, b. Abt. 1845, Wilkes County, North Carolina; d. January 1897, Chico, Texas.
217. iv. WILLIAM TAYLOR LAND, b. Abt. 1848, Wilkes County, North Carolina.

142. NARCISSA[8] LAND *(WILLIAM THOMAS[7], JONATHAN[6], THOMAS[5], THOMAS[4], JOHN[3], CURTIS[2], CURTIS[1])*[323] was born November 08, 1817[323], and died December 1904[323]. She married HENRY HARRISON MILLER[323] October 10, 1837 in Wilkes County, North Carolina[323]. He was born 1814[323], and died Abt. 1850[323].

Children of NARCISSA LAND and HENRY MILLER are:

i. WILLIAM J.[9] MILLER[323], b. Abt. 1838, Wilkes County, North Carolina[323]; d. July 1863, Died in the battle of Gettysburg[323].
218. ii. THOMAS C. MILLER, b. Abt. 1840, Wilkes County, North Carolina; d. February 1907, Wise County, Texas.
iii. HENRY HARRISON MILLER[323], b. June 22, 1842[323]; d. March 11, 1914[323].

More About HENRY HARRISON MILLER:
Burial: Bellview Cemetery, Caldwell County, North Carolina[323]

143. LINVILLE[8] LAND *(WILLIAM THOMAS[7], JONATHAN[6], THOMAS[5], THOMAS[4], JOHN[3], CURTIS[2], CURTIS[1])*[323] was born July 27, 1822[323], and died November 04, 1884[323]. He married RHODA PROFFIT[323] August 14, 1849 in Wilkes County, North Carolina[323]. She was born September 05, 1831 in Wilkes Co. NC[323], and died May 18, 1909[323].

More About LINVILLE LAND:
Occupation: Minister[323]

More About RHODA PROFFIT:
Burial: Mt Pleasant, Tn[323]

Children of LINVILLE LAND and RHODA PROFFIT are:

i. MARY J.[9] LAND[323], b. Abt. 1850[323].
ii. WILSON LAND[323], b. Abt. 1852[323].
219. iii. WILLIAM THOMAS LAND, b. April 17, 1857, Wilkes County, North Carolina; d. March 11, 1928.
iv. CALVIN LAND[323], b. Abt. 1859[323].
220. v. SARAH A. LAND, b. November 06, 1860; d. April 19, 1940.
221. vi. ELLEN LOU LAND, b. 1867, Wilkes County, North Carolina; d. 1902.
vii. MARTHA E. LAND[323], b. Abt. 1870[323].

144. NANCY[8] LAND *(WILLIAM THOMAS[7], JONATHAN[6], THOMAS[5], THOMAS[4], JOHN[3], CURTIS[2], CURTIS[1])*[323] was born November 24, 1830[323], and died April 30, 1903[323]. She married ALEXANDER B. WEST[323] February 04, 1851[323].

More About NANCY LAND:
Burial: Avery County Cemetery, North Carolina[323]

Child of NANCY LAND and ALEXANDER WEST is:

i. THOMAS HARVEY[9] WEST[323], b. Abt. 1858, Wilkes County, North Carolina[323]; d. Abt. 1949[323].

More About THOMAS HARVEY WEST:
Burial: Avery County Cemetery, North Carolina[323]

145. MARTHA CAROLINE[8] LAND *(WILLIAM THOMAS[7], JONATHAN[6], THOMAS[5], THOMAS[4], JOHN[3], CURTIS[2], CURTIS[1])*[323] was born August 02, 1834 in Wilkes County, North Carolina[323], and died August 20, 1904[323]. She married LEANDER J. HENDRICK[323] October 25, 1865[323].

More About MARTHA CAROLINE LAND:

Burial: Hendrick Cemetery[323]

Children of MARTHA LAND and LEANDER HENDRICK are:

i. CARRIE[9] HENDRICK[323].
ii. EDWARD HENDRICK[323].
iii. DELLA HENDRICK[323].
iv. MARTHA HENDRICK[323].
v. CAIN V. HENDRICK[323], b. Abt. 1867[323].
vi. CALVIN JAMES HENDRICK[323], b. Abt. 1867, Wilkes County, North Carolina[323].
vii. WILLIAM T. HENDRICK[323], b. Abt. 1869[323].
viii. MARY E. HENDRICK[323], b. Abt. 1871[323].

146. JAMES CALVIN[8] LAND *(WILLIAM THOMAS[7], JONATHAN[6], THOMAS[5], THOMAS[4], JOHN[3], CURTIS[2], CURTIS[1])* [323] was born July 14, 1837 in Wilkes County, North Carolina[323], and died April 23, 1925[323]. He married NANCY WAGNER[323] November 04, 1866[323]. She was born March 20, 1845 in Taylorsville, Johnson County, Tennessee[323], and died December 06, 1918[323].

More About JAMES CALVIN LAND:
Burial: Mt Pleasant, Tennessee[323]

More About NANCY WAGNER:
Burial: Mt Pleasant, Tennessee[323]

Children of JAMES LAND and NANCY WAGNER are:

222. i. CATHERINE JANE[9] LAND, b. June 06, 1868, Hunting Creek, Wilkes County, North Carolina; d. October 20, 1943.
223. ii. THOMAS DAVID LAND, b. May 18, 1870, Wilkes County, North Carolina; d. June 19, 1948, Mt Pleasant, Tennessee.
224. iii. SALLY CAROLINE LAND, b. December 28, 1876; d. July 28, 1960.
225. iv. MARY ELIZABETH LAND, b. March 10, 1879.

147. HASTING[8] LAND *(JAMES[7], JONATHAN[6], THOMAS[5], THOMAS[4], JOHN[3], CURTIS[2], CURTIS[1])* [323] was born Abt. 1808[323], and died Aft. 1850[323]. He married DELIHA UNKNOWN[323]. She was born Aft. 1807[323].

Children of HASTING LAND and DELIHA UNKNOWN are:

i. WILLIAM[9] LAND[323], b. Abt. 1836[323]; d. Bef. 1865[323].
ii. ELIAS LAND[323], b. Abt. 1839[323].
iii. INEZ LAND[323], b. Abt. 1842[323].
iv. JAMES JEFFERSON LAND[323], b. Abt. 1844[323]; d. 1914, Knox County, Tennessee[323].
Served in the Confederate 63rd Inf.

148. THOMAS[8] LAND *(JAMES[7], JONATHAN[6], THOMAS[5], THOMAS[4], JOHN[3], CURTIS[2], CURTIS[1])* [323] was born 1809[323]. He married MATILDA CARLTON[323] August 30, 1831 in Wilkes County, North Carolina[323]. She was born October 05, 1809[323].

Children of THOMAS LAND and MATILDA CARLTON are:

i. ELIZABETH[9] LAND[323], b. 1837[323]; m. PEARL WIMBLEY[323].
226. ii. WILLIAM LANGLEY LAND, b. December 27, 1838.

149. JR. JAMES[8] LAND *(JAMES[7], JONATHAN[6], THOMAS[5], THOMAS[4], JOHN[3], CURTIS[2], CURTIS[1])* [323] was born Abt. 1814[323], and died Abt. 1885 in Alexander County, North Carolina[323]. He married (1) ANN HALL[323]. He married (2) NANCY ALLISON[323]. She was born in Haywood County, North Carolina[323]. He married (3) JINNEY MURPHY[323] December 21, 1839[323]. She was born in Caroline County, North Carolina[323].

Children of JAMES LAND and JINNEY MURPHY are:

227. i. SARAH[9] LAND, b. Abt. 1842, Wilkes County, North Carolina.
ii. JOHN LAND[324,325], b. Abt. 1846, Alexander County, North Carolina[325]; d. Richmond, Virginia[325].
John died a Confederate soldier in Company B, 11th NC Inf.

228. iii. MARY LAND, b. July 21, 1849, Alexander County, North Carolina; d. March 16, 1947, Alexander County, North Carolina.
iv. NIMROD LAND[325], b. Abt. 1850, Wilkes County, North Carolina[325]; d. Aft. 1910, Alexander County, North Carolina[325].
229. v. JAMES ELI LAND, b. June 17, 1851, Wilkes County, North Carolina; d. April 20, 1933, Alexander County, North Carolina.
230. vi. NOAH LAND, b. Abt. 1852, Alexander County, North Carolina; d. Aft. 1920, Alexander County, North Carolina.
vii. GEORGE LAND[325], b. Abt. 1856[325].

150. NIMROD[8] LAND *(JAMES[7], JONATHAN[6], THOMAS[5], THOMAS[4], JOHN[3], CURTIS[2], CURTIS[1])* [325] was born August 31, 1821 in Alexander County, North Carolina[325], and died September 28, 1883[325]. He married HANNAH MARINDA KERLEY[325] Abt. 1851[325].

More About NIMROD LAND:
Burial: Land Cemetery[325]

Children of NIMROD LAND and HANNAH KERLEY are:
i. ELCANAH BRISON[9] LAND[325], b. April 27, 1852, Alexander County, North Carolina[325]; d. February 03, 1930, Alexander County, North Carolina[325].

More About ELCANAH BRISON LAND:
Burial: Little River Cemetery[325]

231. ii. DAVID V. LAND, b. Abt. 1854.
232. iii. DEWANNA W. LAND, b. September 22, 1856, Alexander County, North Carolina; d. February 12, 1939.
iv. INFANT DAUGHTER LAND[325], b. Abt. 1858[325]; d. Abt. 1858, Alexander County, North Carolina[325].

More About INFANT DAUGHTER LAND:
Burial: Land Cemetery[325]

v. HOWARD COLUMBUS LAND[325], b. August 26, 1860, Alexander County, North Carolina[325]; d. November 12, 1863, Alexander County, North Carolina[325].

More About HOWARD COLUMBUS LAND:
Burial: Land Cemetery[325]

vi. MARY ELIZABETH LAND[325], b. March 30, 1863, Alexander County, North Carolina[325]; d. August 14, 1883, Alexander County, North Carolina[325].

More About MARY ELIZABETH LAND:
Burial: Land Cemetery[325]

151. DAVID[8] LAND *(JAMES[7], JONATHAN[6], THOMAS[5], THOMAS[4], JOHN[3], CURTIS[2], CURTIS[1])* [325] was born 1825 in Wilkes County, North Carolina[325], and died 1900 in Alexander County, North Carolina[325]. He married (1) REBECCA FRANCES KNIGHT[325]. She was born 1823 in Wilkes County, North Carolina [325], and died Aft. 1870[325]. He married (2) SARAH MINERVAKERLEY[325] Abt. 1877[325], daughter of MARY CAROLYN KERLEY. She was born September 24, 1885[325], and died November 27, 1923[325].

Notes for DAVID LAND:
David was a Civil War Veteran, serving in Company I, 13th North Carolina Infantry, CSA. His unit was part of the Lane-Scales-Kirkland North Carolina Brigades, known as "Lee's Tarheels". David enlisted at Camp Vance near Morganton, NC on 5 May, 1861 (for three years - or duration). David was probably wounded at Gettysburg, or became seriously ill during the winter of 1863/64 (his unit sustained a significant number of casualties during Pickett's Charge). In February 1864, David received several pieces of clothing at General Hospital, Camp Winder in Richmond, VA. David was captured on 2 April, 1865 during fighting at Petersburg (captured on the south side of the railroad during the Northern breakthrough). David was processed at City Point, VA on 7 April 1865 and sent to Hart's Island, New York Harbor, where he was confined. David was released on 20 June 1865, after taking the US Oath of Allegiance. David is said to have walked home from the war barefooted. Like most Lands of the time,

David was a farmer and land holder in the Brushy Mountains near Beaver Creek (vicinity of Kings Creek and Lower Creek).

Shown in the scrapbook is the remnant of a Confederate battle-flag carried by the 13th North Carolina Infantry. My great-great-grandfather, David Land served in Company I of this regiment from his muster-in, Feb 14,1864 (he probably volunteered to avoid conscription) till he was captured by advancing Federal troops after rebel lines were broken in front of Petersburg, VA April 2,1865. After being " processed " at City Point, VA on April 7th, David was among some of the first rebel P.O.W.s to arrive at Hart Island ,New York Harbor, hurriedly turned to a prison camp from Yankee training camp to accommodate the influx of Rebel prisoners taken by Gen U.S. Grant since the spring of 1864. Many of the Confederate prisoners apparently didn't believe the Yankees telling them of Lee's surrender on April 9,1865. Many like David didn't take the Oath of Allegiance till weeks or even months later in order to be released and return home. David " took the dog " as it was called, and started home June 19,1865. Another of David's great-great-grandsons and Land researcher, Howard " Doug " Land states while growing up in North Carolina, he could recall hearing of David " walking back to North Carolina barefoot following the Civil War." I've quite a bit of Land Civil War history on other related pages if one is interested. The following description and background is given with the flag photo on another genealogy site I have at " Tribal-Pages. "
Photo : Confederate Battle-Flag of the 13th North Carolina Infantry
Photo provided by Mr. Richard L. Reed. of Lakewood, Colorado. Mr. Reed, a Civil War writer and historian, whose 4th cousin was Captain of Company I (David Land's Company,) Captain R.S. Williams. His great-granduncle was 1st Lieut. W.H. Winchester of Co. I who was mortally wounded on 7-3-1863 at Gettysburg, Pa. His great-grandfather was Pvt. John E. Winchester of Co. I. John was captured with David Land on April 2, 1865. They probably arrived together at the Federal prison on Hart's Island ,N.Y. Both were released and started back to North Carolina the same day. David to Wilkes County, John to Rockingham County. David married Sarah Kerley after the death of his first wife Rebecca Knight. (Hannah was David and Sarah's child)

Notes for SARAH MINERVA KERLEY:
Daniel Kerley and Hannah Barnes played a significant part in our " Land Clan " in North Carolina. Their daughter, Sarah was the 2nd wife of David Land and the mother of his youngest, Hannah. Their daughter, Mary Caroline, was the mother of Sarah Etta Oxford, wife of David`s son, Thomas Clingman Land. Their daughter, Hannah Marinda married David`s brother, Nimrod Land. Household: In the 1880 Census : Name Relation Marital Status Gender Race Age Birthplace Occupation Father`s Birthplace Mother`s Birthplace Daniel W KERLEE Self M Male W 83 NC Farmer VA Hannah KERLEE Wife M Female W 78 NC Housekeeping NC NC Rachael E MEDLOCK Dau W Female W 42 NC Laborer On Farm NC NC Robert Loyd MEDLOCK GSon S Male W 4 NC NC NC Source Information: Census Place Little River, Alexander, North Carolina.

More About SARAH MINERVA KERLEY:
Burial: Wm. Cornelius Crisp Cemetery[325]

Children of DAVID LAND and REBECCA KNIGHT are:
233. i. JAMES LINVILLE[9] LAND, b. 1849, Lenoir, North Carolina; d. 1929.
234. ii. ELI JASON LAND, b. May 14, 1852, Wilkes County, North Carolina; d. July 19, 1940, Wilkes County, North Carolina.
235. iii. ELIZABETH LAND, b. April 07, 1854, Caldwell County, North Carolina; d. November 23, 1942, Mineral, Virginia.
236. iv. MARY SERELDA LAND, b. February 22, 1856, Caldwell County, North Carolina; d. November 06, 1941, Alexander County, North Carolina.
237. v. CYNTHIA ELLEN LAND, b. March 07, 1858; d. December 05, 1936.
238. vi. THOMAS CLINGMAN LAND, b. January 25, 1860, Wilkes County, North Carolina; d. January 11, 1939.
vii. SARAH JANE LAND[325], b. Abt. 1862[325]; m. J.W. CROTTS[325], September 11, 1884[325].

Child of DAVID LAND and SARAH KERLEY is:
239. viii. HANNAH NINABELLE[9] LAND, b. May 23, 1878, Alexander County, North Carolina; d. April 21, 1965, Caldwell County, North Carolina.

152. JOSEPH R.[8] LAND *(JONATHON[7], JONATHAN[6], THOMAS[5], THOMAS[4], JOHN[3], CURTIS[2], CURTIS[1])*[325] was born 1831[325]. He married (1) ANNA PENNELL[325]. He married (2) ANNA ISENHOUR[325] December 16, 1855[325].

Children of JOSEPH LAND and ANNA PENNELL are:

i. MARY M.[9] LAND[325], b. September 1857[325].

ii. MARTHA LOWE LAND[325], b. October 26, 1860, Alexander County, North Carolina[325]; d. May 20, 1954, Alexander County, North Carolina[325].

More About MARTHA LOWE LAND:
Burial: Little River Cemetery[325]

153. ANN[8] LAND *(JONATHON[7], JONATHAN[6], THOMAS[5], THOMAS[4], JOHN[3], CURTIS[2], CURTIS[1])*[325] was born Abt. 1832 in Wilkes Co. NC[325]. She married ANDREW WILSON MCGEE[325].

Children of ANN LAND and ANDREW MCGEE are:

i. BARTLETT[9] MCGEE[325], b. Wilkes Co. NC[325].

ii. J. LINVILLE MCGEE[325], b. Wilkes Co. NC[325].

iii. MARY E. MCGEE[325], b. Wilkes Co. NC[325].

iv. WILLIAM BRADFORD MCGEE[325], b. Wilkes Co. NC[325].

v. CALVIN LEE MCGEE[325], b. December 08, 1865, Wilkes Co. NC[325].

154. ALLISON[8] LAND *(JAMES NOAH[7], THOMAS[6], THOMAS[5], THOMAS[4], JOHN[3], CURTIS[2], CURTIS[1])*[325] was born July 09, 1833 in Monroe Co., Tn[325], and died January 10, 1908 in Monroe Co., Tn[325]. He married SARAH ANN MOSES[325]. She was born September 18, 1833[325], and died June 08, 1898 in Monroe County, Tennessee[325].

More About ALLISON LAND:
Burial: Eleazor Cemetery, Monroe County, Tennessee[325]

More About SARAH ANN MOSES:
Burial: Eleazor Cemetery, Monroe County, Tennessee[325]

Child of ALLISON LAND and SARAH MOSES is:

240. i. JOHN WESLEY[9] LAND, b. October 21, 1875, Monroe County, Tennessee; d. August 31, 1959, Englewood, McMinn County, Tennessee.

155. RAYMOND TIMOTHY[8] LAND *(WILLIAM JEFFERSON[7], JOHN HENRY[6], CHARLES[5], CHARLES[4], CURTIS[3], CURTIS[2], CURTIS[1])*[325,326,327] was born December 31, 1900 in Florida[328], and died January 18, 1965[328]. He married VELMA GILBERT[328,329,330] WFT Est. 1915-1946[331]. She was born WFT Est. 1888-1910[331], and died September 27, 1963.
Facts about this person:
Grandmother
Sweetest person, Grand Grandmother

Children of RAYMOND LAND and VELMA GILBERT are:

241. i. LIVING[9] LAND.

ii. LIVING LAND[333].

iii. LIVING LAND[333].

iv. LIVING LAND[333].

v. LIVING LAND[333].

242. vi. LIVING LAND.

vii. LIVING LAND[334].

243. viii. LIVING LAND.

ix. LIVING LAND[334].

x. JAMES DEWITT LAND[334], b. May 06, 1934[335,336]; d. September 1980[337,338].
Facts about this person:
Twin
Twin to Doris

James Linville Land

Thomas Clingman Land & Sallie Oxford

156. BENJAMIN SMITH[8] LAND *(CETH SMITH[7], CETH SMITH[6], CHARLES[5], CHARLES[4], CURTIS[3], CURTIS[2], CURTIS[1])*[339] was born September 23, 1898[339], and died June 09, 1966[339]. He married (1) JOHNNY MCGILL[339]. He married (2) VIVIAN EADON[339]. She was born July 13, 1898[339], and died December 02, 1950. He married (3) AGATHA ROBINSON IRICK April 23, 1964. She was born February 09, 1912, and died April 23, 1964.

Children of BENJAMIN LAND and AGATHA IRICK are:

i. BENJAMIN SMITH[9] LAND, m. MOZELL S. MOAK.
ii. VIVIAN EADON LAND, m. GEORGE FRASIER WESSEL.

157. JOHN[8] LAND *(CETH SMITH[7], CETH SMITH[6], CHARLES[5], CHARLES[4], CURTIS[3], CURTIS[2], CURTIS[1])*[339] was born August 28, 1904[339], and died April 12, 1961[339]. He married CAROLYN CANTEY[339].

Child of JOHN LAND and CAROLYN CANTEY is:

i. JOHN[9] LAND[339], m. (1) DEE BEST[339]; m. (2) LAURIS ELROD.

158. JOHN THOMAS[8] LAND *(JOHN T.[7], WILLIAM[6], JESSE[5], CHARLES[4], CURTIS[3], CURTIS[2], CURTIS[1])*[339] was born May 04, 1873 in Newberry County, SC. He married (1) EMMA SARAH QUINTON. He married (2) LOIS REBECCA BRICE, daughter of JAMES BRICE and DOUGLASS.

Children of JOHN LAND and EMMA QUINTON are:

i. HAVRIES SELEYN[9] LAND, b. July 17, 1900, South Carolina; d. March 29, 1970, Richmond Co , Hamlet, NC; m. NANCY DOVE.

   More About HAVRIES SELEYN LAND:
   Burial: Richland Co., Hamlet Co. Memorial Park

ii. MAUDE T. LAND, b. 1901.
iii. FRED R. LAND, b. 1902.
iv. NANCY N. LAND, b. 1905.
v. WILLIE C. LAND, b. 1907.

Child of JOHN LAND and LOIS BRICE is:

vi. ELDRIDGE H.[9] LAND, b. 1915

159. JOSEPH LINDSEY[8] LAND *(JOHN THOMAS[7], ELDRIDGE HALL[6], FRANCES[5], JOHN[4], WILLIAM[3], CURTIS[2], CURTIS[1])* was born June 25, 1918 in Vaughn/Moore Co., NC, and died February 02, 1995 in Clearwater/Pinellas, FL. He married VIVIAN OLIVE HICKS June 01, 1942 in Clearwater/Pinellas, FL, daughter of MARION HICKS and MARY BADEN. She was born April 27, 1914 in Live Oak/Suwannee, FL, and died October 26, 2008 in Dunedin, FL.

More About JOSEPH LINDSEY LAND:
Burial: Clearwater/Pinellas, FL

Children of JOSEPH LAND and VIVIAN HICKS are:

i. ROBERT BRICE[9] LAND, b. June 12, 1943, Clearwater/Pinellas, FL.
ii. BONNIE CHARLENE LAND, b. November 06, 1945.

John Thomas Land and Wife Lois Rebecca Brice

J. T. Land, Retired Railroader Takes Life Easy In Aberdeen

After 38 years of work on the railroad, J. T. Land lives at ease and enjoys life at his home in Aberdeen.

Mr. Land who was born in Newberry, South Carolina on May 4, 1873 started his railroad career in 1899 as a laborer on the Seaboard Air Line Railway at [illegible] cents per day with no overtime pay. After 4 years as a laborer he was promoted to section foreman, a position he held until his retirement in 1937 after 38 years of service.

Rich in experiences gained during his many years as a "railroad man," Mr. Land can tell of many a train wreck that will bear comparison with Casey Jones and his famous last run.

Mr. Land has been married three times and is the father of twelve children, nine of whom are living.

He was first married to Miss Emma Quinton to which union eight children were born. Three are dead. The living are Harvies

Continued on page two.

J. T. LAND

J. T. LAND, RETIRED RAILROADER, TAKES THINGS EASY NOW

Continued From Page One)

Land of Aberdeen, Fred Land of Petersburg, Va., Mrs. Maude Wilkins of Aberdeen; Willie Chanceler of Richmond, Va., and Mrs. Nellie Averitt of Aberdeen.

His second marriage was to Miss Lois Brice. To this union four children were born as follows: Mrs. E. B. Rogers of Fayetteville; James Land of Apex who is with the railroad; Eldridge Land of Aberdeen; and J. L. Land of Wildwood, Florida who is also with the railroad.

His third marriage was to Mrs. Janie Dawkins, who died several years ago.

His work on the railroad has included service in the Georgia South Carolina, North Carolina and Virginia divisions.

Mr. Land has retired from the railroad with a goodly pension check coming to his mail box twice monthly which amounts to about four times as much as was his salary when he started his railroad career back in 1899.

Marriage Certificate

FILE NO. 1109-1929

STATE OF SOUTH CAROLINA
CHESTER COUNTY
PROBATE COURT.

To Whom It May Concern:

THIS IS TO CERTIFY, That on the 30 day of March, 1929

at Chester in Chester County, State of South Carolina.

J. T. Land, Aberdeen, N.C., 56 years and
MAN'S NAME — ADDRESS — AGE

Mrs. D. E. Dawkins, Chester, S. C., 50 years
WOMAN'S NAME — ADDRESS — AGE

were united in the Bonds of Matrimony by J. E. Jones

Minister in accordance with the law of South Carolina,
OFFICIAL TITLE

in such cases made and provided, and as shown by the records of this Court in Marriage Register 1911-1936 and Certified; that the information given is that their race is white and their Nationality is American.

Witness my Hand and Seal of said Court, this the 12 day of January, 1960.

A TRUE COPY

Attest: Hattie G. Harden
JUDGE OF PROBATE

FORM 1008 - KEYS PRINTING CO., GREENVILLE, S. C.

ENLISTED RECORD AND REPORT OF SEPARATION — HONORABLE DISCHARGE

1. Last Name—First Name—Middle Initial: Land Eldridge H
2. Army Serial Number: 34 008 380
3. Grade: Sgt
4. Arm or Service: MD
5. Component: Aus
6. Organization: Co B 328th Med Bn
7. Date of Separation: 25 Sep 45
8. Place of Separation: Separation Center Fort Bragg N.C.
9. Permanent Address for Mailing Purposes: Aberdeen N.C. Moore Co.
10. Date of Birth: 11 Aug 15
11. Place of Birth: Chester S.C.
12. Address From Which Employment Will Be Sought: See 9
13. Color Eyes: Brown
14. Color Hair: Brown
15. Height: 5 10
16. Weight: 142 Lbs.
17. No. Depend.: 0
18. Race: White X | Negro | Other (Specify)
19. Marital Status: Single X | Married | Other (Specify)
20. U. S. Citizen: Yes X | No
21. Civilian Occupation and Number: Plumbers Helper (7-32.812)

MILITARY HISTORY

22. Date of Induction: 16 Jan 41
23. Date of Enlistment:
24. Date of Entry Into Active Service: 16 Jan 41
25. Place of Entry Into Service: Fort Bragg N.C.
Selective Service Data: 26. Registered: Yes X | No; 27. Local S. S. Board Number: 1; 28. County and State: Moore Co N.C.
29. Home Address at Time of Entry Into Service: Aberdeen N.C.
30. Military Occupational Specialty and Number: Medical NCO (673)
31. Military Qualification and Date (i.e., infantry, aviation and marksmanship badges, etc.): MM 30 Cal. Rifle M1
32. Battles and Campaigns: Normandy Northern France Rhineland Ardennes Central Europe
33. Decorations and Citations: European African Middle Eastern Campaign Medal with 5 Bronze service stars; [illegible] Service Medal; Bronze Star Medal GO 77 Hq 30th Div [illegible]
34. Wounds Received in Action: None

35. Latest Immunization Dates

Smallpox	Typhoid	Tetanus	Other (Specify)
8 Oct 43	8 Oct 43	3 Nov 44	Typ 15 Jan 45

36. Service Outside Continental U. S. and Return

Date of Departure	Destination	Date of Arrival
12 Feb 44	Europe	[illegible]
10 Sep 45	USA	[illegible]

37. Total Length of Service

Continental Service Years	Months	Days	Foreign Service Years	Months	Days
3	7	3	1	7	7

38. Highest Grade Held: Sergeant
39. Prior Service: None
40. Reason and Authority for Separation: Convenience of Government RR1-1 (Demobilization) AR 615-365 [illegible]
41. Service Schools Attended: None
42. Education (Years): Grammar 7 | High School 3 | College 0

PAY DATA

43. Longevity for Pay Purposes Years	Months	Days	44. Mustering Out Pay Total	This Payment	45. Soldier Deposits	46. Travel Pay	47. Total Amount, Name of Disbursing Officer
4	8	10	$300	$100	None	$2.30	123.[illegible] [illegible]

INSURANCE NOTICE

IMPORTANT—If premium is not paid when due or within thirty-one days thereafter, insurance will lapse. Make checks or money orders payable to the Treasurer of the United States and forward to Collections Subdivision, Veterans' Administration, Washington 25, D. C.

48. Kind of Insurance: Nat. Service	U. S. Govt.	None	49. How Paid: Allotment	Direct to V. A.	50. Effective Date of Allotment Discontinuance	51. Date of Next Premium Due (One month after 50)	52. Premium Due Each Month	53. Intention of Veteran To: Continue	Continue Only	Discontinue
X			X		30 Sep 45	31 Oct 45	$6.90	X		

54.
55. Remarks (This space for completion of above items or entry of other items specified in W. D. Directives): No time lost under AW 107. [illegible] button issued [illegible]

56. Signature of Person Being Separated: Eldridge H Land
57. Personnel Officer (Type name, grade and organization - signature): E M Kopp 1st Lt Aus

I, ______, being duly sworn, depose and say that the foregoing discharge (or certificate of lost discharge) is the original discharge (or certificate of lost discharge) issued to me by the Government of the United States; and no alterations have been made therein, by me, or by any person to my knowledge.

Subscribed and sworn to before me, this ______ day of ______, 19__.

______, Register of Deeds

Filed for registration this 3 day of Oct, 1945, at 11 o'clock A.M., and duly recorded.

Bessie M. Caskill

Register of Deeds, Moore County.

This form supersedes all previous editions of W.D.A.G.O. Forms 53 and 55 for enlisted persons entitled to an honorable discharge, which will not be used after receipt of this revision.

Marriage License

No. 33217

AFFIDAVITS TO OBTAIN LICENSE

STATE OF SOUTH CAROLINA
County of Marlboro

I do solemnly swear that I am legally capacitated to marry; that my full name is John Thomas Land; that my age is 68 years and months; my place of residence is Aberdeen, N.C.; my race is white; my nationality is American.

SWORN to before me this 6th day of September A. D. 1941. J.T.Land

J.F.Kinney (L. S.)
Notary Public for S. C.

STATE OF SOUTH CAROLINA
County of Marlboro

I do solemnly swear that I am legally capacitated to marry; that my full name is Lena Clark Knight; that my age is 41 years and months; my place of residence is Aberdeen, N.C.; my race is white; my nationality is American.

SWORN to before me this 6th day of September A. D. 1941. Lena Clark Knight

J.F.Kinney (L. S.)
Notary Public for S. C.

Marriage License

WHEREAS, IT HAS BEEN MADE TO APPEAR TO ME, John F.Kinney, JUDGE OF PROBATE FOR MARLBORO COUNTY, UPON OATH THAT:

John Thomas Land of Aberdeen, North Carolina

and Lena Clark Knight of Aberdeen, North Carolina

are legally capacitated to contract matrimony, and their ages are respectively 68 years and months and 41 years and months and their race is white and their nationality is Amercian.

THESE ARE THEREFORE, to authorize any person qualified to perform marriage ceremonies to perform the marriage ceremony for the persons above named and for so doing this shall be sufficient warrant.

GIVEN UNDER my Hand and Seal this 6th day of September A. D. 1941.

John F.Kinney
Judge of Probate for Marlboro County

SEABOARD AIR LINE RAILWAY

L. R. POWELL, JR. AND HENRY W. ANDERSON, RECEIVERS

OFFICE OF
CHIEF ENGINEER MAINTENANCE OF WAY

J. L. KIRBY,
CHIEF ENGINEER MAINTENANCE OF WAY

Norfolk, Va., April 20, 1938.

RECEIVED
JUL 9 1938
OFFICE OF SECRETARY
ANNUITY CLAIMS
FILES

Mr. J. T. Land,
Section Foreman,
Aberdeen, N. C.

Dear Mr. Land:

I wish to commend you on the faithful and loyal service you have performed for the Seaboard as Section Foreman during the past 35 years, and I trust when you leave our service within the next 30 days that you will enjoy many years of good health and happiness.

With kind regards and all good wishes, I am,

Sincerely yours,

J. L. Kirby

Chief Engr. M. of W.

CLAIMS SERVICE
RECEIVED
JUL 11 1938
Central Record Unit

1938

Name: Land, John Thomas
Lodge: Roman Eagle, No. 550

Initiated	Suspended
Passed	
Raised	Died July 4, 1957
Admitted March 16, 1939	Demitted
Reinstated	Expelled
Place of Birth	Date of Birth 65 in 1939

Dimitted from Chester Lodge No.18, S.C. to Vaughan Lodge #604 May 12, 1922 and dimitted Nov. 3, 1923 and affiliated with Roman Eagle #550 Jan. 17, 1924 and dimitted May 17, 1934 and came back to #550.

34-1079

Form 3. 104. Rev. 11-15-43

APPLICATION FOR REGISTRATION OF BIRTH

Page 70 STATE OF SOUTH CAROLINA Sep. 9, 1950

(With Instructions)

Full Name: Mavries Selwyn Land
Male: X Female:
Race: White Nationality: American
Present Address: Pinehurst N.C.

Date of Birth: July 17, 1900
Where Born:
City: Chester
County: Chester
State: S.C.

Full Name of Father: John Thomas Land
Nationality: American
Race: White
Present Address: North Carolina

Age Last Birthday: 78
Where Born:
City:
County: Chester
State: S.C.

Maiden Name of Mother: Emma Sarah Quinton
Nationality: American
Race: White
Present Address: Deceased

Age Last Birthday:
Where Born:
City:
County: Chester
State: S.C.

A. If family Bible is used as proof

PHYSICIAN'S CERTIFICATE:
B. I hereby certify that I attended the birth of the above-named child.

Attending Physician.

(C, D, E, F, G, proof or other record.)
STATE OF
County of
Personally appeared before me
who, being first duly sworn, deposes and says that

and that the statement of birth given above is true as copied from said record.
Sworn to and subscribed before me this
day of , 19

Notary Public.

(H. Disinterested, related or unrelated, individual.)
STATE OF South Carolina
County of Chester
Personally appeared before me Mrs. Laura Quinton
who, being first duly sworn, deposes and says that she is 80 years old; that the date of such birth is based on deponent's best memory, information and belief; that deponent is definite and positive of the above facts as to the date and place of birth, and that the statement of birth so given above is true.
Sworn to and subscribed before me this 8th
day of September 1950
Ruby Howell Hurst, Notary Public. x Mrs. Laura Quinton

(H. Disinterested, related or unrelated, individual.)
STATE OF South Carolina
County of Chester
Personally appeared before me Josie Clark
who, being first duly sworn, deposes and says that she is 68 years old; that the date of such birth is based on deponent's best memory, information and belief; that deponent is definite and positive of the above facts as to the date and place of birth, and that the statement of birth so given above is true.
Sworn to and subscribed before me this 8th
day of September 1950
Ruby Howell Hurst, Notary Public. x Josie Clark

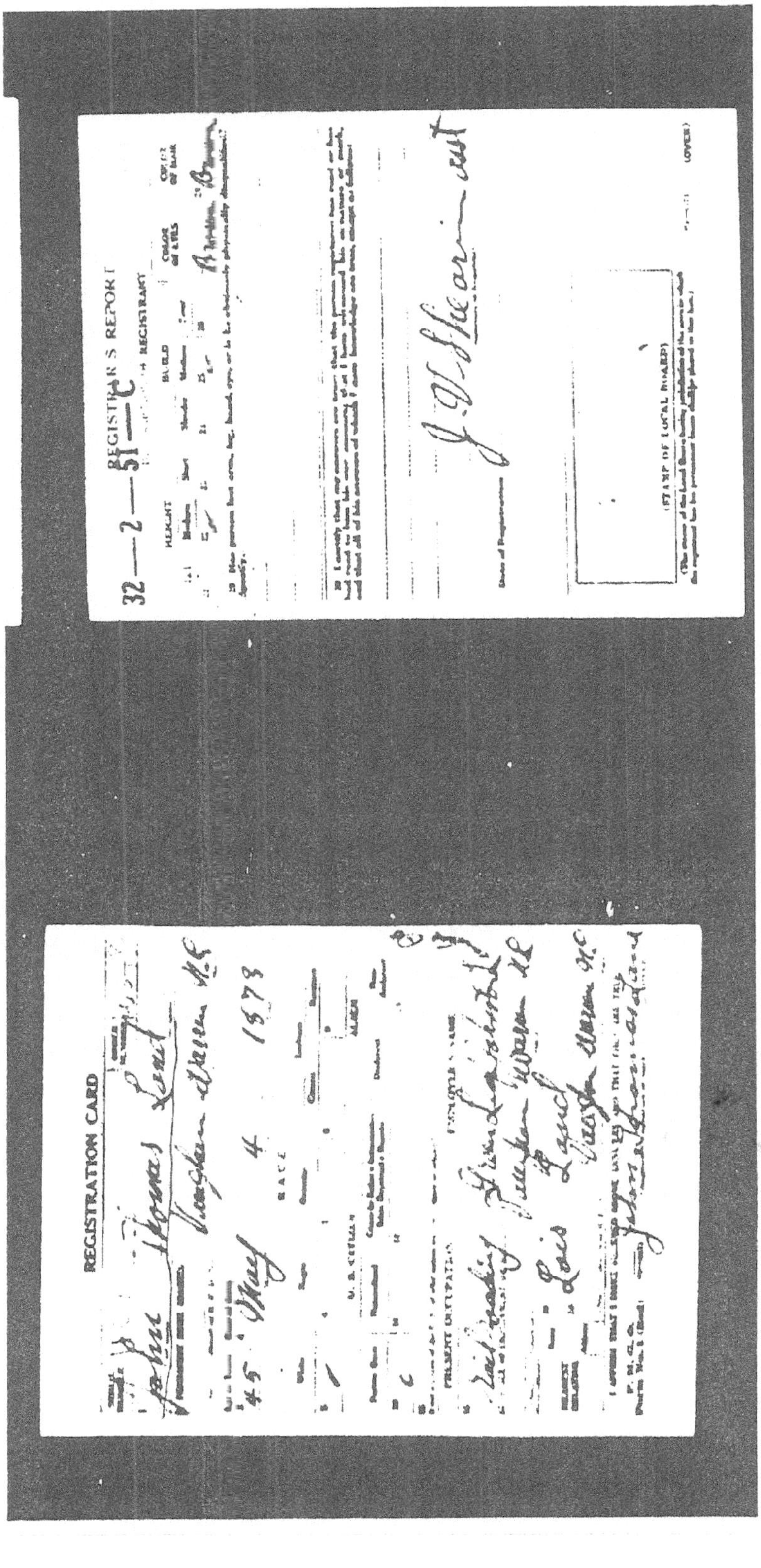

REGISTRATION CARD

John Thomas Land

REGISTRAR'S REPORT

32—2—51—C

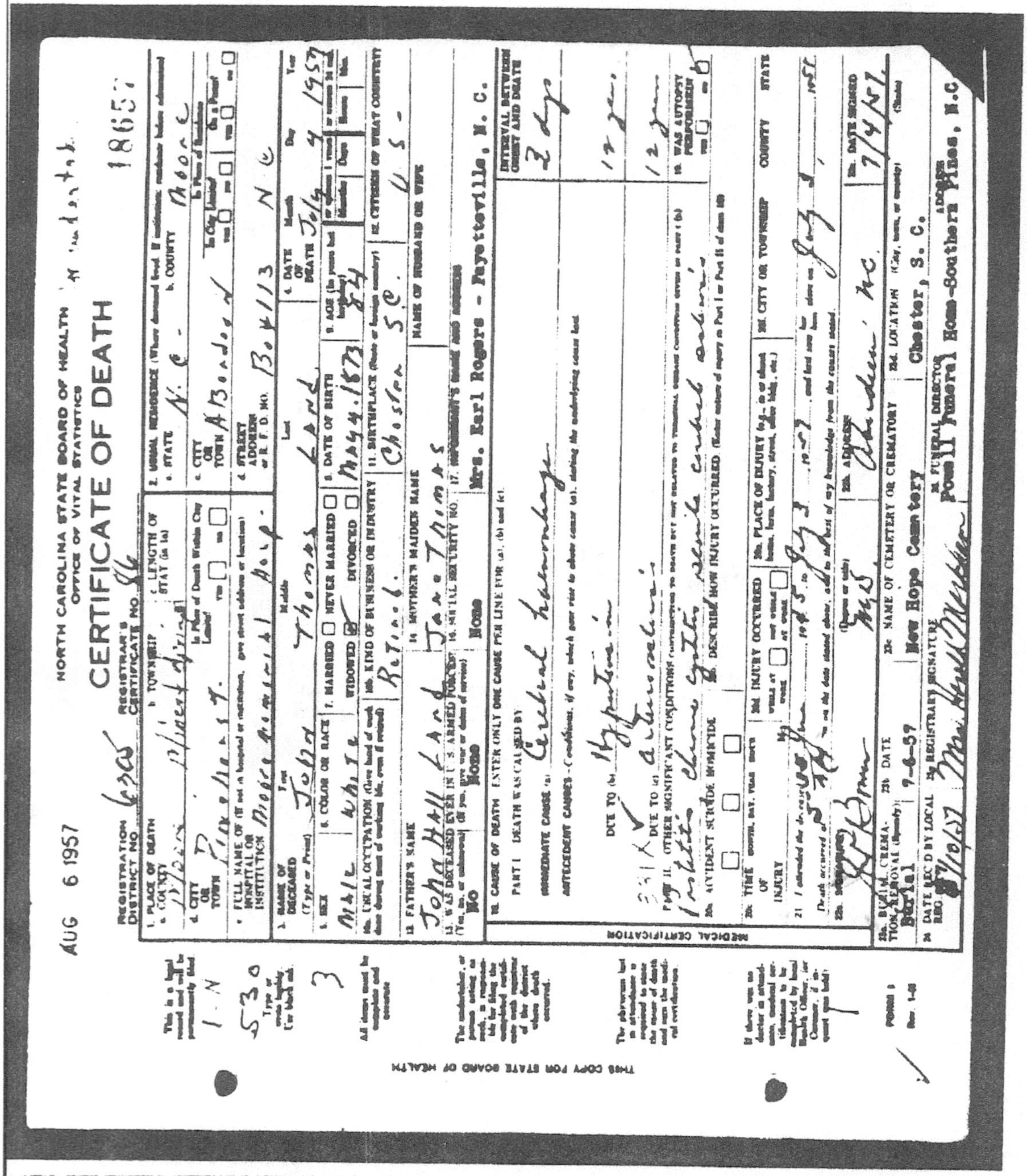

AUG 6 1957

NORTH CAROLINA STATE BOARD OF HEALTH
OFFICE OF VITAL STATISTICS

CERTIFICATE OF DEATH

REGISTRATION DISTRICT NO. 6305 REGISTRAR'S CERTIFICATE NO. 86

18657

1. PLACE OF DEATH a. COUNTY Moore b. TOWNSHIP Mineral Springs
c. CITY OR TOWN Pinehurst
d. FULL NAME OF HOSPITAL OR INSTITUTION Moore Memorial Hosp.

2. USUAL RESIDENCE a. STATE N. C. b. COUNTY Moore
c. CITY OR TOWN Aberdeen
d. STREET ADDRESS Box 113 N. C.

3. NAME OF DECEASED John Thomas Land
4. DATE OF DEATH July 4 1957
5. SEX Male 6. COLOR OR RACE White 7. WIDOWED
8. DATE OF BIRTH May 4, 1873 9. AGE 84
10a. USUAL OCCUPATION 10b. KIND OF BUSINESS OR INDUSTRY Retired
11. BIRTHPLACE Chester S.C. 12. CITIZEN OF WHAT COUNTRY U.S.
13. FATHER'S NAME John Hall Land 14. MOTHER'S MAIDEN NAME Jane Thomas
15. WAS DECEASED EVER IN U.S. ARMED FORCES? No None
16. SOCIAL SECURITY NO. None
17. INFORMANT'S NAME AND ADDRESS Mrs. Earl Rogers - Fayetteville, N. C.

18. CAUSE OF DEATH
PART I. DEATH WAS CAUSED BY
IMMEDIATE CAUSE (a) Cerebral haemorrhage — 2 days
DUE TO (b) Hypertension — 12 years
DUE TO (c) Arteriosclerosis — 12 years
PART II. OTHER SIGNIFICANT CONDITIONS Prostatitis, chronic cystitis, senile cerebral arteriosclerosis

21. I attended the deceased from June 1955 to July 3 1957, and last saw him alive on July 3, 1957
Death occurred at 5 AM on the date stated above.
22a. SIGNATURE R. P. Brown M.D. 22b. ADDRESS Aberdeen NC 22c. DATE SIGNED 7/4/57

23a. BURIAL 23b. DATE 7-6-57 23c. NAME OF CEMETERY New Hope Cemetery 23d. LOCATION Chester, S. C.
24. DATE REC'D BY LOCAL REG. 7/10/57 REGISTRAR'S SIGNATURE Mrs. Harold Matthews
25. FUNERAL DIRECTOR Powell Funeral Home-Southern Pines, N.C

THIS COPY FOR STATE BOARD OF HEALTH

B. V. S. FORM 33
10,000-4-57

North Carolina State Board of Health
BUREAU OF VITAL STATISTICS

No 145022

STANDARD CERTIFICATE OF BIRTH

1. PLACE OF BIRTH—
County Warren Registration District No. 93-2673 Certificate No. 6
Township River or Village
City Vaughan No. St. Ward
(If birth occurred in a hospital or institution, give its name instead of street and number)

2. FULL NAME OF CHILD Joseph Lindsey Land
If child is not yet named, make supplemental report, as directed

3. Sex Male | If plural births | 4. Twin, triplet, or other | 5. Number in order of birth | 6. Premature / Full term | 7. Are parents married. Yes | 8. Date of birth June 25, 1918 (Month, day, year)

FATHER	MOTHER
9. Full name John Thomas Land	18. Full maiden name Lois Rebecca Brice
10. Residence (usual place of abode) (If non-resident, give place and State) Vaughan	19. Residence (usual place of abode) (If non-resident, give place and State) Vaughan
11. Color or race White 12. Age at last birthday – (years)	20. Color or race White 21. Age at last birthday – (years)
13. Birthplace (city or place) S. C. (State or country)	22. Birthplace (City or place) S. C. (State or country)
OCCUPATION 14. Trade, profession or particular kind of work done, as spinner, sawyer, bookkeeper, etc. Truck Foreman	OCCUPATION 23. Trade, profession or particular kind of work done, as housekeeper, typist, nurse, clerk, etc. Housewife
15. Industry or business in which work was done, as silk mill, sawmill, bank, etc.	24. Industry or business in which work was done, as own home, lawyer's office, silk mill, etc.
16. Date (month and year) last engaged in this work 19 17. Total time (years) spent in this work	25. Date (month and year) last engaged in this work 19 26. Total time (years) spent in this work

27. Number of children of this mother (at time of this birth and including this child) (a) Born alive and now living 4 (b) Born alive but now dead (c) Stillborn

CERTIFICATE OF ATTENDING PHYSICIAN OR MIDWIFE

I hereby certify that I attended the birth of this child, who was born alive at 5:A. m. on the date above stated.

WHEN THERE WAS NO ATTENDING PHYSICIAN OR MIDWIFE, THEN THE FATHER, HOUSEHOLDER, ETC., SHOULD MAKE THIS RETURN.

(Signed) L. J. Picot M. D.
or Midwife

Given name added from a supplemental report (Date of) REGISTRAR

Address Littleton, North Carolina

Filed –, 19–. J.H. Harris REGISTRAR

THIS IS TO CERTIFY that the above is a true copy of the birth certificate of Joseph Lindsey Land filed in this office.

J.W.R. Norton
State Registrar.

FILE 725 PAGE 387

Date Issued: 11-24-1958

65

Verified

Marriage License

C. J. No. 13503

CENTRAL BUREAU OF VITAL STATISTICS

State of Florida, Pinellas County

To any Minister of the Gospel, or any Officer Legally Authorized to Solemnize the Rite of Matrimony:

Whereas, *Application having been made to the County Judge of Pinellas County, of the State of Florida, for a license for marriage, and it appearing to the satisfaction of said County Judge that no legal impediments exist to the marriage now sought to be solemnized:*

These are, therefore, *To authorize you to unite in the*

Holy Estate of Matrimony

J. L. Land *and* Vivian Hicks

and that you make return of the same, duly certified under your hand, to the County Judge aforesaid.

Witness *my name as County Judge, and the seal of said Court, at the Courthouse in Clearwater, this* 1st *day of* June *A. D. 19*42 (SEAL) Jack P. White *County Judge.*

CERTIFICATE OF MARRIAGE

I Certify *that the within-named* J. L. Land *and* Vivian Hicks *were by me, the undersigned, duly united in the Holy Estate of Matrimony, by the authority of the within License.*

Done this 1st *day of* June *A. D. 19*42 *at* Clearwater *Florida.*

Witness Mrs. Johnny Williams (SEAL.) John C. Brown - Notary Public

MINISTER OR LEGALLY AUTHORIZED OFFICER

Witness Johnny Williams Clearwater, Fla.

ADDRESS

Returned this 1 *day of* June *A. D. 19*42 *and recorded in Marriage Book* 23 *page* 2

Jack P. White *County Judge*

J.B.

CIRCUIT COURT

PINELLAS COUNTY

NOVEMBER . 09

67

144

Vivian Hicks Land

CERTIFI[illegible]

FLORIDA CERTIFICATE OF DEATH

1. Decedent's Name (First, Middle, Last, Suffix): Vivian Olive Land
2. Sex: Female
3. Date of Birth: April 27, 1914
4a. Age: 94
5. Date of Death: October 26, 2008
6. Social Security Number: 263-01-0181
7. Birthplace: Live Oak, Florida
8. County of Death: Pinellas
9. Place of Death: X Decedent's Home
10. Facility Name: 1627 Paradise Lane Unit C
11a. City, Town, or Location of Death: Dunedin
11b. Inside City Limits: X Yes
12. Marital Status: X Widowed
14a. Residence – State: Florida
14b. County: Pinellas
14c. City, Town, or Location: Dunedin
14d. Street Address: 1627 Paradise Lane Unit C
14f. Zip Code: 34698
14g. Inside City Limits: X Yes
15a. Decedent's Usual Occupation: Bookkeeper
15b. Kind of Business/Industry: Retail Department Store
16. Decedent's Race: X White
17. Decedent of Hispanic or Haitian Origin: X No
18. Decedent's Education: X High school graduate or GED
19. Was Decedent Ever in U.S. Armed Forces: X No
20. Father's Name: Marion Hicks
21. Mother's Name (Maiden Surname): Mary Harriet Baden
22a. Informant's Name: Bonnie Essary
22b. Relationship to Decedent: Daughter
22c. Informant's Mailing – State: Florida
23a. City or Town: Dunedin
23b. Street Address: 1657 Carefree Lane Apt. C
23c. Zip Code: 34698
24. Place of Disposition: Sylvan Abbey Memorial Park
25a. Location – State: Florida
25b. Location – City or Town: Clearwater
26. Method of Disposition: X Burial
27a. License Number: F043034
27b. Signature of Funeral Service Licensee: [signature]
28a. Name of Funeral Facility: Sylvan Abbey Funeral Home
28b. Facility's Mailing – State: Florida
29a. City or Town: Clearwater
29b. Street Address: 2853 Sunset Pt. Rd.
29c. Zip Code: 33759
30. Certifier: X Certifying Physician – To the best of my knowledge, death occurred at the time, date and place, and due to the cause(s) and manner stated.
Signature and Title of Certifier: [signature] MD
31. Date Signed: 10/27/2008
32. Time of Death (24 hr): 0846
34a. License Number: 55727
34b. Certifier's Name: Gregory B. Sidhu
36a. Certifier's State: Florida
36b. City or Town: Clearwater
36c. Street Address: 1969 Sunset Point Road Suite 15
36d. Zip Code: 33765
38. Local Registrar – Signature: [signature]
Date Filed by Registrar: November 05 2008

Barbara M. Sortier

Chief Deputy Registrar, Pinellas County

Issued: Nov. 5, 2008

68

41488457

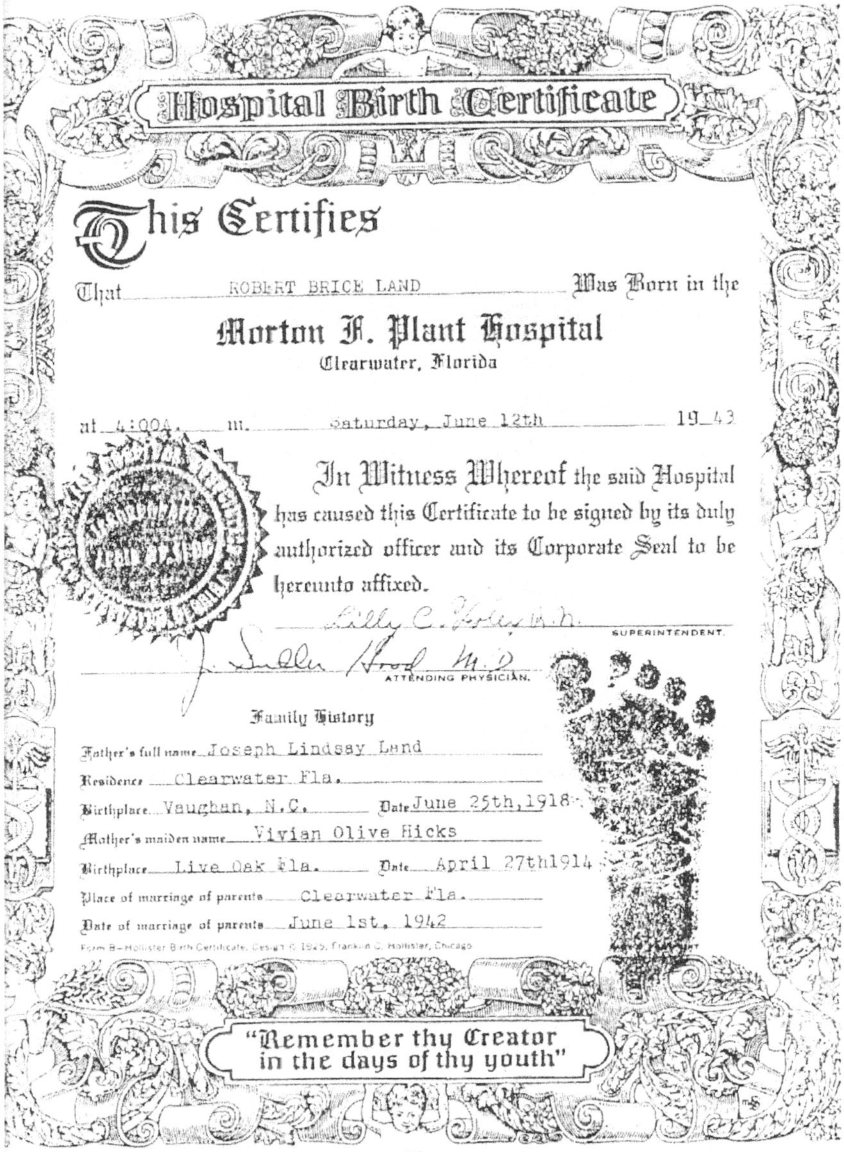

Hospital Birth Certificate

This Certifies

That ROBERT BRICE LAND Was Born in the

Morton F. Plant Hospital
Clearwater, Florida

at 4:00A. m. Saturday, June 12th 1943

In Witness Whereof the said Hospital has caused this Certificate to be signed by its duly authorized officer and its Corporate Seal to be hereunto affixed.

SUPERINTENDENT.

ATTENDING PHYSICIAN.

Family History

Father's full name Joseph Lindsay Land

Residence Clearwater Fla.

Birthplace Vaughan, N.C. Date June 25th, 1918

Mother's maiden name Vivian Olive Hicks

Birthplace Live Oak Fla. Date April 27th 1914

Place of marriage of parents Clearwater Fla.

Date of marriage of parents June 1st. 1942

Form B—Hollister Birth Certificate, Design © 1925, Franklin C. Hollister, Chicago

"Remember thy Creator in the days of thy youth"

69

Joseph Lindsey Land and son Robert Brice Land

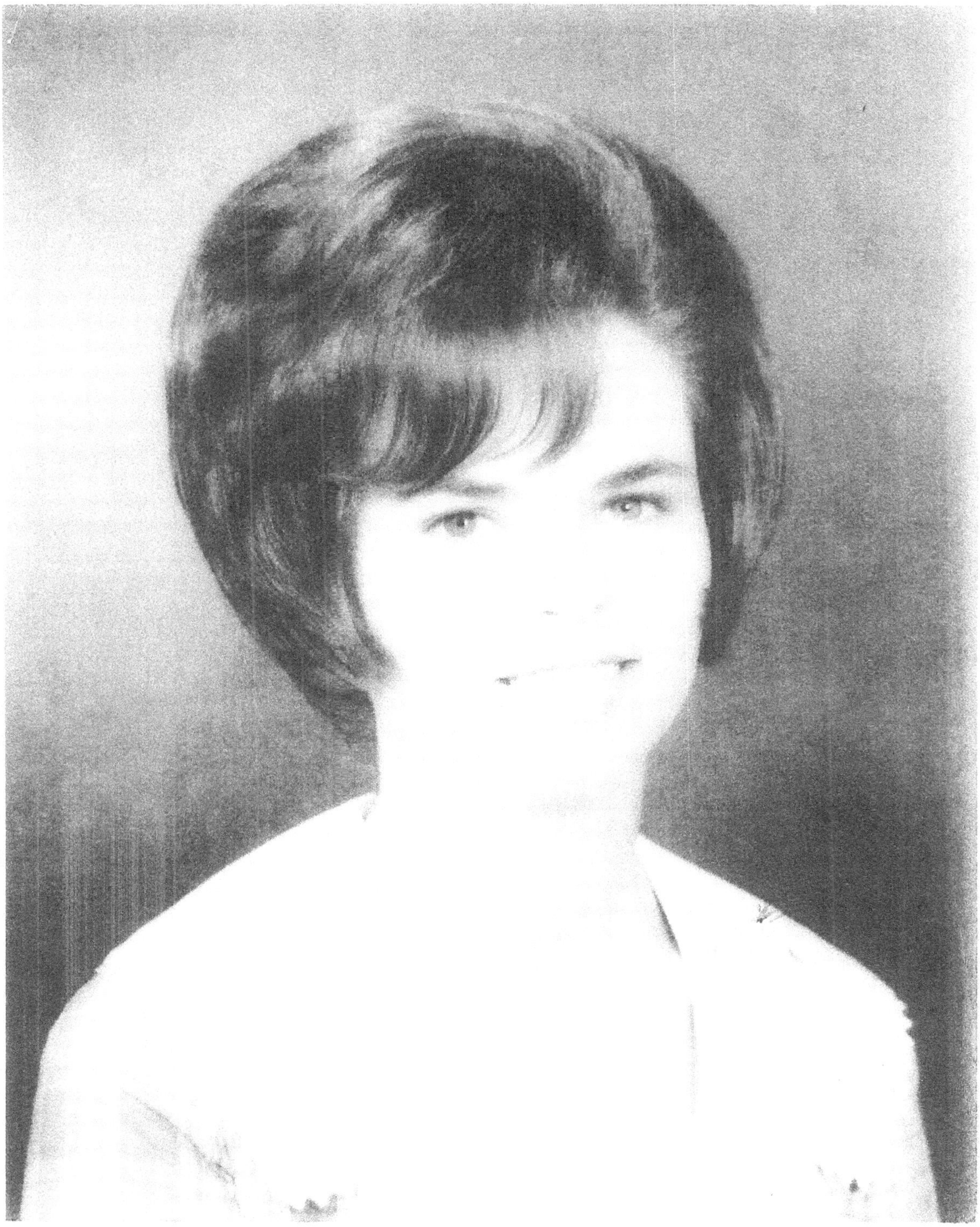

Florida

State Board of Health

BUREAU OF VITAL STATISTICS
JACKSONVILLE

This is to Certify that a Birth Certificate has been filed for

Bonnie Charlene Land Sex Female

Born in Pinellas County, Florida, on November 6, 1945

Child of:

Mr. and Mrs. Joseph Lindsey Land
1910 Overbrook Road
Clearwater, Floriia

This Record is filed in

Book No. 1839
46492
Page No.

Filed November 10, 1945

Wilson T. Sowder
State Health Officer

Director Bureau of Vital Statistics

Robert Brice Land

DEPARTMENT OF THE ARMY

TO ALL WHO SHALL SEE THE PRESENTS, GREETING THIS IS TO CERTIFY THAT THE SECRETARY OF THE ARMY HAS ON THIS DAY AWARDED THE

ARMY COMMENDATION MEDAL

TO

PRIVATE E-2 ROBERT B. LAND

FOR

FOR DISTINGUISHED AND OUTSTANDING PERSONAL ACHIEVEMENT IN THE PERFORMANCE OF YOUR DUTIES WHILE SERVING WITH SERVICE COMPANY, 3RD ARMY

GIVEN UNDER MY HAND IN THE CITY OF WASHINGTON

ON THIS 20TH DAY OF OCTOBER 1965

William A. Hartley
COLONEL, USA, ADJUTANT

Verne L. Bowers
Major General USA

DEPARTMENT OF THE ARMY

TO ALL WHO SHALL SEE THE PRESENTS, GREETING THIS IS TO CERTIFY THAT THE SECRETARY OF THE ARMY HAS ON THIS DAY AWARDED THE

ARMY COMMENDATION MEDAL

TO

STAFF SERGEANT E-6 ROBERT B. LAND

FOR

FOR DISTINGUISHED AND OUTSTANDING PERSONAL ACHIEVEMENT IN THE PERFORMANCE OF YOUR DUTIES WHILE SERVING WITH 3RD ARMY, CAMP BLANDING, FL

GIVEN UNDER MY HAND IN THE CITY OF WASHINGTON, DC

ON THIS 2ND DAY OF FEBRUARY 1967

William A. Hartley
COLONEL, USA, ADJUTANT

Verne L. Bowers
Major General USA

DEPARTMENT OF THE ARMY

THE SECRETARY OF THE ARMY OF THE UNITED STATES OF AMERICA HAS ON THIS DAY AWARDED THE

GOOD CONDUCT MEDAL

TO

SERGEANT ROBERT B. LAND

FOR

YOUR EXEMPLARY CONDUCT, EFFICIENCY, AND FIDELITY IN ACTIVE FEDERAL MILITARY SERVICE

BY EXECUTIVE ORDER 10444 1953, PER COMMANDING OFFICER, 3RD ARMY

GIVEN ON THIS 22ND DAY OF DECEMBER 1966

Robert E. Barnes
CAPT, US ARMY ADJ

Stanley R. Reasor
Secretary of the Army

DA AGCM EO-10444 REN.158

DEPARTMENT OF THE ARMY

THE SECRETARY OF THE ARMY OF THE UNITED STATES OF AMERICA HAS ON THIS DAY AWARDED THE

GOOD CONDUCT MEDAL

TO

SERGEANT ROBERT B. LAND

FOR

YOUR EXEMPLARY CONDUCT, EFFICIENCY, AND FIDELITY IN ACTIVE FEDERAL MILITARY SERVICE

BY EXECUTIVE ORDER 10444 1953, PER COMMANDING OFFICER, 3RD ARMY

GIVEN ON THIS 18TH DAY OF JANUARY 1970

Francis R. Banister
CAPTAIN, US ARMY ADJ

Stanley R. Reasor
Secretary of the Army

DA AGCM EO-10444 REN.158

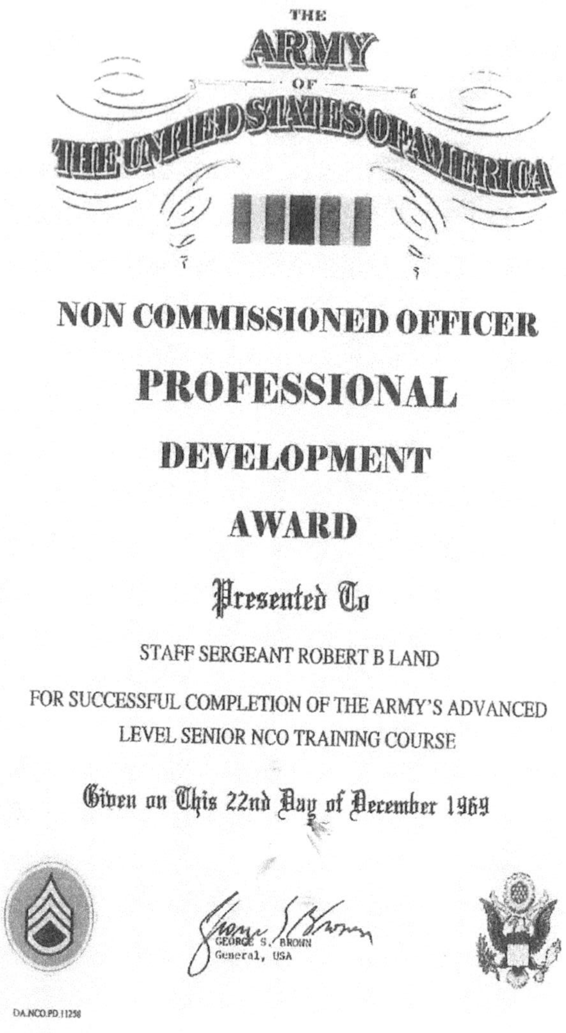
THE ARMY OF THE UNITED STATES OF AMERICA

NON COMMISSIONED OFFICER

PROFESSIONAL

DEVELOPMENT

AWARD

Presented To

STAFF SERGEANT ROBERT B LAND

FOR SUCCESSFUL COMPLETION OF THE ARMY'S ADVANCED LEVEL SENIOR NCO TRAINING COURSE

Given on This 22nd Day of December 1969

GEORGE S. BROWN
General, USA

DA.NCO.PD.11250

THE ARMY OF THE UNITED STATES OF AMERICA

NON COMMISSIONED OFFICER

PROFESSIONAL

DEVELOPMENT

AWARD

Presented To

SERGEANT ROBERT B LAND

FOR SUCCESSFUL COMPLETION OF THE ARMY'S ADVANCED LEVEL NCO TRAINING COURSE

Given on This 1st Day of August 1967

Verne L. Bowers
Major General USA

DA.NCO.PD.11250

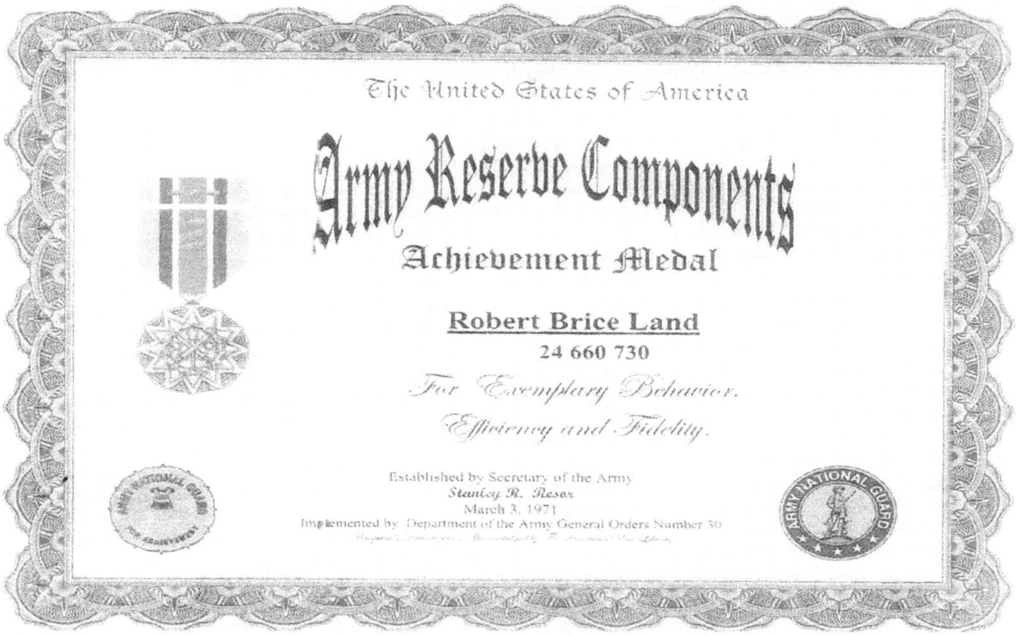

The United States of America

Army Reserve Components

Achievement Medal

Robert Brice Land

24 660 730

For Exemplary Behavior,

Efficiency and Fidelity.

Established by Secretary of the Army

Stanley R. Resor

March 3, 1971

Implemented by Department of the Army General Orders Number 30

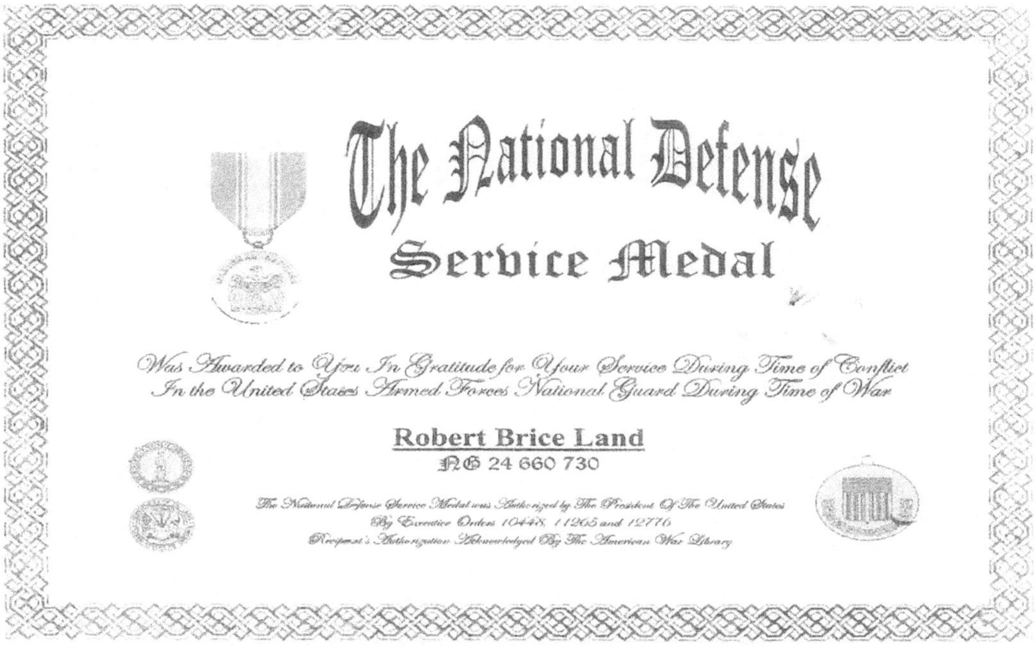

The National Defense

Service Medal

Was Awarded to You In Gratitude for Your Service During Time of Conflict
In the United States Armed Forces National Guard During Time of War

Robert Brice Land

NG 24 660 730

The National Defense Service Medal was Authorized by The President Of The United States
By Executive Orders 10448, 11265 and 12776
Recipient's Authorization Acknowledged By The American War Library

THE UNITED STATES OF AMERICA

THE SECRETARY OF THE ARMY TAKES PLEASURE IN PRESENTING THE

MERITORIOUS SERVICE MEDAL

TO

STAFF SERGEANT ROBERT B. LAND

FOR

DISTINGUISHED AND OUTSTANDING MERITORIOUS SERVICE IN THE PERFORMANCE OF YOUR DUTIES WHILE SERVING WITH THE U.S. ARMY SOUTHERN COMMAND, REPUBLIC OF PANAMA

By Order of the Secretary of the Army

GIVEN UNDER MY HAND IN THE CITY OF WASHINGTON, DC

ON THIS 29TH DAY OF JULY 1974

Carl P. Cook,
Colonel, USA ADJ

Howard H Callaway
SECRETARY OF THE ARMY

DEPARTMENT OF THE ARMY

THE SECRETARY OF THE ARMY TAKES PLEASURE IN AWARDING THE

ARMY ACHIEVEMENT MEDAL

TO

STAFF SERGEANT ROBERT B. LAND

FOR

EXERCISING THROUGH KNOWLEDGE AND PROFESSIONAL SKILL BY HIS SOUND JUDGMENT AND DEVOTION TC DUTY, WHILE ASSIGNED TO THE SOUTHERN COMMAND, REPUBLIC OF PANAMA

GIVEN UNDER MY HAND IN THE CITY OF WASHINGTON DC

ON THIS 9TH DAY OF AUGUST 1974

WILLIAM C CLIFFORD
MAJOR USA ADJ

JOHN O. MARSH JR
SECRETARY OF THE ARMY

DEPARTMENT OF THE ARMY

THE SECRETARY OF THE ARMY TAKES PLEASURE IN AWARDING THE

ARMY ACHIEVEMENT MEDAL

TO

STAFF SERGEANT ROBERT B. LAND

FOR

DEVOTION TO DUTY, SOUND JUDGMENT AND PROFESSIONAL SKILLS WHILE ASSIGNED TO THE 3RD ARMY, CAMP BLANDING, FLORIDA

GIVEN UNDER MY HAND IN THE CITY OF WASHINGTON, DC

ON THIS 3RD DAY OF FEBRUARY 1976

Michael R. McGinnis LTC
USA, Executive Office

HOWARD H GALLAWAY
SECRETARY OF THE ARMY

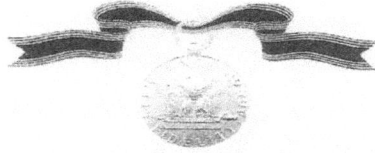

DEPARTMENT OF THE ARMY

THE SECRETARY OF THE ARMY OF THE UNITED STATES OF AMERICA HAS ON THIS DAY AWARDED THE

GOOD CONDUCT MEDAL

TO

STAFF SERGEANT ROBERT B. LAND

FOR

YOUR EXEMPLARY CONDUCT, EFFICIENCY, AND FIDELITY IN ACTIVE FEDERAL MILITARY SERVICE

BY EXECUTIVE ORDER 10444 1953, PER COMMANDING OFFICER, 53RD ARMORED BRIGADE

GIVEN ON THIS 15TH DAY OF JUNE 1977

William E. Player
MAJOR, US ARMY ADJ

JOHN O. MARSH JR
SECRETARY OF THE ARMY

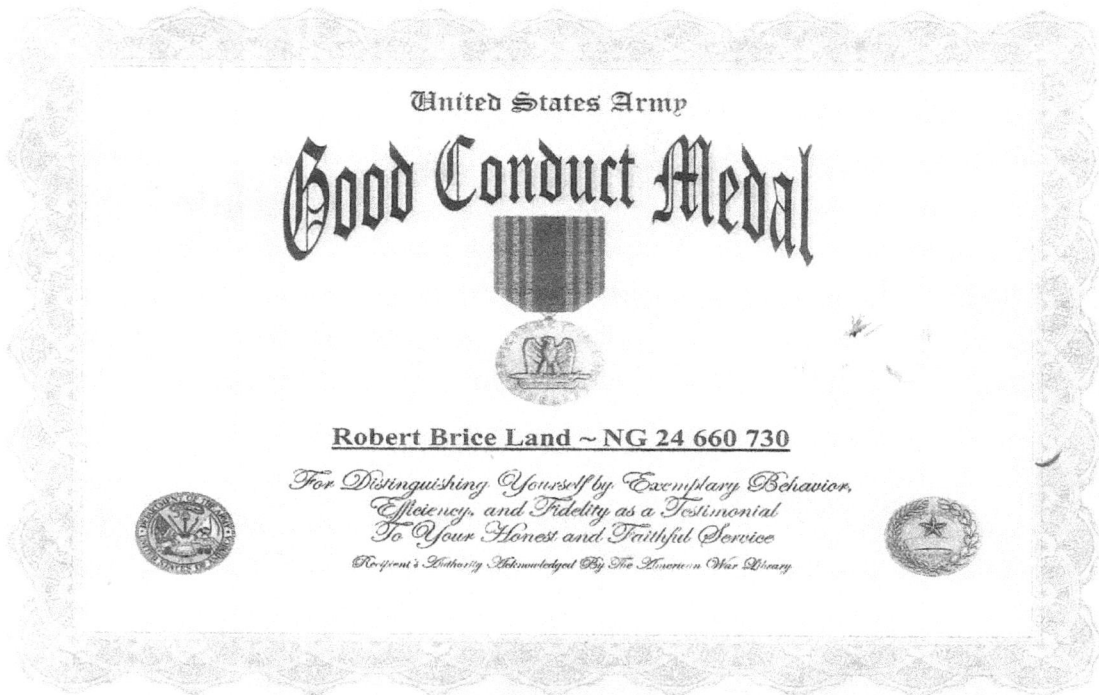

DA AGCM EO 10444 REN 158

United States Army

Good Conduct Medal

Robert Brice Land ~ NG 24 660 730

For Distinguishing Yourself by Exemplary Behavior,
Efficiency, and Fidelity as a Testimonial
To Your Honest and Faithful Service

Recipient's Authority Acknowledged By The American War Library

UNITED STATES
NATIONAL DEFENSE FORCE SUPPORT COMMAND

The
ARMED FORCES EXPEDITIONARY MEDAL CITATION
Is
Awarded To:

SSG. Robert B. Land

FOR FAITHFUL AND HONORABLE SERVICE WITH AN ARMED EXPEDITIONARY FORCE OF THE UNITED STATES ARMED FORCES ON FOREIGN SOIL PROTECTING AND DEFENDING THE NATIONAL SECURITY AND INTERESTS OF THE UNITED STATES OF AMERICA, THIS AWARD IS MADE TO THE RECIPIENT ON BEHALF OF THE PRESIDENT OF THE UNITED STATES, THE DEPARTMENT OF DEFENSE AND THE CITIZENS OF A GRATEFUL NATION

Service Branch: U.S. ARMY-Cuban Missile Crisis
Date: January 16, 2006
Certificate: 109

Lieutenant General
Director: Veterans Recognition Program
United States
National Defense Force Support Command
(Separate)

*Replacement Certificate
*Verification Required

Form: U.S.-DOD-AFEM-02

THE UNITED STATES OF AMERICA

TO ALL WHO SHALL SEE THESE PRESENTS, GREETING; THIS IS TO CERTIFY THAT THE SECRETARY OF THE DEPARTMENT OF DEFENSE HAS AWARDED THE

ARMED FORCES RESERVE MEDAL

TO

STAFF SERGEANT ROBERT B LAND

FOR

HONORABLE AND SATISFACTORY SERVICE AS A MEMBER OF U.S. ARMY INFANTRY, 53RD ARMORED BRIGADE

GIVEN UNDER MY HAND IN THE CITY OF WASHINGTON
ON THIS 11TH DAY OF FEBRUARY 1978

ROBERT L. WHITE, JR.
LTC, AG
Chief, Military Awards Branch

FOR SECRETARY OF DEFENSE
JAMES L. JAMERSON, MAJ GEN,
COMMANDING GENERAL

UNITED STATES
NATIONAL DEFENSE FORCE SUPPORT COMMAND

The
ARMED FORCES EXPEDITIONARY MEDAL CITATION
Is
Awarded To:

SSG. Robert B. Land

FOR FAITHFUL AND HONORABLE SERVICE WITH AN ARMED EXPEDITIONARY FORCE OF THE UNITED STATES ARMED FORCES ON FOREIGN SOIL PROTECTING AND DEFENDING THE NATIONAL SECURITY AND INTERESTS OF THE UNITED STATES OF AMERICA, THIS AWARD IS MADE TO THE RECIPIENT ON BEHALF OF THE PRESIDENT OF THE UNITED STATES, THE DEPARTMENT OF DEFENSE AND THE CITIZENS OF A GRATEFUL NATION

Service Branch: U.S. ARMY-Cuban Missile Crisis
Date: January 16, 2006
Certificate: 109

Lieutenant General
Director: Veterans Recognition Program
United States
National Defense Force Support Command
(Separate)

*Replacement Certificate
*Verification Required

Form: U.S.-DOD-AFEM-02

THE UNITED STATES OF AMERICA

TO ALL WHO SHALL SEE THESE PRESENTS, GREETING: THIS IS TO CERTIFY THAT THE SECRETARY OF THE DEPARTMENT OF DEFENSE HAS AWARDED THE

ARMED FORCES RESERVE MEDAL

TO

STAFF SERGEANT ROBERT B LAND

FOR

HONORABLE AND SATISFACTORY SERVICE AS A MEMBER OF U.S. ARMY INFANTRY, 53RD ARMORED BRIGADE

GIVEN UNDER MY HAND IN THE CITY OF WASHINGTON
ON THIS 11TH DAY OF FEBRUARY 1978

ROBERT L. WHITE, JR.
LTC, AG
Chief, Military Awards Branch

FOR SECRETARY OF DEFENSE
JAMES L. JAMERSON, MAJ GEN,
COMMANDING GENERAL

THE ARMY OF THE UNITED STATES OF AMERICA

THIS IS TO CERTIFY THAT THE SECRETARY OF THE ARMY
HAS ON THIS DAY AWARDED THE

ARMY SERVICE RIBBON

ESTABLISHED ON 10 APRIL 1981 BY THE SECRETARY OF THE ARMY

TO

STAFF SERGEANT ROBERT B. LAND

FOR

SUCCESSFUL COMPLETION OF THE UNITED STATES ARMY INITIAL ENTRY TRAINING AND COMPLETION OF YOUR PRIMARY MOS COURSE WHILE SERVING WITH COMPANY B, 2ND BATTALION, 6TH REGIMENT, FORT JACKSON, SOUTH CAROLINA

GIVEN AT THE US ARMY TRAINING CENTER AND SCHOOL

ON THIS 20TH DAY OF AUGUST 1993

GEORGE E. FRIED
MAJOR, US ARMY, ADJ

FRANK P. BLAIR
MAJ GENERAL, USA
Commanding General
Infantry Training

DOD DA ASR REN-2104

DEPARTMENT OF THE ARMY

THE SECRETARY OF THE ARMY

WASHINGTON

THE SECRETARY OF THE ARMY HAS ON THIS DAY AWARDED THE

OVERSEAS SERVICE RIBBON

ESTABLISHED ON 10 APRIL1981 BY THE SECRETARY OF THE ARMY

TO

STAFF SERGEANT ROBERT B. LAND

FOR

SUCCESSFUL COMPLETION OF AN OVERSEAS TOUR WITH SOUTHERN COMMAND, REPUBLIC OF PANAMA

GIVEN IN THE CITY OF WASHINGTON, DC

ON THIS 1ST DAY OF AUGUST 1984

Reno D. Ayers
MAJ GENERAL USA, ADJ

JOHN O. MARSG JR
SECRETARY OF THE ARMY

DA OSS-R 1650.18A

UNITED STATES
NATIONAL DEFENSE FORCE SUPPORT COMMAND
*** **Separate** ***

The
COLD WAR SERVICE MEDAL CITATION
Is
Awarded To:
SSG. Robert B. Land
U.S. ARMY-Ret.

FOR PATRIOTIC AND FAITHFUL MILITARY SERVICE WITH THE ACTIVE DUTY ARMED FORCES, RESERVE FORCES OR NATIONAL GUARD FORCES DURING THE COLD WAR PERIOD 2 SEPTEMBER 1945 TO 26 DECEMBER 1991, THEREBY PROTECTING THE CITIZENS OF THE UNITED STATES OF AMERICA AGAINST THE THREAT OF COMMUNISM AND NUCLEAR WAR BY THE FORMER SOVIET UNION. THIS AWARD OF THE COLD WAR SERVICE MEDAL IS MADE TO THE RECEIPIENT ON BEHALF OF A GRATEFUL NATION.

Service Branch: U.S. ARMY
Date: January 20, 2005
Certificate: 1687

Lieutenant General
Director
Veterans Recognition Program

Form: CWSM-02

UNITED STATES
NATIONAL DEFENSE FORCE SUPPORT COMMAND
*** **Separate** ***

The
NATIONAL HOMELAND SECURITY SERVICE MEDAL CITATION
Is
Awarded To:

SSG. Robert B. Land
U.S.ARMY-Ret.

FOR PATRIOTIC INVOLVEMENT IN THE HOMELAND SECURITY PROGRAM EFFORTS TO PROTECT THE CITIZENS OF THE UNITED STATES OF AMERICA FROM THE THREATS OF DOMESTIC AND FOREIGN TERRORISM AND FOR REAFFIRMING A DEDICATION TO SERVE THE COMMUNITY AND NATION IN TIMES OF CRISIS ON BEHALF OF ITS MOST GRATEFUL CITIZENS.

Date: January 20, 2005
Certificate: 305

Lieutenant General
Director
Veterans Recognition Program
United States National Defense Force Support Command
(Separate)

Form: U.S.-NHSSM-02

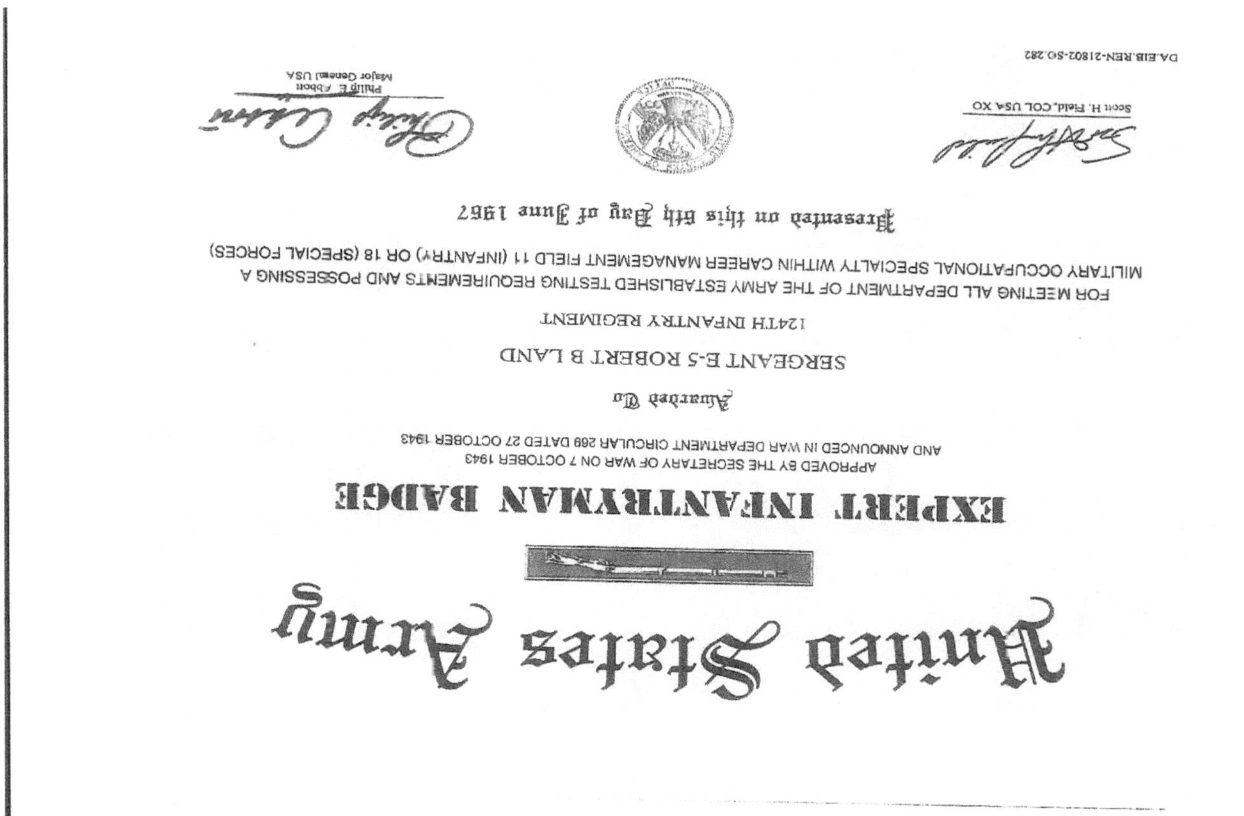

United States Army

EXPERT INFANTRYMAN BADGE

APPROVED BY THE SECRETARY OF WAR ON 7 OCTOBER 1943
AND ANNOUNCED IN WAR DEPARTMENT CIRCULAR 269 DATED 27 OCTOBER 1943

Awarded To

SERGEANT E-5 ROBERT B LAND

124TH INFANTRY REGIMENT

FOR MEETING ALL DEPARTMENT OF THE ARMY ESTABLISHED TESTING REQUIREMENTS AND POSSESSING A MILITARY OCCUPATIONAL SPECIALTY WITHIN CAREER MANAGEMENT FIELD 11 (INFANTRY) OR 18 (SPECIAL FORCES)

Presented on this 6th Day of June 1967

Scott H. Field, COL USA XO

Philip E. Abbott
Major General USA

DA.EIB.REN-21802-SO.282

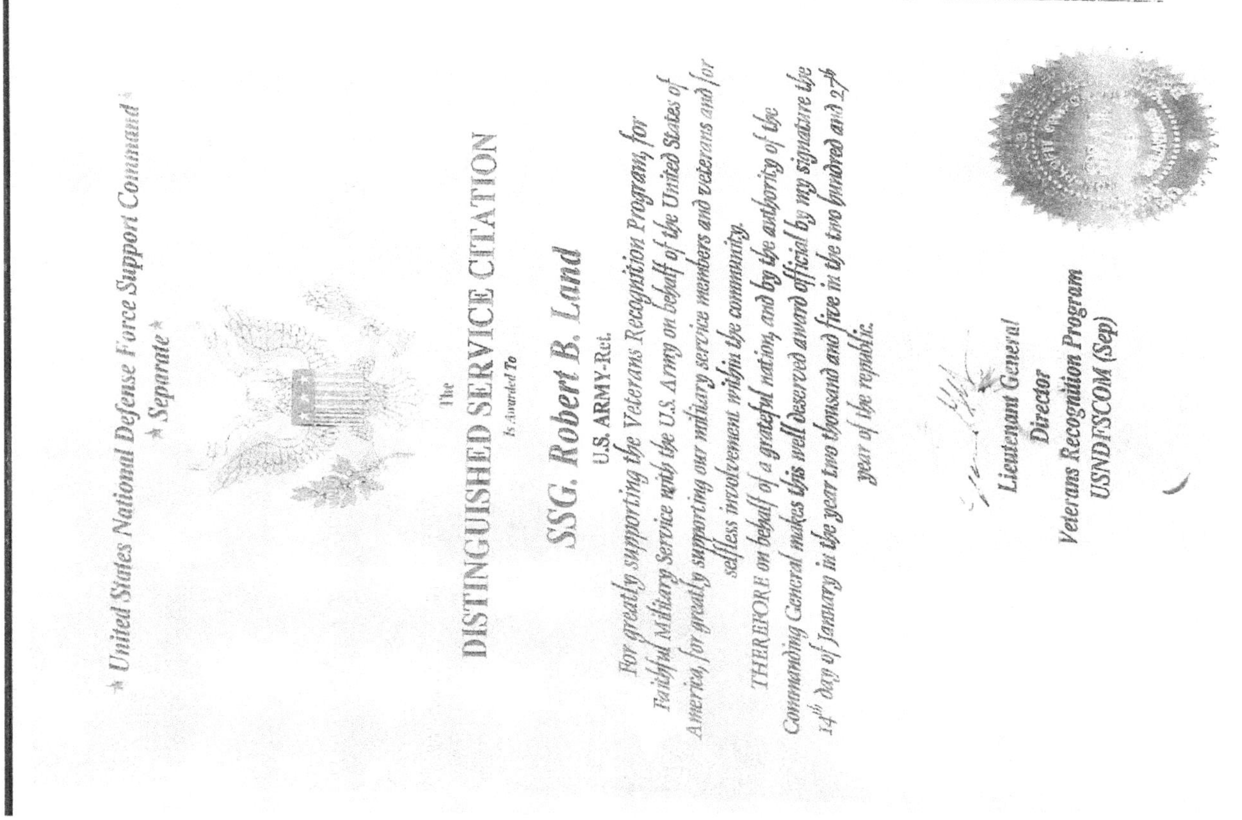

★ United States National Defense Force Support Command ★
★ Separate ★

The
DISTINGUISHED SERVICE CITATION
Is Awarded To

SSG. Robert B. Land
U.S. ARMY-Ret.

For greatly supporting the Veterans Recognition Program, for Faithful Military Service with the U.S. Army on behalf of the United States of America, for greatly supporting our military service members and veterans and for selfless involvement within the community.

THEREFORE on behalf of a grateful nation, and by the authority of the Commanding General makes this well deserved award official by my signature the 14th day of January in the year two thousand and five in the two hundred and 27th year of the republic.

Lieutenant General
Director
Veterans Recognition Program
USNDFSCOM (Sep)

VIRGINIA
gratitude for
your service for
our freedom!
George Allen
U.S. Senator

Best Wishes.
Bill Clinton

To SSG Robert B. Land USA(Ret)
With grateful appreciation for your
service in defense of our country -
Floyd Spence
Chairman HASC

To Staff Sgt Robert Land
Charlie Rangel
2d Inf Div
Good Luck

Symbolism of the SAR Medal

Membership in the Sons of the American Revolution entitles you to wear the medal of the SAR. I now take great pride in describing the symbolism behind the Cross of Malta. The cross is composed of horizontal and vertical bars. The vertical bar represents the commandment, "You Shall Love Your God." The horizontal bar represents the commandment, "You Shall Love Your Neighbor as Yourself." Let us focus on the intersection of the bars to remind us the "Love of God and Neighbor" are in fact one and the same love.

There are four limbs of the cross. The limbs remind us of the four cardinal virtues. The first virtue is prudence, learned by studying the past in order to regulate the present and plan for the future. Prudence allows one to understand the fallacy in allowing a lesser evil to avoid a greater evil, because the accumulation of lesser evils will eventually exceed the hypothetical greater evil. The second virtue is justice. There is an art and science in being just. The art comes from the recognition of the true worth of fellow man. The science involves the concept of impartiality and always begs the question: Is it fair to all concerned? True justice is underscored by integrity of life. The third virtue is temperance or moderation in all of our actions, including the senses, especially the sensual desires. The fourth virtue is fortitude, with magnanimity and courage to serve God.

There are eight points of the Maltese Cross. Each point represents one of the beatitudes recounted for the Knight of Malta by the initiator who would proclaim the following annunciation: "This cross was given white to us as a sign of purity, which you must carry in your heart as you wear it externally, without spot or blemish. The eight points that you see in this are signs of the eight beatitudes that you must always have within you, and they are:

1. To have spiritual contentment
2. To live without malice
3. To weep over your sins
4. To humble yourself at insults
5. To love justice
6. To be merciful
7. To be sincere and open-hearted
8. To suffer persecution

All these virtues you must engrave upon your heart for conservation and preservation of your soul, and for that reason I command you to wear it openly sewn on your clothing on the left-hand side of the heart and never abandon it."

Lastly, our medal has the bust of George Washington at the intersection of the two bars of the cross. This reminds us of our great leader at the time of the American Revolution. Surrounding his bust are the words, "LIBERTAS ET PATRIA," reminding us of our Declaration of Independence and Constitution.

2

The National Society,
Sons of the American Revolution

1000 South Fourth Street, Louisville, KY 40203

Greetings: **Robert Brice Land**

It is a pleasure to inform you that your application for membership in this Society has been approved by the Registrar General, under National Number 177686 and FL Society. Your membership certificate will be prepared and sent to you through your State Society.

We cordially welcome you, and hope that you will participate in the meetings and programs of our Society.

Fraternally,

J. David Sympson

President General

Membership Registered: August 05, 2010

International Headquarters

Sons of Confederate Veterans

Columbia, Tennessee

1861 CONFEDERATE SONS OF VETERANS 1896 1865

To all who shall see these presents, Greetings:

This is to Certify, that

Robert Brice Land

has been elected a member of

Stonewall Jackson Camp No. 1381

Sons of Confederate Veterans

upon the record of his Confederate Ancestor,

Private James Henry Brice

Co. G, F, 12th South Carolina Infantry Regiment

and is entitled to all the rights and privileges of the Confederation.

SONS OF CONFEDERATE VETERANS · DEO VINDICE · RICHMOND, VA., JULY 1, 1896

In witness whereof this certificate is given under the hand and seal of the Commander-in-Chief, duly attested by the Adjutant-in-Chief, at International Headquarters, Columbia, Tennessee this the 13th *day of* June . 2006

Commander-in-Chief

Adjutant-in-Chief

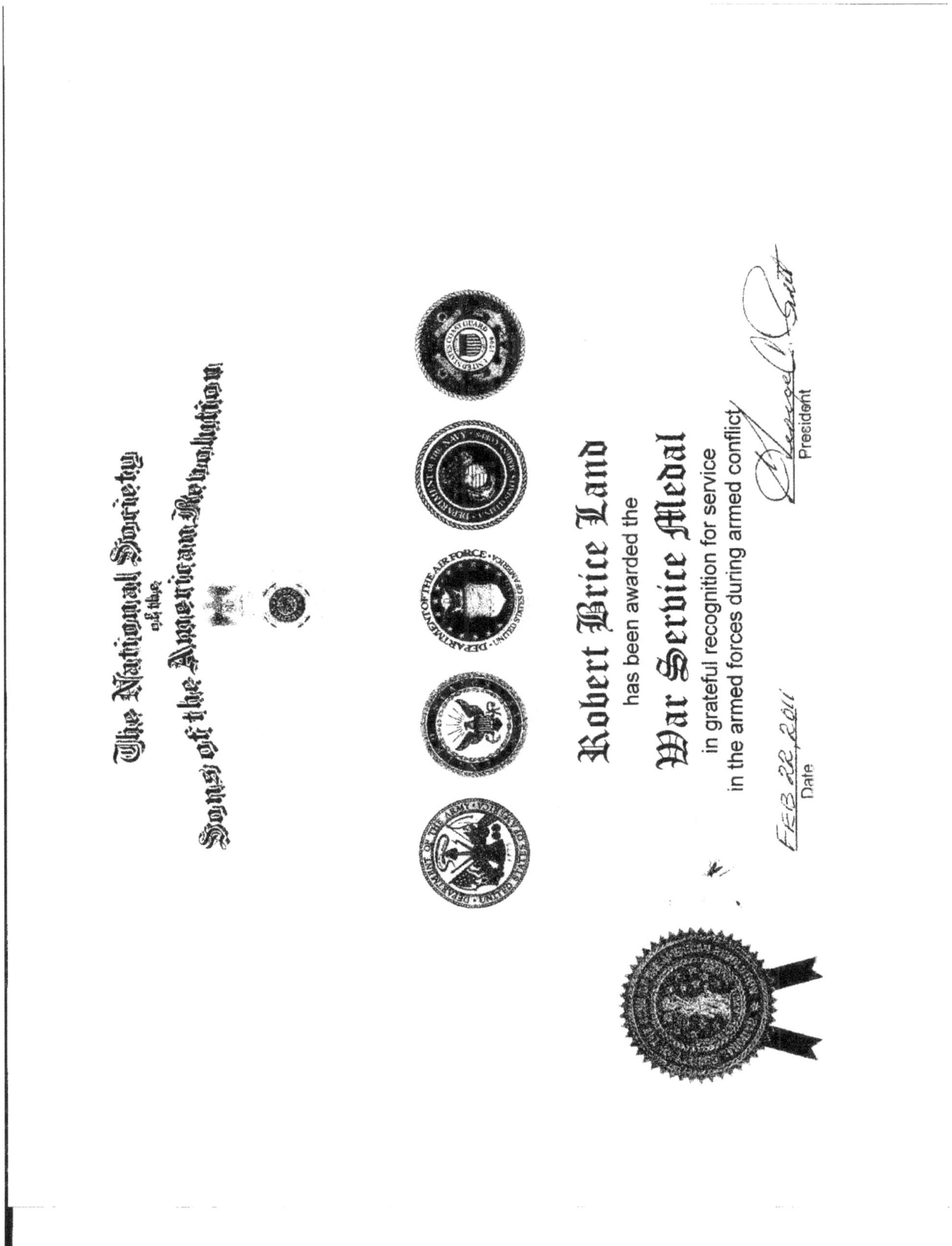

The National Society
of the
Sons of the American Revolution

Robert Brice Land
has been awarded the
War Service Medal
in grateful recognition for service
in the armed forces during armed conflict

FEB 22, 2011
Date

President

The National Society
of the
Sons of the American Revolution

This certifies that

Robert Brice Land

is a member of

The Florida Society

By descent from **John Baden**

Date of Admission **August 05, 2010**

National Number **177686**

President General

State President

Secretary General

State Secretary

William O. Brice

William Oscar Brice, CBE, (December 10, 1898 - January 30, 1972) was a United States Marine Corps General and a veteran of the Korean War, the World War II fight for the Solomon Islands and pre-war expeditionary duty in Haiti and China. He last served at Pearl Harbor as Commanding General, Fleet Marine Force, Pacific, after more than three years at Headquarters Marine Corps, Washington, D.C., as Director of Marine Aviation, Assistant Commandant of the Marine Corps for Air and Assistant Chief of Naval Operations for Marine Aviation.

The general served in Korea as Assistant Commander of the 1st Marine Aircraft Wing from April to October 1951. In World War II, when the Marines were fighting at Guadalcanal in America's first offensive against Japan, he commanded all United States Army, Navy, Marine and Royal New Zealand Air Force search, bombing and torpedo planes based on that island. He also headed Marine Aircraft Group 14 during its support of the New Georgia and Bougainville invasions and directed all Solomons-based Army, Navy, Marine and New Zealand fighter operations against Rabaul, Japan's biggest base in the Southwest Pacific.

Brice was awarded the Distinguished Service Medal for actions at Guadalcanal, the Legion of Merit with Combat "V" as head of the Fighter Command, the Air Medal for combat flights in the Solomons between December 1942, and February 1944, and the Order of the British Empire (with rank of Honorary Commander, Military Division) for his service with the New Zealand Air Force. In addition, he earned the Bronze Star with Combat "V" in the final months of the war as Chief of Staff, Air, Fleet Marine Force, Pacific.

William Oscar Brice

December 10, 1898 – January 30, 1972 (aged 73)

William O. Brice

Place of birth	Columbia, South Carolina
Place of death	Ft. Jackson, South Carolina
Allegiance	United States of America
Service/branch	United States Marine Corps
Years of service	1921-1956 (USMC)
Rank	General
Commands held	Marine Corps Aviation (1952-1959) Assistant Commandant of the Marine Corps Assistant Chief of Naval Operations Fleet Marine Force Pacific
Battles/wars	World War I (US Army) World War II Korean War
Awards	Distinguished Service Medal Legion of Merit Bronze Star Order of the British Empire

Biography

William Brice was born on December 10, 1898, in Columbia, South Carolina. He attended Mt. Zion Institute at Winnsboro, South Carolina from 1913 to 1917. He then served in the U.S. Army in the latter part of World War I. After the war, he resumed his education, graduating from The Citadel at Charleston, South Carolina in 1921.[1] On September 25 of that year, he reported for active duty as a U.S. Marine second lieutenant and was assigned to the Company Officers School at Quantico, Virginia. Graduating from the school in July 1922, he was stationed at the Marine Barracks, Parris Island, South Carolina until May 1923, when he joined the 1st Marine Brigade in Haiti. He returned from that country in February 1924, to enter flight training at Pensacola, Florida, where he was designated an aviator that August.

In June 1925, after further instruction at Pensacola and service with Observation Squadron 3 at Quantico, the Brice began another overseas tour of duty, this time with Scouting Squadron 1 on Guam. From Guam he was ordered to China in April 1927, when most of the squadron was sent there to help protect Americans and other foreigners during the Chinese Civil War. The squadron was withdrawn to the Philippines in May while arrangements for a flying field were made with the Chinese government, and the next month it returned to China to begin operating from Hsin Ho in support of the 3rd Marine Brigade.

Returning to the United States in December 1927, Brice was assigned the following month to Fighter Squadron 9-M at Quantico where he remained until October 1931. On November 2 of that year, he reported aboard the aircraft carrier *Lexington* in command of Scouting Squadron 15-M, which thus began its service as one of the first two Marine squadrons to be based on Navy carriers. (The other unit, Scouting Squadron 14-M, boarded the "Saratoga" the same day.)

Brice remained on the *Lexington* until January 1933. In June 1933, after six month at San Diego, he returned to Quantico. There, during the next three years, he served on aviation duty, completed the Junior Course and was a member of the War Plans Section. He entered the Army Air Corps Tactical School at Maxwell Field, Montgomery, Alabama in August 1936, and upon graduation in June of the following year, returned to Quantico to serve as Executive Officer and later, Commander, of Scouting Squadron 1. After that he was an instructor at Pensacola from June 1939 to August 1941, when he returned to Quantico, this time as Operations Officer of Marine Aircraft Group 11 (MAG-11).

Brice moved with MAG-11 to San Diego in December 1941, and there, in March 1942, he assumed command of Marine Aircraft Group 12. He headed that unit until September 1942, when he rejoined Marine Aircraft Group 11 as its commander, and the following month he sailed with it (via New Caledonia) for the New Hebrides Islands, where the group began feeding planes and pilots into Guadalcanal. In December 1942, he moved to Guadalcanal to take command of Marine Aircraft Group 14 and all the search, bombing and torpedo planes based there, remaining until April 1943, when he departed for New Zealand with the group.

Brice returned to the Solomons with MAG-14 in August 1943, to support the New Georgia and Bougainville operations. The group became the nucleus of the Solomons Fighter Command, and that October Brice was assigned additional duties as head of that organization. He relinquished his command of the group in January 1944, but continued to head the Fighter Command until he returned to the United States in March 1944.

In September 1944, after service in various capacities at the Marine Corps Air Station, Cherry Point, North Carolina, General Brice reported to Marine Corps Headquarters, where he served as Executive Officer of the Division of Plans and Policies until June 1945. The same year he was promoted to brigadier general at the age of 46, which made him the youngest general officer then in the Marine Corps, and that July he arrived in Hawaii to take over as Chief of Staff, Air, Fleet Marine Force, Pacific. He held that post until May 1947, and the following month, returned to Marine Corps Headquarters as Assistant Director of Marine Aviation.

Leaving Headquarters in May 1949, the general's next tour of duty was at Glenview, Illinois, as a Commander of Marine Air Reserve Training from that July until April 1951, when he left for Korea to become Assistant Commander of the 1st Marine Aircraft Wing. Promoted to major general that August, he returned to Hawaii in October as Deputy Commander, Fleet Marine Force, Pacific, serving in that capacity until March 1952, when he returned to the United States. He became Director of Aviation the following month, and in August 1953, when that post was elevated to a lieutenant general's billet, he was promoted to that rank. He left Washington, D.C. in July 1955, and assumed his final command on September 9 of that year. He retired in 1956 and was advanced to the rank of General.[2]

General Brice died on January 30, 1972 at the U.S. Army Hospital, Ft. Jackson, South Carolina.

Awards

General Brice has been awarded:

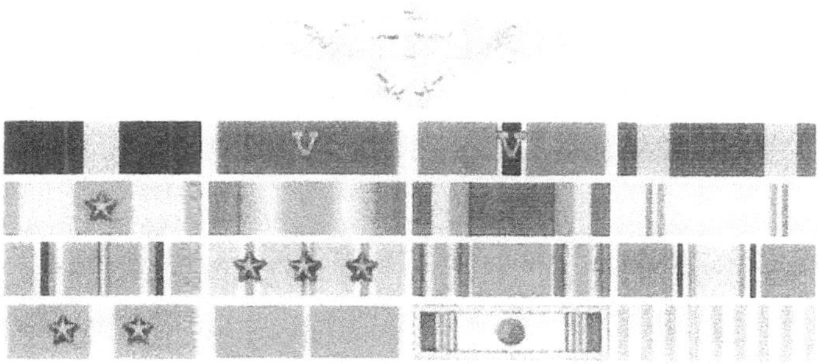

Naval Aviator Badge

Navy Distinguished Service Medal	Legion of Merit w/ valor device	Bronze Star w/ valor device	Air Medal
Marine Corps Expeditionary Medal w/ 1 service star	World War I Victory Medal	Yangtze Service Medal	American Defense Service Medal
American Campaign Medal	Asiatic-Pacific Campaign Medal w/ 3 service stars	World War II Victory Medal	National Defense Service Medal
Korean Service Medal w/ 2 service stars	Commander, Order of the British Empire	Korean Presidential Unit Citation	United Nations Korea Medal

160. Lucy[8] Land *(John G.[7], Bird[6], Littleberry[5], Bird[4], Curtis[3], Curtis[2], Curtis[1])*[339]. She married (1) Freeman Oliver[339]. She married (2) Fred Jefferies[339].

Child of Lucy Land and Fred Jefferies is:

i. Ethel[9] Jefferies[339].

161. Louis Curl[8] Penry *(Nancy[7] Land, Bird[6], Littleberry[5], Bird[4], Curtis[3], Curtis[2], Curtis[1])*[339] was born October 24, 1864 in Noxubee County, Mississippi[339]. He married Ena Montgomery October 25, 1885, daughter of William Montgomery and Anna Wortham. She was born February 12, 1868 in Greenville, Mississippi, and died June 18, 1935 in Encino, New Mexico.

Children of Louis Penry and Ena Montgomery are:

i. Lucille[9] Penry.
ii. Allene Penry, b. August 22, 1887, Waco, Texas; d. June 02, 1989, Santa Fe, New Mexico.
iii. Mildred Penry, b. April 06, 1902; d. October 1982; m. Frank Bigbee.
iv. Dorothy Penry, b. August 01, 1908, Plainview, Texas; d. August 25, 1959, Los Angeles, California.

162. Leopold[8] Weill *(Elmira Sherman[7] Land, Bird[6], Littleberry[5], Bird[4], Curtis[3], Curtis[2], Curtis[1])*[339] was born 1859[339]. He married Bess Sims.

Child of Leopold Weill and Bess Sims is:

i. Frank Lee[9] Weill, b. September 13, 1899, Brandon, Rankin Co., Mississippi; d. 1975, Boston, Massachusetts.

163. Mary[8] Hargrove *(Samuel Henry[7], Sally[6] Land, Littleberry[5], Bird[4], Curtis[3], Curtis[2], Curtis[1])*[340] was born May 07, 1852 in Edgecombe Co. NC[340], and died January 03, 1876 in Edgecombe Co. NC[340].

More About Mary Hargrove:
Record Change: January 08, 2004[340]

Child of Mary Hargrove is:

244. i. James L.[9] Ruffin, b. June 1874, Edgecombe Co. NC.

164. Lucinda[8] Hargrove *(Samuel Henry[7], Sally[6] Land, Littleberry[5], Bird[4], Curtis[3], Curtis[2], Curtis[1])*[340] was born March 09, 1859 in Edgecombe Co. NC[340]. She married William Calvin Spicer[340] 1877 in Edgecombe Co. NC. He was born 1856 in Edgecombe Co. NC[340].

Children of Lucinda Hargrove and William Spicer are:

i. Harriet[9] Spicer[340], b. November 01, 1878, Edgecombe Co. NC[340]; d. Bef. 1898, Edgecombe Co. NC[340].
ii. Henry Spicer[340], b. March 18, 1880, Edgecombe Co. NC[340]; d. Bef. 1900, Edgecombe Co. NC[340].
iii. Lena Spicer[340], b. September 26, 1881, Edgecombe Co. NC[340]; d. June 19, 1883, Edgecombe Co. NC[340].
iv. Mary Spicer[340], b. December 01, 1883, Edgecombe Co. NC[340]; m. Oliver Chromwell Cummings[340]; b. May 30, 1881, Edgecombe Co. NC[340].
v. Rosa Spicer[340], b. July 25, 1885, Edgecombe Co. NC[340].
vi. Prudy Spicer[340], b. September 30, 1891, Edgecombe Co. NC[340].
vii. Ernest Spicer[340], b. September 05, 1896, Edgecombe Co. NC[340].
viii. Emma Spicer[340], b. September 05, 1896, Edgecombe Co. NC[340].

165. Robert Gray[8] Hargrove *(Samuel Henry[7], Sally[6] Land, Littleberry[5], Bird[4], Curtis[3], Curtis[2], Curtis[1])*[340] was born December 06, 1868 in Edgecombe Co. NC[340], and died March 06, 1934 in Edgecombe Co. NC[340]. He married Winnafred Lassiter[340]. She was born in Edgecombe Co. NC[340].

Children of Robert Hargrove and Winnafred Lassiter are:

i. Samuel H.[9] Hargrove[340], b. 1910, Edgecombe Co. NC[340]; m. Nettie G. Unknown[340]; b. 1913, Edgecombe Co. NC[340].
ii. Nellie Hargrove[340], b. 1913[340].

166. ROBERT HENRY[8] HARGROVE *(GRAY LEMON[7], SALLY[6] LAND, LITTLEBERRY[5], BIRD[4], CURTIS[3], CURTIS[2], CURTIS[1])*[340] was born March 21, 1855[340], and died December 07, 1923[340]. He married (1) DELLA EDMONDSON[340]. She died October 24, 1907 in Martin County, NC[340]. He married (2) DORA MAE KRIDER[340]. She was born December 14, 1878[340].

Notes for ROBERT HENRY HARGROVE:
Dr. Robert Henry Hargrove, M.D. was born on a farm about five miles from Tarboro, N.C. He attended high school in Tarboro taught by Frank S. Wilkerson and received his academic training at Trinity College (Duke University). He graduated in medicine at the University of Maryland in 18 77. He did post-graduate work in the Bellevue Hospital Medical College, N. Y., giving special attention to surgical work. After graduation he practice medicine in Rocky Mount, N.C. and later moved to Robersonville, N.C. to make his home and his contribution to the common good of the community and its people.
Dr. Hargrove's practice was in the "horse and buggy days," which saw hi m at his busiest with four horses. He often drove them double on long trips, which extended over a
radius about 15 miles. For many years he was the only doctor between Williamston and Tarboro, and Hamilton and Greenville.
One of the incidents which his friends loved to hear him relate concerned the time that his horses jumped the bridge and started upstream at the crossing of what is now known
as Sam Everett's Creek. One of his closer calls happened when attacked at Collie Swamp, although he was not hurt in the affray.
Dr. Hargrove was active in civic and fraternal affairs of the community. He was a member of the Odd Fellows, Kappa Sigma social fraternity, N.C. Medical Society of the United States and Martin County Medical Society. He served as the first president of the Martin County Medical Society when it was formed in April 29, 1904. he was also a member of other professional organizations.
He was an active member of the First Christian Church, serving as chairman of the board for several years and as a Sunday School teacher. He helped to build every church that was built in the surrounding communities from the time he took up his there to the time of his death.
Dr. Hargrove served as a director of the Bank of Robersonvile and was one of its early presidents. He also served as President of the Robersonville Tobacco Warehouse Company in the early 1900's.
Among the first in the Robersonville community, he built the first brick store and laid the first concrete sidewalk. He owned the first automobile in Martin County. This little red two passenger automobile created quite some excitement in its day. It was shipped in by freight and a man came all the way from Chicago to teach the doctor to drive. Many amusing stories have circulated throughout the section as to the reaction of the people and their team to this new device.
Except for a brief stay in Kinston , N.C. where he practiced with his brother Dr. W.F. Hargrove, Dr. Bob Hargrove maintained his office and practice in Robersonville until his death on December 7, 1923. His hobbies in addition to his love of fine horses were fishing and hunting. He was never too busy to listen to or tell a good fish story.
Dora Mae Krider came to Robersonville as a high school teacher in 1908. She was the first Latin teacher in the Robersonville High School. Her higher education was received
at Mont Amonena Seminary, Mt. Pleasant, N.C. and Claremont College, Hickory, N.C. She was salutatorian of her graduating class .
She was born in Rowan County, Providence Township near Salisbury, N.C. and was the daughter of William Robert Krider and Georgia Ann Hudson. She was confirmed in the Union Lutheran Church at 13 years of age. Her ancestors had been members of this church since coming from Pennsylvania to North Carolina in early 1700."
----Mae Krider Hargrove Pope[2882706.ged]

Children of ROBERT HARGROVE and DELLA EDMONDSON are:

i. LENA BRUCE[9] HARGROVE[340], b. May 21, 1883[340]; d. May 15, 1892[340].
ii. ROBERT HENRY HARGROVE[340], b. April 01, 1893[340]; d. June 25, 1893[340].
iii. MANSE LEROY HARGROVE[340], b. May 01, 1895[340]; d. October 24, 1896[340].

Child of ROBERT HARGROVE and DORA KRIDER is:

245. iv. MAE KRIDER[9] HARGROVE, b. February 16, 1912.

167. JOHN DAVID[8] HARGROVE *(GRAY LEMON[7], SALLY[6] LAND, LITTLEBERRY[5], BIRD[4], CURTIS[3], CURTIS[2], CURTIS[1])*[340] was born March 24, 1856 in Edgecombe Co. NC[340], and died February 23, 1932 in Edgecombe Co. NC[340]. He married SUSAN JANE THIGPEN[340]. She was born August 17, 1859 in Edgecombe Co. NC[340], and died November 11, 1929 in Edgecombe Co. NC[340].

Children of JOHN HARGROVE and SUSAN THIGPEN are:

i. MUSA DORA[9] HARGROVE[340], b. October 06, 1878, Edgecombe Co. NC[340]; d. October 13, 1888, Edgecombe Co. NC[340].

ii. LOSSIE JANE HARGROVE[340], b. January 30, 1886, Edgecombe Co. NC[340]; d. November 25, 1888, Edgecombe Co. NC[340].

iii. LEE DAVID HARGROVE[340], b. May 11, 1887, Edgecombe Co. NC[340]; d. March 05, 1945, Edgecombe Co. NC[340]; m. MINNIE SAVAGE[340]; b. 1893[340].

iv. FRANK LESLEY HARGROVE[340], b. December 10, 1889, Edgecombe Co. NC[340]; m. VIRGINIA SHEFFIELD[340].

246. v. WALTER CLARK HARGROVE, b. February 11, 1891, Edgecombe Co. NC; d. July 15, 1960, Tarboro, NC.

168. LUCY ELLA[8] HARGROVE *(GRAY LEMON[7], SALLY[6] LAND, LITTLEBERRY[5], BIRD[4], CURTIS[3], CURTIS[2], CURTIS[1])*[340] was born September 07, 1864 in Edgecombe Co. NC[340], and died Aft. April 11, 1930 in Wake County, North Carolina[340]. She married JOHN H. UZZLE[340]. He was born September 12, 1854 in Franklin Co., North Carolina[340], and died April 27, 1915 in Franklin Co., North Carolina[340].

Notes for LUCY ELLA HARGROVE:
Name: Joseph A. 'Joe' UZZELL 1 Sex: M Title: Dr. Birth: MAR 1886 in Franklin Co., North Carolina 1 Death: ABT 1922 in Baltimore, Maryland
Note:
[Earl Jobe File.FTW]
1900 -Franklin Co., NC, Louisburg, ED#49, District 6, page 5B (enumerated June 7, 1900)
John H. UZZELL head, Sept ,1854 45 m/14yrs, owns, farmer NC
Lucy wife, Sept.1865 35 m/14yrs, 1 child 1 living NC
Joseph son Mar.1886 13 in school NC
*Joseph is age 13 - listed with parents.

1910 -Franklin Co., NC, Louisburg, page 2B, #35-35 (enumerated Ma y 16, 1910)
John H. UZZELL head, 55 m/24yrs, farmer owns, NC
Lucy wife 45 m/24yrs, 1 child 1 living NCNCNC
Joe A. son, 23 single Physician NCNCNC
*Joe is age 23, unmarried, listed with parents.
----
*He died quite young while studying to be a doctor.[2882706.ged]

Notes for JOHN H. UZZLE:
[Earl Jobe File.FTW]
-per research of Jean Hill:
"John Uzzell was Mapleville postmaster and lived at Mapleville in Franklin Co., NC in home occupied mid to late 1900's by Shack and Hazel Harris. His wife, Lucy Ella Hargrove (daughter of Gray Lemon Hargrove and Felicia Little), was from Tarboro, Edgecombe Co., NC. They had only one child, a son, Joe who became a MD and died in Baltimore, MD at age 2 6 without marrying. Joe was born 14 Nov 1886 and died 22 Oct 1912. He is buried at Maple Springs Church Cemetery."
"Lucy Ella Hargrove Uzzell, John's wife, was born 7 Sept 1864 ad died at St. Lukes Home in Wake Co., NC. In later year s, she lived upstairs in the family home at Mapleville and scared the people who lived downstairs by pitching the hot coals and ashes from her wood stove out the window."

1860 -Franklin Co., NC, Harris District, page 80A, #579-52
3 (enumerated Aug 31, 1860)
Wm.B. UZZLE 38 overseer, 350 2500 NC
Mary E. 33 NC
James E. 14 NC
Mary E. 11 NC
Martha A. 9 NC
Asia 7 f. NC

John H. 5 NC
Otelia 3 NC
Fannie 1 NC
*John H. is age 5 - listed with parents.

1870 -Franklin Co., NC, Louisburg, p age 40, #378-378 (enumerated Sept 1870)
W. B. UZZEL 49 w/m farmer 2500 3500 NC
Amanda 40 w/f k/h NC
Mary 22 w/f at home NC
Asia 18 w/f at school NC
Joh n 16 w/m at school NC
Otelia 13 w/f at school NC
Fannie 11 w/f at school NC
Allice 4 w/f at home NC
Agnes 4 w/f at home NC
Emma 2 w/f at home NC
*John i s age 16 - listed with parents.

1880 -Franklin Co., NC, Louis burg, page 665D
Wm. B. UZZLE Self M Male W 58 NC Farmer NC NC
Amanda C. UZZL E Wife M Female W 50 NC Keeps House NC NC
Jno. H. UZZLE Son S Male W 25 NC Merchant NC NC
Alice UZZLE Dau S Female W 15 NC At Home NC NC
Agnes UZZLE Dau S Female W 15 NC At Home NC NC
Emma UZZLE Dau S Female W 12 NC At Home NC NC
Wm. B. UZZLE, JR. Son S Male W 8 NC At Home NC NC
Gene VA BALL Other Female W 24 NC School Teacher NC NC
*John is age 25 - listed with father and stepmother.

1900 -Franklin Co., NC, Louisburg, ED#49, District 6 , page 5B (enumerated June 7, 1900)
John H. UZZELL head, Sept,1854 45 m/14yr s, owns, farmer NC NC NC
Lucy wife, Sept.1865 35 m/14yrs, 1 child 1 living N C NC NC
Joseph son Mar.1886 13 in school NCNCNC

1910 -Franklin Co., NC, Louisburg, page 2B, #35-35 (enumerated May 16, 1910)
John H. UZZELL head, 55 m/24yrs, farmer owns, NCNCNC
Lucy wife 45 m/24yrs, 1 child 1 living NCNCNC
Joe A. son, 23 single Physician NCNCNC

1930 -Franklin Co., NC, Louisburg, ED#17, page 8A, #118-118
Lucy UZZELL head, 65 wd. $2 500, n/radio NCNCNC
Hal B. PERRY boarder, 38 single farmer w/WW NCNCNC
------ -----------
Sources:
1) Personal Correspondence/Researcher/Descendant of Jean Hill (April 2003) <jbh5@psu.edu>
2) 1860 Franklin Co., NC
3) 1870 Franklin Co., NC
4) 1880 Franklin Co., NC
5) 1900 Franklin Co., NC
6) 1910 Franklin Co., NC
7) 1930 Franklin Co., NC[2882706.ged]

More About JOHN H. UZZLE:
Burial: Maple Springs Baptist Church Cemetery, Franklin Co., NC[340]

Child of LUCY HARGROVE and JOHN UZZLE is:
i. JOSEPH A.[9] UZZLE[340], b. March 1886[340].

169. SALLIE CAPITOLA[8] HARGROVE *(GRAY LEMON[7], SALLY[6] LAND, LITTLEBERRY[5], BIRD[4], CURTIS[3], CURTIS[2], CURTIS[1])*[340] was born August 01, 1868[340]. She married WILLIAM EDWARDS[340] July 27, 1887. He was born January 1864 in Nash Co., NC[340].

Children of SALLIE HARGROVE and WILLIAM EDWARDS are:
247. i. OPIE GRAY[9] EDWARDS, b. September 1891, Nash Co., NC.
248. ii. HELEN MARIE EDWARDS, b. July 1894, Spring Hope, NC; d. 1942, Edgecombe Co. NC.

170. HATTIE IDORA[8] HARGROVE *(GRAY LEMON[7], SALLY[6] LAND, LITTLEBERRY[5], BIRD[4], CURTIS[3], CURTIS[2], CURTIS[1])*[340] was born October 06, 1876 in Edgecombe Co. NC[340]. She married SR. AUGUSTINE CLARK HUGHES[340]. He was born 1878[340].

Children of HATTIE HARGROVE and AUGUSTINE HUGHES are:
i. MARY[9] HUGHES[340].
ii. JR. AUGUSTINE CLARK HUGHES[340], m. CLARA LEE WATSON[340], December 02, 1923.
iii. GRAY HUGHES[340].

171. LOGAN JASPER[8] BARNHILL *(FLORENCE ANNA[7] HARGROVE, SALLY[6] LAND, LITTLEBERRY[5], BIRD[4], CURTIS[3], CURTIS[2], CURTIS[1])*[340] was born March 11, 1879 in Edgecombe Co. NC[340], and died April 16, 1954 in Enfield, Nash Co., NC[340]. He married REBIE ELIZABETH PETTIT[340] Abt. 1904. She was born March 05, 1884[340], and died January 05, 1962[340].

Child of LOGAN BARNHILL and REBIE PETTIT is:
i. ROBERT EDWIN[9] BARNHILL[340], b. February 02, 1905, Halifax Co., NC[340]; d. February 01, 1967, Rocky Mount, Edgecombe County, North Carolina[340]; m. LILLIAN HAMILL[340], September 06, 1930; b. September 06, 1910, Halifax Co., NC[340]; d. November 21, 1974, Norfolk, Norfolk County, Virginia[340].

172. DAVID W.[8] BARNHILL *(FLORENCE ANNA[7] HARGROVE, SALLY[6] LAND, LITTLEBERRY[5], BIRD[4], CURTIS[3], CURTIS[2], CURTIS[1])*[340] was born 1882 in Edgecombe Co. NC[340], and died September 04, 1966[340]. He married REBECCA ELANE[340]. She was born March 07, 1883[340], and died March 1983[340].

Child of DAVID BARNHILL and REBECCA ELANE is:
i. IRENE[9] BARNHILL[340], b. 1905[340].

173. ORA[8] JOYNER *(BURRELL HILDSMAN[7], AMY[6] LAND, LITTLEBERRY[5], BIRD[4], CURTIS[3], CURTIS[2], CURTIS[1])* was born November 23, 1869 in Edgecombe, North Carolina, and died April 18, 1907. She married JOHN FARMER BATTS.

Children of ORA JOYNER and JOHN BATTS are:
i. SUSAN J.[9] BATTS, b. July 13, 1897.
ii. JOHN F. BATTS, b. August 29, 1899.
iii. BURRELL THOMAS BATTS, b. June 20, 1901.
iv. SALLY ANN ELIZABETH BATTS, b. November 25, 1904.

174. SAMUEL SIBLEY[8] LAND *(HENRY GREY[7], BURRELL[6], LITTLEBERRY[5], BIRD[4], CURTIS[3], CURTIS[2], CURTIS[1])*[341] was born December 01, 1871 in Noxubee County, Mississippi[341], and died July 21, 1937 in Noxubee County, Mississippi[341]. He married ALMA PEARL BELL[341]. She was born January 01, 1883[341].

Children of SAMUEL LAND and ALMA BELL are:
249. i. LULU ELIZABETH[9] LAND, b. November 22, 1904, Noxubee Co., Mississippi.
ii. HENRY BURRELL LAND[341], b. 1902[341]; d. Abt. 1940[341].
250. iii. LITTLE GRACE LAND, b. 1903; d. 1943.

175. SARAH BIRT[8] LAND *(HENRY GREY[7], BURRELL[6], LITTLEBERRY[5], BIRD[4], CURTIS[3], CURTIS[2], CURTIS[1])* [341] was born November 29, 1875 in Noxubee County, Mississippi[341], and died in Noxubee County, Mississippi[341]. She married WILLIAM B. HARE[341] December 19, 1894[341].

Children of SARAH LAND and WILLIAM HARE are:

- i. WOODROW WILSON[9] HARE[341].
- ii. JOHN L. HARE[341].
- iii. BENJAMIN HARE[341].
- iv. LIVING HARE[341].

176. DANIEL BURRELL[8] LAND *(HENRY GREY[7], BURRELL[6], LITTLEBERRY[5], BIRD[4], CURTIS[3], CURTIS[2], CURTIS[1])* [341] was born November 29, 1875 in Noxubee County, Mississippi[341], and died December 13, 1953 in Noxubee County, Mississippi[341]. He married HUTCHINSON October 21, 1901[341].

Children of DANIEL LAND and HUTCHINSON are:

251. i. SAMUEL BURRELL "DOCK"[9] LAND.
252. ii. DANIEL PAUL LAND, b. 1907, Mississippi.

177. HENRY GREY[8] LAND *(HENRY GREY[7], BURRELL[6], LITTLEBERRY[5], BIRD[4], CURTIS[3], CURTIS[2], CURTIS[1])* [341] was born December 19, 1877 in Noxubee County, Mississippi[341], and died July 24, 1955 in Noxubee County, Mississippi[341]. He married BIRDIE LEE BELL[341] January 17, 1906[341]. She was born April 18, 1887[341].

More About HENRY GREY LAND:
Burial: Odd Fellows Cemetery[341]

Children of HENRY LAND and BIRDIE BELL are:

- i. ETHEL MAE[9] LAND[341], b. January 30, 1906[341]; d. Aft. 1955, Birmingham, Alabama[341].
- ii. HENRY STRONG LAND[341], b. January 31, 1909, Noxubee County, Mississippi[341]; d. Aft. 1955, Anniston, Alabama[341].
- iii. EMMETT BURRELL LAND[341], b. January 11, 1911, Noxubee County, Mississippi[341]; d. Aft. 1955, DeKalb County, Illinois[341].
- iv. BIRDIE BELL LAND[341], b. December 26, 1913, Noxubee County, Mississippi[341]; d. Aft. 1855, Anniston, Alabama[341].
- v. HAROLD LAND[341], b. April 05, 1922[341]; d. 1950[341].

178. MARY LUCY[8] LAND *(HENRY GREY[7], BURRELL[6], LITTLEBERRY[5], BIRD[4], CURTIS[3], CURTIS[2], CURTIS[1])* [341] was born January 27, 1880 in Noxubee County, Mississippi[341]. She married JOHN WILLIAMS CLARK[341] January 25, 1899 in Noxubee County, Mississippi[341].

Children of MARY LAND and JOHN CLARK are:

- i. LIVING[9] CLARK[341].
- ii. LIVING CLARK[341].
- iii. LIVING CLARK[341].
- iv. LIVING CLARK[341].
- v. LIVING CLARK[341].
- vi. LIVING CLARK[341].
- vii. LIVING CLARK[341].
- viii. LIVING CLARK[341].

179. ELIZABETH JANE[8] LAND *(HENRY GREY[7], BURRELL[6], LITTLEBERRY[5], BIRD[4], CURTIS[3], CURTIS[2], CURTIS[1])* [341] was born February 18, 1882 in Noxubee County, Mississippi[341]. She married DAVID BIRT FOX[341] July 15, 1903[341].

Children of ELIZABETH LAND and DAVID FOX are:

- i. LIVING[9] FOX[341].
- ii. LIVING FOX[341].
- iii. LIVING FOX[341].
- iv. LIVING FOX[341].
- v. LIVING FOX[341].

vi. LIVING FOX[341].
vii. LIVING FOX[341].

180. MILDRED JEFFERSON[8] LAND *(HENRY GREY[7], BURRELL[6], LITTLEBERRY[5], BIRD[4], CURTIS[3], CURTIS[2], CURTIS[1])*[341] was born October 12, 1884 in Noxubee County, Mississippi[341]. She married WALTER GILBERT[341] September 20, 1905[341].

Children of MILDRED LAND and WALTER GILBERT are:
i. LIVING[9] GILBERT[341].
ii. LIVING GILBERT[341].
iii. LIVING GILBERT[341].
iv. LIVING GILBERT[341].

181. MARY MILDRED "MAGGIE"[8] LAND *(WILLIAM BURT[7], BURRELL[6], LITTLEBERRY[5], BIRD[4], CURTIS[3], CURTIS[2], CURTIS[1])*[341] was born 1852 in Louisana[341], and died April 18, 1885 in Noxubee County, Mississippi[341]. She married GEORGE COMODORE VANDEVENDER[342,343] February 17, 1881[343]. He was born Abt. 1850 in Kemper County, Mississippi[343], and died July 29, 1924 in Preston, Kemper County, Mississippi[343].

More About MARY MILDRED "MAGGIE" LAND:
Burial: Near Kellis' Store in private graveyard on Widow Small's farm[343]

More About GEORGE COMODORE VANDEVENDER:
Burial: July 30, 1924, Pleasant Springs Cemetery, Kemper County, Mississippi[343]

Children of MARY LAND and GEORGE VANDEVENDER are:
i. LESLIE OLNEY[9] VANDEVENDER[343], b. December 03, 1881, Kemper County, Mississippi[343]; d. August 14, 1882, Kemper County, Mississippi[343].
253. ii. EFFIE LAVINA VANDEVENDER, b. August 30, 1884, Dekalb County, Alabama; d. April 05, 1968, Forrest City, St. Francis County, Arkansas.
254. iii. MARY MILDRED VANDEVENDER, b. April 18, 1885, Kemper County, Mississippi; d. October 12, 1969.

182. HENRY TAYLOR[8] LAND *(WILLIAM BURT[7], BURRELL[6], LITTLEBERRY[5], BIRD[4], CURTIS[3], CURTIS[2], CURTIS[1])*[343] was born May 1861 in Richland Parrish, Louisiana[343], and died 1928 in Winston County, Mississippi[343]. He married (1) ANNA JANE VANDERVENDER[343] December 23, 1883[343]. She was born September 11, 1865 in Kemper County, Mississippi[343]. He married (2) LAURA HAILEY[343] November 10, 1898 in Kemper County, Mississippi[343]. She was born 1876 in Mississippi[343].

Children of HENRY LAND and ANNA VANDERVENDER are:
i. OSCAR MELVIN[9] LAND[343], b. September 1884, Mississippi[343]; d. March 30, 1955, Jasper County, Missouri[343].
ii. DORA LAND[343], b. July 07, 1887, Kemper County, Mississippi[343]; d. April 24, 1907, Kemper County, Mississippi[343].

More About DORA LAND:
Burial: Old Salem Cemetery, Kemper County, Mississippi[343]

iii. HENRY CLAYTON LAND[343], b. 1889, Kemper County, Mississippi[343]; d. 1962, Orange County, California[343].
iv. WILLIAM CARTER LAND[343], b. May 15, 1891, Kemper County, Mississippi[343]; d. December 01, 1956, Dawson County, Texas[343].

Child of HENRY LAND and LAURA HAILEY is:
v. EDWIN GARNER[9] LAND[343], b. January 29, 1905, Winston County, Mississippi[343]; d. April 14, 1982, Winston County, Mississippi[343].

183. LITTLEBERRY JOHN[8] LAND *(WILLIAM BURT[7], BURRELL[6], LITTLEBERRY[5], BIRD[4], CURTIS[3], CURTIS[2], CURTIS[1])*[343] was born August 01, 1876 in Louisana[343], and died November 19, 1919 in Richland Parrish, Louisiana[343]. He married ELIZA JANE THARP[343] November 16, 1899 in Richland Parrish, Louisiana[343]. She was born November 30, 1883[343].

Children of LITTLEBERRY LAND and ELIZA THARP are:

i. LIVING[9] LAND[343].
ii. LIVING LAND[343], m. LIVING POLLARD[343].
iii. LIVING LAND[343].
iv. MAGGIE GUSHIN LAND[343], b. July 28, 1900, Richland Parrish, Louisiana[343]; d. 1985, Tallulah, Louisiana[343].
v. JOHN LITTLEBERRY LAND[343], b. August 17, 1902, Richland Parrish, Louisiana[343]; d. December 17, 1973, Delhi Parrish, Louisiana[343]; m. LIVING NEWTON[343].
vi. NELLIE LAND[343], b. April 1904, Richland Parrish, Louisiana[343]; d. 1911, Richland Parrish, Louisiana[343].
vii. ALBERT LAND[343], b. December 07, 1905, Richland Parrish, Louisiana[343]; d. April 13, 1972, Tallulah, Louisiana[343].
viii. I.C. LAND[343], b. 1910, Richland Parrish, Louisiana[343]; d. 1911[343].
ix. TWIN SON LAND[343], b. 1919[343]; d. 1919[343].
x. TWIN DAUGHTER LAND[343], b. 1919[343]; d. 1919[343].

184. SOLOMON R.[8] LAND *(THOMAS C.[7], JOHN[6], CHARLES[5], CHARLES[4], CURTIS[3], CURTIS[2], CURTIS[1])* was born May 1868 in NC, and died Aft. 1900 in Wilson, NC. He married DENISE WINSTEAD. She was born February 1873 in NC, and died Aft. 1900 in Wilson, NC.

Children of SOLOMON LAND and DENISE WINSTEAD are:
i. MARY[9] LAND.
ii. JAMES C. LAND.

185. WILLIAM H.[8] LAND *(THOMAS C.[7], JOHN[6], CHARLES[5], CHARLES[4], CURTIS[3], CURTIS[2], CURTIS[1])* was born June 1870, and died Aft. 1900 in Wilson, NC. He married LOUISIANA. She was born July 1870 in NC, and died Aft. 1900 in Wilson, NC.

Children of WILLIAM LAND and LOUISIANA are:
i. ETHEL[9] LAND.
ii. MAGGIE LAND.
iii. DORETHA LAND.

186. JOSIAH JOSEPH B.[8] LAND *(THOMAS C.[7], JOHN[6], CHARLES[5], CHARLES[4], CURTIS[3], CURTIS[2], CURTIS[1])* was born 1879 in NC, and died Aft. 1910 in Edgecombe, North Carolina. He married MARY Abt. 1906. She was born 1891, and died Aft. 1910 in Nash, North Carolina.

Child of JOSIAH LAND and MARY is:
i. JAMES[9] LAND.

187. TURNER[8] LAND *(WILLIE G.[7], JOHN[6], CHARLES[5], CHARLES[4], CURTIS[3], CURTIS[2], CURTIS[1])* was born 1837 in NC. He married DELLA. She was born August 1864 in NC, and died Aft. 1910 in Nash, North Carolina.

Child of TURNER LAND and DELLA is:
i. F.[9] LAND, b. June 1884, NC; d. Wilson, NC.

Notes for F. LAND:
He was a doctor.

188. RHODES[8] BAILEY *(WILLIAM W.[7], ELIZABETH[6] LAND, LEWIS[5], BIRD[4], CURTIS[3], CURTIS[2], CURTIS[1])*[344] was born Abt. 1855[344], and died WFT Est. 1889-1965[344]. He married MATILDA ALLISON[344] WFT Est. 1887-1920[344]. She was born October 10, 1865 in Ravenden Springs, Ar.[344], and died March 20, 1936[344].

Child of RHODES BAILEY and MATILDA ALLISON is:
255. i. LIVING[9] BAILEY.

189. GEORGE WASHINGTON[8] BAILEY *(WILLIAM W.[7], ELIZABETH[6] LAND, LEWIS[5], BIRD[4], CURTIS[3], CURTIS[2], CURTIS[1])* was born January 25, 1857.

Children of GEORGE WASHINGTON BAILEY are:
256. i. JAMES THEADORE[9] BAILEY, b. September 03, 1882; d. May 19, 1955.
257. ii. FRANKIE ZULA BAILEY, b. September 29, 1887.

258. iii. FANNIE LULA BAILEY, b. September 29, 1887.
259. iv. WILLIAM SOLOMON BAILEY, b. November 11, 1889; d. January 25, 1958.
260. v. TILDA PEARL BAILEY, b. November 01, 1893.
261. vi. ALBERT DONALD BAILEY, b. March 24, 1896; d. May 26, 1964.
262. vii. VIRGIL BAILEY, b. December 24, 1899; d. 1967.
viii. ELLA BAILEY, b. April 24, 1897.
ix. IRENE BAILEY, b. February 24, 1901.

190. ALLEN A.^{8} BAILEY *(WILLIAM W.^{7}, ELIZABETH^{6} LAND, LEWIS^{5}, BIRD^{4}, CURTIS^{3}, CURTIS^{2}, CURTIS^{1})* was born Abt. 1864 in Arkansas. He married KATIE PALMER November 03, 1881. She was born in Randolph Co. Arkansas.

Children of ALLEN BAILEY and KATIE PALMER are:
263. i. FREDERICK^{9} BAILEY.
ii. BERTHA BAILEY, m. GEORGE MUPHEY.
iii. MRYTLE BAILEY.
iv. MANDA BAILEY, b. 1890, Arkansas.
v. GERTIE BAILEY, b. 1898.
vi. ELMER BAILEY, b. 1901; m. MYRTLE BAILEY DAVIS.
vii. MAUDE BAILEY, m. GLEN MILLER.

191. MARTHA C.^{8} BAILEY *(WILLIAM W.^{7}, ELIZABETH^{6} LAND, LEWIS^{5}, BIRD^{4}, CURTIS^{3}, CURTIS^{2}, CURTIS^{1})* was born Abt. 1867. She married WILLIAM MILLER.

Children of MARTHA BAILEY and WILLIAM MILLER are:
i. EVA^{9} MILLER.
ii. FRANK MILLER.
iii. IRA MILLER.
iv. VIRGIL MILLER.
v. CORA MILLER, m. UNKNOWN RUSK.
vi. WILLIE MILLER.
vii. ETHEL LOTTIE MILLER, m. UNKNOWN THOMPSON.

192. MOSES^{8} BAILEY *(WILLIAM W.^{7}, ELIZABETH^{6} LAND, LEWIS^{5}, BIRD^{4}, CURTIS^{3}, CURTIS^{2}, CURTIS^{1})* was born September 1869 in Arkansas. He married KATE (BAILEY).

Children of MOSES BAILEY and KATE (BAILEY) are:
i. CLIFFORD^{9} BAILEY, b. 1895.
ii. CLARENCE BAILEY, b. 1897.
iii. MAZIE BAILEY, b. 1899.
iv. TOLA BAILEY, b. 1906.
v. MAYBORN BAILEY, b. 1910.
vi. OLEN BAILEY.

193. SUSAN "SUSIE"^{8} BAILEY *(WILLIAM W.^{7}, ELIZABETH^{6} LAND, LEWIS^{5}, BIRD^{4}, CURTIS^{3}, CURTIS^{2}, CURTIS^{1})* was born Abt. 1872. She married LEE MCILROY.

Children of SUSAN BAILEY and LEE MCILROY are:
i. HITE^{9} MCILROY, m. UNKNOWN MOORE.
ii. LELA MCILROY.
iii. ALMA MCILROY, m. HOUSTON BROWN.
iv. EVAMCILROY, m. VIRGIL CRAWFORD.
v. IRENE MCILROY, m. WELLS WADDELL.
vi. PAULINE MCILROY, m. GROVR MILAM.

194. MARY ELIZABETH "MATILDA"^{8} BAILEY *(WILLIAM W.^{7}, ELIZABETH^{6} LAND, LEWIS^{5}, BIRD^{4}, CURTIS^{3}, CURTIS^{2}, CURTIS^{1})* was born Abt. 1876. She married "BILL" W. A. DAVIS.

Children of MARY BAILEY and "BILL" DAVIS are:
i. ZONA^{9} DAVIS.
ii. LELIA DAVIS.

iii. MOLLY DAVIS.
264. iv. WILLIAM CLARK DAVIS.

195. WARNER DAVID^{8} PARRIS *(SUSANNAH^{7} LAND, STEPHEN^{6}, LEWIS^{5}, BIRD^{4}, CURTIS^{3}, CURTIS^{2}, CURTIS^{1})* [345] was born October 1871[345]. He married (2) ADDIE THEODOSA AUSTIN September 12, 1891 in Georgia. She was born December 03, 1871 in Georgia, and died December 05, 1913 in Georgia.

Children of WARNER DAVID PARRIS are:
265. i. ROBERT DAVID^{9} PARRIS, b. August 26, 1913, Marietta, Georgia; d. November 13, 1984, SaVAnnah, Tennessee.
266. ii. WILLIAM BENSON PARRIS, b. October 20, 1920.
267. iii. HAROLD LESTER PARRIS, b. June 23, 1923.
268. iv. HAZEL CORNELIA PARRIS, b. September 03, 1924.

Children of WARNER PARRIS and ADDIE AUSTIN are:
v. OTIS CLIFTON^{9} PARRIS.
vi. ALBERT CLARENCE PARRIS.
vii. CECIL LEO PARRIS.
viii. NELLIE OCTAVIA PARRIS.
ix. LOIS THEODOSIA PARRIS.

196. RONEY JEFFERSON^{8} PARRIS *(ELIZABETH JANE^{7} LAND, STEPHEN^{6}, LEWIS^{5}, BIRD^{4}, CURTIS^{3}, CURTIS^{2}, CURTIS^{1})* [345]. He married AELAIDE REID.

Child of RONEY PARRIS and AELAIDE REID is:
269. i. ANNA MAE BELL^{9} PARRIS.

197. JOEL CAMERON^{8} LAND *(JAMES B.^{7}, KINSON^{6}, LEWIS^{5}, BIRD^{4}, CURTIS^{3}, CURTIS^{2}, CURTIS^{1})* [345]. He married ELIZABETH DAVIS[345].

Child of JOEL LAND and ELIZABETH DAVIS is:
i. JOEL CAMERON^{9} LAND[345].

198. REBECCA^{8} LAND *(JORDON^{7}, KINSON^{6}, LEWIS^{5}, BIRD^{4}, CURTIS^{3}, CURTIS^{2}, CURTIS^{1})* [345] was born December 06, 1874 in Arkansas[345], and died January 15, 1930[345]. She married (1) LEMMONS[345]. She married (2) JOE LARUE[345].

More About REBECCA LAND:
Burial: Oaklawn Cemetery, Batesville, Arkansas[345]

Children of REBECCA LAND and LEMMONS are:
i. LUCY^{9} LEMMONS[345], b. February 1891[345].
ii. ORA LEMMONS[345], b. June 06, 1894[345]; d. January 28, 1978[345]; m. IRA WILSON[345]; b. August 23, 1888[345]; d. August 15, 1956[345].

More About ORA LEMMONS:
Burial: Oaklawn Cemetery, Batesville, Arkansas[345]

199. LUCRETIA (LOU CRECY) JANE^{8} LAND *(JORDON^{7}, KINSON^{6}, LEWIS^{5}, BIRD^{4}, CURTIS^{3}, CURTIS^{2}, CURTIS^{1})* [345] was born May 20, 1877 in Pocahontas, Arkansas[345], and died September 15, 1957 in Batesville, Independence County, Arkansas[345]. She married CHARLES MONROE REED[346,347] June 16, 1895 in Lawrence County, Arkansas[347]. He was born April 22, 1869 in Texas[347], and died December 01, 1949 in Batesville, Arkansas[347].

Children of LUCRETIA LAND and CHARLES REED are:
i. GLADES MAE^{9} REED[347], b. July 04[347].
270. ii. CLYDE REED, b. October 10, 1892; d. January 15, 1969, Swifton, Arkansas.
271. iii. JOE LUTHER REED, b. January 03, 1903; d. December 11, 1937, Egypt, Arkansas.
272. iv. JAMES ALVIS REED, b. December 04, 1904; d. February 22, 1985, Illinois.
273. v. BESSIE TENNESSEE REED, b. May 26, 1906; d. August 1972.
274. vi. ORA DELLAR REED, b. November 26, 1909; d. November 23, 2003, Rolling Hills Nursing Home.
275. vii. MATTIE BEATRICE REED, b. September 22, 1911; d. December 1939, Rosie, Arkansas.

276. viii. Frank Carter Reed, b. December 10, 1914; d. August 22, 1975, Illinois.
277. ix. Walter Collins Reed, b. December 22, 1918, Batesville, Arkansas; d. December 11, 1999, Batesville, Independence County, Arkansas.
278. x. Charles Jett Reed, b. April 12, 1922; d. August 27, 1951, Batesville, Independence County, Arkansas.

200. Joseph James Rufus[8] Tyler *(Martha Matilda Rosetta[7] Land, Kinson[6] Lewis[5] Bird[4] Curtis[3] Curtis[2] Curtis[1])* was born February 24, 1890 in Randolph Co. Arkansas, and died May 08, 1974 in Pocahontas, Randolph Co., Arkansas. He married Edna Laura Prevett November 20, 1918, daughter of Absalom Prevett and Alice Blackwell. She was born January 14, 1894 in Water Valley, Randolph, Arkansas, and died March 24, 1971 in Pocahontas, Randolph Co., Arkansas.

Children of Joseph Tyler and Edna Prevett are:

279. i. Noami Evelyn[9] Tyler, b. July 11, 1920.
ii. Harold Eugene Tyler.
iii. Edward Leo Tyler.
iv. Agnes Faye Tyler.
v. Gerald Cloyce Tyler.
vi. Alice Rose Tyler.
vii. Joseph James Rufus Tyler, Jr..
viii. Glendon Ray Tyler.

201. Bertha Deliah[8] Tyler *(Martha Matilda Rosetta[7] Land, Kinson[6] Lewis[5] Bird[4] Curtis[3] Curtis[2] Curtis[1])*[348] was born 1891[348], and died WFT Est. 1918-1985[348]. She married William Jones[348] WFT Est. 1904-1934[348]. He was born February 18, 1884[348], and died June 1974[348].

Children of Bertha Tyler and William Jones are:

280. i. James Gerald[9] Jones, b. June 29, 1914; d. May 29, 1994, St. Bernards Hospital, Jonesboro, Ar..
ii. Lehman Jones.
iii. Juanita Jones.
iv. Oneida Jones.
v. Vera Jones.
vi. Billy Joe Jones.
vii. Carson Jones.
viii. Gene Jones.

202. Luther Edward[8] Tyler *(Martha Matilda Rosetta[7] Land, Kinson[6] Lewis[5] Bird[4] Curtis[3] Curtis[2] Curtis[1])* was born April 02, 1895, and died December 21, 1980. He married Nellie Henderson. She was born December 18, 1887, and died February 08, 1973.

Children of Luther Tyler and Nellie Henderson are:

i. William Woodrow[9] Tyler, b. June 25, 1917.
ii. John Lawson Tyler, b. May 01, 1919.
281. iii. Leslie Wade Tyler, b. July 15, 1921.
iv. Luther "Bea" Tyler, b. October 07, 1923.
v. Veda Iretha Tyler, b. October 28, 1923.
vi. Clyde Abe Tyler, b. October 28, 1930.

203. James Curtis[8] Tyler *(Martha Matilda Rosetta[7] Land, Kinson[6] Lewis[5] Bird[4] Curtis[3] Curtis[2] Curtis)* was born 1900. He married Irene Hogue.

Children of James Tyler and Irene Hogue are:

i. Wilma[9] Tyler.
ii. Ernest Levi Tyler.

204. John Paris[8] Tyler *(Martha Matilda Rosetta[7] Land, Kinson[6], Lewis[5], Bird[4] Curtis[3] Curtis[2] Curtis)* was born 1901. He married Opal Hefner.

Child of John Tyler and Opal Hefner is:

282. i. MODENE[9] TYLER.

205. JAMES EDGAR[8] HUGHES *("DONA" FRANCIS CALDONIA[7] LAND, KINSON[6], LEWIS[5], BIRD[4], CURTIS[3], CURTIS[2], CURTIS[1])* was born May 1891, and died in Yuma, AZ.

Child of JAMES EDGAR HUGHES is:

i. EUGENE[9] HUGHES.

206. MARTHA ANNA[8] HUGHES *("DONA" FRANCIS CALDONIA[7] LAND, KINSON[6], LEWIS[5], BIRD[4], CURTIS[3], CURTIS[2], CURTIS[1])* was born March 04, 1893, and died September 19, 1946. She married JOHN MONROE WHITE March 16, 1913 in Randolph Co., Arkansas. He was born December 20, 1884 in Randolph Co. Arkansas, and died February 27, 1964. Burial: Brady Cemetery, Randolph Co. Arkansas

Children of MARTHA HUGHES and JOHN WHITE are:

i. ADAM[9] WHITE.
ii. CARL WHITE.
iii. LUKE WHITE.
iv. RUSSELL WHITE.
v. WILLARD WHITE.
vi. PEARL WHITE.
vii. PAULINE WHITE.
viii. JOHN MONROE WHITE, JR..

207. MARY EMMA[8] HUGHES *("DONA" FRANCIS CALDONIA[7] LAND, KINSON[6], LEWIS[5], BIRD[4], CURTIS[3], CURTIS[2], CURTIS[1])* was born December 1896 in Randolph Co. Arkansas, and died May 15, 1979 in Jacksboro, Texas. She married JAMES CALVIN HACKWORTH September 02, 1914 in Randolph Co., Arkansas. He was born March 01, 1893 in Missouri, and died January 28, 1976 in Russellville, Arkansas.

More About JAMES CALVIN HACKWORTH:
Burial: Jane Cemetery

Children of MARY HUGHES and JAMES HACKWORTH are:

i. ELMER[9] HACKWORTH.
ii. ALMON HACKWORTH.
iii. JERRY HACKWORTH.
iv. JOHN HACKWORTH.
v. THELMA HACKWORTH.
vi. IRENE HACKWORTH.
vii. RUBY HACKWORTH.
viii. MARY HACKWORTH.

208. ROSY[8] HUGHES *("DONA" FRANCIS CALDONIA[7] LAND, KINSON[6], LEWIS[5], BIRD[4], CURTIS[3], CURTIS[2], CURTIS[1])* was born December 1899. She married WILLIAM CARRELL RIDDLE November 01, 1914 in Randolph Co., Arkansas, son of MEREDITH RIDDLE and MARY LEMASTIS. He was born January 18, 1896 in Randolph Co. Arkansas.

Children of ROSY HUGHES and WILLIAM RIDDLE are:

283. i. ERVIN LEE[9] RIDDLE, b. Randolph Co. Arkansas; d. March 20, 2000.
ii. EARL MONROE RIDDLE, b. April 09, 1919.
iii. RAY RIDDLE.
iv. FAYE RIDDLE.
v. MILDRED RIDDLE.
vi. JEAN RIDDLE.
vii. LOUISA LUCEILLE RIDDLE.

209. HENRY F.[8] HUGHES *("DONA" FRANCIS CALDONIA[7] LAND, KINSON[6], LEWIS[5], BIRD[4], CURTIS[3], CURTIS[2], CURTIS[1])* was born June 04, 1901 in Randolph Co. Arkansas, and died November 06, 1989 in Sulphur Rock, Independence Co., AR.

Child of HENRY F. HUGHES is:

i. HAROLD[9] HUGHES.

210. BIRDIE[8] HUGHES *("DONA" FRANCIS CALDONIA[7] LAND, KINSON[6], LEWIS[5], BIRD[4], CURTIS[3], CURTIS[2], CURTIS[1])* was born 1904. She married MARION AUTHOR GANN March 21, 1920 in Randolph Co., Arkansas, son of RALEIGH GANN and MARY RODGERS. He was born May 02, 1900 in Randolph Co. Arkansas, and died February 11, 1983.

Children of BIRDIE HUGHES and MARION GANN are:

i. EARL[9] GANN.
ii. RUSSELL GANN.
iii. DELMER GANN.
iv. HELEN GANN.
v. MURIAM GANN.

211. THOMAS JEFFERSON[8] HUGHES *("DONA" FRANCIS CALDONIA[7] LAND, KINSON[6], LEWIS[5], BIRD[4], CURTIS[3], CURTIS[2], CURTIS[1])* was born January 20, 1906 in Randolph Co. Arkansas, and died October 24, 1970 in Randolph Co. Arkansas. He married NETTIE EVALINE BENNETT 1934 in Ravenden Springs, Randolph Co., AR, daughter of JAMES BENNETT and ROXIE WATLEY. She was born April 05, 1912 in Water Valley, Randolph, Arkansas.

More About THOMAS JEFFERSON HUGHES:
Burial: Jane Cemetery

Children of THOMAS HUGHES and NETTIE BENNETT are:

284. i. IMOGENE EVELYN[9] HUGHES, b. 1936.
285. ii. JAMES HENRY HUGHES, b. April 13, 1938, Ravenden Springs, Randolph Co., AR.
286. iii. BETTY JOYCE HUGHES, b. 1940.
287. iv. THOMAS DAIL HUGHES, b. 1942.
288. v. RONNIE HUGHES, b. 1944.
289. vi. BUDDY CARSON HUGHES, b. July 27, 1947.

Generation No. 9

212. JAMES MONROE[9] LAND *(HENDERSON P.[8], FOUNTAIN[7], JOHN[6], THOMAS[5], THOMAS[4], JOHN[3], CURTIS[2], CURTIS[1])*[349] was born 1855[349]. He married LINDSY BRANNON[349]. She was born 1857[349].

Children of JAMES LAND and LINDSY BRANNON are:

i. LENORA[10] LAND[349], b. September 18, 1874[349].
ii. LEANN LAND[349], b. 1875[349].
iii. LUTER LAND[349], b. 1887[349].

213. HENRY FOUNTAIN[9] LAND *(HENDERSON P.[8], FOUNTAIN[7], JOHN[6], THOMAS[5], THOMAS[4], JOHN[3], CURTIS[2], CURTIS[1])*[349] was born 1867[349], and died 1951[349]. He married CELIA AMY RUYLE[349]. She was born 1871[349], and died 1965[349].

Children of HENRY LAND and CELIA RUYLE are:

i. CLAUDE EARL[10] LAND[349], b. 1893[349]; d. 1913[349].
290. ii. CLYDE ERR LAND, b. 1896; d. 1988.

214. MARY LOUISE[9] LAND *(WILSON[8], WILLIAM THOMAS[7], JONATHAN[6], THOMAS[5], THOMAS[4], JOHN[3], CURTIS[2], CURTIS[1])*[349] was born May 28, 1838 in Stoney Fork, Watauga County, North Carolina[349], and died October 25, 1901 in Lenoir/ Caldwell County, North Carolina[349]. She married GEORGE WASHINGTON TRIPLETT[349] Abt. 1855[349].

Children of MARY LAND and GEORGE TRIPLETT are:

i. THOMAS WILSON[10] TRIPLETT[349], b. Abt. 1856, Lenoir County, North Carolina[349]; d. Abt. 1926, Bend, Oregon[349].
ii. MARTHA ALICE TRIPLETT[349], b. Abt. 1858, Caldwell County, North Carolina[349].
iii. ELIZABETH TRIPLETT[349], b. Abt. 1861, Caldwell County, North Carolina[349].
iv. MOLTEN TRIPLETT[349], b. September 02, 1863, Lenoir County, North Carolina[349]; d. September 02, 1863, San Jose, California[349].

v. MILLIARD TAYLOR TRIPLETT[349], b. May 1869, Bull's Gap, Tennessee[349]; d. January 15, 1951, Bend, Oregon[349].

More About MILLIARD TAYLOR TRIPLETT:
Burial: Pilot Butte Cemetery, Bend, Oregon[349]

vi. ONEY W. TRIPLETT[349], b. Abt. 1873[349].
vii. CARLISLE COLUMBUS TRIPLETT[349], b. April 03, 1878, Lenoir County, North Carolina[349]; d. 1919[349].
viii. CREED M. TRIPLETT[349], b. November 05, 1880, Lenoir County, North Carolina[349].

215. MARTHA JANE[9] LAND *(WILSON[8], WILLIAM THOMAS[7], JONATHAN[6], THOMAS[5], THOMAS[4], JOHN[3], CURTIS[2], CURTIS[1])*[349] was born September 03, 1840 in Wilkes County, North Carolina[349], and died in Texas[349]. She married (1) JAMES WELLINGTON TRIPLETT[349] May 06, 1858[349]. She married (2) HUBBARD BROWN[349] 1880[349].

Children of MARTHA LAND and JAMES TRIPLETT are:
i. CALVIN CARTER[10] TRIPLETT[349], b. July 24, 1859, Lenoir County, North Carolina[349]; d. December 18, 1943[349].

More About CALVIN CARTER TRIPLETT:
Burial: Collier Methodist Cemetery, Caldwell County, North Carolina[349]

ii. SARAH JANE TRIPLETT[349], b. Abt. 1863[349].

216. ELIZABETH[9] LAND *(WILSON[8], WILLIAM THOMAS[7], JONATHAN[6], THOMAS[5], THOMAS[4], JOHN[3], CURTIS[2], CURTIS[1])*[349] was born Abt. 1845 in Wilkes County, North Carolina[349], and died January 1897 in Chico, Texas[349]. She married THOMAS C. MILLER[349], son of HENRY MILLER and NARCISSA LAND. He was born Abt. 1840 in Wilkes County, North Carolina[349], and died February 1907 in Wise County, Texas[349].

Children of ELIZABETH LAND and THOMAS MILLER are:
i. JUNIUS[10] MILLER[349], b. 1867[349]; d. Abt. 1927, Wise County, Texas[349].
ii. LAWRENCE MILLER[349], b. Abt. 1874[349].
iii. REBECCA ANN MILLER[349], b. Abt. 1877[349].
iv. EMMETT MILLER[349], b. Abt. 1884[349].

217. WILLIAM TAYLOR[9] LAND *(WILSON[8], WILLIAM THOMAS[7], JONATHAN[6], THOMAS[5], THOMAS[4], JOHN[3], CURTIS[2], CURTIS[1])*[349] was born Abt. 1848 in Wilkes County, North Carolina[349]. He married ELIZABETH A. UNKNOWN[349].

Children of WILLIAM LAND and ELIZABETH UNKNOWN are:
i. JAMES L.[10] LAND[349], b. Abt. 1867[349].
ii. PICKENS O. LAND[349], b. Abt. 1871[349].
iii. JASPER H. LAND[349], b. Abt. 1872[349].
iv. REBECCA G. LAND[349], b. Abt. 1874[349].
v. ELIZABETH LAND[349], b. Abt. 1876[349].
vi. CALVIN C. LAND[349], b. Abt. 1879[349].

218. THOMAS C.[9] MILLER *(NARCISSA[8] LAND, WILLIAM THOMAS[7], JONATHAN[6], THOMAS[5], THOMAS[4], JOHN[3], CURTIS[2], CURTIS[1])*[349] was born Abt. 1840 in Wilkes County, North Carolina[349], and died February 1907 in Wise County, Texas[349]. He married ELIZABETH LAND[349], daughter of WILSON LAND and REBECCA MILLER. She was born Abt. 1845 in Wilkes County, North Carolina[349], and died January 1897 in Chico, Texas[349].

Children are listed above under (216) Elizabeth Land.

219. WILLIAM THOMAS[9] LAND *(LINVILLE[8], WILLIAM THOMAS[7], JONATHAN[6], THOMAS[5], THOMAS[4], JOHN[3], CURTIS[2], CURTIS[1])*[349] was born April 17, 1857 in Wilkes County, North Carolina[349], and died March 11, 1928[349]. He married JANE SOPHENA DULA[349]. She was born June 07, 1860 in Wilkes County, North Carolina[349], and died May 08, 1926[349].

More About WILLIAM THOMAS LAND:
Burial: Elk County Cemetery[349]
Occupation: Shopkeeper/Gauger - Sparks Creek Distillery[349]

More About JANE SOPHENA DULA:
Burial: Elk County Cemetery[349]

Children of WILLIAM LAND and JANE DULA are:

i. AUGUSTA B.[10] LAND[349], b. March 1885[349]; d. 1910[349]; m. WILLIAM S. BENSON[349].

291. ii. THOMAS LINVILLE LAND, b. July 15, 1887, Wilkes County, North Carolina; d. January 11, 1979.

iii. LIZZIE MAE LAND[349], b. April 01, 1891[349]; d. 1920, Alexander County, North Carolina[349]; m. EDWARD LEONARD HIGHT[349].

iv. VENZUELLA LAND[349], b. November 05, 1893, Wilkes County, North Carolina[349]; d. 1942[349]; m. ODUS FINLEY ANNAS[349].

v. MOLLIE LAND[349], b. 1895, Wilkes County, North Carolina[349]; d. 1919, Robeson County, North Carolina[349]; m. J.M. KINLAW[349].

vi. MARTHA A. LAND[349], b. January 05, 1896, Wilkes County, North Carolina[349]; d. July 18, 1984[349]; m. WILLIARD WINFRED FERGUSON[349].

More About MARTHA A. LAND:
Burial: Zion Cemetery[349]

vii. VERA ALMA LAND[349], b. March 19, 1898[349]; d. 1921, Moore County, North Carolina[349]; m. G.E. DAVIDSON[349].

viii. FLORENCE LAND[349], b. January 01, 1902, Wilkes County, North Carolina[349]; d. June 07, 1931, Caldwell County, North Carolina[349]; m. JAMES BLAINE PEARSON[349].

220. SARAH A.[9] LAND *(LINVILLE[8], WILLIAM THOMAS[7], JONATHAN[6], THOMAS[5], THOMAS[4], JOHN[3], CURTIS[2], CURTIS[1])*[349] was born November 06, 1860[349], and died April 19, 1940[349]. She married JAMES JEFFERSON MARLEY[349].

More About SARAH A. LAND:
Burial: Mt Pleasant, Tennessee[349]

Children of SARAH LAND and JAMES MARLEY are:

i. LIVING[10] MARLEY[349].

ii. FRANCES MARLEY[349], b. December 19, 1880, Wilkes County, North Carolina[349]; d. February 08, 1944, Wilkes County, North Carolina[349].

More About FRANCES MARLEY:
Burial: New Hope Cemetery[349]

iii. ISABELL MARLEY[349], b. Abt. 1885[349].

iv. LOMAS J. MARLEY[349], b. Abt. 1888[349].

v. WILLIAM H. MARLEY[349], b. Abt. 1890[349].

vi. MINNIE MARLEY[349], b. Abt. 1893[349].

vii. JADEN MARLEY[349], b. Abt. 1895[349].

viii. MISTY MARLEY[349], b. Abt. 1898[349].

ix. BENJAMIN MARLEY[349], b. Abt. 1899[349].

221. ELLEN LOU[9] LAND *(LINVILLE[8], WILLIAM THOMAS[7], JONATHAN[6], THOMAS[5], THOMAS[4], JOHN[3], CURTIS[2], CURTIS[1])*[349] was born 1867 in Wilkes County, North Carolina[349], and died 1902[349]. She married DAVID RICHARD RECTOR[349].

Children of ELLEN LAND and DAVID RECTOR are:

i. FRANCES[10] RECTOR[349].

ii. BESSIE RECTOR[349], b. Abt. 1894[349].

iii. ROBERT RECTOR[349], b. Abt. 1896[349].

222. CATHERINE JANE[9] LAND *(JAMES CALVIN[8], WILLIAM THOMAS[7], JONATHAN[6], THOMAS[5], THOMAS[4], JOHN[3], CURTIS[2], CURTIS[1])*[349] was born June 06, 1868 in Hunting Creek, Wilkes County, North Carolina[349], and died October 20, 1943[349]. She married CHARLES CALVIN WRIGHT[349]. He was born August 14, 1862 in Hunting Creek, Wilkes County, North Carolina[349], and died 1933[349].

Children of CATHERINE LAND and CHARLES WRIGHT are:

i. LIVING[10] WRIGHT[349], m. EVELYN WILBURN[349]; b. 1914[349].

More About EVELYN WILBURN:
Burial: Edgewood Baptist Church[349]

ii. MARY DORIS WRIGHT[349], b. 1892[349]; d. 1913[349].
292. iii. JAMES THOMAS CARR WRIGHT, b. 1894; d. July 14, 1963, Perkinsville, North Carolina.
iv. DAVID RALPH WRIGHT[349], b. 1896[349]; d. 1966[349]; m. EULA BUMGARDNER[349]; b. 1898[349]; d. 1966[349].
v. CLYDE ROBERT WRIGHT[349], b. 1901[349]; d. 1978[349]; m. LIVING WOODRUFF[349].

223. THOMAS DAVID[9] LAND *(JAMES CALVIN[8], WILLIAM THOMAS[7], JONATHAN[6], THOMAS[5], THOMAS[4], JOHN[3], CURTIS[2], CURTIS[1])*[349] was born May 18, 1870 in Wilkes County, North Carolina[349], and died June 19, 1948 in Mt Pleasant, Tennessee[349]. He married MIRA SUZANNE ROBINETT[349] August 01, 1915[349]. She was born August 21, 1891 in Wilkes County, North Carolina[349], and died October 30, 1978 in Nashville, Tennessee[349].

More About THOMAS DAVID LAND:
Burial: Arlington Cemetery, Mt Pleasant, Tennessee[349]
Nickname: Dave[349]
Occupation: Farmer[349]

More About MIRA SUZANNE ROBINETT:
Burial: Arlington Cemetery, Mt Pleasant, Tennessee[349]
Nickname: Annie[349]
Occupation: Teacher[349]

Children of THOMAS LAND and MIRA ROBINETT are:
293. i. LIVING[10] LAND.
294. ii. LIVING LAND.
295. iii. LIVING LAND.
iv. CALVIN HENDERSON LAND[349], b. April 15, 1916, Stony Fork Creek, North Carolina[349]; d. July 22, 1944, England[349]; m. LIVING MITCHELL[349].
296. v. THOMAS MERIDETH LAND, b. January 28, 1918, Mt Pleasant, Tennessee; d. February 23, 1984, Fort Smith, Arkansas.

224. SALLY CAROLINE[9] LAND *(JAMES CALVIN[8], WILLIAM THOMAS[7], JONATHAN[6], THOMAS[5], THOMAS[4], JOHN[3], CURTIS[2], CURTIS[1])*[349] was born December 28, 1876[349], and died July 28, 1960[349]. She married JAMES CICERO PARSONS[349].

Children of SALLY LAND and JAMES PARSONS are:
i. MARY DORRIS[10] PARSONS[349].
ii. LIVING PARSONS[349].
iii. LIVING PARSONS[349].
iv. LIVING PARSONS[349].
v. LIVING PARSONS[349], m. LIVING RHYNE[349].

225. MARY ELIZABETH[9] LAND *(JAMES CALVIN[8], WILLIAM THOMAS[7], JONATHAN[6], THOMAS[5], THOMAS[4], JOHN[3], CURTIS[2], CURTIS[1])*[349] was born March 10, 1879[349]. She married ROMULUS ZEBULON ROBINETT[349] June 01, 1904[349]. He was born October 15, 1882[349], and died October 06, 1962[349].

Child of MARY LAND and ROMULUS ROBINETT is:
i. LIVING[10] ROBINETT[349].

226. WILLIAM LANGLEY[9] LAND *(THOMAS[8], JAMES[7], JONATHAN[6], THOMAS[5], THOMAS[4], JOHN[3], CURTIS[2], CURTIS[1])*[349] was born December 27, 1838[349]. He married LUCINDA HEDRLTRA CLEMMONS[349] February 22, 1874[349].

Children of WILLIAM LAND and LUCINDA CLEMMONS are:
297. i. SAMUEL[10] LAND, b. December 17, 1874.
ii. MARY ELLEN LAND[349], b. November 26, 1876[349]; m. LUTHER TEETERS[349].
iii. JESSE TILDEN LAND[349], b. January 15, 1879[349]; m. MARY CATHERINE SCOTT[349].
iv. EMMA JANE LAND[349], b. August 03, 1881[349]; m. JOHN AUSTIN[349].
v. WILLIAM RODRICK LAND[349], b. July 03, 1884[349]; m. GUSTAVE TEETERS[349].
vi. ALICA TABITHA LAND[349], b. January 31, 1887[349]; m. ROBERT HILLIS[349].

vii. GRACE LEANN LAND[349], b. July 20, 1889[349]; m. HENDERSON ELLIOTT[349].
viii. GEORGE WASHINGTON LAND[349], b. January 23, 1892[349]; m. MARY JANE WHITLOW[349].

227. SARAH[9] LAND *(JAMES[8], JAMES[7], JONATHAN[6], THOMAS[5], THOMAS[4], JOHN[3], CURTIS[2], CURTIS[1])* [349] was born Abt. 1842 in Wilkes County, North Carolina[349]. She married JORDON LIVINGSTON [350,351] Abt. 1861[351].

Jordon Livingston, a CSA Veteran in North Carolina's Bethel Regiment, was married to David's distant cousin, Sarah Land, daughter of James Land's son, James Land, Jr. (David's brother). Both James Junior and Sarah Livingston's younger brother, Jordon Livingston, were in the same regiment - and both were taken prisoner on 2 April 1865. Both eventually died in prison. It is believed that a Jonathan Livingston was Sarah's and Jordon's father. Their mother is not known at this time.

Child of SARAH LAND and JORDON LIVINGSTON is:
i. MARY JANE[10] LIVINGSTON[351], b. August 16, 1865, Caldwell County, North Carolina[351].

228. MARY[9] LAND *(JAMES[8], JAMES[7], JONATHAN[6], THOMAS[5], THOMAS[4], JOHN[3], CURTIS[2], CURTIS[1])* [351] was born July 21, 1849 in Alexander County, North Carolina[351], and died March 16, 1947 in Alexander County, North Carolina[351]. She married JACOB SIPE[351] February 25, 1877[351].

More About MARY LAND:
Burial: Three Forks Cemetery[351]

Child of MARY LAND and JACOB SIPE is:
i. JAMES OSCAR[10] SIPE[351], b. Abt. 1878[351].

229. JAMES ELI[9] LAND *(JAMES[8], JAMES[7], JONATHAN[6], THOMAS[5], THOMAS[4], JOHN[3], CURTIS[2], CURTIS[1])* [351] was born June 17, 1851 in Wilkes County, North Carolina[351], and died April 20, 1933 in Alexander County, North Carolina[351]. He married ELIZABETH FORTNER[351] Abt. 1870[351].

More About JAMES ELI LAND:
Burial: Three Forks Cemetery[351]

Children of JAMES LAND and ELIZABETH FORTNER are:
i. JAMES WILLIAM[10] LAND[351], b. Abt. 1872[351].
298. ii. AARON CARTER LAND, b. February 07, 1874; d. July 18, 1945, Alexander County, North Carolina.
299. iii. JUDITH ROSELLEN LAND, b. August 19, 1876; d. May 22, 1956, Alexander County, North Carolina.
iv. SARAH ELMIRA LAND[351], b. Abt. 1879[351].
300. v. BRYSON HENDERSON LAND, b. Abt. 1882.

230. NOAH[9] LAND *(JAMES[8], JAMES[7], JONATHAN[6], THOMAS[5], THOMAS[4], JOHN[3], CURTIS[2], CURTIS[1])* [351] was born Abt. 1852 in Alexander County, North Carolina[351], and died Aft. 1920 in Alexander County, North Carolina[351]. He married LAURA KING[351] September 18, 1888[351].

Children of NOAH LAND and LAURA KING are:
i. JAMES W.[10] LAND[351], b. Abt. 1888[351].
301. ii. MARY JANE LAND, b. August 25, 1892, Alexander County, North Carolina; d. November 18, 1945, Alexander County, North Carolina.
302. iii. ROBERT LEE LAND, b. September 18, 1893, Alexander County, North Carolina; d. July 02, 1967, Caldwell County, North Carolina.
303. iv. GEORGE WASHINGTON LAND, b. September 11, 1894, Alexander County, North Carolina; d. April 18, 1959, Caldwell County, North Carolina.
v. JONATHAN LAND[351], b. Abt. 1899[351].
vi. ELIZABETH LAND[351], b. Abt. 1901, Alexander County, North Carolina[351]; d. Alexander County, North Carolina[351].

More About ELIZABETH LAND:
Burial: Three Forks Cemetery[351]

231. DAVID V.[9] LAND *(NIMROD[8], JAMES[7], JONATHAN[6], THOMAS[5], THOMAS[4], JOHN[3], CURTIS[2], CURTIS[1])*[351] was born Abt. 1854[351]. He married MARY A. LANEY[351].

Children of DAVID LAND and MARY LANEY are:

i. EULA MATTIE[10] LAND[351], b. April 25, 1889[351].
ii. WILLIAM ROBERT LAND[351], b. May 22, 1893[351].

232. DEWANNA W.[9] LAND *(NIMROD[8], JAMES[7], JONATHAN[6], THOMAS[5], THOMAS[4], JOHN[3], CURTIS[2], CURTIS[1])*[351] was born September 22, 1856 in Alexander County, North Carolina[351], and died February 12, 1939[351]. She married M.D. JOHN MCLEOD OXFORD[351] September 25, 1873[351]. He was born July 15, 1841 in Caldwell County, North Carolina[351], and died September 16, 1928 in Alexander County, North Carolina[351].

More About DEWANNA W. LAND:
Burial: February 1939, Three Forks Baptist Church, Taylorsville, Alexander County, North Carolina[351]

Children of DEWANNA LAND and JOHN OXFORD are:

i. MARY LOU[10] OXFORD[351], b. June 24, 1874[351]; d. October 11, 1878[351].
ii. MINNIE DORA OXFORD[351], b. November 27, 1877[351]; d. February 28, 1965[351].

More About MINNIE DORA OXFORD:
Burial: February 1965, Three Forks Baptist Church, Taylorsville, Alexander County, North Carolina[351]

iii. LINNIE BELL OXFORD[351], b. November 27, 1877[351]; d. August 07, 1942[351].
iv. JENNER ARGUILE OXFORD[351], b. March 17, 1880[351]; d. July 15, 1970[351].
v. FREDDIE ROSTON OXFORD[351], b. April 28, 1885[351]; d. June 19, 1886[351].

More About FREDDIE ROSTON OXFORD:
Burial: Land Cemetery, Alexander County, North Carolina[351]

233. JAMES LINVILLE[9] LAND *(DAVID[8], JAMES[7], JONATHAN[6], THOMAS[5], THOMAS[4], JOHN[3], CURTIS[2], CURTIS[1])*[351] was born 1849 in Lenoir, North Carolina[351], and died 1929[351]. He married CYNTHIA ELIZABETH COX[351]. She was born 1849 in Washington County, Tennessee[351], and died 1930[351].

Notes for JAMES LINVILLE LAND:
THE LANDS IN THE 1850 CENSUS :
In the 1850 census of Wilkes County, N.C. recorded Oct.31.1850, the children of my great-great-great grandfather, James Linville Land are listed and living within " shoutin distance " of one another. Household # 1812 HASTING LAND 42, DELILAH 43, WILLIAM 14, ELIAS 11, LUCY 8, JAMES 6. Household # 1813 JAMES (LINVILLE JR.) LAND 36, JANE 28, SARAH 8, MARY 6, JOHN 4, NIMROD 3. Household # 1814 NIMROD LAND 29, EDEY (my gr,gr,gr,grandmother, Edith Livingston Land) 65, MILLIE BARLOW 19. Household # 1815 DAVID LAND (my gr,gr,grandfather) 25 Rebecca 25. Their first child, a son, also named James Linville (my great-grandfather) would be born the following February. Household # 1817 was the family of their uncle, Jonathan Land Jr. The daughters of James Linville & Edith Livingston Land were : MAHALA, born abt 1807 married REUBIN KNIGHT. MALINDA born abt 1809, married JAMES HOLESCLAW. MILLIE born abt 1811 married HARVIN MOONEY. CYNTHIA born abt 1817 married THOMAS MALTBA (Y). Another brother, THOMAS J. LAND born abt 1809 died in 1841 shortly after moving his family to Marion (later Sequatchie) County, Tennessee. (see related page on the Civil War experience of his sons William and Jesse Land and their brother-in-law, Pearl Wimberly.)
THE HASTING LAND FAMILY came to my " neck of the woods " in upper East Tennessee in the mid-1850's. They may have been on their way farther south to " kin " in Monroe or Sequatchie Counties. Like his brother Thomas, Hasting apparently died shortly after coming to Tennessee. I've not found any information on his older sons, William and Elias but have been able to glean some nuggets of info on their youngest son, JAMES JEFFERSON LAND and his sister, LUCY along with their mother DELILA. James is counted in the 1860 census of Greene County, Tennessee as member of a household by the name of HAYS and occupation " farmhand." while Lucy is listed in Greene County as a member of a ARMSTRONG household occupation " domestic " On a lighter side, the head of the Armstrong family born in 1800 is actually named LANTZ ARMSTRONG !!!! Greene County Tennessee by the way, is the home of future President Andrew Johnson. James served as a Confederate soldier in the

Civil War in Co .D 63rd Tenn Inf. In 1905 a destitute and disabled James applied for and received a Confederate pension from the State of Tennessee. The examining doctor saying, " He leans heavily on his staff, cannot dress or care for himself without assistance, the old soldier deserves a pension." James states in his pension he was " born in Wilkes County, North Carolina in 1844." and " came to Tennessee with his parents when he was 10 years old." His Confederate service is as follows :

Son of Hasting (oldest brother of my gr,gr,grandfather) & Delila Land. Born in Wilkes County, North Carolina abt.1844. Enlisted, Jonesboro,Tenn. (oldest town in Tennessee) May 13,1862. Mustered at Knoxville, age 18,May 22,1862. March-April 1863 ' sick in Camp ' (Strawbery Plains, Tenn.)' present ' till Aug.22,1863 ' sent to hospital in Knoxville by order of company surgeon ' ' present ' Jan-Feb 1864 till ' absent AWOL since Oct 20,1864. Returned and paid $ 100.00 bounty ' Nov.-Dec.1864. Name appears on the roll of prisoners of war belonging to the Army of Northern Virginia who have this day (April 9,1865) been surrendered by Gen Robert E. Lee C.S.A. commanding said army to Gen.U.S. Grant commanding armies of the U.S. Dated April 11,1865 Hd.Qrs .McComb's Brigade. James was one of only 28 enlisted men remaining of the 63rd that surrendered at Appomattox. One of only 7 of Company D. Later occupation : Brakeman on the railroad in East Tenn. Died 1914 in Knox County,Tenn. James was a nephew of my g,g,grandfather, David Land (Co.I, 13th N.C. Inf.)

James and his family in the 1880 census of Greene County, Tenn : James J. LAND Self M Male W 36 NC Brakeman On R. R. NC NC Susan LAND Wife M Female W 37 TN Keeping House TN NC Minnie LAND Dau S Female W 9 TN NC TN Addie LAND Dau S Female W 7 TN NC TN Thomas LAND Son S Male W 5 TN NC TN This family was not with James in 1905. He speaks of only a " wife and 14 year-old daughter " James' second wife, BIRDIE J. KNIGHT of North Carolina. She drew a Confederate widow's pension from the State of Tennessee.

About 1875 Lucy C. Land became the 2nd wife of James Hagan Morrow (1837 - 1902) of Washington County, Tennessee. The Morrows came to Tennessee from South Carolina. James served as a Confederate Soldier in the Civil War until being discharged before war's end for health reasons. James served as a Private in Co. B of the " Fightin " 19th Tenn Inf. Ironically several ancestor / relatives on the maternal side of my family tree in Tennessee, including my great-great-grandfather, served in this same company and regiment. James' brother, John became 2nd.Lt. of Co. B while brother, Benjamin served as sergeant of Co. K 60th Tennessee. In the 1880 census of Washington County, Tennessee 75 year-old DELILA LAND is numbered as a member of her son-in-law's household : VENA age 4,is a daughter of James and Lucy. Her brothers, born later, were ALEXANDER born 29 May,1882 and JAMES FRANKLIN born 6 July, 1884.

James H. MORROW Self M Male W 42 SC Farming SC NC Lucy C. MORROW Wife M Female W 37 NC Keeping House NC NC John MORROW Son S Male W 13 TN Farming SC NC Drury MORROW Son S Male W 11 TN Farming SC NC Sarah A. MORROW Dau S Female W 9 TN SC NC Vena MORROW Dau S Female W 4 TN SC NC Delila LAND MotherL W Female W 75 NC NC NC Frank RUPE Other S Male W 27 TN Laborer TN TN

Our Ancestor / Relatives and Dan'l Boone The following comes from Howard Douglass (Doug) Land of Stafford, Virginia. Doug is a great-grandson of Thomas Clingman Land, youngest brother of my great- grandfather, James Linville Land. The research is courtesy his friend, Lynn Huber : Dear Doug, The will of a Benjamin Howard - Wilkes County Will Book 4. pp. 119, dated November 1828, shows this Benjamin Howard to be the father of Discretion Howard, wife of Thomas Isbell. He's also the father of a Cornelius Howard.. It's stated on the net that a Cornelius Howard is reported in the Draper Manuscripts as married to Mary Bryan, sister of Rebecca Bryan Boone. It's also stated on the net that the 1768 Rowan County Tax List shows a Cornelius Howard in the tax company of Morgan Bryan Jr., an uncle of Rebecca Bryan Boone. If so, Daniel Boone, in visiting with Benjamin Howard, was possibly visiting with the family of his wife's brother-in-law, who was also a brother-in-law to your Thomas Isbell. He was married to Cornelius and Mary Bryan Howard's sister/sister-in-law, Discretion Howard Isbell I would guess the name Daniel Boone probably came into the Land and Oxford families through their connection to the Isbells. The Isbells were apparently closely related to the family of Daniel Boone through marriage, and also closely involved with the Boones. John Preston Arthur wrote A History of North Carolina in 1914. In Chapter IV, he said: Daniel Boone, circa 1767, moved 65 miles west of Dutchman's Creek, in the Yadkin Settlement, where he'd been living, to just above the mouth of Beaver Creek on the upper Yadkin River. Daniel Boones's cabin there was in a small horseshoe shaped swamp and canebreak, surrounding the point of a ridge, and with the ridge projecting into the swamp and canebreak. Colonel James Isbell said Daniel Boone lived 6 miles below present (1909-1914) home of James Isbell, on Beaver Creek, 1 mile from where it flows into the Yadkin, near Holman's Ford.. Colonel Isbell also reported Daniel Boone often stayed with Benjamin Howard, at the mouth of Elk Creek, near Elksville. Benjamin Howard is the man who ranged cattle in the mountains near the village of Boone. The Howards are related

to the Isbells. One of Colonel Isbell's grandmother's was a Howard - I believe, but am not 100% certain, the daughter of this Benjamin Howard. In 1914, Alfred Foster owned the land where Boone's cabin had been located. In 1914, there were people in Lenoir descended from Daniel Boone, and others there descended from a brother of his who'd also lived in the area. The earliest Daniel Boone Oxford I found was one born in 1869. He was a brother of your ancestress, Sarah Etta Oxford, wife of Thomas Clingman Land, and so a son of Adam Barnes Oxford.
My great-grandfather, James Linville Land (named for his grandfather) was David and Rebecca Knight Land's first child. James was born in Wilkes County, N.C. Feb 1851 and died in Johnson City, (Washington County) Tenn Feb 1929. James was just past 10 yrs old at the outbreak of the Civil War in April 1861. He may have seen his father, David leave for the Rebel Army and the front lines in Virginia on his 13th birthday Feb.1864. All the old photos of Linville as he was known, show a hardened exterior and a grim and determined face. He would have been the " man of the house " in David's absence. Western North Carolina, Southwest Virginia, Eastern Kentucky, and East Tennessee were DANGEROUS places during the " late unpleasantness." Some nuggets I was able to glean over the years from older distant cousins and my aunts Louise and Clara who remembered him : He was very strict on the granddaughters in the family who were " scared to death of him " but let the grandsons " get by with murder. " My uncle Howard and his cousins Fred Land and Jess Shipley said their grandpa was a " pack rat, never threw away anything. " The only way they could make him mad was to " bother his pile of junk in the barn." "Once, he let some of the grandsons take an old " hog killin rifle " to the woods where they spent the day playing cowboy and army and pointing the thing at one another and yelling BANG YOUR DEAD. " At the end of the day their grandmaw Land discovered the old gun ACTUALLY HAD A SHELL IN IT !!!!! Linville got a lecture from the only one who could (and would) talk back to him. Needless to say guardian angels worked overtime that day. The old homeplace near " Haws Crossroads " still stands and is occupied by renters. Linville was known to neighbors as " the old bear hunter." was a " rock-ribbed southern conservative democrat " had no use for northerners, black folk, and republicans. He was a great fan of the legendary boxer Jack Dempsey. The photo shown was taken before August 25,1926 because my grandfather, George Land Sr. is included with his siblings. George, born on June 11,1892, the baby in the family. He was electrocuted on the job in Johnson City, Tennessee. The following brief article appeared in the city newspaper :
George Land Sr 30,employed here by the Tennessee Eastern Electric Co. as assistant master mechanic was instantly killed about 8 am at the company's plant when his head came in contact with a live wire while he was working under a trolley car.
George was married abt 1914 to my grandmother, Annie Blakely. Their children were LOUISE born April 12,1915. died July 23,1990. CLARA born Aug 10,1917 died Nov 30,1995. HOWARD born April 16,1920 was a twice wounded G.I. in the European theatre of World War Two. Receiving his 2nd wound during the " Battle of the Bulge " He died in March of 1984. GEORGE JR. born Nov.2,1926 after the death of his father. George was my Dad. He passed away Nov 24, 1991.

Children of JAMES LAND and CYNTHIA COX are:

i. AMANDA SERILDA[10] LAND[351], b. 1874[351]; d. 1965[351]; m. JESSE STATIN[351].
ii. SARAH REBECCA LAND[351], b. 1876[351]; d. 1953[351]; m. MELVIN WHITAKER[351].
iii. JOHN DAVID LAND[351], b. 1878[351]; d. 1953, Missouri[351]; m. LAURA BARTON[351].
iv. THOMAS LAND[351], b. 1880[351] d. 1959[351]; m. LEIRA HALE[351].
v. ELIZABETH LAND[351], b. 1883[351]; d. 1961[351]; m. LIBON SHIPLEY[351].
vi. IDA LAND[351], b. 1885[351]; d. 1974[351]; m. OSCAR WHITLOCK[351].
304. vii. CHARLES CLEVELAND LAND, b. November 1887; d. 1961.
viii. ROY C. LAND[351], b. August 1890[351]; d. 1963[351]; m. MAUD SNODGRASS[351].
305. ix. SR. GEORGE EDWARD LAND, b. June 1892; d. April 1926.
x. JOHN LAND, b. 1894.
xi. REBECCA LAND, b. 1896; m. MELVIN WHITAKER[351].

234. ELI JASON[9] LAND *(DAVID[8], JAMES[7], JONATHAN[6], THOMAS[5], THOMAS[4], JOHN[3], CURTIS[2], CURTIS[1])*[351] was born May 14, 1852 in Wilkes County, North Carolina[351], and died July 19, 1940 in Wilkes County, North Carolina[351]. He married CLARISSA SERALDA ANDREWS[351].

More About ELI JASON LAND:
Burial: Little Rock Church Cemetery[351]

Children of ELI LAND and CLARISSA ANDREWS are:

306. i. THOMAS WILLIAM[10] LAND, b. September 24, 1880, Wilkes County, North Carolina; d. January 26, 1960, Wilkes County, North Carolina.
307. ii. DAVID LAND, b. August 04, 1885, Wilkes County, North Carolina; d. June 11, 1949, Wilkes County, North Carolina.
308. iii. PARTEE VANCE LAND, b. February 14, 1888, Caldwell County, North Carolina; d. June 02, 1968, Wilkes County, North Carolina.
309. iv. JAMES EDGAR LAND, b. May 24, 1889, Caldwell County, North Carolina; d. May 06, 1965, Wilkes County, North Carolina.
310. v. FRED COLUMBUS LAND, b. August 12, 1892, Caldwell County, North Carolina; d. February 23, 1970, Catawba County, North Carolina.
vi. ROBY CRISP LAND[351], b. March 11, 1896, Caldwell County, North Carolina[351]; d. March 18, 1959, Catawba County, North Carolina[351]; m. LIVING BRITTAIN[351].

More About ROBY CRISP LAND:
Burial: Fairview Cemetery[351]

vii. NORA LAND[351], b. Abt. 1897, Caldwell County, North Carolina[351]; m. RAY HARRIS[351].
viii. CORA LAND[351], b. Abt. 1899, Caldwell County, North Carolina[351]; m. GAITHER BESHEARS[351].

235. ELIZABETH[9] LAND *(DAVID[8], JAMES[7], JONATHAN[6], THOMAS[5], THOMAS[4], JOHN[3], CURTIS[2], CURTIS[1])*[351] was born April 07, 1854 in Caldwell County, North Carolina[351], and died November 23, 1942 in Mineral, Virginia[351]. She married THOMAS ALVAANDREWS[351] January 21, 1875[351].

Children of ELIZABETH LAND and THOMAS ANDREWS are:
i. REBECCA ANN[10] ANDREWS[351], b. March 02, 1876, Caldwell County, North Carolina[351].
ii. SARAH E. ANDREWS[351], b. November 29, 1877, Caldwell County, North Carolina[351]; d. June 15, 1963, Caldwell County, North Carolina[351].
iii. JANE B. ANDREWS[351], b. November 26, 1881, Caldwell County, North Carolina[351]; d. October 31, 1885, Caldwell County, North Carolina[351].
iv. COLUMBUS ANDREWS[351], b. October 17, 1885, Caldwell County, North Carolina[351].
v. MCGRUDER ANDREWS[351], b. October 20, 1887, Caldwell County, North Carolina[351]; d. April 1903, Caldwell County, North Carolina[351].
vi. ESTELLE PEARL ANDREWS[351], b. March 09, 1894, Caldwell County, North Carolina[351]; d. December 20, 1894, Caldwell County, North Carolina[351].
vii. THOMAS CARL ANDREWS[351], b. June 23, 1896, Caldwell County, North Carolina[351].

236. MARY SERELDA[9] LAND *(DAVID[8], JAMES[7], JONATHAN[6], THOMAS[5], THOMAS[4], JOHN[3], CURTIS[2], CURTIS[1])*[351] was born February 22, 1856 in Caldwell County, North Carolina[351], and died November 06, 1941 in Alexander County, North Carolina[351]. She married WALTER S. BRADBURN[351].

More About MARY SERELDA LAND:
Burial: Antioch Baptist Cemetery[351]

Children of MARY LAND and WALTER BRADBURN are:
i. AMANDA[10] BRADBURN[351], b. Abt. 1884[351]; m. MARLONE WALKER[351].
ii. MARJORIE JOSIE BRADBURN[351], b. December 02, 1888, Dover Baptist Church Cemetery[351]; d. February 11, 1918[351].

237. CYNTHIA ELLEN[9] LAND *(DAVID[8], JAMES[7], JONATHAN[6], THOMAS[5], THOMAS[4], JOHN[3], CURTIS[2], CURTIS[1])*[351] was born March 07, 1858[351], and died December 05, 1936[351]. She married JEFFERSON D. BRADBURN[351] February 12, 1880[351].

Children of CYNTHIA LAND and JEFFERSON BRADBURN are:
i. ELIZABETH[10] BRADBURN[351], b. October 19, 1882, Alexander County, North Carolina[351]; d. October 22, 1969, Catawba County, North Carolina[351]; m. CHARLES KNOX SIPES[351].
ii. SARAH BRADBURN[351], b. Abt. 1884[351].
iii. ETTA BRADBURN[351], b. Abt. 1885[351].
iv. GERTRUDE BRADBURN[351], b. Abt. 1889[351].

238. THOMAS CLINGMAN[9] LAND *(DAVID[8], JAMES[7], JONATHAN[6], THOMAS[5], THOMAS[4], JOHN[3], CURTIS[2], CURTIS[1])* [351]was born January 25, 1860 in Wilkes County, North Carolina[351], and died January 11, 1939[351]. He married (1) MARY CAROLYN KERLEY[351]. She was born August 09, 1840[351], and died November 15, 1908[351]. He married (2) SARAH ETTA "SALLIE" OXFORD[351] 1889 [351], daughter of MARY CAROLYN KERLEY. She was born March 02, 1872 in Alexander County, North Carolina[351], and died February 17, 1960 in Caldwell County, North Carolina[351].

Notes for THOMAS CLINGMAN LAND:
David and Rebecca's youngest son was THOMAS CLINGMAN LAND (1860 - 1939) Thomas carried on the " tradition " by being the son named Thomas in David`s line. ( going back to David`s great-grandfather Thomas in the first U.S. census in 1790.) There is also a part of " Grandfather Mountain," located in our native Western North Carolina known as " Clingman`s Dome." There was also a Confederate General and popular politician following the Civil War from that part of North Carolina named Thomas Clingman. David Land may have held him in high regard enough to name a son for him. Tom was very tall and strong, as were many of David Land's kinfolk. another of David's sons, Eli Jason Land was at least 7 feet tall. They had to make him a special casket when he died in 1942. Tom was married to Sarah Oxford, a lady of short stature. She was a daughter of Adam Barnes Oxford and Mary Caroline Kerley. Mary was actually Adam`s 2nd wife. His first wife was : Marriage 1 Barbara MCLEOD b: 14 FEB 1806 in NC Married: 05 JAN 1830 in Burke Co, NC. Sons born to this marriage and Confederate Service for Adam`s oldest sons and Sallie`s half brothers : Hugh A. Oxford Alexander County NC; a 30 year-old Teacher. Enlisted on 7/11/1861 at Alexander County, NC as a PriVAte. On 7/11/1861 he mustered into 'K" Co. NC 7th Infantry He was Killed on 5/3/1863 at Chancellorsville, VA Promotions: * Sergt 8/12/1862 Other Information: born in Lincoln County, NC (Buried with four other soldiers in one trench on the Chancellorsville, VA battlefield.) James Henry Oxford Residence Alexander County NC; a 27 year-old Farmer. Enlisted on 8/16/1862 at Alexander County, NC as a Private. On 8/16/1862 he mustered into "E" Co. NC 58th P. Rangers Infantry (date and method of discharge not given) He was listed as: * On rolls 4/30/1864 (place not stated) * POW 6/22/1864 Kolb`s Farm, GA * Confined 6/25/1864 Nashville, TN * Transferred 7/14/1864 Louisville, KY * Transferred 7/16/1864 Camp Douglas, IL * Oath Allegiance 6/16/1865 Camp Douglas, IL (Released) John M. Oxford Residence was not listed; 20 years old. Enlisted on 8/16/1862 at Alexander County, NC as a Private. On 8/16/1862 he mustered into "E" Co. NC 58th P. Rangers Infantry (date and method of discharge not given) (No further record) He was listed as: * 10/15/1862 Johnson`s Station, TN (Estimated day, bitten by rattlesnake William C. Oxford Residence was not listed; a 33 year-old Farmer. Enlisted on 7/5/1862 at Caldwell County, NC as a Private. On 7/2/1862 he mustered into "E" Co. NC 58th P. Rangers Infantry (date and method of discharge not given) He was listed as: * On rolls 4/30/1864 (place not stated) * Wounded 5/14/1864 Resaca, GA (Wounded in jaw) * Returned 9/1/1864 (place not stated) (No further record) Other Information: born in Caldwell County, NC.

More About THOMAS CLINGMAN LAND:
Burial: Lower Creek Baptist Church Cemetery[351]

More About SARAH ETTA "SALLIE" OXFORD:
Burial: Land Family Cemetery, Lower Creek Baptist Church[351]

Children of THOMAS LAND and SARAH OXFORD are:

i. PEARL[10] LAND[351], d. Deceased[351]; m. HEDRICK[351].

311. ii. LIVING LAND.

312. iii. HAYDEN JAMES LAND, b. 1885, Wilkes County, North Carolina; d. 1968, Dallas, Texas.

iv. DEWEY LAND[351], b. May 15, 1890, Caldwell County, North Carolina[351]; d. January 09, 1919, Lower Creek, North Carolina[351].

More About DEWEY LAND:
Burial: Lower Creek Baptist Church Cemetery[351]

v. ROSS VANCE LAND[351], b. February 06, 1891[351]; d. December 25, 1969[351]; m. NOLA HENDRICK[351]; b. August 16, 1896[351]; d. September 08, 1966[351].

More About ROSS VANCE LAND:
Occupation: Broyhill Industries in Lenoir; Occupation: Furniture Designer[351]

313. vi. SR. FRED LAND, b. May 28, 1891, Caldwell County, North Carolina; d. December 07, 1967, Caldwell County, North Carolina.

314. vii. RALPH CALDWELL LAND, b. March 02, 1895, Caldwell County, North Carolina; d. March 29, 1982, Lenoir, North Carolina.

viii. MARY LEE LAND[351], b. April 04, 1905[351]; d. March 07, 1921[351].

More About MARY LEE LAND:
Burial: Lower Creek Baptist Church Cemetery[351]

315. ix. VERA LAND, b. May 01, 1908, Wilkes County, North Carolina; d. February 21, 1993, Catawba County, North Carolina.

239. HANNAH NINABELLE[9] LAND *(DAVID[8], JAMES[7], JONATHAN[6], THOMAS[5], THOMAS[4], JOHN[3], CURTIS[2], CURTIS[1])* [351] was born May 23, 1878 in Alexander County, North Carolina[351], and died April 21, 1965 in Caldwell County, North Carolina[351]. She married WILLIAM CORNELIUS CRISP[351] December 20, 1902[351].

More About HANNAH NINABELLE LAND:
Burial: William Corneilus Crisp Cemetery[351]

Children of HANNAH LAND and WILLIAM CRISP are:

i. LIVING[10] CRISP[351].

ii. FAYE LAND CRISP, b. October 29, 1903.

240. JOHN WESLEY[9] LAND *(ALLISON[8], JAMES NOAH[7], THOMAS[6], THOMAS[5], THOMAS[4], JOHN[3], CURTIS[2], CURTIS[1])* [351] was born October 21, 1875 in Monroe County, Tennessee[351], and died August 31, 1959 in Englewood, McMinn County, Tennessee[351]. He married MARY ANN TORBETT[351] July 29, 1900[351]. She was born November 08, 1882 in Monroe County, Tennessee[351], and died July 04, 1973 in Englewood, McMinn County, Tennessee[351].

More About JOHN WESLEY LAND:
Burial: Notchy Creek Cemetery, Monroe County, TN[351]

More About MARY ANN TORBETT:
Burial: Eleazor Cemetery, Monroe County, Tennessee[351]

Children of JOHN LAND and MARY TORBETT are:

i. LIVING[10] LAND[351].

ii. LIVING LAND[351].

iii. LIVING LAND[351].

iv. MINNIE BELLE LAND[351], b. August 05, 1901[351]; d. August 08, 1924[351].

316. v. ELLA MAE LAND, b. October 09, 1903, Monroe County, Tennessee; d. February 03, 1992, Blount County, Tennessee.

vi. GUSSIE JANE LAND[351], b. January 20, 1909, Monroe County, Tennessee[351]; d. August 30, 1999, Englewood, McMinn County, Tennessee[351].

317. vii. GRACIE ALICE LAND, b. March 16, 1911, Monroe County, Tennessee; d. November 10, 2001, Maryville, Tennessee.

viii. MAGGIE EDNA LAND[351], b. May 05, 1913, Monroe County, Tennessee[351]; d. June 12, 2001, McMinn County, Tennessee[351].

ix. CLARENCE RAMON LAND[351], b. April 21, 1917, Monroe County, Tennessee[351]; d. October 1982, Monroe County, Tennessee[351].

x. FRANCES LOUISE LAND[351], b. June 01, 1921, Monroe County, Tennessee[351]; d. June 18, 1995, McMinn County, Tennessee[351].

xi. FRANK HENRY LAND[351], b. June 01, 1921, Monroe County, Tennessee[351]; d. June 09, 2001, Prineville, Crook County, Oregon[351].

xii. ALFRED HOMER LAND[351], b. March 13, 1923[351]; d. 1927[351].

xiii. JOHNNY ROSS LAND[351], b. September 09, 1925, Monroe County, Tennessee[351]; d. October 01, 1933, McMinn County, Tennessee[351].

241. LIVING[9] LAND *(RAYMOND TIMOTHY[8], WILLIAM JEFFERSON[7], JOHN HENRY[6], CHARLES[5], CHARLES[4], CURTIS[3], CURTIS[2], CURTIS[1])*[352]. She married DANIEL SCOTT FARTHING[352,353]. He was born November 04, 1921[354,355], and died November 24, 1975 in Dickson, Tn.[356,357].

Children of LIVING LAND and DANIEL FARTHING are:
318. i. LIVING[10] FARTHING.
ii. LIVING FARTHING[358].
iii. LIVING FARTHING[358].
iv. LIVING FARTHING[358].

242. LIVING[9] LAND *(RAYMOND TIMOTHY[8], WILLIAM JEFFERSON[7], JOHN HENRY[6], CHARLES[5], CHARLES[4], CURTIS[3], CURTIS[2], CURTIS[1])*[359]. She married DANIEL SCOTT FARTHING[360,361]. He was born November 04, 1921[362,363], and died November 24, 1975 in Dickson, Tn.[364,365].

Children of LIVING LAND and DANIEL FARTHING are:
319. i. LIVING[10] FARTHING.
ii. LIVING FARTHING[365].
iii. LIVING FARTHING[365].
iv. LIVING FARTHING[365].

243. LIVING[9] LAND *(RAYMOND TIMOTHY[8], WILLIAM JEFFERSON[7], JOHN HENRY[6], CHARLES[5], CHARLES[4], CURTIS[3], CURTIS[2], CURTIS[1])*[365]. He married LIVING PATTERSON[366].

Children of LIVING LAND and LIVING PATTERSON are:
320. i. LIVING[10] LAND.
321. ii. LIVING LAND.
322. iii. LIVING LAND.
323. iv. LIVING LAND.

244. JAMES L.[9] RUFFIN *(MARY[8] HARGROVE, SAMUEL HENRY[7], SALLY[6] LAND, LITTLEBERRY[5], BIRD[4], CURTIS[3], CURTIS[2], CURTIS[1])*[367] was born June 1874 in Edgecombe Co. NC[367]. He married LOUISA L. UNKNOWN[367]. She was born November 1879 in Edgecombe Co. NC[367].

Child of JAMES RUFFIN and LOUISA UNKNOWN is:
i. ROBERT G.[10] RUFFIN[367], b. October 1898, Edgecombe Co. NC[367].

245. MAE KRIDER[9] HARGROVE *(ROBERT HENRY[8], GRAY LEMON[7], SALLY[6] LAND, LITTLEBERRY[5], BIRD[4], CURTIS[3], CURTIS[2], CURTIS[1])*[367] was born February 16, 1912[367]. She married JR. HENRY H. POPE[367] April 04, 1945. He was born December 23, 1911[367].

Children of MAE HARGROVE and HENRY POPE are:
324. i. LIVING[10] POPE.
ii. III LIVING POPE.
iii. LIVING POPE.
325. iv. LIVING POPE.
v. III LIVING POPE[367].
vi. LIVING POPE[367].

246. WALTER CLARK[9] HARGROVE *(JOHN DAVID[8], GRAY LEMON[7], SALLY[6] LAND, LITTLEBERRY[5], BIRD[4], CURTIS[3], CURTIS[2], CURTIS[1])*[367] was born February 11, 1891 in Edgecombe Co. NC[367], and died July 15, 1960 in Tarboro, NC[367]. He married (1) HELEN MARIE EDWARDS[367] June 24, 1916, daughter of WILLIAM EDWARDS and SALLIE HARGROVE. She was born July 1894 in Spring Hope, NC[367], and died 1942 in Edgecombe Co. NC[367]. He married (2) SARAH PARKER BARHAM[367] 1952. She was born June 14, 1910 in Norfolk, VA[367].

Notes for WALTER CLARK HARGROVE:
The following was a newspaper article from The Rocky Mount, N.C. Telegram, Sunday December 13, 1959.:
During a public ceremony last Wednesday, the head of the NC Medical Care Commission handed Walter Clark Hargrove a license to operate Edgecombe General Hospital.

The document, giving official permission to open the first county-owned hospital in Edgecombe's history, was a milestone for Hargrove and the people of the county.
As chairman of the Board of Commissioner for 23 years , he has had a strong role in shaping the county's future. As head of government, he has, in turn, seen advancements and setbacks. He regards the new hospital as a definite advancement.
Soon, the new medical center will be regarded as just another working part that makes Edgecombe a functioning unit. Hargrove and the commissioners will be busy with other problems which in their time and place, will be just as necessary as the hospital. With the voters' permission and they have never turned him down, Walter Hargrove will serve five more years. Before he steps down he wants to see a new headquarter for the county. First it was a county nursing home, then a hospital and now a courthouse.
Walter Hargrove has spent all of his 68 years in Edgecombe County. He has held public office of one kind or another for 26 years. He has seen the county break its shell of aristocracy, at least to a degree, and emerge as a working unit. Though he owns and sees to the farming of 1500 acres, the chairman feels the need for diversification. There is no answer to the farmer's dilemma, he says, as long as there are too many farmers producing more and more each year.
He was born at a crossroads called Logsboro in the north of the county. He attended Wilkinson Academy, that once stood on Tarboro' s Common. He also studied at Massey Business College in Richmond, VA. He worked first for the Pinetops Bank for a year and a half. He spent seven years as an Eastern Carolina Railroad conductor, and another stretch as a yardmaster for the Atlantic Coast Line.
In 1916, he married Helen Edwards, of Spring Hope. She gave him two children, Walter Jr. and a daughter who is now Mrs . Herbert Bailey (Sally Gray Hargrove), before her death in 1942.
In 1919, he began a small mercantile house in Tarboro. During WW II, he opened a hardware store here, but both businesses have been discontinued.
Editorial from The Rocky Mount, N.C. Telegram, Tues, July 26, 1960:
Leadership is Eternal
Last week, Edgecombe citizens closed a chapter in their history that began in the depths of The Great Depression and ended in the throes of the county's rebirth.
Taken from the scene was a leader who held the reins of county government 24 years. But as the county mourned the loss of Walter Clark Hargrove, it found new leadership to guide it into what could be an era of unprecedented progress. That is as it should be, for leadership is, and must be an eternal quality that flows from man to man.
Since he was elected to the Board of Commissioners and picked as its chairman in 1932, Walter Hargrove had become a fixture wherever important decisions were made. An intelligent, patient man, he was beloved for his ability to mix a working knowledge of human nature with keen administrative insight. A numbness spread over the county when he was stricken suddenly at 68. It was Walter Hargrove who did things in the county. When he was serving as Tarboro's mayor, 1928-31, he pushed a program to continue municipal production of electricity. He converted the town's plant from coal to diesel engines and the plant showed a $60,000 profit at the end of a year.
As a commissioner, he immediately launched a drive to provide a new nursing home for the aged. In 1935, the new facility was a reality.
His third dream for the people of Edgecombe.
More About WALTER CLARK HARGROVE:
Burial: July 18, 1960, Greenwood Cemetery Tarboro, NC[367]
Record Change: May 10, 2004[367]

More About HELEN MARIE EDWARDS:
Burial: Greenwood Cemetery Tarboro, NC[367]
Record Change: May 10, 2004[367]

Notes for SARAH PARKER BARHAM:
Sarah was granddaddy's second wife. She was a fun loving person and doted on Walter and the grandchildren.[2882706.ged]

Children of WALTER HARGROVE and HELEN EDWARDS are:
326. i. SALLY GRAY[10] HARGROVE, b. September 19, 1918, Spring Hope, NC; d. July 15, 1992, Greenville, NC.
327. ii. WALTER CLARK HARGROVE, b. June 20, 1920, Tarboro, Edgecombe Co., NC; d. May 19, 1969, Edgecombe Co. NC.

247. OPIE GRAY[9] EDWARDS *(SALLIE CAPITOLA[8] HARGROVE, GRAY LEMON[7], SALLY [6]LAND, LITTLEBERRY[5], BIRD[4], CURTIS[3], CURTIS[2], CURTIS[1])*[367] was born September 1891 in Nash Co., NC[367]. He married NELLIE B. JACOBS [367] June 20, 1917.

Children of OPIE EDWARDS and NELLIE JACOBS are:
- i. WILLIAM[10] EDWARDS[367], b. 1917, Nash Co., NC[367].
- ii. JR. OPIE GRAY EDWARDS[367], b. 1923, Nash Co., NC[367].

248. HELEN MARIE[9] EDWARDS *(SALLIE CAPITOLA[8] HARGROVE, GRAY LEMON[7], SALLY [6]LAND, LITTLEBERRY[5], BIRD[4], CURTIS[3], CURTIS[2], CURTIS[1])*[367] was born July 1894 in Spring Hope, NC[367], and died 1942 in Edgecombe Co. NC[367]. She married WALTER CLARK HARGROVE[367] June 24, 1916, son of JOHN HARGROVE and SUSAN THIGPEN. He was born February 11, 1891 in Edgecombe Co. NC[367], and died July 15, 1960 in Tarboro, NC[367].

More About HELEN MARIE EDWARDS:
Burial: Greenwood Cemetery Tarboro, NC[367]

Children are listed above under (246) Walter Clark Hargrove.

249. LULU ELIZABETH[9] LAND *(SAMUEL SIBLEY[8], HENRY GREY[7], BURRELL[6], LITTLEBERRY[5], BIRD[4], CURTIS[3], CURTIS[2], CURTIS[1])*[368] was born November 22, 1904 in Noxubee Co., Mississippi. She married JOHN EARL MCDAVID[368] April 01, 1927 in Kemper County, Mississippi.

Child of LULU LAND and JOHN MCDAVID is:
- i. JOHN LAND[10] MCDAVID[368], b. 1930.

250. LITTLE GRACE[9] LAND *(SAMUEL SIBLEY[8], HENRY GREY[7], BURRELL[6], LITTLEBERRY[5], BIRD[4], CURTIS[3], CURTIS[2], CURTIS[1])*[368] was born 1903[368], and died 1943[368]. She married HUNTER C. MCCANN[368] 1922.

Child of LITTLE LAND and HUNTER MCCANN is:
- i. LAURENCE[10] MCCANN[368], b 1923; d. 1943.

251. SAMUEL BURRELL "DOCK"[9] LAND *(DANIEL BURRELL[8], HENRY GREY[7], BURRELL[6], LITTLEBERRY[5], BIRD[4], CURTIS[3], CURTIS[2], CURTIS[1])*[368]. He married ELIZABETH KELLY HESTER[368].

Notes for ELIZABETH KELLY HESTER:
Daughter of Dr. F. L. Hester

Child of SAMUEL LAND and ELIZABETH HESTER is:
- i. HESTER BURRELL[10] LAND[368], b. 1925; d. 1945.

252. DANIEL PAUL[9] LAND *(DANIEL BURRELL[8], HENRY GREY[7], BURRELL[6], LITTLEBERRY[5], BIRD[4], CURTIS[3], CURTIS[2], CURTIS[1])*[368] was born 1907 in Mississippi. He married JEANETTE HELEN POUNDSTONE[368] October 14, 1928 in Tuscaloosa, Alabama.

Child of DANIEL LAND and JEANETTE POUNDSTONE is:
- i. ITANI JENETTE[10] LAND[368], b. 1945.

253. EFFIE LAVINA[9] VANDEVENDER *(MARY MILDRED "MAGGIE"[8] LAND, WILLIAM BURT[7], BURRELL[6], LITTLEBERRY[5], BIRD[4], CURTIS[3], CURTIS[2], CURTIS[1])*[369,370] was born August 30, 1884 in Dekalb County, Alabama[370], and died April 05, 1968 in Forrest City, St. Francis County, Arkansas[370]. She married (1) WILLIAM IVY MILAM[370] February 14, 1913 in Kemper County, Mississippi[370]. He was born September 10, 1872 in Alexander City, Tallapoosa County, Alabama[370], and died August 10, 1922 in Parkin, St. Francis County, Arkansas[370]. She married (2) JOHN MINOR[370] Aft. 1922[370].

More About EFFIE LAVINA VANDEVENDER:
Burial: Tyre Cemetery, between Cherry Valley & Harrisburg, Arkansas[370]

More About WILLIAM IVY MILAM:
Burial: Tyre Cemetery, between Cherry Valley & Harrisburg, Arkansas[370]

Children of EFFIE VANDEVENDER and WILLIAM MILAM are:
328. i. LIVING[10] MILAM.
ii. ERMA LENA MILAM[370], b. December 13, 1913[370]; d. 1916[370].
iii. RUSSELL MAURICE MILAM[370], b. April 10, 1915[370]; d. February 14, 1920[370].
iv. EDNA PEARL MILAM[370], b. January 29, 1916[370]; d. 1916[370].
329. v. SYBLE WAYNE MILAM, b. December 16, 1918, Arkansas; d. May 13, 2003, Memphis, Shelby County, Tennessee.

254. MARY MILDRED[9] VANDEVENDER *(MARY MILDRED "MAGGIE"[8] LAND, WILLIAM BURT[7], BURRELL[6], LITTLEBERRY[5], BIRD[4], CURTIS[3], CURTIS[2], CURTIS[1])*[370] was born April 18, 1885 in Kemper County, Mississippi[370], and died October 12, 1969[370]. She married STEPHEN CHESLEY PALMER[370] November 1904 in Kemper County, Mississippi[370]. He was born May 08, 1883 in Kemper County, Mississippi[370].

Children of MARY VANDEVENDER and STEPHEN PALMER are:
330. i. LIVING[10] PALMER.
ii. LIVING PALMER[370].
iii. LIVING PALMER[370].
iv. LIVING PALMER[370].
v. LIVING PALMER[370].
vi. LIVING PALMER[370].
vii. LESTER OTIS "BUCK" PALMER[370], b. July 19, 1908[370]; d. May 27, 1985[370].
viii. SARAH IRENE PALMER[370], b. March 30, 1911[370]; d. February 1994[370].
ix. MADIE PALMER[370], b. July 23, 1914[370]; d. April 1992[370].
x. HOMER DEWITT PALMER[370], b. September 23, 1916[370]; d. June 06, 1917[370].
xi. EDNA HORTENSE PALMER[370], b. March 28, 1920[370]; d. August 20, 1995[370].

255. LIVING[9] BAILEY *(RHODES[8], WILLIAM W.[7], ELIZABETH[6] LAND, LEWIS[5], BIRD[4], CURTIS[3], CURTIS[2], CURTIS[1])*[371]. She married HENRY HORSEMAN[371]. He was born Private.

Child of LIVING BAILEY and HENRY HORSEMAN is:
331. i. LILA[10] HORSEMAN.

256. JAMES THEADORE[9] BAILEY *(GEORGE WASHINGTON[8], WILLIAM W.[7], ELIZABETH[6] LAND, LEWIS[5], BIRD[4], CURTIS[3], CURTIS[2], CURTIS[1])* was born September 03, 1882, and died May 19, 1955. He married BERTIE WELLS. She was born September 13, 1883, and died June 21, 1964.

Children of JAMES BAILEY and BERTIE WELLS are:
332. i. JAMES BURLEY[10] BAILEY, b. December 13, 1905.
ii. JEWEL BAILEY.
333. iii. EUGENE BAILEY.
334. iv. ARLENE BAILEY.
335. v. RUBY BAILEY.
336. vi. DONALD BAILEY.
vii. NOBLE BAILEY, m. JUANITA RAINS.
337. viii. BIRDIE BAILEY.

257. FRANKIE ZULA[9] BAILEY *(GEORGE WASHINGTON[8], WILLIAM W.[7], ELIZABETH[6] LAND, LEWIS[5], BIRD[4], CURTIS[3], CURTIS[2], CURTIS[1])* was born September 29, 1887. She married OSCAR WILLIAMS.

Children of FRANKIE BAILEY and OSCAR WILLIAMS are:
i. HARRY[10] WILLIAMS, m. VIRGINIA BLACK.
ii. ROBERTA WILLIAMS.

258. FANNIE LULA[9] BAILEY *(GEORGE WASHINGTON[8], WILLIAM W.[7], ELIZABETH[6] LAND, LEWIS[5], BIRD[4], CURTIS[3], CURTIS[2], CURTIS[1])* was born September 29, 1887. She married (1) STAIRETT HARRISON. She married (2) UNKNOWN POSEY. She married (3) JASPER KELLETT.

Children of FANNIE BAILEY and STAIRETT HARRISON are:
338. i. ELGIN[10] HARRISON.
339. ii. LOIS MARIE HARRISON.

259. WILLIAM SOLOMON[9] BAILEY *(GEORGE WASHINGTON[8], WILLIAM W.[7], ELIZABETH[6] LAND, LEWIS[5], BIRD[4], CURTIS[3], CURTIS[2], CURTIS[1])* was born November 11, 1889, and died January 25, 1958. He married JULIA FAYE BOWEN November 26, 1909 in Randolph Co., Arkansas, daughter of RUFUS BOWEN and LUCINDA KELLETT. She was born July 09, 1890, and died December 08, 1979.

Child of WILLIAM BAILEY and JULIA BOWEN is:
340. i. WILLIAM MILLARD[10] BAILEY, b. July 03, 1914.

260. TILDA PEARL[9] BAILEY *(GEORGE WASHINGTON[8], WILLIAM W.[7], ELIZABETH[6] LAND, LEWIS[5], BIRD[4], CURTIS[3], CURTIS[2], CURTIS[1])* was born November 0[illegible], 1893. She married CLARENCE WELLS. He was born 1891, and died 1973.

More About CLARENCE WELLS:
Burial: Masonic Cemetery, Pocahontas, Randolph Co., Arkansas

Child of TILDA BAILEY and CLARENCE WELLS is:
i. PRESTON[10] WELLS.

261. ALBERT DONALD[9] BAILEY *(GEORGE WASHINGTON[8], WILLIAM W.[7], ELIZABETH[6] LAND, LEWIS[5], BIRD[4], CURTIS[3], CURTIS[2], CURTIS[1])* was born March 24, 1896, and died May 26, 1964. He married BEULAH MAE NIXON.

Children of ALBERT BAILEY and BEULAH NIXON are:
341. i. SIBYL[10] BAILEY.
342. ii. MANLEY BAILEY.
343. iii. CLEO BAILEY.
344. iv. MILDRED BAILEY.
345. v. ALDEAN BAILEY.

262. VIRGIL[9] BAILEY *(GEORGE WASHINGTON[8], WILLIAM W.[7], ELIZABETH[6] LAND, LEWIS[5], BIRD[4], CURTIS[3], CURTIS[2], CURTIS[1])* was born December 24, 1899, and died 1967. He married BLANCHE JANES, daughter of MACK JANES and FANNIE.

Child of VIRGIL BAILEY and BLANCHE JANES is:
346. i. GUY[10] BAILEY.

263. FREDERICK[9] BAILEY *(ALLEN A.[8], WILLIAM W.[7], ELIZABETH[6] LAND, LEWIS[5], BIRD[4], CURTIS[3], CURTIS[2], CURTIS[1])* He married RETTIE VICTORIA MURPHEY.

Child of FREDERICK BAILEY and RETTIE MURPHEY is:
347. i. EVALENA[10] BAILEY.

264. WILLIAM CLARK[9] DAVIS *(MARY ELIZABETH "MATILDA"[8] BAILEY, WILLIAM W.[7], ELIZABETH[6] LAND, LEWIS[5], BIRD[4], CURTIS[3], CURTIS[2], CURTIS[1])*

Child of WILLIAM CLARK DAVIS is:
348. i. THELMA NEL[10] DAVIS.

265. ROBERT DAVID[9] PARRIS *(WARNER DAVID[8], SUSANNAH[7] LAND, STEPHEN[6], LEWIS[5], BIRD[4], CURTIS[3], CURTIS[2], CURTIS[1])* was born August 26, 1913 in Marietta, Georgia, and died November 13, 1984 in SaVAnnah, Tennessee.

He married JUANITA BELLE DELLMAN June 19, 1937 in Sioux Falls, South Dakota. She was born August 19, 1917 in Sioux Falls, South Dakota.

Children of ROBERT PARRIS and JUANITA DELLMAN are:
349. i. ROBERT DAVID[10] PARRIS, b. November 09, 1939, Sioux Falls, South Dakota.
350. ii. JIM WARNER PARRIS, b. December 18, 1945, Sioux Falls, South Dakota.

266. WILLIAM BENSON[9] PARRIS *(WARNER DAVID[8], SUSANNAH[7] LAND, STEPHEN[6], LEWIS[5], BIRD[4], CURTIS[3], CURTIS[2], CURTIS[1])* was born October 20, 1920. He married SARAH ANITA GRIFFIN April 20, 1950. She was born July 03, 1929 in Gillisville, GA.

Children of WILLIAM PARRIS and SARAH GRIFFIN are:
i. SUSAN VIRGINIA[10] PARRIS, b. November 26, 1951.
ii. ELIZABETH ELAINE PARRIS, b. March 30, 1954.
351. iii. WILLIAM GRIFFIN PARRIS, b. April 17, 1957, Savannah, Tennessee.
352. iv. BENSON LAMAR PARRIS, b. February 25, 1959, Savannah, Tennessee.

267. HAROLD LESTER[9] PARRIS *(WARNER DAVID[8], SUSANNAH[7] LAND, STEPHEN[6], LEWIS[5], BIRD[4], CURTIS[3], CURTIS[2], CURTIS[1])* was born June 23, 1923. He married VIRGINIA RUTHERFORD April 12, 1945 in Marietta, Georgia.

Notes for HAROLD LESTER PARRIS:
Navy Corpsman US Marines WII.

Child of HAROLD PARRIS and VIRGINIA RUTHERFORD is:
353. i. DONALD LESTER[10] PARRIS, b. January 29, 1947, Atlanta, Georgia.

268. HAZEL CORNELIA[9] PARRIS *(WARNER DAVID[8], SUSANNAH[7] LAND, STEPHEN[6], LEWIS[5], BIRD[4], CURTIS[3], CURTIS[2], CURTIS[1])* was born September 03, 1924. She married BRYON LAMAR PADGETT February 06, 1945. He was born June 23, 1921 in Georgia, and died in Georgia.

Notes for BRYON LAMAR PADGETT:
US Marines WWII and Korea.

Children of HAZEL PARRIS and BRYON PADGETT are:
354. i. CHRIS LAMAR[10] PADGETT, b. March 09, 1950, Georgia.
355. ii. KATHY CORNELIA PADGETT, b. September 26, 1951.
356. iii. MARK JOHN PADGETT, b. March 16, 1958, Georgia.

269. ANNA MAE BELL[9] PARRIS *(RONEY JEFFERSON[8], ELIZABETH JANE[7] LAND, STEPHEN[6], LEWIS[5], BIRD[4], CURTIS[3], CURTIS[2], CURTIS[1])* She married FRED FLOYD REGISTER.

Child of ANNA PARRIS and FRED REGISTER is:
i. BARBARA[10] REGISTER.

270. CLYDE[9] REED *(LUCRETIA (LOU CRECY) JANE[8] LAND, JORDON[7], KINSON[6], LEWIS[5], BIRD[4], CURTIS[3], CURTIS[2], CURTIS[1])*[372] was born October 10, 1892[372], and died January 15, 1969 in Swifton, Arkansas[372]. He married (1) DOLLIE UNKNOWN[372]. He married (2) TRESSIE UNKNOWN[372]. She was born March 30, 1916[372], and died November 23, 1995 in Swifton, Arkansas[372].

More About CLYDE REED:
Burial: Swifton Cemetery[372]

More About TRESSIE UNKNOWN:
Burial: Swifton Cemetery[372]

Child of CLYDE REED and DOLLIE UNKNOWN is:
i. LIVING[10] REED[372].

271. JOE LUTHER[9] REED *(LUCRETIA (LOU CRECY) JANE[8] LAND, JORDON[7], KINSON[6], LEWIS[5], BIRD[4], CURTIS[3], CURTIS[2], CURTIS[1])*[372] was born January 03, 1903[372], and died December 11, 1937 in Egypt, Arkansas[372]. He married SARAH VADA GARVER[372]. She was born October 29, 1907[372], and died June 12, 1985 in Illinois[372].

More About JOE LUTHER REED:
Burial: Oaklawn Cemetery, Batesville, Arkansas[372]

More About SARAH VADA GARVER:
Burial: Garver Cemetery, Decatur, Illinois[372]

Children of JOE REED and SARAH GARVER are:
357. i. LIVING[10] REED.
358. ii. LIVING REED.
iii. GIRL REED[372], b. July 05, 1926[372]; d. July 05, 1926[372].
iv. MARTIN LUTHER REED[372], b. June 06, 1927[372]; d. June 06, 1927[372].
359. v. JESSIE JAMES REED, b. May 10, 1932; d. October 31, 1985, Illinois.

272. JAMES ALVIS[9] REED *(LUCRETIA (LOU CRECY) JANE[8] LAND, JORDON[7], KINSON[6], LEWIS[5], BIRD[4], CURTIS[3], CURTIS[2], CURTIS[1])*[372] was born December 04, 1904[372], and died February 22, 1985 in Illinois[372]. He married ELLIE GERTRUDE WHATLEY[372]. She was born July 23, 1913[372], and died August 29, 1997[372].

Children of JAMES REED and ELLIE WHATLEY are:
360. i. LIVING[10] REED.
ii. LIVING REED[372].

273. BESSIE TENNESSEE[9] REED *(LUCRETIA (LOU CRECY) JANE[8] LAND, JORDON[7], KINSON[6], LEWIS[5], BIRD[4], CURTIS[3], CURTIS[2], CURTIS[1])*[372] was born May 26, 1906[372], and died August 1972[372]. She married (1) LIVING CURTIS[372]. She married (2) LIVING STROTHER[372].

More About BESSIE TENNESSEE REED:
Burial: Hutchison Cemetery, Arkansas[372]

Child of BESSIE REED and LIVING CURTIS is:
361. i. LIVING[10] CURTIS.

Child of BESSIE REED and LIVING STROTHER is:
362. ii. LIVING[10] STROTHER.

274. ORA DELLAR[9] REED *(LUCRETIA (LOU CRECY) JANE[8] LAND, JORDON[7], KINSON[6], LEWIS[5], BIRD[4], CURTIS[3], CURTIS[2], CURTIS[1])*[373,374] was born November 26, 1909[374], and died November 23, 2003 in Rolling Hills Nursing Home[374]. She married WALTER JACKSON COKER[374] February 13, 1926 in Independence County, Arkansas[374]. He was born June 28, 1900 in Hutchinson Mountain, Independence County, Arkansas[374], and died May 30, 1975[374].

I was born in my Grandparents home, Jordon & Rebecca Land, the doctor said I was dead so he wrapped me up in a blanket and laid me on the table. He told my grandparents to clean my mother up and she did. Then after the doctor left she said I can't leave that baby laying over there dirty so she got me and washed my front side then turned me over and washed my back when she did I cried.

More About ORA DELLAR REED:
Burial: November 26, 2003, Wyatt Cemetery[374]

More About WALTER JACKSON COKER:
Burial: Wyatt Cemetery[374]

Children of ORA REED and WALTER COKER are:

363. i. LIVING[10] COKER.
ii. LIVING COKER[374].
364. iii. LIVING COKER.
365. iv. LIVING COKER.
366. v. JAMES WALTER COKER, b. September 24, 1929; d. August 18, 1982, Washington.
367. vi. HELEN JANE COKER, b. July 23, 1933; d. February 19, 2002, Saldo, Arkansas.
vii. EULARD GERTRUDE COKER[374], b. October 05, 1935[374]; d. June 22, 1941[374].

More About EULARD GERTRUDE COKER:
Burial: Wyatt Cemetery[374]

275. MATTIE BEATRICE[9] REED *(LUCRETIA (LOU CRECY) JANE[8] LAND, JORDON[7], KINSON[6], LEWIS[5], BIRD[4], CURTIS[3], CURTIS[2], CURTIS[1])*[374] was born September 22, 1911[374], and died December 1939 in Rosie, Arkansas[374]. She married (1) LARKIN H. HUTCHISON[374] December 06, 1928 in Independence County, Arkansas[374]. He was born December 03, 1908[374], and died November 25, 1970 in Cash, Arkansas[374]. She married (2) JOHN CRABTREE[374] December 09, 1935[374]. He was born Abt. 1870[374], and died Abt. 1937[374].

More About MATTIE BEATRICE REED:
Burial: Wyatt Cemetery, Rosie, Independence County, Arkansas[374]

More About LARKIN H. HUTCHISON:
Burial: Johnson Cemetery, Cash, Craighead County, Arkansas[374]

Children of MATTIE REED and LARKIN HUTCHISON are:
i. LIVING[10] HUTCHISON[374].
ii. CHARLES HENRY HUTCHISON[374], b. April 22, 1931[374]; d. August 23, 1964[374]; m. LIVING UNKNOWN[374].

More About CHARLES HENRY HUTCHISON:
Burial: Johnson Cemetery, Cash, Craighead County, Arkansas[374]

Child of MATTIE REED and JOHN CRABTREE is:
368. iii. LIVING[10] CRABTREE.

276. FRANK CARTER[9] REED *(LUCRETIA (LOU CRECY) JANE[8] LAND, JORDON[7], KINSON[6], LEWIS[5], BIRD[4], CURTIS[3], CURTIS[2], CURTIS[1])*[374] was born December 10, 1914[374], and died August 22, 1975 in Illinois[374]. He married WILLIE ELMS[374]. She was born March 28, 1923[374], and died June 02, 1996[374].

More About FRANK CARTER REED:
Burial: Wyatt Cemetery, Rosie, Independence County, Arkansas[374]

More About WILLIE ELMS:
Burial: Garver Cemetery, Decatur, Illinois[374]

Children of FRANK REED and WILLIE ELMS are:
i. LIVING[10] REED[374].
ii. LIVING REED[374].
iii. LIVING REED[374], m. KENNETH WHITE[374]; d. March 22, 2001, Lincoln, Illinois[374].

More About KENNETH WHITE:
Burial: Garver Cemetery, Decatur, Illinois[374]

277. WALTER COLLINS[9] REED *(LUCRETIA (LOU CRECY) JANE[8] LAND, JORDON[7], KINSON[6], LEWIS[5], BIRD[4], CURTIS[3], CURTIS[2], CURTIS[1])*[375,376] was born December 22, 1918 in Batesville, Arkansas[376], and died December 11, 1999 in Batesville, Independence County, Arkansas[376]. He married LIVING HOOVER[376].

More About WALTER COLLINS REED:
Burial: Locust Grove Cemetery[376]

Children of WALTER REED and LIVING HOOVER are:

- i. LIVING[10] REED[376], m. LIVING MITCHUM[376].
- 369. ii. LIVING REED.
- 370. iii. LIVING REED.
- iv. LIVING REED[376], m. LIVING GIPSON[376].

278. CHARLES JETT[9] REED *(LUCRETIA (LOU CRECY) JANE[8] LAND, JORDON[7], KINSON[6], LEWIS[5], BIRD[4], CURTIS[3], CURTIS[2], CURTIS[1])*[377,378] was born April 12, 1922[378], and died August 27, 1951 in Batesville, Independence County, Arkansas[378]. He married LIVING SHANKS[378].

Notes for CHARLES JETT REED:
[2847174.ged]

An article from Batesville Guard dated Aug 28, 1951. A 29 year old Locust Grove man, Jett Reed, was found dead shot to death in front of Sisk's Store on East Main Street yesterday afternoon in what Deputy Coroner John Davies said was a suicide. Reed had been living in Illinois and had returned to the county about two weeks ago and was living with his mother at Locust Grove. Funeral will be in the Crouch Chapel at 2:30 Wednesday.

Children of CHARLES REED and LIVING SHANKS are:

- i. LIVING[10] REED[378].
- ii. LIVING REED[378].

279. NOAMI EVELYN[9] TYLER *(JOSEPH JAMES RUFUS[8], MARTHA MATILDA ROSETTA[7] LAND, KINSON[6], LEWIS[5], BIRD[4], CURTIS[3], CURTIS[2], CURTIS[1])* was born July 11, 1920. She married LEVI AUGUSTUS HOGUE August 22, 1938. He was born September 24, 1910, and died May 02, 1975.

Children of NOAMI TYLER and LEVI HOGUE are:

- i. L. J.[10] HOGUE.
- ii. WILLARD RAY HOGUE.
- iii. SHIRLEY EVON HOGUE.

280. JAMES GERALD[9] JONES *(BERTHA DELIAH[8] TYLER, MARTHA MATILDA ROSETTA[7] LAND, KINSON[6], LEWIS[5], BIRD[4], CURTIS[3], CURTIS[2], CURTIS[1])*[379] was born June 29, 1914[379], and died May 29, 1994 in St. Bernards Hospital, Jonesboro, Ar.[379]. He married LILA HORSEMAN[379], daughter of HENRY HORSEMAN and LIVING BAILEY.

Facts about this person:
Burial June 1994
Ravenden Springs, Ar.

Child of JAMES JONES and LILA HORSEMAN is:

- 371. i. LIVING[10] JONES.

281. LESLIE WADE[9] TYLER *(LUTHER EDWARD[8], MARTHA MATILDA ROSETTA[7] LAND, KINSON[6], LEWIS[5], BIRD[4], CURTIS[3], CURTIS[2], CURTIS[1])* was born July 15, 192[illegible]. He married LEOLA BREWER August 19, 1942.

Children of LESLIE TYLER and LEOLA BREWER are:

- i. LESLIE ELVIN[10] TYLER, b. December 24, 1946.
- ii. PASH LYNN TYLER, b. May 05, 1948.
- iii. BRENDA LEA TYLER, b. December 12, 1949.

282. MODENE[9] TYLER *(JOHN PARIS[8], MARTHA MATILDA ROSETTA[7] LAND, KINSON[6], LEWIS[5], BIRD[4], CURTIS[3], CURTIS[2], CURTIS[1])* She married JOHN WESLEY MITCHELL.

Children of MODENE TYLER and JOHN MITCHELL are:

- 372. i. PAULINE[10] MITCHELL.
- ii. JOHN WILSON MITCHELL.
- iii. MARY GLEE MITCHELL.
- iv. VIRGINIA MITCHELL.

v. JAMES DAVID MITCHELL.

283. ERVIN LEE[9] RIDDLE *(ROSY[8] HUGHES, "DONA" FRANCIS CALDONIA [7]LAND, KINSON[6], LEWIS[5], BIRD[4], CURTIS[3], CURTIS[2], CURTIS[1])* was born in Randolph Co. Arkansas, and died March 20, 2000. He married BERNICE OMA ROBERTS.

Children of ERVIN RIDDLE and BERNICE ROBERTS are:

i. ERVIN LEE[10] RIDDLE.
ii. VIRGINIA RIDDLE.
iii. PLYLLIS LAVERNE RIDDLE.
iv. LINDA OMA RIDDLE.

284. IMOGENE EVELYN[9] HUGHES *(THOMAS JEFFERSON[8], "DONA" FRANCIS CALDONIA [7]LAND, KINSON[6], LEWIS[5], BIRD[4], CURTIS[3], CURTIS[2], CURTIS[1])* was born 1936. She married MAYLON WHITE. He was born 1930 in Arkansas.

Children of IMOGENE HUGHES and MAYLON WHITE are:

373. i. DEBORAH[10] WHITE.
ii. RICKY WHITE.
iii. PAUL WHITE.

285. JAMES HENRY[9] HUGHES *(THOMAS JEFFERSON[8], "DONA" FRANCIS CALDONIA [7]LAND, KINSON[6], LEWIS[5], BIRD[4], CURTIS[3], CURTIS[2], CURTIS[1])* was born April 13, 1938 in Ravenden Springs, Randolph Co., AR. He married VERNADEAN PICKETT April 12, 1961 in Lawrence Co., Arkansas, daughter of DWELL PICKETT and MILDRED MERDITH. She was born September 27, 1938 in Lawrence Co., Arkansas, and died January 26, 1998 in Randolph Co. Arkansas.

More About VERNADEAN PICKETT:
Burial: Bennett Cemetery

Children of JAMES HUGHES and VERNADEAN PICKETT are:

i. JAMES HENRY[10] HUGHES, JR., b. November 12, 1966.
374. ii. BONNIE SUE HUGHES, b. December 03, 1970.

286. BETTY JOYCE[9] HUGHES *(THOMAS JEFFERSON[8], "DONA" FRANCIS CALDONIA[7] LAND, KINSON[6], LEWIS[5], BIRD[4], CURTIS[3], CURTIS[2], CURTIS[1])* was born 1940. She married (1) BILL MCGUIRE. She married (2) LINDELL RICHARDSON 2000.

Children of BETTY HUGHES and BILL MCGUIRE are:

i. JEFF[10] MCGUIRE.
ii. PEGGY SUE MCGUIRE, b. January 11, 1966.
iii. LAURA LEA MCGUIRE, b. August 17, 1967.

287. THOMAS DAIL[9] HUGHES *(THOMAS JEFFERSON[8], "DONA" FRANCIS CALDONIA [7]LAND, KINSON[6], LEWIS[5], BIRD[4], CURTIS[3], CURTIS[2], CURTIS[1])* was born 1942. He married ALICE A. OWENS 1965, daughter of ARTHUR OWENS and FLORA MAY.

Children of THOMAS HUGHES and ALICE OWENS are:

375. i. DONNA CAROL[10] HUGHES, b. December 30, 1965.
ii. PATRICIA DAIL HUGHES, b. July 24, 1968.
iii. JOSEPH BRIAN HUGHES, b. November 1979.
376. iv. THOMAS HUGHES, b. 1971.

288. RONNIE[9] HUGHES *(THOMAS JEFFERSON[8], "DONA" FRANCIS CALDONIA[7] LAND, KINSON[6], LEWIS[5], BIRD[4], CURTIS[3], CURTIS[2], CURTIS[1])* was born 1944. He married CATHY.

Children of RONNIE HUGHES and CATHY are:

i. MICHAEL[10] HUGHES, b. 1970.

ii. CRYSTAL HUGHES.

289. BUDDY CARSON[9] HUGHES *(THOMAS JEFFERSON[8], "DONA" FRANCIS CALDONIA[7] LAND, KINSON[6], LEWIS[5], BIRD[4], CURTIS[3], CURTIS[2], CURTIS[1])* was born July 27, 1947. He married CATHERINE VIRGINIA PICKETT December 30, 1972, daughter of ERNEST PICKETT and DOROTHY BELL. She was born October 23, 1954.

Children of BUDDY HUGHES and CATHERINE PICKETT are:

377. i. SHELIA RENEE[10] HUGHES, b. March 30, 1974.
ii. VIRGINIA DENISE HUGHES, b. August 13, 1975.
iii. CHERYL LYNN HUGHES, b. July 18, 1981.

Generation No. 10

290. CLYDE ERR[10] LAND *(HENRY FOUNTAIN[9], HENDERSON P.[8], FOUNTAIN[7], JOHN[6], THOMAS[5], THOMAS[4], JOHN[3], CURTIS[2], CURTIS[1])*[380] was born 1896[380], and died 1988[380]. He married LOUISE BAKER[380] 1921[380]. She was born 1896[380], and died 1978[380].

Child of CLYDE LAND and LOUISE BAKER is:

i. LIVING[11] LAND[380].

291. THOMAS LINVILLE[10] LAND *(WILLIAM THOMAS[9], LINVILLE[8], WILLIAM THOMAS[7], JONATHAN[6], THOMAS[5], THOMAS[4], JOHN[3], CURTIS[2], CURTIS[1])*[380] was born July 15, 1887 in Wilkes County, North Carolina[380], and died January 11, 1979[380]. He married DOLCIE IRENE POARCH[380].

More About THOMAS LINVILLE LAND:
Burial: Union County Cemetery[380]

Children of THOMAS LAND and DOLCIE POARCH are:

i. LIVING[11] LAND[380].
ii. LIVING LAND[380].
iii. LIVING LAND[380].
iv. LIVING LAND[380].
v. LIVING LAND[380].
378. vi. LIVING LAND.
vii. LIVING LAND[380].
379. viii. LIVING LAND.
380. ix. LIVING LAND.
381. x. WILLIAM ADAM LAND, b. February 08, 1908, Caldwell County, North Carolina; d. February 19, 1993, Caldwell County, North Carolina.

292. JAMES THOMAS CARR[10] WRIGHT *(CATHERINE JANE[9] LAND, JAMES CALVIN[8], WILLIAM THOMAS[7], JONATHAN[6], THOMAS[5], THOMAS[4], JOHN[3], CURTIS[2], CURTIS[1])*[380] was born 1894[380], and died July 14, 1963 in Perkinsville, North Carolina[380]. He married SINESCA MASTIN[380] May 1917[380]. She died 1992[380].

More About JAMES THOMAS CARR WRIGHT:
Burial: Mount Lawn Cemetery[380]
Occupation: Teacher[380]

Children of JAMES WRIGHT and SINESCA MASTIN are:

i. LIVING[11] WRIGHT[380].
ii. LIVING WRIGHT[380].
iii. LIVING WRIGHT[380].

293. LIVING[10] LAND *(THOMAS DAVID[9], JAMES CALVIN[8], WILLIAM THOMAS[7], JONATHAN[6], THOMAS[5], THOMAS[4], JOHN[3], CURTIS[2], CURTIS[1])*[380]. He married LIVING MILLER[380].

Children of LIVING LAND and LIVING MILLER are:

382. i. LIVING[11] LAND.
383. ii. LIVING LAND.
384. iii. LIVING LAND.
385. iv. LIVING LAND.

294. LIVING[10] LAND *(THOMAS DAVID[9], JAMES CALVIN[8], WILLIAM THOMAS[7], JONATHAN[6], THOMAS[5], THOMAS[4], JOHN[3], CURTIS[2], CURTIS[1])*[380]. She married LIVING JONES[380].

Children of LIVING LAND and LIVING JONES are:
386. i. LIVING[11] JONES.
387. ii. LIVING JONES.

295. LIVING[10] LAND *(THOMAS DAVID[9], JAMES CALVIN[8], WILLIAM THOMAS[7], JONATHAN[6], THOMAS[5], THOMAS[4], JOHN[3], CURTIS[2], CURTIS[1])*[380]. He married LIVING BRAGG[380].

Children of LIVING LAND and LIVING BRAGG are:
i. LIVING[11] LAND[380].
388. ii. LIVING LAND.
iii. LIVING LAND[380].
389. iv. LIVING LAND.

296. THOMAS MERIDETH[10] LAND *(THOMAS DAVID[9], JAMES CALVIN[8], WILLIAM THOMAS[7], JONATHAN[6], THOMAS[5], THOMAS[4], JOHN[3], CURTIS[2], CURTIS[1])*[380] was born January 28, 1918 in Mt Pleasant, Tennessee[380], and died February 23, 1984 in Fort Smith, Arkansas[380]. He married LIVING FERGUSON[380].

Children of THOMAS LAND and LIVING FERGUSON are:
390. i. LIVING[11] LAND.
391. ii. LIVING LAND.

297. SAMUEL[10] LAND *(WILLIAM LANGLEY[9], THOMAS[8], JAMES[7], JONATHAN[6], THOMAS[5], THOMAS[4], JOHN[3], CURTIS[2], CURTIS[1])*[380] was born December 17, 1874[380]. He married EMMALINE LOCKHART[380] July 30, 1889[380].

Children of SAMUEL LAND and EMMALINE LOCKHART are:
i. LIVING[11] LAND[380].
ii. LIVING LAND[380].
iii. LIVING LAND[380].
iv. LIVING LAND[380].
v. MILTON LAND[380], b. May 04, 1899[380].

298. AARON CARTER[10] LAND *(JAMES ELI[9], JAMES[8], JAMES[7], JONATHAN[6], THOMAS[5], THOMAS[4], JOHN[3], CURTIS[2], CURTIS[1])*[380] was born February 07, 1874[380], and died July 18, 1945 in Alexander County, North Carolina[380]. He married LITA JOHNSON[380] August 08, 1915[380].

Children of AARON LAND and LITA JOHNSON are:
i. LIVING[11] LAND[380].
ii. LIVING LAND[380].
392. iii. LIVING LAND.
393. iv. LIVING LAND.

299. JUDITH ROSELLEN[10] LAND *(JAMES ELI[9], JAMES[8], JAMES[7], JONATHAN[6], THOMAS[5], THOMAS[4], JOHN[3], CURTIS[2], CURTIS[1])*[380] was born August 19, 1876[380], and died May 22, 1956 in Alexander County, North Carolina[380]. She married NATHAN BARNES[380] September 01, 1894[380].

Children of JUDITH LAND and NATHAN BARNES are:
i. PETER[11] BARNES[380], b. Alexander County, North Carolina[380]; d. Alexander County, North Carolina[380].

More About PETER BARNES:
Burial: Three Forks Cemetery[380]

ii. LIVING BARNES[380].
iii. LIVING BARNES[380].
iv. LIVING BARNES[380].
v. LIVING BARNES[380].
vi. OSIE A. BARNES[380], b. Abt. 1903[380]; d. Alexander County, North Carolina - Poplar Springs[380].
vii. SMITH J. BARNES[380], b. August 08, 1904, Alexander County, North Carolina[380]; d. April 02, 1991, Alexander County, North Carolina[380].

More About SMITH J. BARNES:
Burial: Mountain Ridge Cemetery[380]

viii. FRED ELI BARNES[380], b. January 27, 1913[380]; d. April 08, 1964, Alexander County, North Carolina[380].

More About FRED ELI BARNES:
Burial: Oxford Memorial Cemetery[380]

300. BRYSON HENDERSON[10] LAND *(JAMES ELI[9], JAMES[8], JAMES[7], JONATHAN[6], THOMAS[5], THOMAS[4], JOHN[3], CURTIS[2], CURTIS[1])*[380] was born Abt. 1882[380]. He married EMMA ELIZABETH AUTON[380].

Child of BRYSON LAND and EMMA AUTON is:
i. LIVING[11] LAND[380].

301. MARY JANE[10] LAND *(NOAH[9], JAMES[8], JAMES[7], JONATHAN[6], THOMAS[5], THOMAS[4], JOHN[3], CURTIS[2], CURTIS[1])*[380] was born August 25, 1892 in Alexander County, North Carolina[380], and died November 18, 1945 in Alexander County, North Carolina[380]. She married JAMES JEFFERSON FOX[380] January 04, 1910[380].

More About MARY JANE LAND:
Burial: Three Forks Cemetery[380]

Children of MARY LAND and JAMES FOX are:
i. LIVING[11] FOX[380].
ii. LIVING FOX[380].
iii. LIVING FOX[380].
iv. LIVING FOX[380].
v. HARVEY ALEXANDER FOX[380], b. December 18, 1910, Alexander County, North Carolina[380]; d. September 22, 1992, Alexander County, North Carolina[380].

More About HARVEY ALEXANDER FOX:
Burial: Three Forks Cemetery[380]

vi. LEVINA LUNA FOX[380], b. December 08, 1912, Alexander County, North Carolina[380]; d. December 20, 1986, Alexander County, North Carolina[380].
vii. GEORGE W. FOX[380], b. September 15, 1915, Alexander County, North Carolina[380]; d. November 08, 1925, Alexander County, North Carolina[380].

More About GEORGE W. FOX:
Burial: Three Forks Cemetery[380]

viii. CHARLIE LEE FOX[380], b. June 13, 1918, Alexander County, North Carolina[380]; d. March 03, 1998, Alexander County, North Carolina[380].
ix. ROBERT DOUGHTON FOX[380], b. March 18, 1921, Alexander County, North Carolina[380]; d. January 05, 1980, Alexander County, North Carolina[380].

302. ROBERT LEE[10] LAND *(NOAH[9], JAMES[8], JAMES[7], JONATHAN[6], THOMAS[5], THOMAS[4], JOHN[3], CURTIS[2], CURTIS[1])*[380] was born September 18, 1893 in Alexander County, North Carolina[380], and died July 02, 1967 in Caldwell County, North Carolina[380]. He married LIVING DYSON[380].

More About ROBERT LEE LAND:
Burial: Dover Baptist Church Cemetery[380]

Children of ROBERT LAND and LIVING DYSON are:

394. i. LIVING[11] LAND.
 ii. LIVING LAND[380], m. LIVING CHURCH[380].
395. iii. LIVING LAND.
396. iv. LIVING LAND.
 v. LIVING LAND[380].
397. vi. LIVING LAND.

303. GEORGE WASHINGTON[10] LAND *(NOAH[9], JAMES[8], JAMES[7], JONATHAN[6], THOMAS[5], THOMAS[4], JOHN[3], CURTIS[2], CURTIS[1])*[380] was born September 11, 1894 in Alexander County, North Carolina[380], and died April 18, 1959 in Caldwell County, North Carolina[380]. He married JULIE EVAPENNELL[380].

More About GEORGE WASHINGTON LAND:
Burial: Dover Baptist Church Cemetery[380]

Children of GEORGE LAND and JULIE PENNELL are:

398. i. LIVING[11] LAND.
 ii. LIVING LAND[380].

304. CHARLES CLEVELAND[10] LAND *(JAMES LINVILLE[9], DAVID[8], JAMES[7], JONATHAN[6], THOMAS[5], THOMAS[4], JOHN[3], CURTIS[2], CURTIS[1])*[380] was born November 1887[380], and died 1961[380]. He married MARY NELL[380].

Child of CHARLES LAND and MARY NELL is:

 i. LIVING[11] LAND[380].

305. SR. GEORGE EDWARD[10] LAND *(JAMES LINVILLE[9], DAVID[8], JAMES[7], JONATHAN[6], THOMAS[5], THOMAS[4], JOHN[3], CURTIS[2], CURTIS[1])*[380] was born June 1892[380], and died April 1926[380]. He married ANNIE BLAKLEY[380]. She was born 1893[380], and died 1975[380].

More About SR. GEORGE EDWARD LAND:
Cause of Death: Johnson City, Tennessee[380]

Children of GEORGE LAND and ANNIE BLAKLEY are:

 i. LIVING[11] LAND[380], m. LIVING HOOD[380].
 ii. LIVING LAND[380], m. LIVING COX[380].
 iii. LIVING LAND[380], m. LIVING CARROLL[380].
399. iv. JR. GEORGE EDWARD LAND, b. November 02, 1926; d. November 1991, Melbourne, Florida.

306. THOMAS WILLIAM[10] LAND *(ELI JASON[9], DAVID[8], JAMES[7], JONATHAN[6], THOMAS[5], THOMAS[4], JOHN[3], CURTIS[2], CURTIS[1])*[380] was born September 24, 1880 in Wilkes County, North Carolina[380], and died January 26, 1960 in Wilkes County, North Carolina[380]. He married EMMA CARLTON[380].

More About THOMAS WILLIAM LAND:
Burial: Little Rock Church Cemetery[380]

Children of THOMAS LAND and EMMA CARLTON are:

 i. LIVING[11] LAND[380], m. LIVING CARLTON[380].
 ii. LIVING LAND[380].
 iii. KATY DELA LAND[380], b. April 26, 1918, Wilkes County, North Carolina[380]; d. August 30, 1991, Wilkes County, North Carolina[380]; m. LIVING YOHO[380].

 More About KATY DELA LAND:
 Burial: Little Rock Church Cemetery[380]

 iv. JOHNNY FRANKLIN LAND[380], b. November 21, 1925, Wilkes County, North Carolina[380]; d. September 02, 1990, Caldwell County, North Carolina[380].

307. DAVID[10] LAND *(ELI JASON[9], DAVID[8], JAMES[7], JONATHAN[6], THOMAS[5], THOMAS[4], JOHN[3], CURTIS[2], CURTIS[1])*[380] was born August 04, 1885 in Wilkes County, North Carolina[380], and died June 11, 1949 in Wilkes County, North Carolina[380]. He married CALLIE ESTELLA KNIGHT[380].

Children of DAVID LAND and CALLIE KNIGHT are:

400. i. LIVING[11] LAND.
401. ii. LIVING LAND.
402. iii. LIVING LAND.
403. iv. LIVING LAND.
404. v. LIVING LAND.
405. vi. LIVING LAND.
406. vii. LIVING LAND.
407. viii. LIVING LAND.
408. ix. LIVING LAND.
409. x. CLARA REBECCA LAND, b. September 19, 1914, Wilkes County, North Carolina; d. June 14, 1968, Wilkes County, North Carolina.
410. xi. JAMES HERBERT LAND, b. November 29, 1918; d. June 18, 1980, Caldwell County, North Carolina.
xii. VALECIE LAND[380], b. December 03, 1921, Wilkes County, North Carolina[380]; d. July 06, 1924[380].
xiii. DAVID ALBERT LAND[389], b. December 05, 1923, Wilkes County, North Carolina[380]; d. January 04, 1924, Wilkes County, North Carolina[389].

308. PARTEE VANCE[10] LAND *(ELI JASON[9], DAVID[8], JAMES[7], JONATHAN[6], THOMAS[5], THOMAS[4], JOHN[3], CURTIS[2], CURTIS[1])*[380] was born February 14, 1888 in Caldwell County, North Carolina[380], and died June 02, 1968 in Wilkes County, North Carolina[380]. He married CALLIE O. LIVINGSTON[380] January 21, 1912[380].

More About PARTEE VANCE LAND:
Burial: Little Rock Church Cemetery[380]

Children of PARTEE LAND and CALLIE LIVINGSTON are:

411. i. LIVING[11] LAND.
ii. LIVING LAND[380].
412. iii. LIVING LAND.
iv. LIVING LAND[380], m. LIVING ROBERTS[380].
v. JAMES HOWARD LAND[380], b. August 31, 1923, Wilkes County, North Carolina[380]; d. June 24, 1981, Wilkes County, North Carolina[380].

More About JAMES HOWARD LAND:
Burial: Little Rock Church Cemetery[380]

309. JAMES EDGAR[10] LAND *(ELI JASON[9], DAVID[8], JAMES[7], JONATHAN[6], THOMAS[5], THOMAS[4], JOHN[3], CURTIS[2], CURTIS[1])*[380] was born May 24, 1889 in Caldwell County, North Carolina[380], and died May 06, 1965 in Wilkes County, North Carolina[380]. He married ELIZABETH CARLTON[380].

More About JAMES EDGAR LAND:
Burial: Little Rock Church Cemetery[380]

Child of JAMES LAND and ELIZABETH CARLTON is:
i. LIVING[11] LAND[380].

310. FRED COLUMBUS[10] LAND *(ELI JASON[9], DAVID[8], JAMES[7], JONATHAN[6], THOMAS[5], THOMAS[4], JOHN[3], CURTIS[2], CURTIS[1])*[380] was born August 12, 1892 in Caldwell County, North Carolina[380], and died February 23, 1970 in Catawba County, North Carolina[380]. He married LIVING COX[380].

More About FRED COLUMBUS LAND:
Burial: Catawba Memorial Cemetery[380]

Children of FRED LAND and LIVING COX are:
i. LIVING[11] LAND[380], m. LIVING WHITE[380].
ii. LIVING LAND[380], m. LIVING JEAN[380].

311. LIVING[10] LAND *(THOMAS CLINGMAN[9], DAVID[8], JAMES[7], JONATHAN[6], THOMAS[5], THOMAS[4], JOHN[3], CURTIS[2], CURTIS[1])*[380]. He married LIVING UNKNOWN[380].

Children of LIVING LAND and LIVING UNKNOWN are:

i. LIVING[11] LAND[380].
ii. LIVING LAND[380].
iii. LIVING LAND[380].

312. HAYDEN JAMES[10] LAND *(THOMAS CLINGMAN[9], DAVID[8], JAMES[7], JONATHAN[6], THOMAS[5], THOMAS[4], JOHN[3], CURTIS[2], CURTIS[1])*[381,382] was born 1885 in Wilkes County, North Carolina[382], and died 1968 in Dallas, Texas[382]. He married LIVING UPTMORE[382].
Hayden was once a US Marine, assigned to Quantico MCB, Virginia - where he was on the Marine Corps Football Team in the early 1930's.

Children of HAYDEN LAND and LIVING UPTMORE are:

i. LIVING[11] LAND[382], m. LIVING PATTERSON[382].
ii. LIVING LAND[382].
iii. LIVING LAND[382].

313. SR. FRED[10] LAND *(THOMAS CLINGMAN[9], DAVID[8], JAMES[7], JONATHAN[6], THOMAS[5], THOMAS[4], JOHN[3], CURTIS[2], CURTIS[1])*[383,384] was born May 28, 1891 in Caldwell County, North Carolina[384], and died December 07, 1967 in Caldwell County, North Carolina[384]. He married GRACE MALTA WEEKS[384]. She was born in Caldwell County, North Carolina[384].
A piano player with Tommy Dorsey Band

More About SR. FRED LAND:
Burial: Blue Ridge Memorial Park[384]

Children of FRED LAND and GRACE WEEKS are:

i. BETTY[11] LAND[384], b. Lenoir, North Carolina[384]; d. Collettesville, North Carolina[384].
ii. LIVING LAND[384].
iii. JR. FRED LAND[384], b. Wilkes County, North Carolina[384]; d. Atlanta, Georgia[384].
iv. JACK L. LAND[384], b. Watauga[384]; d. Asheville, North Carolina[384].
v. WILLOWDEAN LAND[384], b. Wilkes County, North Carolina[384]; d. Greensboro, North Carolina[384]; m. LIVING BARTUS[384].

314. RALPH CALDWELL[10] LAND *(THOMAS CLINGMAN[9], DAVID[8], JAMES[7], JONATHAN[6], THOMAS[5], THOMAS[4], JOHN[3], CURTIS[2], CURTIS[1])*[384] was born March 02, 1895 in Caldwell County, North Carolina[385,386], and died March 29, 1982 in Lenoir, North Carolina[386]. He married (1) MINNIE BARLOW[386]. She was born in Wilkes County, North Carolina[386], and died in after giving birth[386]. He married (2) BERTHA MALISSA PENNELL[386]. She was born August 05, 1900 in Kings Creek, Caldwell County, North Carolina[386], and died May 17, 1972 in Lenoir, Caldwell County, North Carolina[386].

More About RALPH CALDWELL LAND:
Burial: Lower Creek Cemetery, Lenoir, North Carolina[386]
Occupation: Professional Carpenter[386]

More About BERTHA MALISSA PENNELL:
Burial: Lower Creek Cemetery, Lenoir, North Carolina[386]
Occupation: Professional School Teacher[386]

Child of RALPH LAND and MINNIE BARLOW is:

i. BABY[11] LAND[386].

Children of RALPH LAND and BERTHA PENNELL are:

413. ii. LIVING[11] LAND.

414. iii. Living Land.
415. iv. Sr. Howard Douglas Land, b. November 12, 1922, Lenoir, Caldwell County, North Carolina; d. May 08, 1995, Newport News, Virginia.

315. Vera[10] Land *(Thomas Clingman[9], David[8], James[7], Jonathan[6], Thomas[5], Thomas[4], John[3], Curtis[2], Curtis[1])*[386] was born May 01, 1908 in Wilkes County, North Carolina[386], and died February 21, 1993 in Catawba County, North Carolina[386]. She married Living Bishop[386].

Children of Vera Land and Living Bishop are:
- i. Living[11] Bishop[386].
- ii. Living Bishop[386].
- iii. Living Bishop[386].
- iv. Living Bishop[386].

316. Ella Mae[10] Land *(John Wesley[9], Allison[8], James Noah[7], Thomas[6], Thomas[5], Thomas[4], John[3], Curtis[2], Curtis[1])*[386] was born October 09, 1903 in Monroe County, Tennessee[386], and died February 03, 1992 in Blount County, Tennessee[386]. She married James Franklin Raper[386] October 01, 1918 in Monroe County, Tennessee[386]. He was born October 16, 1897[386].

More About Ella Mae Land:
Burial: Clarks Grove Cemetery, Maryville, Blount County, Tennessee[386]

Children of Ella Land and James Raper are:
- i. Living[11] Raper[386].
- ii. Living Raper[386].
- iii. Living Raper[386].
- iv. Living Raper[386].

317. Gracie Alice[10] Land *(John Wesley[9], Allison[8], James Noah[7], Thomas[6], Thomas[5], Thomas[4], John[3], Curtis[2], Curtis[1])*[386] was born March 16, 1911 in Monroe County, Tennessee[386], and died November 10, 2001 in Maryville, Tennessee[386]. She married Edgar Huskey[386] January 01, 1930[386]. He was born June 12, 1899[386].

More About Gracie Alice Land:
Burial: Liberty Baptist Church Cemetery, Blount County, Tennessee[386]

Children of Gracie Land and Edgar Huskey are:
- i. Living[11] Huskey[386].
- ii. Living Huskey[386].
- iii. Living Huskey[386].
- iv. Living Huskey[386].
- v. Living Huskey[386].
- vi. Living Huskey[386].
- vii. Living Huskey[386].
- viii. Living Huskey[386].
- ix. Living Huskey[386].
- x. Living Huskey[386].

318. Living[10] Farthing *(Living[9] Land, Raymond Timothy[8], William Jefferson[7], John Henry[6], Charles[5], Charles[4], Curtis[3], Curtis[2], Curtis[1])*[387]. He married Big Cheese Living Wall[387,388].

Children of Living Farthing and Living Wall are:
- i. Living[11] Farthing[389].

416. ii. Living Farthing.
- iii. Living Farthing[389].

319. Living[10] Farthing *(Living[9] Land, Raymond Timothy[8], William Jefferson[7], John Henry[6], Charles[5], Charles[4], Curtis[3], Curtis[2], Curtis[1])*[390]. He married Big Cheese Living Wall[391,392].

Children of Living Farthing and Living Wall are:

i. LIVING[11] FARTHING[392].
417. ii. LIVING FARTHING.
iii. LIVING FARTHING[392].

320. LIVING[10] LAND *(LIVING[9], RAYMOND TIMOTHY[8], WILLIAM JEFFERSON[7], JOHN HENRY[6], CHARLES[5], CHARLES[4], CURTIS[3], CURTIS[2], CURTIS[1])*[392]. She married LIVING BANES[392].

Child of LIVING LAND and LIVING BANES is:
418. i. LIVING[11] BANES.

321. LIVING[10] LAND *(LIVING[9], RAYMOND TIMOTHY[8], WILLIAM JEFFERSON[7], JOHN HENRY[6], CHARLES[5], CHARLES[4], CURTIS[3], CURTIS[2], CURTIS[1])*[392]. She married LIVING BROCK[392].

Children of LIVING LAND and LIVING BROCK are:
419. i. LIVING[11] BROCK.
ii. LIVING BROCK[392].
iii. LIVING BROCK[392].

322. LIVING[10] LAND *(LIVING[9], RAYMOND TIMOTHY[8], WILLIAM JEFFERSON[7], JOHN HENRY[6], CHARLES[5], CHARLES[4], CURTIS[3], CURTIS[2], CURTIS[1])*[392]. She married LIVING HENRY[392].

Children of LIVING LAND and LIVING HENRY are:
i. LIVING[11] HENRY[392].
ii. LIVING HENRY[392].
iii. LIVING HENRY[392].

323. LIVING[10] LAND *(LIVING[9], RAYMOND TIMOTHY[8], WILLIAM JEFFERSON[7], JOHN HENRY[6], CHARLES[5], CHARLES[4], CURTIS[3], CURTIS[2], CURTIS[1])*[392]. She married LIVING WASHBURN[392].

Child of LIVING LAND and LIVING WASHBURN is:
i. LIVING[11] WASHBURN[392].

324. LIVING[10] POPE *(MAE KRIDER[9] HARGROVE, ROBERT HENRY[8], GRAY LEMON[7], SALLY[6] LAND, LITTLEBERRY[5], BIRD[4], CURTIS[3], CURTIS[2], CURTIS[1])* She married JR. LIVING CROWDER.

Children of LIVING POPE and LIVING CROWDER are:
i. LIVING[11] CROWDER.
ii. LIVING CROWDER.

325. LIVING[10] POPE *(MAE KRIDER[9] HARGROVE, ROBERT HENRY[8], GRAY LEMON[7], SALLY[6] LAND, LITTLEBERRY[5], BIRD[4], CURTIS[3], CURTIS[2], CURTIS[1])*[393]. She married JR. LIVING CROWDER[393].

Children of LIVING POPE and LIVING CROWDER are:
i. LIVING[11] CROWDER[393].
ii. LIVING CROWDER[393].

326. SALLY GRAY[10] HARGROVE *(WALTER CLARK[9], JOHN DAVID[8], GRAY LEMON[7], SALLY[6] LAND, LITTLEBERRY[5], BIRD[4], CURTIS[3], CURTIS[2], CURTIS[1])*[393] was born September 19, 1918 in Spring Hope, NC[393], and died July 15, 1992 in Greenville, NC[393]. She married SR. HERBERT THEODORE BAILEY[393] June 08, 1940. He was born April 04, 1912[393], and died May 17, 1974 in Tarboro, NC[393].

Notes for SR. HERBERT THEODORE BAILEY:
The Raleigh News & Observer
August 26, 1962
Tar Heel of the Week
H. T. Bailey of Tarboro
By Roy Parker, Jr.
"Tarboro is a proud old town, it takes about 15 years to break in," says H. T. Bailey.

With a grin, Bailey admits: "I was a newcomer until I got elected mayor."
The 50-year-old Bailey, a native of Hobgood just down the road from proud Tarboro, "broke in" fast as the community's mayor, and his administration coincided with a great leap forward in Tarboro's economy. Proud of the record, although giving major credit to Tarboro's new generation of leaders, Bailey is out of the public position right now.
"I've got four children to send through college. I'm going to lay out of politics for awhile, but I'll be back in", he promises.
Bailey means he will stick to business as the sales director of Southern Concrete Products Company of Rocky Mount , of Stevenson Brick and Block of New Bern, and Goldsboro Block Company. A ll three firms provide building materials for schools, hospitals, and other big public projects in eastern North Carolina.
MAIN INTEREST
Moving from the job of helping Tarboro meet the challenges of a new day to the job of working for his children's education, Bailey's main interest now is in East Carolina
College. He has no less thatn three sons at the Greenville institution, and most of his conversations these days is apt to be about the activities on the Greenville campus. One son, Bill, is slated to be the ECC football team 's first string fullback this fall. Another, Herbert Jr., has one more year at ECC, and then plans a career as an English professor. Reynolds Bailey, an ECC freshman, wants to be an accountant. Back home in Tarboro, daughter Sally Gray is a junior at Tarboro High.
Typical of the man-of-all-talents type of community leaders who are pushing their towns to meet the need of the modern day, Bailey has been active in the entire spectrum of
community activities.
Industry-hunting was the main effort during his tenure as mayor, from 159 until last year. Tarboro's first families, men whose wealth was made from the broad tobacco lands of the Roanoke Valley area, turned their outlook toward the future, and the city which had been known for its ancient charm burst into a frenzy of modern activity.
LANDED INDUSTRY.
In two years, Tarboro landed three big industries, adding nearly 1,000 jobs to its economy. The community set up an industrial development organization that has been the envy of its neighbors, staffed by a $15,000-a-year executive. Bailey as mayor and longtime chamber and merchants association leader, was in the thick of the industry-hunting activities. He is proud that Tarboro has pulled itself up by its own bootstraps. "We did it all with local capital," he says, and gives full credit to the enlightening willingness to take a chance of the community's wealthier citizens who could have continued in their old ways.
"There were some who held Tarboro back, but they are on the go now," he says.
Bailey credits his wife, school teacher Sally Gray Hargrove Bailey, with "pushing me into these jobs." Whoever is responsible Tarboro folks say Bailey was one of the first
"newcomers" to preach the line that Tarboro needed to keep up with the times.
Just after World War II, he headed the chamber of commerce. He organized the local Jaycees in 1947 and was its first president. That same year, he helped organize the
Tarboro High School band. He worked on the board of the Tarboro federal housing project, one of eastern North Carolina's first public housing programs. The project provided 100 housing units, 50 for Negroes.
PENCHANT FOR POLITICS.
His penchant for politics came naturally, too. Bailey's father is still active.

Children of SALLY HARGROVE and HERBERT BAILEY are:

- i. SR. LIVING[11] BAILEY.
- ii. JR. LIVING BAILEY.
- iii. LIVING BAILEY.
- iv. LIVING BAILEY.
- v. SR. LIVING BAILEY[393].
- vi. JR. LIVING BAILEY[393].
- vii. LIVING BAILEY[393].
- viii. LIVING BAILEY[393].

327. WALTER CLARK[10] HARGROVE *(WALTER CLARK[9], JOHN DAVID[8], GRAY LEMON[7], SALLY[6] LAND, LITTLEBERRY[5], BIRD[4], CURTIS[3], CURTIS[2], CURTIS[1])*[393] was born June 20, 1920 in Tarboro, Edgecombe Co., NC[393], and died May 19, 1969 in Edgecombe Co. NC[393]. He married ALICE LEIGH BLOW[393] June 05, 1943 in Greenville, NC. She was born 1922[393].

Children of WALTER HARGROVE and ALICE BLOW are:
i. III LIVING[11] HARGROVE.
ii. LIVING HARGROVE.
iii. LIVING HARGROVE.
iv. III LIVING HARGROVE[393].
v. LIVING HARGROVE[393].
vi. LIVING HARGROVE[393].

328. LIVING[10] MILAM *(EFFIE LAVINA[9] VANDEVENDER, MARY MILDRED "MAGGIE"[8] LAND, WILLIAM BURT[7], BURRELL[6], LITTLEBERRY[5], BIRD[4], CURTIS[3], CURTIS[2], CURTIS[1])*[394]. She married (1) LOYAL AUGUSTUS DANIEL[394]. He was born November 08, 1914 in Ochlocknee, Thomas County, Georgia[394], and died June 24, 1991 in Panama City, Bay County, Florida[394]. She married (2) LIVING AMES[394].

More About LOYAL AUGUSTUS DANIEL:
Burial: June 26, 1991, Kent Forest Cemetery, Panama City, Bay County, Florida[394]

Children of LIVING MILAM and LOYAL DANIEL are:
420. i. LIVING[11] DANIEL.
421. ii. LIVING DANIEL.
422. iii. LIVING DANIEL.

Children of LIVING MILAM and LIVING AMES are:
iv. LIVING[11] AMES[394].
v. LIVING AMES[394].
vi. LIVING AMES[394].
vii. LIVING AMES[394].
viii. LIVING AMES[394].

329. SYBLE WAYNE[10] MILAM *(EFFIE LAVINA[9] VANDEVENDER, MARY MILDRED "MAGGIE"[8] LAND, WILLIAM BURT[7], BURRELL[6], LITTLEBERRY[5], BIRD[4], CURTIS[3], CURTIS[2], CURTIS[1])*[395,396] was born December 16, 1918 in Arkansas[396], and died May 13, 2003 in Memphis, Shelby County, Tennessee[396]. She married ROBERT LANCE MURPHY[396] in Arkansas[396]. He was born June 11, 1915 in Calhoun City, Calhoun County, Mississippi[396], and died October 30, 1984 in Arkansas[396].

More About SYBLE WAYNE MILAM:
Burial: May 19, 2003, Crittenden Memorial Cemetery, Marion, Arkansas[396]

More About ROBERT LANCE MURPHY:
Burial: Crittenden Memorial Cemetery, Marion, Arkansas[396]

Children of SYBLE MILAM and ROBERT MURPHY are:
423. i. LIVING[11] MURPHY.
424. ii. LIVING MURPHY.
425. iii. LIVING MURPHY.
426. iv. LIVING MURPHY.

330. LIVING[10] PALMER *(MARY MILDRED[9] VANDEVENDER, MARY MILDRED "MAGGIE"[8] LAND, WILLIAM BURT[7], BURRELL[6], LITTLEBERRY[5], BIRD[4], CURTIS[3], CURTIS[2], CURTIS[1])*[396]. He married LIVING JOHNSON[396].

Child of LIVING PALMER and LIVING JOHNSON is:
i. LIVING[11] PALMER[396].

331. LILA[10] HORSEMAN *(LIVING[9] BAILEY, RHODES[8], WILLIAM W.[7], ELIZABETH[6] LAND, LEWIS[5], BIRD[4], CURTIS[3], CURTIS[2], CURTIS[1])*[397]. She married JAMES GERALD JONES[397], son of WILLIAM JONES and BERTHA TYLER. He was born June 29, 1914[397], and died May 29, 1994 in St. Bernards Hospital, Jonesboro, Ar.[397].
Facts about this person:
Burial June 1994

Ravenden Springs, Ar.

Child is listed above under (280) James Gerald Jones.

332. JAMES BURLEY[10] BAILEY *(JAMES THEADORE[9], GEORGE WASHINGTON[8], WILLIAM W.[7], ELIZABETH[6] LAND, LEWIS[5], BIRD[4], CURTIS[3], CURTIS[2], CURTIS[1])* was born December 13, 1905. He married MAZIE ENGLISH. She was born December 13, 1905.

Children of JAMES BAILEY and MAZIE ENGLISH are:

i. GLENN[11] BAILEY.
ii. GORDON BAILEY.

333. EUGENE[10] BAILEY *(JAMES THEADORE[9], GEORGE WASHINGTON[8], WILLIAM W.[7], ELIZABETH[6] LAND, LEWIS[5], BIRD[4], CURTIS[3], CURTIS[2], CURTIS[1])* He married OMA FREEMAN.

Child of EUGENE BAILEY and OMA FREEMAN is:

i. BILL[11] BAILEY.

334. ARLENE[10] BAILEY *(JAMES THEADORE[9], GEORGE WASHINGTON[8], WILLIAM W.[7], ELIZABETH[6] LAND, LEWIS[5], BIRD[4], CURTIS[3], CURTIS[2], CURTIS[1])* She married MILLARD BLANSETT, son of WILLIAM BLANSETT and SARAH SMITH. He was born November 11, 1903 in Water Valley, Randolph, Arkansas, and died May 14, 1967.

Children of ARLENE BAILEY and MILLARD BLANSETT are:

i. MILDRED ARLENE[11] BLANSETT.
ii. LEON BLANSETT.

335. RUBY[10] BAILEY *(JAMES THEADORE[9], GEORGE WASHINGTON[8], WILLIAM W.[7], ELIZABETH[6] LAND, LEWIS[5], BIRD[4], CURTIS[3], CURTIS[2], CURTIS[1])* She married SOL BRADFORD.

Children of RUBY BAILEY and SOL BRADFORD are:

i. SHIRLEY[11] BRADFORD.
ii. ELBERT BRADFORD.
iii. MICHAEL BRADFORD.
iv. CAROL BRADFORD.

336. DONALD[10] BAILEY *(JAMES THEADORE[9], GEORGE WASHINGTON[8], WILLIAM W.[7], ELIZABETH[6] LAND, LEWIS[5], BIRD[4], CURTIS[3], CURTIS[2], CURTIS[1])* He married DORIS BAILEY.

Children of DONALD BAILEY and DORIS BAILEY are:

i. JAMES[11] BAILEY.
ii. SHERRIL BAILEY.
iii. JEWELETTA BAILEY.
iv. PATRICIA BAILEY.

337. BIRDIE[10] BAILEY *(JAMES THEADORE[9], GEORGE WASHINGTON[8], WILLIAM W.[7], ELIZABETH[6] LAND, LEWIS[5], BIRD[4], CURTIS[3], CURTIS[2], CURTIS[1])* She married ERNEST RICE.

Children of BIRDIE BAILEY and ERNEST RICE are:

i. NOVELLA[11] RICE.
ii. OLA RICE.
iii. GAY RICE.

338. ELGIN[10] HARRISON *(FANNIE LULA[9] BAILEY, GEORGE WASHINGTON[8], WILLIAM W.[7], ELIZABETH[6] LAND, LEWIS[5], BIRD[4], CURTIS[3], CURTIS[2], CURTIS[1])*

Child of ELGIN HARRISON is:

i. STEVE[11] HARRISON.

339. LOIS MARIE[10] HARRISON *(FANNIE LULA[9] BAILEY, GEORGE WASHINGTON[8], WILLIAM W.[7], ELIZABETH [6]LAND, LEWIS[5], BIRD[4], CURTIS[3], CURTIS[2], CURTIS[1])* She married WILLIAM TURNER.

Children of LOIS HARRISON and WILLIAM TURNER are:

i. ONALEE[11] TURNER.
ii. JR. TURNER WILLIAM.
iii. RONALD TURNER.

340. WILLIAM MILLARD[10] BAILEY *(WILLIAM SOLOMON[9], GEORGE WASHINGTON[8], WILLIAM W.[7], ELIZABETH [6]LAND, LEWIS[5], BIRD[4], CURTIS[3], CURTIS[2], CURTIS[1])* was born July 03, 1914. He married MIRIAM RICKMAN June 27, 1936. She was born May 18, 1915.

Children of WILLIAM BAILEY and MIRIAM RICKMAN are:

i. CAROL[11] BAILEY, b. November 02, 1941.
ii. WILLIAM MILLARD "BILL" BAILEY, b. December 23, 1945.

341. SIBYL[10] BAILEY *(ALBERT DONALD[9], GEORGE WASHINGTON[8], WILLIAM W.[7], ELIZABETH [6]LAND, LEWIS[5], BIRD[4], CURTIS[3], CURTIS[2], CURTIS[1])* She married JOHN KING.

Children of SIBYL BAILEY and JOHN KING are:

i. LEON[11] KING.
ii. STANLEY KING.

342. MANLEY[10] BAILEY *(ALBERT DONALD[9], GEORGE WASHINGTON[8], WILLIAM W.[7], ELIZABETH [6]LAND, LEWIS[5], BIRD[4], CURTIS[3], CURTIS[2], CURTIS[1])* He married JEAN BROWN.

Children of MANLEY BAILEY and JEAN BROWN are:

i. DONALD[11] BAILEY.
ii. CARL BAILEY.
iii. GAIL BAILEY.
iv. ROGER BAILEY.
v. CAROL BAILEY.
vi. BRENDA BAILEY.
vii. HAROLD BAILEY.
viii. ANNA BAILEY.

343. CLEO[10] BAILEY *(ALBERT DONALD[9], GEORGE WASHINGTON[8], WILLIAM W.[7], ELIZABETH [6]LAND, LEWIS[5], BIRD[4], CURTIS[3], CURTIS[2], CURTIS[1])* She married WANDA HEPLER, son of RALPH HEPLER and WILLIE BAIRD.

Children of CLEO BAILEY and WANDA HEPLER are:

i. RANDAL[11] HEPLER.
ii. PATRICIA HEPLER.
iii. SHARON HEPLER.

344. MILDRED[10] BAILEY *(ALBERT DONALD[9], GEORGE WASHINGTON[8], WILLIAM W.[7], ELIZABETH [6]LAND, LEWIS[5], BIRD[4], CURTIS[3], CURTIS[2], CURTIS[1])* She married J. R. "BOB" DAIL.

Children of MILDRED BAILEY and J. DAIL are:

i. JOHNNIE[11] DAIL.
ii. ROBIN DAIL.
iii. DENNIS DAIL.
iv. JANE LYNN DAIL.

345. ALDEAN[10] BAILEY *(ALBERT DONALD[9], GEORGE WASHINGTON[8], WILLIAM W.[7], ELIZABETH [6]LAND, LEWIS[5], BIRD[4], CURTIS[3], CURTIS[2], CURTIS[1])* She married ALMUS HOGAN.

Children of ALDEAN BAILEY and ALMUS HOGAN are:

i. RONNIE[11] HOGAN.
ii. KAREN HOGAN.

iii. Melissa Hogan
iv. Paula Hogan.

346. Guy[10] Bailey *(Virgil[9], George Washington[8], William W.[7], Elizabeth[6] Land, Lewis[5], Bird[4], Curtis[3], Curtis[2], Curtis[1])* He married Mildred.

Children of Guy Bailey and Mildred are:
427. i. Dailey[11] Bailey.
ii. Lucille Bailey.
428. iii. Bettie Marie Bailey.

347. Evalena[10] Bailey *(Frederick[9], Allen A.[8], William W.[7], Elizabeth[6] Land, Lewis[5], Bird[4], Curtis[3], Curtis[2], Curtis[1])* She married Wayne Fry Horsman, son of Newton Horsman and Isabelle Fry.

Children of Evalena Bailey and Wayne Horsman are:
i. Freddie Fry[11] Horsman, b. July 16, 1934; d. September 21, 1984.
ii. Carma Jane Horsman, d. June 09, 1972.

More About Carma Jane Horsman:
Burial: McIlroy Cemetery, Randolph Co., Arkansas

iii. Allen Horsman.

348. Thelma Nel[10] Davis *(William Clark[9], Mary Elizabeth "Matilda"[8] Bailey, William W.[7], Elizabeth[6] Land, Lewis[5], Bird[4], Curtis[3], Curtis[2], Curtis[1])* She married G. W. Butler.

Child of Thelma Davis and G. Butler is:
i. Ruth Anne[11] Butler.

349. Robert David[10] Parris *(Robert David[9], Warner David[8], Susannah[7] Land, Stephen[6], Lewis[5], Bird[4], Curtis[3], Curtis[2], Curtis[1])* was born November 09, 1939 in Sioux Falls, South Dakota. He married Anna Gayle Love. She was born September 08, 1943 in Hardin Co., TN.

Children of Robert Parris and Anna Love are:
i. Gregory David[11] Parris, b. July 02, 1963.
ii. James Michael Parris, b. November 1967.

350. Jim Warner[10] Parris *(Robert David[9], Warner David[8], Susannah[7] Land, Stephen[6], Lewis[5], Bird[4], Curtis[3], Curtis[2], Curtis[1])* was born December 18, 1945 in Sioux Falls, South Dakota. He married Ruth Dorothy Rodriguez June 23, 1979 in Rogers, Arkansas. She was born November 10, 1952 in Tela, Honduras.

Children of Jim Parris and Ruth Rodriguez are:
i. Lucas Martin[11] Parris, b. October 10, 1981.
ii. Caroline Anne Parris, b. September 10, 1985.
iii. Jubal Robert Parris, b. August 15, 1987.

351. William Griffin[10] Parris *(William Benson[9], Warner David[8], Susannah[7] Land, Stephen[6], Lewis[5], Bird[4], Curtis[3], Curtis[2], Curtis[1])* was born April 17, 1957 in Savannah, Tennessee. He married Carla.

Children of William Parris and Carla are:
i. Sarah Elizabeth[11] Parris, b. 1991.

Notes for Sarah Elizabeth Parris:
Adopted

ii. Kathleen Parris, b. 1993.

Notes for Kathleen Parris:

Adopted

352. BENSON LAMAR[10] PARRIS *(WILLIAM BENSON[9], WARNER DAVID[8], SUSANNAH[7] LAND, STEPHEN[6], LEWIS[5], BIRD[4], CURTIS[3], CURTIS[2], CURTIS[1])* was born February 25, 1959 in Savannah, Tennessee. He married DENISE POLLARD June 04, 1985 in Tennessee. She was born October 10, 1962 in Memphis, TN.

Children of BENSON PARRIS and DENISE POLLARD are:
- i. NATHANIEL BENSON[11] PARRIS, b. March 10, 1988.
- ii. CHANDLER CHRISTENE PARRIS, b. November 11, 1991.
- iii. AUSTIN BROOK PARRIS, b. January 15, 1995.
- iv. NOAH JACKSON PARRIS, b. August 08, 1997.

353. DONALD LESTER[10] PARRIS *(HAROLD LESTER[9], WARNER DAVID[8], SUSANNAH[7] LAND, STEPHEN[6], LEWIS[5], BIRD[4], CURTIS[3], CURTIS[2], CURTIS[1])* was born January 29, 1947 in Atlanta, Georgia. He married RUTH REVELISE February 18, 1979. She was born October 01, 1946.

Child of DONALD PARRIS and RUTH REVELISE is:
- i. MAX WARNER[11] PARRIS, b. December 19, 1980, Hilton Head, SC.

354. CHRIS LAMAR[10] PADGETT *(HAZEL CORNELIA[9] PARRIS, WARNER DAVID[8], SUSANNAH[7] LAND, STEPHEN[6], LEWIS[5], BIRD[4], CURTIS[3], CURTIS[2], CURTIS[1])* was born March 09, 1950 in Georgia. He married CAROL HIX March 08, 1975 in Georgia. She was born November 25, 1953 in Georgia.

Children of CHRIS PADGETT and CAROL HIX are:
- i. MINDY JOY[11] PADGETT, b. October 27, 1980.
- ii. TARA ELAINE PADGETT, b. April 01, 1986.

355. KATHY CORNELIA[10] PADGETT *(HAZEL CORNELIA[9] PARRIS, WARNER DAVID[8], SUSANNAH[7] LAND, STEPHEN[6], LEWIS[5], BIRD[4], CURTIS[3], CURTIS[2], CURTIS[1])* was born September 26, 1951. She married LYNN MEREL LEWIS June 16, 1974 in Georgia. He was born December 12, 1951.

Child of KATHY PADGETT and LYNN LEWIS is:
- i. NICHOLE[11] LEWIS, b. 1975.

356. MARK JOHN[10] PADGETT *(HAZEL CORNELIA[9] PARRIS, WARNER DAVID[8], SUSANNAH[7] LAND, STEPHEN[6], LEWIS[5], BIRD[4], CURTIS[3], CURTIS[2], CURTIS[1])* was born March 16, 1958 in Georgia. He married SUZIE.

Child of MARK PADGETT and SUZIE is:
- i. ?[11] PADGETT.

357. LIVING[10] REED *(JOE LUTHER[9], LUCRETIA (LOU CRECY) JANE[8] LAND, JORDON[7], KINSON[6], LEWIS[5], BIRD[4], CURTIS[3], CURTIS[2], CURTIS[1])*[398]. He married LIVING DEPEW[398].

Children of LIVING REED and LIVING DEPEW are:

429. i. LIVING[11] REED.
430. ii. LIVING REED.
431. iii. LIVING REED.
432. iv. LIVING REED.

358. LIVING[10] REED *(JOE LUTHER[9], LUCRETIA (LOU CRECY) JANE[8] LAND, JORDON[7], KINSON[6], LEWIS[5], BIRD[4], CURTIS[3], CURTIS[2], CURTIS[1])*[398]. She married LIVING SAPP[398].

Children of LIVING REED and LIVING SAPP are:

433. i. LIVING[11] SAPP.
434. ii. LIVING SAPP.

359. JESSIE JAMES[10] REED *(JOE LUTHER[9], LUCRETIA (LOU CRECY) JANE[8] LAND, JORDON[7], KINSON[6], LEWIS[5], BIRD[4], CURTIS[3], CURTIS[2], CURTIS[1])*[398] was born May 10, 1932[398], and died October 31, 1985 in Illinois[398]. He married ALICE MARIE MYERS[398] November 30, 1949[398]. She was born May 11, 1930[398].

More About ALICE MARIE MYERS:
Burial: Garver Cemetery, Decatur, Illinois[398]

Children of JESSIE REED and ALICE MYERS are:
435. i. LIVING[11] REED.
436. ii. LIVING REED.
iii. LIVING REED[398], m. LIVING GREER[398].
iv. HARRY JAMES REED[398], b. January 11, 1952[398]; d. January 22, 1952[398].

360. LIVING[10] REED *(JAMES ALVIS[9], LUCRETIA (LOU CRECY) JANE[8] LAND, JORDON[7], KINSON[6], LEWIS[5], BIRD[4], CURTIS[3], CURTIS[2], CURTIS[1])*[398]. She married LIVING COLLINS[398].

Children of LIVING REED and LIVING COLLINS are:
i. LIVING[11] COLLINS[398], m. LIVING NUDO[398].
ii. LIVING COLLINS[398].
iii. LIVING COLLINS[398].
iv. LIVING COLLINS[398].
v. LIVING COLLINS[398], m. LIVING LITTLE[398].
vi. LIVING COLLINS[398].
vii. LIVING COLLINS[398], m. LIVING SHOEMAKER[398].
viii. LIVING COLLINS[398].
ix. LIVING COLLINS[398], m. (1) JR. LIVING KING[398]; m. (2) LIVING KENDRICK[398].

361. LIVING[10] CURTIS *(BESSIE TENNESSEE[9] REED, LUCRETIA (LOU CRECY) JANE[8] LAND, JORDON[7], KINSON[6], LEWIS[5], BIRD[4], CURTIS[3], CURTIS[2], CURTIS[1])*[398]. She married (1) BILLY QUILLMAN[398]. He was born December 27, 1936[398], and died March 1981 in Batesville, Arkansas[398]. She married (2) RUSSELL STAGGS[398]. He was born September 20, 1927[398], and died October 1980 in Cave City, Arkansas[398].

More About BILLY QUILLMAN:
Burial: Pleasant Valley Cemetery, Cushman, Arkansas[398]

Child of LIVING CURTIS and BILLY QUILLMAN is:
i. LIVING[11] QUILLMAN[398].

Child of LIVING CURTIS and RUSSELL STAGGS is:
437. ii. LIVING[11] STAGGS.

362. LIVING[10] STROTHER *(BESSIE TENNESSEE[9] REED, LUCRETIA (LOU CRECY) JANE[8] LAND, JORDON[7], KINSON[6], LEWIS[5], BIRD[4], CURTIS[3], CURTIS[2], CURTIS[1])*[398]. He married LIVING RORIE[398].

Child of LIVING STROTHER and LIVING RORIE is:
i. LIVING[11] STROTHER[398].

363. LIVING[10] COKER *(ORA DELLAR[9] REED, LUCRETIA (LOU CRECY) JANE[8] LAND, JORDON[7], KINSON[6], LEWIS[5], BIRD[4], CURTIS[3], CURTIS[2], CURTIS[1])*[398]. He married (1) LIVING RICHERSON[398]. He married (2) MARIE GLADIS ADAMS[398]. She died June 2002 in California[398].

Child of LIVING COKER and LIVING RICHERSON is:
438. i. LIVING[11] COKER.

Children of LIVING COKER and MARIE ADAMS are:
439. ii. LIVING[11] COKER.

440. iii. LIVING COKER.
441. iv. LIVING COKER.
442. v. LIVING COKER.
vi. LIVING COKER[398].
vii. LIVING COKER[398].

364. LIVING[10] COKER *(ORA DELLAR[9] REED, LUCRETIA (LOU CRECY) JANE[8] LAND, JORDON[7], KINSON[6], LEWIS[5], BIRD[4], CURTIS[3], CURTIS[2], CURTIS[1])*[398]. She married BILL THOMAS WILSON[398]. He was born April 28, 1921 in Buffalo, Arkansas[398], and died May 13, 1998[398].

More About BILL THOMAS WILSON:
Burial: Edgar Cemetery, Independence County, Arkansas[398]

Children of LIVING COKER and BILL WILSON are:
443. i. LIVING[11] WILSON.
444. ii. LIVING WILSON.
445. iii. LIVING WILSON.
446. iv. LIVING WILSON.
447. v. LIVING WILSON.
vi. LIVING WILSON[398].
448. vii. LIVING WILSON.

365. LIVING[10] COKER *(ORA DELLAR[9] REED, LUCRETIA (LOU CRECY) JANE[8] LAND, JORDON[7], KINSON[6], LEWIS[5], BIRD[4], CURTIS[3], CURTIS[2], CURTIS[1])*[398]. She married FRANKLIN NATHANIEL HAWKINS[398]. He was born August 04, 1934[398], and died February 13, 2002[398].

Children of LIVING COKER and FRANKLIN HAWKINS are:
449. i. LIVING[11] HAWKINS.
450. ii. LIVING HAWKINS.
451. iii. LIVING HAWKINS.
iv. LIVING HAWKINS[398].
v. LIVING HAWKINS[398].

366. JAMES WALTER[10] COKER *(ORA DELLAR[9] REED, LUCRETIA (LOU CRECY) JANE[8] LAND, JORDON[7], KINSON[6], LEWIS[5], BIRD[4], CURTIS[3], CURTIS[2], CURTIS[1])*[398] was born September 24, 1929[398], and died August 18, 1982 in Washington[398]. He married BARBARA ELOIS HATTAN[398] October 22, 1949[398]. She was born February 11, 1934[398], and died October 01, 1989 in Oherhurst, California[398].

Children of JAMES COKER and BARBARA HATTAN are:
452. i. LIVING[11] COKER.
453. ii. LIVING COKER.
454. iii. LIVING COKER.

367. HELEN JANE[10] COKER *(ORA DELLAR[9] REED, LUCRETIA (LOU CRECY) JANE[8] LAND, JORDON[7], KINSON[6], LEWIS[5], BIRD[4], CURTIS[3], CURTIS[2], CURTIS[1])*[398] was born July 23, 1933[398], and died February 19, 2002 in Saldo, Arkansas[398]. She married (1) LIVING SAMPLES[398]. She married (2) LIVING CARROLL[398]. She married (3) LIVING HAYS[398].

More About HELEN JANE COKER:
Burial: February 22, 2002, Egner Cemetery, Saldo, Arkansas[398]

Child of HELEN COKER and LIVING SAMPLES is:
455. i. LIVING[11] SAMPLES.

368. LIVING[10] CRABTREE *(MATTIE BEATRICE[9] REED, LUCRETIA (LOU CRECY) JANE[8] LAND, JORDON[7], KINSON[6], LEWIS[5], BIRD[4], CURTIS[3], CURTIS[2], CURTIS[1])*[398]. She married ARNOLD STEWART MARTIN[398]. He was born November 16, 1928 in Rosie, Arkansas[398], and died April 19, 1996 in Batesville, Arkansas[398].

More About ARNOLD STEWART MARTIN:
Burial: Wyatt Cemetery[398]

Children of LIVING CRABTREE and ARNOLD MARTIN are:
456. i. LIVING[11] MARTIN.
457. ii. LIVING MARTIN.
458. iii. LIVING MARTIN.
iv. LIVING MARTIN[398], m. LIVING YOPP[398].
459. v. LIVING MARTIN.
460. vi. LIVING MARTIN.
461. vii. LIVING MARTIN.

369. LIVING[10] REED *(WALTER COLLINS[9], LUCRETIA (LOU CRECY) JANE[8] LAND, JORDON[7], KINSON[6], LEWIS[5], BIRD[4], CURTIS[3], CURTIS[2], CURTIS[1])*[398]. He married (1) LIVING WILSON[398]. He married (2) LIVING RAMSEY[398].

Children of LIVING REED and LIVING WILSON are:
462. i. LIVING[11] REED.
463. ii. LIVING REED.

370. LIVING[10] REED *(WALTER COLLINS[9], LUCRETIA (LOU CRECY) JANE[8] LAND, JORDON[7], KINSON[6], LEWIS[5], BIRD[4], CURTIS[3], CURTIS[2], CURTIS[1])*[398]. He married LIVING FLOYD[398].

Child of LIVING REED and LIVING FLOYD is:
i. LIVING[11] REED[398].

371. LIVING[10] JONES *(JAMES GERALD[9], BERTHA DELIAH[8] TYLER, MARTHA MATILDA ROSETTA[7] LAND, KINSON[6], LEWIS[5], BIRD[4], CURTIS[3], CURTIS[2], CURTIS[1])*[399]. She married ZANUEL WHITE[399]. He was born July 29, 1935 in Pocahontas , AR[399], and died January 1991 in Jonesboro, AR.[399].

Children of LIVING JONES and ZANUEL WHITE are:
464. i. LIVING[11] WHITE.
ii. LIVING WHITE[399], m. LIVING GATES[399].
465. iii. LIVING WHITE.

372. PAULINE[10] MITCHELL *(MODENE[9] TYLER, JOHN PARIS[8], MARTHA MATILDA ROSETTA[7] LAND, KINSON[6], LEWIS[5], BIRD[4], CURTIS[3], CURTIS[2], CURTIS[1])* She married JOHN TRIBBLE.

Children of PAULINE MITCHELL and JOHN TRIBBLE are:
i. WESLEY ALLEN[11] TRIBBLE.
ii. NOVELENE TRIBBLE.
iii. DAVID TRIBBLE.
iv. CAROLYN TRIBBLE.
v. IRENE TRIBBLE.
vi. PAULETTE TRIBBLE.

373. DEBORAH[10] WHITE *(IMOGENE EVELYN[9] HUGHES, THOMAS JEFFERSON[8], "DONA" FRANCIS CALDONIA[7] LAND, KINSON[6], LEWIS[5], BIRD[4], CURTIS[3], CURTIS[2], CURTIS[1])* She married RONNIE TAYLOR.

Child of DEBORAH WHITE and RONNIE TAYLOR is:
i. AMY[11] TAYLOR.

374. BONNIE SUE[10] HUGHES *(JAMES HENRY[9], THOMAS JEFFERSON[8], "DONA" FRANCIS CALDONIA[7] LAND, KINSON[6], LEWIS[5], BIRD[4], CURTIS[3], CURTIS[2], CURTIS[1])* was born December 03, 1970. She married TIMOTHY MILLS.

Child of BONNIE HUGHES and TIMOTHY MILLS is:
i. COLLIN TIMOTHY[11] MILLS.

375. DONNA CAROL[10] HUGHES *(THOMAS DAIL[9], THOMAS JEFFERSON[8], "DONA" FRANCIS CALDONIA[7] LAND, KINSON[6], LEWIS[5], BIRD[4], CURTIS[3], CURTIS[2], CURTIS[1])* was born December 30, 1965. She married NOLAND BALDRIDGE.

Children of DONNA HUGHES and NOLAND BALDRIDGE are:

i. FELICIA[11] BALDRIDGE.

ii. COREY BALDRIDGE.

376. THOMAS[10] HUGHES *(THOMAS DAIL[9], THOMAS JEFFERSON[8], "DONA" FRANCIS CALDONIA[7] LAND, KINSON[6], LEWIS[5], BIRD[4], CURTIS[3], CURTIS[2], CURTIS[1])* was born 1971. He married REBECCA THACKER.

Child of THOMAS HUGHES and REBECCA THACKER is:

i. DILLION[11] HUGHES.

377. SHELIA RENEE[10] HUGHES *(BUDDY CARSON[9], THOMAS JEFFERSON[8], "DONA" FRANCIS CALDONIA[7] LAND, KINSON[6], LEWIS[5], BIRD[4], CURTIS[3], CURTIS[2], CURTIS[1])* was born March 30, 1974. She married TIM RANDALL.

Child of SHELIA HUGHES and TIM RANDALL is:

i. SARAH ANN[11] RANDALL.

Generation No. 11

378. LIVING[11] LAND *(THOMAS LINVILLE[10], WILLIAM THOMAS[9], LINVILLE[8], WILLIAM THOMAS[7], JONATHAN[6], THOMAS[5], THOMAS[4], JOHN[3], CURTIS[2], CURTIS[1])*[400]. He married LIVING MONTGOMERY[400].

Children of LIVING LAND and LIVING MONTGOMERY are:

i. LIVING[12] LAND[400].

ii. LIVING LAND[400].

iii. LIVING LAND[400].

379. LIVING[11] LAND *(THOMAS LINVILLE[10], WILLIAM THOMAS[9], LINVILLE[8], WILLIAM THOMAS[7], JONATHAN[6], THOMAS[5], THOMAS[4], JOHN[3], CURTIS[2], CURTIS[1])*[400]. He married LIVING REID[400].

Children of LIVING LAND and LIVING REID are:

i. LIVING[12] LAND[400].

ii. LIVING LAND[400].

iii. LIVING LAND[400].

iv. LIVING LAND[400].

v. LIVING LAND[400].

380. LIVING[11] LAND *(THOMAS LINVILLE[10], WILLIAM THOMAS[9], LINVILLE[8], WILLIAM THOMAS[7], JONATHAN[6], THOMAS[5], THOMAS[4], JOHN[3], CURTIS[2], CURTIS[1])*[400]. She married LIVING TURNMIRE[400].

Children of LIVING LAND and LIVING TURNMIRE are:

i. LIVING[12] TURNMIRE[400].

ii. LIVING TURNMIRE[400].

iii. LIVING TURNMIRE[400].

iv. LIVING TURNMIRE[400].

381. WILLIAM ADAM[11] LAND *(THOMAS LINVILLE[10], WILLIAM THOMAS[9], LINVILLE[8], WILLIAM THOMAS[7], JONATHAN[6], THOMAS[5], THOMAS[4], JOHN[3], CURTIS[2], CURTIS[1])*[400] was born February 08, 1908 in Caldwell County, North Carolina[400], and died February 19, 1993 in Caldwell County, North Carolina[400]. He married LIVING LEFEVERS[400].

More About WILLIAM ADAM LAND:
Burial: Blue Ridge Cemetery[400]

Child of WILLIAM LAND and LIVING LEFEVERS is:

i. LIVING[12] LAND[400].

382. LIVING[11] LAND *(LIVING[10], THOMAS DAVID[9], JAMES CALVIN[8], WILLIAM THOMAS[7], JONATHAN[6], THOMAS[5], THOMAS[4], JOHN[3], CURTIS[2], CURTIS[1])*[400]. He married LIVING YATES[400].

Child of LIVING LAND and LIVING YATES is:

i. LIVING[12] LAND[400].

383. LIVING[11] LAND *(LIVING[10], THOMAS DAVID[9], JAMES CALVIN[8], WILLIAM THOMAS[7], JONATHAN[6], THOMAS[5], THOMAS[4], JOHN[3], CURTIS[2], CURTIS[1])*[400]. She married (1) LIVING DAVIS[400]. She married (2) JR. LIVING TUCKER[400].

Children of LIVING LAND and LIVING DAVIS are:

i. LIVING[12] DAVIS[400].
ii. LIVING DAVIS[400].

384. LIVING[11] LAND *(LIVING[10], THOMAS DAVID[9], JAMES CALVIN[8], WILLIAM THOMAS[7], JONATHAN[6], THOMAS[5], THOMAS[4], JOHN[3], CURTIS[2], CURTIS[1])*[400]. She married LIVING PUCCINI[400].

Children of LIVING LAND and LIVING PUCCINI are:

i. LIVING[12] PUCCINI[400].
ii. LIVING PUCCINI[400].
iii. LIVING PUCCINI[400].

385. LIVING[11] LAND *(LIVING[10], THOMAS DAVID[9], JAMES CALVIN[8], WILLIAM THOMAS[7], JONATHAN[6], THOMAS[5], THOMAS[4], JOHN[3], CURTIS[2], CURTIS[1])*[400]. He married (1) LIVING JACOBS[400]. He married (2) LIVING RICHARDSON[400].

Children of LIVING LAND and LIVING JACOBS are:

i. LIVING[12] LAND[400].
ii. LIVING LAND[400].
iii. LIVING LAND[400].

386. LIVING[11] JONES *(LIVING[10] LAND, THOMAS DAVID[9], JAMES CALVIN[8], WILLIAM THOMAS[7], JONATHAN[6], THOMAS[5], THOMAS[4], JOHN[3], CURTIS[2], CURTIS[1])*[400]. She married LIVING MCFARLAND[400].

Child of LIVING JONES and LIVING MCFARLAND is:

i. LIVING[12] MCFARLAND[400].

387. LIVING[11] JONES *(LIVING[10] LAND, THOMAS DAVID[9], JAMES CALVIN[8], WILLIAM THOMAS[7], JONATHAN[6], THOMAS[5], THOMAS[4], JOHN[3], CURTIS[2], CURTIS[1])*[400]. She married (1) LIVING FUDGE[400]. She married (2) LIVING HAMMOND[400].

Children of LIVING JONES and LIVING FUDGE are:

i. LIVING[12] FUDGE[400].
ii. LIVING FUDGE[400].
iii. LIVING FUDGE[400].

388. LIVING[11] LAND *(LIVING[10], THOMAS DAVID[9], JAMES CALVIN[8], WILLIAM THOMAS[7], JONATHAN[6], THOMAS[5], THOMAS[4], JOHN[3], CURTIS[2], CURTIS[1])*[400]. She married LIVING GRESSLEY[400].

Children of LIVING LAND and LIVING GRESSLEY are:

i. LIVING[12] GRESSLEY[400].
ii. LIVING GRESSLEY[400].
iii. LIVING GRESSLEY[400].
iv. LIVING GRESSLEY[400].

389. LIVING[11] LAND *(LIVING[10], THOMAS DAVID[9], JAMES CALVIN[8], WILLIAM THOMAS[7], JONATHAN[6], THOMAS[5], THOMAS[4], JOHN[3], CURTIS[2], CURTIS[1])*[400]. She married LIVING MARTIN[400].

Children of LIVING LAND and LIVING MARTIN are:

i. LIVING[12] MARTIN[400].

ii. LIVING MARTIN[400].
iii. LIVING MARTIN[400].
iv. LIVING MARTIN[400].

390. LIVING[11] LAND *(THOMAS MERIDETH[10], THOMAS DAVID[9], JAMES CALVIN[8], WILLIAM THOMAS[7], JONATHAN[6], THOMAS[5], THOMAS[4], JOHN[3], CURTIS[2], CURTIS[1])*[400]. She married (1) LIVING BARNETT[400]. She married (2) LIVING SOLOMAN[400]. She married (3) LIVING KLEIN[400].

Child of LIVING LAND and LIVING SOLOMAN is:
i. LIVING[12] SOLOMAN[400].

391. LIVING[11] LAND *(THOMAS MERIDETH[10], THOMAS DAVID[9], JAMES CALVIN[8], WILLIAM THOMAS[7], JONATHAN[6], THOMAS[5], THOMAS[4], JOHN[3], CURTIS[2], CURTIS[1])*[400]. She married (1) LIVING CROUSE[400]. She married (2) LIVING DAVIS[400].

Child of LIVING LAND and LIVING DAVIS is:
i. LIVING[12] DAVIS[400].

392. LIVING[11] LAND *(AARON CARTER[10], JAMES ELI[9], JAMES[8], JAMES[7], JONATHAN[6], THOMAS[5], THOMAS[4], JOHN[3], CURTIS[2], CURTIS[1])*[400]. He married LIVING ADAMS[400].

Child of LIVING LAND and LIVING ADAMS is:
i. LIVING[12] LAND[400].

393. LIVING[11] LAND *(AARON CARTER[10], JAMES ELI[9], JAMES[8], JAMES[7], JONATHAN[6], THOMAS[5], THOMAS[4], JOHN[3], CURTIS[2], CURTIS[1])*[400]. She married LIVING UNKNOWN[400].

Children of LIVING LAND and LIVING UNKNOWN are:
i. LIVING[12] UNKNOWN[400].
ii. LIVING UNKNOWN[400].

394. LIVING[11] LAND *(ROBERT LEE[10], NOAH[9], JAMES[8], JAMES[7], JONATHAN[6], THOMAS[5], THOMAS[4], JOHN[3], CURTIS[2], CURTIS[1])*[400]. She married LIVING HOLSCLAW[400].

Children of LIVING LAND and LIVING HOLSCLAW are:
i. LIVING[12] HOLSCLAW[400].
ii. LIVING HOLSCLAW[400].
iii. LIVING HOLSCLAW[400].
iv. LIVING HOLSCLAW[400].
v. LIVING HOLSCLAW[400].
vi. LIVING HOLSCLAW[400].
vii. LIVING HOLSCLAW[400].

395. LIVING[11] LAND *(ROBERT LEE[10], NOAH[9], JAMES[8], JAMES[7], JONATHAN[6], THOMAS[5], THOMAS[4], JOHN[3], CURTIS[2], CURTIS[1])*[400]. He married LIVING WATSON[400].

Children of LIVING LAND and LIVING WATSON are:
i. LIVING[12] LAND[400].
ii. LIVING LAND[400].
iii. LIVING LAND[400].
iv. LIVING LAND[400].
v. LIVING LAND[400].
vi. LIVING LAND[400].

396. LIVING[11] LAND *(ROBERT LEE[10], NOAH[9], JAMES[8], JAMES[7], JONATHAN[6], THOMAS[5], THOMAS[4], JOHN[3], CURTIS[2], CURTIS[1])*[400]. He married LIVING SUDDRETH[400].

Children of LIVING LAND and LIVING SUDDRETH are:

i. LIVING[12] LAND[400].
ii. LIVING LAND[400].

397. LIVING[11] LAND *(ROBERT LEE[10], NOAH[9], JAMES[8], JAMES[7], JONATHAN[6], THOMAS[5], THOMAS[4], JOHN[3], CURTIS[2], CURTIS[1])*[400]. He married LIVING CLARK[400].

Child of LIVING LAND and LIVING CLARK is:

i. LIVING[12] LAND[400].

398. LIVING[11] LAND *(GEORGE WASHINGTON[10], NOAH[9], JAMES[8], JAMES[7], JONATHAN[6], THOMAS[5], THOMAS[4], JOHN[3], CURTIS[2], CURTIS[1])*[400]. He married LIVING YOW[400].

Child of LIVING LAND and LIVING YOW is:

i. LIVING[12] LAND[400].

399. JR. GEORGE EDWARD[11] LAND *(GEORGE EDWARD[10], JAMES LINVILLE[9], DAVID[8], JAMES[7], JONATHAN[6], THOMAS[5], THOMAS[4], JOHN[3], CURTIS[2], CURTIS[1])*[400] was born November 02, 1926[400], and died November 1991 in Melbourne, Florida[400]. He married (1) LIVING UNKNOWN[400]. He married (2) LIVING COX[400].

Child of GEORGE LAND and LIVING UNKNOWN is:

i. LIVING[12] LAND[400].

Child of GEORGE LAND and LIVING COX is:

ii. SR. LIVING[12] LAND[400].

400. LIVING[11] LAND *(DAVID[10], ELI JASON[9], DAVID[8], JAMES[7], JONATHAN[6], THOMAS[5], THOMAS[4], JOHN[3], CURTIS[2], CURTIS[1])*[400]. He married LIVING RECTOR[400].

Child of LIVING LAND and LIVING RECTOR is:

i. LIVING[12] LAND[400].

401. LIVING[11] LAND *(DAVID[10], ELI JASON[9], DAVID[8], JAMES[7], JONATHAN[6], THOMAS[5], THOMAS[4], JOHN[3], CURTIS[2], CURTIS[1])*[400]. He married LIVING HARTLEY[400].

Children of LIVING LAND and LIVING HARTLEY are:

i. LIVING[12] LAND[400].
ii. LIVING LAND[400].

402. LIVING[11] LAND *(DAVID[10], ELI JASON[9], DAVID[8], JAMES[7], JONATHAN[6], THOMAS[5], THOMAS[4], JOHN[3], CURTIS[2], CURTIS[1])*[400]. He married LIVING GOBLE[400].

Children of LIVING LAND and LIVING GOBLE are:

i. LIVING[12] LAND[400].
ii. LIVING LAND[400].

403. LIVING[11] LAND *(DAVID[10], ELI JASON[9], DAVID[8], JAMES[7], JONATHAN[6], THOMAS[5], THOMAS[4], JOHN[3], CURTIS[2], CURTIS[1])*[400]. She married LIVING BEAN[400].

Children of LIVING LAND and LIVING BEAN are:

i. LIVING[12] BEAN[400].
ii. LIVING BEAN[400].
iii. LIVING BEAN[400].

404. LIVING[11] LAND *(DAVID[10], ELI JASON[9], DAVID[8], JAMES[7], JONATHAN[6], THOMAS[5], THOMAS[4], JOHN[3], CURTIS[2], CURTIS[1])*[400]. He married LIVING GREER[400].

Children of LIVING LAND and LIVING GREER are:

i. LIVING[12] LAND[400].
ii. LIVING LAND[400].
iii. LIVING LAND[400].
iv. LIVING LAND[400].

405. LIVING[11] LAND *(DAVID[10], ELI JASON[9], DAVID[8], JAMES[7], JONATHAN[6], THOMAS[5], THOMAS[4], JOHN[3], CURTIS[2], CURTIS[1])*[400]. He married LIVING DEGANA[400].

Children of LIVING LAND and LIVING DEGANA are:

i. LIVING[12] LAND[400].
ii. LIVING LAND[400].
iii. LIVING LAND[400].

406. LIVING[11] LAND *(DAVID[10], ELI JASON[9], DAVID[8], JAMES[7], JONATHAN[6], THOMAS[5], THOMAS[4], JOHN[3], CURTIS[2], CURTIS[1])*[400]. He married LIVING MALTBA[400].

Children of LIVING LAND and LIVING MALTBA are:

i. LIVING[12] LAND[400].
ii. LIVING LAND[400].

407. LIVING[11] LAND *(DAVID[10], ELI JASON[9], DAVID[8], JAMES[7], JONATHAN[6], THOMAS[5], THOMAS[4], JOHN[3], CURTIS[2], CURTIS[1])*[400]. She married LIVING CROUCH[400].

Children of LIVING LAND and LIVING CROUCH are:

i. LIVING[12] CROUCH[400].
ii. LIVING CROUCH[400].
iii. LIVING CROUCH[400].

408. LIVING[11] LAND *(DAVID[10], ELI JASON[9], DAVID[8], JAMES[7], JONATHAN[6], THOMAS[5], THOMAS[4], JOHN[3], CURTIS[2], CURTIS[1])*[400]. He married LIVING HENNESSEE[400].

Child of LIVING LAND and LIVING HENNESSEE is:

i. LIVING[12] LAND[400].

409. CLARA REBECCA[11] LAND *(DAVID[10], ELI JASON[9], DAVID[8], JAMES[7], JONATHAN[6], THOMAS[5], THOMAS[4], JOHN[3], CURTIS[2], CURTIS[1])*[400] was born September 19, 1914 in Wilkes County, North Carolina[400], and died June 14, 1968 in Wilkes County, North Carolina[400]. She married LIVING KAYLOR[400].

Children of CLARA LAND and LIVING KAYLOR are:

i. LIVING[12] KAYLOR[400].
ii. LIVING KAYLOR[400].
iii. LIVING KAYLOR[400].

410. JAMES HERBERT[11] LAND *(DAVID[10], ELI JASON[9], DAVID[8], JAMES[7], JONATHAN[6], THOMAS[5], THOMAS[4], JOHN[3], CURTIS[2], CURTIS[1])*[400] was born November 29, 1918[400], and died June 18, 1980 in Caldwell County, North Carolina[400]. He married LIVING PIERCY[400].

More About JAMES HERBERT LAND:
Burial: Kings Creek Cemetery[400]

Children of JAMES LAND and LIVING PIERCY are:

i. LIVING[12] LAND[400].
ii. LIVING LAND[400].
iii. LIVING LAND[400].

411. LIVING[11] LAND *(PARTEE VANCE[10], ELI JASON[9], DAVID[8], JAMES[7], JONATHAN[6], THOMAS[5], THOMAS[4], JOHN[3], CURTIS[2], CURTIS[1])*[400]. She married LIVING AUTON[400].

Children of LIVING LAND and LIVING AUTON are:

i. LIVING[12] AUTON[400].
ii. LIVING AUTON[400].
iii. LIVING AUTON[400].

412. LIVING[11] LAND *(PARTEE VANCE[10], ELI JASON[9], DAVID[8], JAMES[7], JONATHAN[6], THOMAS[5], THOMAS[4], JOHN[3], CURTIS[2], CURTIS[1])*[400]. She married LIVING POPE[400].

Child of LIVING LAND and LIVING POPE is:

i. LIVING[12] POPE[400].

413. LIVING[11] LAND *(RALPH CALDWELL[10], THOMAS CLINGMAN[9], DAVID[8], JAMES[7], JONATHAN[6], THOMAS[5], THOMAS[4], JOHN[3], CURTIS[2], CURTIS[1])*[400]. He married LIVING THOMPSON[400].

Children of LIVING LAND and LIVING THOMPSON are:

i. LIVING[12] LAND[400].
ii. LIVING LAND[400].
iii. LIVING LAND[400].

414. LIVING[11] LAND *(RALPH CALDWELL[10], THOMAS CLINGMAN[9], DAVID[8], JAMES[7], JONATHAN[6], THOMAS[5], THOMAS[4], JOHN[3], CURTIS[2], CURTIS[1])*[400]. He married (1) LIVING CARRE[400]. He married (2) LIVING THOMPSON[400].

Child of LIVING LAND and LIVING CARRE is:

i. LIVING[12] CARRE-LAND[400].

Child of LIVING LAND and LIVING THOMPSON is:

ii. JR. LIVING[12] LAND[400].

415. SR. HOWARD DOUGLAS[11] LAND *(RALPH CALDWELL[10], THOMAS CLINGMAN[9], DAVID[8], JAMES[7], JONATHAN[6], THOMAS[5], THOMAS[4], JOHN[3], CURTIS[2], CURTIS[1])*[401 402] was born November 12, 1922 in Lenoir, Caldwell County, North Carolina[402], and died May 08, 1995 in Newport News, Virginia[402]. He married GEORGIA GRACE BARLOW[402]. She was born November 29, 1921 in Lenoir, Caldwell County, North Carolina[402], and died November 13, 1995 in Newport News, Virginia[402].

CMSGT USAF (Ret).
Former Army Special Forces Pioneer and Air Force Combat Controller; retired from Air Force in 1973 as a professional military Non Commissioned Officer. Last residence was Newport News, Virginia.

Howard led a long and distinguished military career as a paratrooper and Special Forces Pioneer working for founder and former OSS member, Alan Bank. Howard was a Veteran of WWII, Korea and Vietnam. Howard also helped establish, operate, and manage the Air Force's elite Combat Control Teams.

Children of HOWARD LAND and GEORGIA BARLOW are:

i. JR. LIVING[12] LAND[402].
ii. LIVING LAND[402].

416. LIVING[11] FARTHING *(LIVING[10], LIVING[9] LAND, RAYMOND TIMOTHY[8], WILLIAM JEFFERSON[7], JOHN HENRY[6], CHARLES[5], CHARLES[4], CURTIS[3], CURTIS[2], CURTIS[1])*[403]. She married LIVING SHIVELY[403].

Child of LIVING FARTHING and LIVING SHIVELY is:

i. LIVING[12] SHIVELY[403].

417. LIVING[11] FARTHING *(LIVING[10], LIVING[9] LAND, RAYMOND TIMOTHY[8], WILLIAM JEFFERSON[7], JOHN HENRY[6], CHARLES[5], CHARLES[4], CURTIS[3], CURTIS[2], CURTIS[1])*[404]. She married LIVING SHIVELY[404].

Child of LIVING FARTHING and LIVING SHIVELY is:

i. LIVING[12] SHIVELY[404].

418. LIVING[11] BANES *(LIVING[10] LAND, LIVING[9], RAYMOND TIMOTHY[8], WILLIAM JEFFERSON[7], JOHN HENRY[6], CHARLES[5], CHARLES[4], CURTIS[3], CURTIS[2], CURTIS[1])*[404]. She married (1) LIVING STOCKS[404]. She married (2) LIVING MOHLER[404].

Child of LIVING BANES and LIVING STOCKS is:
i. LIVING[12] STOCKS[404].

Child of LIVING BANES and LIVING MOHLER is:
ii. LIVING[12] MOHLER[404].

419. LIVING[11] BROCK *(LIVING[10] LAND, LIVING[9], RAYMOND TIMOTHY[8], WILLIAM JEFFERSON[7], JOHN HENRY[6], CHARLES[5], CHARLES[4], CURTIS[3], CURTIS[2], CURTIS[1])*[404]. She married LIVING KIRBY[404].

Children of LIVING BROCK and LIVING KIRBY are:
i. LIVING[12] KIRBY[404].
ii. LIVING KIRBY[404].
iii. LIVING KIRBY[404].

420. LIVING[11] DANIEL *(LIVING[10] MILAM, EFFIE LAVINA[9] VANDEVENDER, MARY MILDRED "MAGGIE"[8] LAND, WILLIAM BURT[7], BURRELL[6], LITTLEBERRY[5], BIRD[4], CURTIS[3], CURTIS[2], CURTIS[1])*[405]. She married LIVING HENSLEY[405].

Child of LIVING DANIEL and LIVING HENSLEY is:
i. LIVING[12] HENSLEY[405].

421. LIVING[11] DANIEL *(LIVING[10] MILAM, EFFIE LAVINA[9] VANDEVENDER, MARY MILDRED "MAGGIE"[8] LAND, WILLIAM BURT[7], BURRELL[6], LITTLEBERRY[5], BIRD[4], CURTIS[3], CURTIS[2], CURTIS[1])*[405]. He married LIVING WAIDHAS[405].

Child of LIVING DANIEL and LIVING WAIDHAS is:
i. LIVING[12] DANIEL[405].

422. LIVING[11] DANIEL *(LIVING[10] MILAM, EFFIE LAVINA[9] VANDEVENDER, MARY MILDRED "MAGGIE"[8] LAND, WILLIAM BURT[7], BURRELL[6], LITTLEBERRY[5], BIRD[4], CURTIS[3], CURTIS[2], CURTIS[1])*[405]. He married LIVING WRIGHT[405].

Children of LIVING DANIEL and LIVING WRIGHT are:
i. LIVING[12] DANIEL[405].
ii. LIVING DANIEL[405].

423. LIVING[11] MURPHY *(SYBLE WAYNE[10] MILAM, EFFIE LAVINA[9] VANDEVENDER, MARY MILDRED "MAGGIE"[8] LAND, WILLIAM BURT[7], BURRELL[6], LITTLEBERRY[5], BIRD[4], CURTIS[3], CURTIS[2], CURTIS[1])*[405]. She married (1) LIVING STEELE[405]. She married (2) LIVING WATTS[405].

Child of LIVING MURPHY and LIVING STEELE is:
i. LIVING[12] STEELE[405].

424. LIVING[11] MURPHY *(SYBLE WAYNE[10] MILAM, EFFIE LAVINA[9] VANDEVENDER, MARY MILDRED "MAGGIE"[8] LAND, WILLIAM BURT[7], BURRELL[6], LITTLEBERRY[5], BIRD[4], CURTIS[3], CURTIS[2], CURTIS[1])*[405]. She married ROBERT WINFORD TRUE[405]. He died January 04, 2001[405].

Child of LIVING MURPHY and ROBERT TRUE is:
i. LIVING[12] TRUE[405].

425. LIVING[11] MURPHY *(SYBLE WAYNE[10] MILAM, EFFIE LAVINA[9] VANDEVENDER, MARY MILDRED "MAGGIE"[8] LAND, WILLIAM BURT[7], BURRELL[6], LITTLEBERRY[5], BIRD[4], CURTIS[3], CURTIS[2], CURTIS[1])*[405]. He married LIVING CLARK[405].

Children of LIVING MURPHY and LIVING CLARK are:
i. JR. LIVING[12] MURPHY[405].
ii. LIVING MURPHY[405].
iii. LIVING MURPHY[405].

426. LIVING[11] MURPHY *(SYBLE WAYNE[10] MILAM, EFFIE LAVINA[9] VANDEVENDER, MARY MILDRED "MAGGIE"[8] LAND, WILLIAM BURT[7], BURRELL[6], LITTLEBERRY[5], BIRD[4], CURTIS[3], CURTIS[2], CURTIS[1])*[405]. She married (1) LIVING DARNELL[405]. She married (2) LIVING HARE[405].

Child of LIVING MURPHY and LIVING DARNELL is:

i. LIVING[12] DARNELL[405].

Child of LIVING MURPHY and LIVING HARE is:

ii. LIVING[12] HARE[405].

427. DAILEY[11] BAILEY *(GUY[10], VIRGIL[9], GEORGE WASHINGTON[8], WILLIAM W.[7], ELIZABETH[6] LAND, LEWIS[5], BIRD[4], CURTIS[3], CURTIS[2], CURTIS[1])* He married EVELYN BAILEY.

Children of DAILEY BAILEY and EVELYN BAILEY are:

i. RICHARD[12] BAILEY.
ii. GARY BAILEY.
iii. DANNY BAILEY.
iv. GERALD BAILEY.

428. BETTIE MARIE[11] BAILEY *(GUY[10], VIRGIL[9], GEORGE WASHINGTON[8], WILLIAM W.[7], ELIZABETH[6] LAND, LEWIS[5], BIRD[4], CURTIS[3], CURTIS[2], CURTIS[1])* She married RAY COBLE.

Children of BETTIE BAILEY and RAY COBLE are:

i. LISA[12] COBLE.
ii. LAURIE COBLE.
iii. RONALD COBLE.
iv. DAVID COBLE.

429. LIVING[11] REED *(LIVING[10], JOE LUTHER[9], LUCRETIA (LOU CRECY) JANE[8] LAND, JORDON[7], KINSON[6], LEWIS[5], BIRD[4], CURTIS[3], CURTIS[2], CURTIS[1])*[405]. He married LIVING GISINGER[405].

Children of LIVING REED and LIVING GISINGER are:

i. LIVING[12] REED[405].
ii. LIVING REED[405].
iii. LIVING REED[405].

430. LIVING[11] REED *(LIVING[10], JOE LUTHER[9], LUCRETIA (LOU CRECY) JANE[8] LAND, JORDON[7], KINSON[6], LEWIS[5], BIRD[4], CURTIS[3], CURTIS[2], CURTIS[1])*[405]. She married MIKE WINK[405]. He was born December 20[405].

Child of LIVING REED and MIKE WINK is:

i. LIVING[12] WINK[405].

431. LIVING[11] REED *(LIVING[10], JOE LUTHER[9], LUCRETIA (LOU CRECY) JANE[8] LAND, JORDON[7], KINSON[6], LEWIS[5], BIRD[4], CURTIS[3], CURTIS[2], CURTIS[1])*[405]. She married (1) LIVING WORTMAN[405]. She married (2) LIVING LEINHART[405].

Child of LIVING REED and LIVING WORTMAN is:

i. LIVING[12] WORTMAN[405].

432. LIVING[11] REED *(LIVING[10], JOE LUTHER[9], LUCRETIA (LOU CRECY) JANE[8] LAND, JORDON[7], KINSON[6], LEWIS[5], BIRD[4], CURTIS[3], CURTIS[2], CURTIS[1])*[405]. He married LIVING MOORE[405].

Children of LIVING REED and LIVING MOORE are:

i. LIVING[12] REED[405].
ii. LIVING REED[405].

433. LIVING[11] SAPP *(LIVING[10] REED, JOE LUTHER[9], LUCRETIA (LOU CRECY) JANE[8] LAND, JORDON[7], KINSON[6], LEWIS[5], BIRD[4], CURTIS[3], CURTIS[2], CURTIS[1])*[405]. He married (1) LIVING NEAL[405]. He married (2) LIVING LANE[405].

Children of LIVING SAPP and LIVING NEAL are:
- i. LIVING[12] SAPP[405].
- ii. LIVING SAPP[405].

Children of LIVING SAPP and LIVING LANE are:
- iii. LIVING[12] SAPP[405].
- iv. LIVING SAPP[405].
- v. LIVING SAPP[405].
- vi. LIVING SAPP[405].
- vii. LIVING SAPP[405].
- viii. LIVING SAPP[405].
- ix. LIVING SAPP[405].

434. LIVING[11] SAPP *(LIVING[10] REED, JOE LUTHER[9], LUCRETIA (LOU CRECY) JANE[8] LAND, JORDON[7], KINSON[6], LEWIS[5], BIRD[4], CURTIS[3], CURTIS[2], CURTIS[1])*[405]. He married LIVING LANGFORD[405].

Children of LIVING SAPP and LIVING LANGFORD are:
- i. LIVING[12] SAPP[405].
- ii. LIVING SAPP[405].

435. LIVING[11] REED *(JESSIE JAMES[10], JOE LUTHER[9], LUCRETIA (LOU CRECY) JANE[8] LAND, JORDON[7], KINSON[6], LEWIS[5], BIRD[4], CURTIS[3], CURTIS[2], CURTIS[1])*[405]. He married SUSIE[405]. She was born September 28[405].

Children of LIVING REED and SUSIE are:
- i. LIVING[12] REED[405].
- ii. LIVING REED[405].
- iii. LIVING REED[405].

436. LIVING[11] REED *(JESSIE JAMES[10], JOE LUTHER[9], LUCRETIA (LOU CRECY) JANE[8] LAND, JORDON[7], KINSON[6], LEWIS[5], BIRD[4], CURTIS[3], CURTIS[2], CURTIS[1])*[405]. She married LIVING SLONAKER[405].

Child of LIVING REED and LIVING SLONAKER is:
- i. LIVING[12] SLONAKER[405].

437. LIVING[11] STAGGS *(LIVING[10] CURTIS, BESSIE TENNESSEE[9] REED, LUCRETIA (LOU CRECY) JANE[8] LAND, JORDON[7], KINSON[6], LEWIS[5], BIRD[4], CURTIS[3], CURTIS[2], CURTIS[1])*[405]. He married LIVING THOMISON[405].

Child of LIVING STAGGS and LIVING THOMISON is:
- i. LIVING[12] STAGGS[405].

438. LIVING[11] COKER *(LIVING[10], ORA DELLAR[9] REED, LUCRETIA (LOU CRECY) JANE[8] LAND, JORDON[7], KINSON[6], LEWIS[5], BIRD[4], CURTIS[3], CURTIS[2], CURTIS[1])*[405]. She married LIVING WEATHERLY[405].

Children of LIVING COKER and LIVING WEATHERLY are:
- i. LIVING[12] WEATHERLY[405].
- ii. LIVING WEATHERLY[405].
- iii. LIVING WEATHERLY[405].

439. LIVING[11] COKER *(LIVING[10], ORA DELLAR[9] REED, LUCRETIA (LOU CRECY) JANE[8] LAND, JORDON[7], KINSON[6], LEWIS[5], BIRD[4], CURTIS[3], CURTIS[2], CURTIS[1])*[405]. She married LIVING SCHRAEDER[405].

Child of LIVING COKER and LIVING SCHRAEDER is:
- i. LIVING[12] SCHRAEDER[405].

440. LIVING[11] COKER *(LIVING[10], ORA DELLAR[9] REED, LUCRETIA (LOU CRECY) JANE[8] LAND, JORDON[7], KINSON[6], LEWIS[5], BIRD[4], CURTIS[3], CURTIS[2], CURTIS[1])*[405]. She married (1) LIVING SWANSON[405]. She married (2) LIVING RONNIE[405].

Child of LIVING COKER and LIVING SWANSON is:

i. LIVING[12] SWANSON[405].

441. LIVING[11] COKER *(LIVING[10], ORA DELLAR[9] REED, LUCRETIA (LOU CRECY) JANE[8] LAND, JORDON[7], KINSON[6], LEWIS[5], BIRD[4], CURTIS[3], CURTIS[2], CURTIS[1])*[405]. She married LIVING BOHANON[405].

Child of LIVING COKER and LIVING BOHANON is:

i. LIVING[12] BOHANON[405].

442. LIVING[11] COKER *(LIVING[10], ORA DELLAR[9] REED, LUCRETIA (LOU CRECY) JANE[8] LAND, JORDON[7], KINSON[6], LEWIS[5], BIRD[4], CURTIS[3], CURTIS[2], CURTIS[1])*[405]. She married (1) LIVING BARNETT[405]. She married (2) JOE BOYD[405]. He died June 18, 1987[405].

Child of LIVING COKER and LIVING BARNETT is:

i. LIVING[12] BARNETT[405].

Child of LIVING COKER and JOE BOYD is:

ii. LIVING[12] BOYD[405].

443. LIVING[11] WILSON *(LIVING[10] COKER, ORA DELLAR[9] REED, LUCRETIA (LOU CRECY) JANE[8] LAND, JORDON[7], KINSON[6], LEWIS[5], BIRD[4], CURTIS[3], CURTIS[2], CURTIS[1])*[405]. He married LIVING FLEMING[405].

Children of LIVING WILSON and LIVING FLEMING are:

i. LIVING[12] WILSON[405].
ii. LIVING WILSON[405].
iii. LIVING WILSON[405].

444. LIVING[11] WILSON *(LIVING[10] COKER, ORA DELLAR[9] REED, LUCRETIA (LOU CRECY) JANE[8] LAND, JORDON[7], KINSON[6], LEWIS[5], BIRD[4], CURTIS[3], CURTIS[2], CURTIS[1])*[405]. He married (1) LIVING UNKNOWN[405]. He married (2) LIVING CASHAW[405].

Children of LIVING WILSON and LIVING UNKNOWN are:

i. LIVING[12] WILSON[405].
ii. LIVING WILSON[405].

Children of LIVING WILSON and LIVING CASHAW are:

iii. LIVING[12] WILSON[405].
iv. LIVING WILSON[405].

445. LIVING[11] WILSON *(LIVING[10] COKER, ORA DELLAR[9] REED, LUCRETIA (LOU CRECY) JANE[8] LAND, JORDON[7], KINSON[6], LEWIS[5], BIRD[4], CURTIS[3], CURTIS[2], CURTIS[1])*[405]. She married LIVING KNIGHT[405].

Child of LIVING WILSON and LIVING KNIGHT is:

i. LIVING[12] KNIGHT[405].

446. LIVING[11] WILSON *(LIVING[10] COKER, ORA DELLAR[9] REED, LUCRETIA (LOU CRECY) JANE[8] LAND, JORDON[7], KINSON[6], LEWIS[5], BIRD[4], CURTIS[3], CURTIS[2], CURTIS[1])*[405]. He married (1) LIVING GODFREY[405]. He married (2) LIVING DUNCAN[405].

Children of LIVING WILSON and LIVING GODFREY are:

i. LIVING[12] WILSON[405].
ii. LIVING WILSON[405].

Child of LIVING WILSON and LIVING DUNCAN is:

iii. LIVING[12] WILSON[405].

447. Living[11] Wilson *(Living[10] Coker, Ora Dellar[9] Reed, Lucretia (Lou Crecy) Jane[8] Land, Jordon[7], Kinson[6], Lewis[5], Bird[4], Curtis[3], Curtis[2], Curtis[1])*[405]. She married (1) Living Wilson[405]. She married (2) Living Laurement[405].

Children of Living Wilson and Living Wilson are:

i. Living[12] Wilson[405].
ii. Living Wilson[405].

Child of Living Wilson and Living Laurement is:

iii. Living[12] Laurement[405].

448. Living[11] Wilson *(Living[10] Coker, Ora Dellar[9] Reed, Lucretia (Lou Crecy) Jane[8] Land, Jordon[7], Kinson[6], Lewis[5], Bird[4], Curtis[3], Curtis[2], Curtis[1])*[405]. She married Living Parott[405].

Children of Living Wilson and Living Parott are:

i. Living[12] Parott[405].
ii. Living Parott[405].
iii. Living Parott[405].

449. Living[11] Hawkins *(Living[10] Coker, Ora Dellar[9] Reed, Lucretia (Lou Crecy) Jane[8] Land, Jordon[7], Kinson[6], Lewis[5], Bird[4], Curtis[3], Curtis[2], Curtis[1])*[405].

Child of Living Hawkins is:

i. Living[12] Mullins[405].

450. Living[11] Hawkins *(Living[10] Coker, Ora Dellar[9] Reed, Lucretia (Lou Crecy) Jane[8] Land, Jordon[7], Kinson[6], Lewis[5], Bird[4], Curtis[3], Curtis[2], Curtis[1])*[405]. He married Living Cullen[405].

Children of Living Hawkins and Living Cullen are:

i. Living[12] Hawkins[405].
ii. Living Hawkins[405].

451. Living[11] Hawkins *(Living[10] Coker, Ora Dellar[9] Reed, Lucretia (Lou Crecy) Jane[8] Land, Jordon[7], Kinson[6], Lewis[5], Bird[4], Curtis[3], Curtis[2], Curtis[1])*[405]. He married Living[405].

Child of Living Hawkins and Living is:

i. Living[12] Hawkins[405].

452. Living[11] Coker *(James Walter[10], Ora Dellar[9] Reed, Lucretia (Lou Crecy) Jane[8] Land, Jordon[7], Kinson[6], Lewis[5], Bird[4], Curtis[3], Curtis[2], Curtis[1])*[405]. She married Living Miles[405].

Children of Living Coker and Living Miles are:

i. Living[12] Miles[405].
ii. Living Miles[405].
iii. Living Miles[405].

453. Living[11] Coker *(James Walter[10], Ora Dellar[9] Reed, Lucretia (Lou Crecy) Jane[8] Land, Jordon[7], Kinson[6], Lewis[5], Bird[4], Curtis[3], Curtis[2], Curtis[1])*[405]. She married Living Armstrong[405].

Child of Living Coker and Living Armstrong is:

i. Living[12] Armstrong[405].

454. Living[11] Coker *(James Walter[10], Ora Dellar[9] Reed, Lucretia (Lou Crecy) Jane[8] Land, Jordon[7], Kinson[6], Lewis[5], Bird[4], Curtis[3], Curtis[2], Curtis[1])*[405]. She married Living Lesk[405].

Child of Living Coker and Living Lesk is:

i. Living[12] Lesk[405].

455. Living[11] Samples *(Helen Jane[10] Coker, Ora Dellar[9] Reed, Lucretia (Lou Crecy) Jane[8] Land, Jordon[7], Kinson[6], Lewis[5], Bird[4], Curtis[3], Curtis[2], Curtis[1])*[405]. She married Living Mead[405].

Child of Living Samples and Living Mead is:

i. Living[12] Mead[405].

456. Living[11] Martin *(Living[10] Crabtree, Mattie Beatrice[9] Reed, Lucretia (Lou Crecy) Jane[8] Land, Jordon[7], Kinson[6], Lewis[5], Bird[4], Curtis[3], Curtis[2], Curtis[1])*[405]. She married (1) Living Smart[405]. She married (2) Living Prickett[405].

Children of Living Martin and Living Smart are:

i. Living[12] Smart[405].
ii. Living Smart[405].
iii. Living Smart[405].

457. Living[11] Martin *(Living[10] Crabtree, Mattie Beatrice[9] Reed, Lucretia (Lou Crecy) Jane[8] Land, Jordon[7], Kinson[6], Lewis[5], Bird[4], Curtis[3], Curtis[2], Curtis[1])*[405]. He married Living Crowson[405].

Children of Living Martin and Living Crowson are:

i. Living[12] Martin[405].
ii. Living Martin[405].

458. Living[11] Martin *(Living[10] Crabtree, Mattie Beatrice[9] Reed, Lucretia (Lou Crecy) Jane[8] Land, Jordon[7], Kinson[6], Lewis[5], Bird[4], Curtis[3], Curtis[2], Curtis[1])*[405]. She married (1) Living Heath[405]. She married (2) Living Brown[405].

Child of Living Martin and Living Heath is:

i. Living[12] Heath[405].

459. Living[11] Martin *(Living[10] Crabtree, Mattie Beatrice[9] Reed, Lucretia (Lou Crecy) Jane[8] Land, Jordon[7], Kinson[6], Lewis[5], Bird[4], Curtis[3], Curtis[2], Curtis[1])*[405]. He married (1) Living Holder[405]. He married (2) Rita Jean Reynolds[405]. She was born February 18[405].

Children of Living Martin and Rita Reynolds are:

i. Living[12] Martin[405].
ii. Living Martin[405].

460. Living[11] Martin *(Living[10] Crabtree, Mattie Beatrice[9] Reed, Lucretia (Lou Crecy) Jane[8] Land, Jordon[7], Kinson[6], Lewis[5], Bird[4], Curtis[3], Curtis[2], Curtis[1])*[405]. She married Living Guynes[405].

Children of Living Martin and Living Guynes are:

i. Living[12] Guynes[405].
ii. Living Guynes[405].

461. Living[11] Martin *(Living[10] Crabtree, Mattie Beatrice[9] Reed, Lucretia (Lou Crecy) Jane[8] Land, Jordon[7], Kinson[6], Lewis[5], Bird[4], Curtis[3], Curtis[2], Curtis[1])*[405]. He married (1) Living Guynes[405]. He married (2) Living McPherson[405].

Children of Living Martin and Living Guynes are:

i. Living[12] Martin[405].
ii. Living Martin[405].

462. Living[11] Reed *(Living[10], Walter Collins[9], Lucretia (Lou Crecy) Jane[8] Land, Jordon[7], Kinson[6], Lewis[5], Bird[4], Curtis[3], Curtis[2], Curtis[1])*[405]. She married (1) Living Wood[405]. She married (2) Living Johnson[405].

Children of Living Reed and Living Wood are:

i. Living[12] Wood[405].

ii. LIVING WOOD[405].
iii. LIVING WOOD[405].

463. LIVING[11] REED *(LIVING[10], WALTER COLLINS[9], LUCRETIA (LOU CRECY) JANE [8]LAND, JORDON[7], KINSON[6], LEWIS[5], BIRD[4], CURTIS[3], CURTIS[2], CURTIS[1])*[405]. He married (1) LIVING ELUMBAUGH[405]. He married (2) LIVING PIETY[405].

Children of LIVING REED and LIVING ELUMBAUGH are:
i. LIVING[12] REED[405].
ii. LIVING REED[405].

Child of LIVING REED and LIVING PIETY is:
iii. LIVING[12] REED[405].

464. LIVING[11] WHITE *(LIVING[10] JONES, JAMES GERALD[9], BERTHA DELIAH [8]TYLER, MARTHA MATILDA ROSETTA [7]LAND, KINSON[6], LEWIS[5], BIRD[4], CURTIS[3], CURTIS[2], CURTIS[1])*[406]. She married LIVING HOLLOWAY[406].

Child of LIVING WHITE and LIVING HOLLOWAY is:
i. LIVING[12] HOLLOWAY[406].

465. LIVING[11] WHITE *(LIVING[10] JONES, JAMES GERALD[9], BERTHA DELIAH [8]TYLER, MARTHA MATILDA ROSETTA [7]LAND, KINSON[6], LEWIS[5], BIRD[4], CURTIS[3], CURTIS[2], CURTIS[1])*[406]. She married (1) LIVING WILLIAMS[406]. She married (2) LIVING EVELAND[406].

Child of LIVING WHITE and LIVING WILLIAMS is:
i. LIVING[12] WILLIAMS[406].

Endnotes

1. hargrovebailey1.FTW, Date of Import: Apr 7, 2011.
2. 2882706.ged, Date of Import: Apr 8, 2011.
3. v53t0914.ged, Date of Import: Apr 9, 2011.
4. hargrovebailey1.FTW, Date of Import: Apr 7, 2011.
5. 2882706.ged, Date of Import: Apr 8, 2011.
6. hargrovebailey1.FTW, Date of Import: Apr 7, 2011.
7. 2882706.ged, Date of Import: Apr 8, 2011.
8. v92t0207.ged, Date of Import: Apr 9, 2011.
9. v65t0520.ged, Date of Import: Apr 9, 2011.
10. v53t0914.ged, Date of Import: Apr 9, 2011.
11. 2882706.ged, Date of Import: Apr 8, 2011.
12. hargrovebailey1.FTW, Date of Import: Apr 7, 2011.
13. 2882706.ged, Date of Import: Apr 8, 2011.
14. 2847174.ged, Date of Import: Apr 8, 2011.
15. 2882706.ged, Date of Import: Apr 8, 2011.
16. 2847174.ged, Date of Import: Apr 8, 2011.
17. 2882706.ged, Date of Import: Apr 8, 2011.
18. 2847174.ged, Date of Import: Apr 8, 2011.
19. 2882706.ged, Date of Import: Apr 8, 2011.
20. 2847174.ged, Date of Import: Apr 8, 2011.
21. 2882706.ged, Date of Import: Apr 8, 2011.
22. 2847174.ged, Date of Import: Apr 8, 2011.
23. 2882706.ged, Date of Import: Apr 8, 2011.
24. v53t0914.ged, Date of Import: Apr 9, 2011.
25. 2882706.ged, Date of Import: Apr 8, 2011.
26. 2847174.ged, Date of Import: Apr 8, 2011.
27. v92t0207.ged, Date of Import: Apr 9, 2011.
28. 2847174.ged, Date of Import: Apr 8, 2011.

29. 2882706.ged, Date of Import: Apr 8, 2011.
30. 2847174.ged, Date of Import: Apr 8, 2011.
31. 2882706.ged, Date of Import: Apr 8, 2011.
32. v65t0520.ged, Date of Import: Apr 9, 2011.
33. 2847174.ged, Date of Import: Apr 8, 2011.
34. v65t0520.ged, Date of Import: Apr 9, 2011.
35. 2882706.ged, Date of Import: Apr 8, 2011.
36. 2847174.ged, Date of Import: Apr 8, 2011.
37. 2882706.ged, Date of Import: Apr 8, 2011.
38. 2847174.ged, Date of Import: Apr 8, 2011.
39. 2882706.ged, Date of Import: Apr 8, 2011.
40. 2847174.ged, Date of Import: Apr 8, 2011.
41. v53t0914.ged, Date of Import: Apr 9, 2011.
42. 2847174.ged, Date of Import: Apr 8, 2011.
43. v53t0914.ged, Date of Import: Apr 9, 2011.
44. 2847174.ged, Date of Import: Apr 8, 2011.
45. v53t0914.ged, Date of Import: Apr 9, 2011.
46. 2847174.ged, Date of Import: Apr 8, 2011.
47. v53t0914.ged, Date of Import: Apr 9, 2011.
48. v65t0520.ged, Date of Import: Apr 9, 2011.
49. v53t0914.ged, Date of Import: Apr 9, 2011.
50. 2847174.ged, Date of Import: Apr 8, 2011.
51. v53t0914.ged, Date of Import: Apr 9, 2011.
52. v65t0520.ged, Date of Import: Apr 9, 2011.
53. 2847174.ged, Date of Import: Apr 8, 2011.
54. 2882706.ged, Date of Import: Apr 8, 2011.
55. 2847174.ged, Date of Import: Apr 8, 2011.
56. 2882706.ged, Date of Import: Apr 8, 2011.
57. 2847174.ged, Date of Import: Apr 8, 2011.
58. v65t0520.ged, Date of Import: Apr 9, 2011.
59. 2847174.ged, Date of Import: Apr 8, 2011.
60. v53t0914.ged, Date of Import: Apr 9, 2011.
61. v65t0520.ged, Date of Import: Apr 9, 2011.
62. 2847174.ged, Date of Import: Apr 8, 2011.
63. v53t0914.ged, Date of Import: Apr 9, 2011.
64. v65t0520.ged, Date of Import: Apr 9, 2011.
65. 2882706.ged, Date of Import: Apr 8, 2011.
66. 2847174.ged, Date of Import: Apr 8, 2011.
67. 2882706.ged, Date of Import: Apr 8, 2011.
68. 2847174.ged, Date of Import: Apr 8, 2011.
69. 2882706.ged, Date of Import: Apr 8, 2011.
70. 2847174.ged, Date of Import: Apr 8, 2011.
71. 2882706.ged, Date of Import: Apr 8, 2011.
72. 2847174.ged, Date of Import: Apr 8, 2011.
73. v53t0914.ged, Date of Import: Apr 9, 2011.
74. v65t0520.ged, Date of Import: Apr 9, 2011.
75. 2847174.ged, Date of Import: Apr 8, 2011.
76. v53t0914.ged, Date of Import: Apr 9, 2011.
77. v65t0520.ged, Date of Import: Apr 9, 2011.
78. 2847174.ged, Date of Import: Apr 8, 2011.
79. 2882706.ged, Date of Import: Apr 8, 2011.
80. 2847174.ged, Date of Import: Apr 8, 2011.
81. 2882706.ged, Date of Import: Apr 8, 2011.
82. 2847174.ged, Date of Import: Apr 8, 2011.
83. v53t0914.ged, Date of Import: Apr 9, 2011.
84. v65t0520.ged, Date of Import: Apr 9, 2011.
85. 2847174.ged, Date of Import: Apr 8, 2011.
86. v53t0914.ged, Date of Import: Apr 9, 2011.
87. v65t0520.ged, Date of Import: Apr 9, 2011.
88. 2882706.ged, Date of Import: Apr 8, 2011.
89. v92t0207.ged, Date of Import: Apr 9, 2011.
90. 2847174.ged, Date of Import: Apr 8, 2011.

91. 2882706.ged, Date of Import: Apr 8, 2011.
92. 2847174.ged, Date of Import: Apr 8, 2011.
93. 2882706.ged, Date of Import: Apr 8, 2011.
94. v92t0207.ged, Date of Import: Apr 9, 2011.
95. 2847174.ged, Date of Import: Apr 8, 2011.
96. 2882706.ged, Date of Import: Apr 8, 2011.
97. 2847174.ged, Date of Import: Apr 8, 2011.
98. 2882706.ged, Date of Import: Apr 8, 2011.
99. 2847174.ged, Date of Import: Apr 8, 2011.
100. 2882706.ged, Date of Import: Apr 8, 2011.
101. 2847174.ged, Date of Import: Apr 8, 2011.
102. 2882706.ged, Date of Import: Apr 8, 2011.
103. 2847174.ged, Date of Import: Apr 8, 2011.
104. 2882706.ged, Date of Import: Apr 8, 2011.
105. 2847174.ged, Date of Import: Apr 8, 2011.
106. 2882706.ged, Date of Import: Apr 8, 2011.
107. 2847174.ged, Date of Import: Apr 8, 2011.
108. 2882706.ged, Date of Import: Apr 8, 2011.
109. 2847174.ged, Date of Import: Apr 8, 2011.
110. 2882706.ged, Date of Import: Apr 8, 2011.
111. 2847174.ged, Date of Import: Apr 8, 2011.
112. 2882706.ged, Date of Import: Apr 8, 2011.
113. 2847174.ged, Date of Import: Apr 8, 2011.
114. 2882706.ged, Date of Import: Apr 8, 2011.
115. 2847174.ged, Date of Import: Apr 8, 2011.
116. 2882706.ged, Date of Import: Apr 8, 2011.
117. 2847174.ged, Date of Import: Apr 8, 2011.
118. 2882706.ged, Date of Import: Apr 8, 2011.
119. 2847174.ged, Date of Import: Apr 8, 2011.
120. 2882706.ged, Date of Import: Apr 8, 2011.
121. 2847174.ged, Date of Import: Apr 8, 2011.
122. 2882706.ged, Date of Import: Apr 8, 2011.
123. 2847174.ged, Date of Import: Apr 8, 2011.
124. 2882706.ged, Date of Import: Apr 8, 2011.
125. 2847174.ged, Date of Import: Apr 8, 2011.
126. 2882706.ged, Date of Import: Apr 8, 2011.
127. 2847174.ged, Date of Import: Apr 8, 2011.
128. v65t0520.ged, Date of Import: Apr 9, 2011.
129. v53t0914.ged, Date of Import: Apr 9, 2011.
130. 2847174.ged, Date of Import: Apr 8, 2011.
131. v53t0914.ged, Date of Import: Apr 9, 2011.
132. v65t0520.ged, Date of Import: Apr 9, 2011.
133. v53t0914.ged, Date of Import: Apr 9, 2011.
134. v65t0520.ged, Date of Import: Apr 9, 2011.
135. v53t0914.ged, Date of Import: Apr 9, 2011.
136. v65t0520.ged, Date of Import: Apr 9, 2011.
137. 2847174.ged, Date of Import: Apr 8, 2011.
138. v53t0914.ged, Date of Import: Apr 9, 2011.
139. v65t0520.ged, Date of Import: Apr 9, 2011.
140. v53t0914.ged, Date of Import: Apr 9, 2011.
141. v65t0520.ged, Date of Import: Apr 9, 2011.
142. v53t0914.ged, Date of Import: Apr 9, 2011.
143. v65t0520.ged, Date of Import: Apr 9, 2011.
144. 2847174.ged, Date of Import: Apr 8, 2011.
145. 2882706.ged, Date of Import: Apr 8, 2011.
146. 2847174.ged, Date of Import: Apr 8, 2011.
147. 2882706.ged, Date of Import: Apr 8, 2011.
148. 2847174.ged, Date of Import: Apr 8, 2011.
149. 2882706.ged, Date of Import: Apr 8, 2011.
150. 2847174.ged, Date of Import: Apr 8, 2011.
151. 2882706.ged, Date of Import: Apr 8, 2011.
152. 2847174.ged, Date of Import: Apr 8, 2011.

153. 2882706.ged, Date of Import: Apr 8, 2011.
154. 2847174.ged, Date of Import: Apr 8, 2011.
155. 2882706.ged, Date of Import: Apr 8, 2011.
156. 2847174.ged, Date of Import: Apr 8, 2011.
157. 2882706.ged, Date of Import: Apr 8, 2011.
158. 2847174.ged, Date of Import: Apr 8, 2011.
159. 2882706.ged, Date of Import: Apr 8, 2011.
160. 2847174.ged, Date of Import: Apr 8, 2011.
161. 2882706.ged, Date of Import: Apr 8, 2011.
162. 2847174.ged, Date of Import: Apr 8, 2011.
163. 2882706.ged, Date of Import: Apr 8, 2011.
164. 2847174.ged, Date of Import: Apr 8, 2011.
165. 2882706.ged, Date of Import: Apr 8, 2011.
166. Reynolds Gray Bailey.
167. 2847174.ged, Date of Import: Apr 8, 2011.
168. 2882706.ged, Date of Import: Apr 8, 2011.
169. 2847174.ged, Date of Import: Apr 8, 2011.
170. 2882706.ged, Date of Import: Apr 8, 2011.
171. 2847174.ged, Date of Import: Apr 8, 2011.
172. 2882706.ged, Date of Import: Apr 8, 2011.
173. 2847174.ged, Date of Import: Apr 8, 2011.
174. 2882706.ged, Date of Import: Apr 8, 2011.
175. 2847174.ged, Date of Import: Apr 8, 2011.
176. 2882706.ged, Date of Import: Apr 8, 2011.
177. 2847174.ged, Date of Import: Apr 8, 2011.
178. 2882706.ged, Date of Import: Apr 8, 2011.
179. 2847174.ged, Date of Import: Apr 8, 2011.
180. Reynolds Gray Bailey.
181. 2847174.ged, Date of Import: Apr 8, 2011.
182. 2882706.ged, Date of Import: Apr 8, 2011.
183. 2847174.ged, Date of Import: Apr 8, 2011.
184. 2882706.ged, Date of Import: Apr 8, 2011.
185. 2847174.ged, Date of Import: Apr 8, 2011.
186. Reynolds Gray Bailey.
187. 2847174.ged, Date of Import: Apr 8, 2011.
188. 2882706.ged, Date of Import: Apr 8, 2011.
189. 2847174.ged, Date of Import: Apr 8, 2011.
190. 2882706.ged, Date of Import: Apr 8, 2011.
191. 2847174.ged, Date of Import: Apr 8, 2011.
192. 2882706.ged, Date of Import: Apr 8, 2011.
193. 2847174.ged, Date of Import: Apr 8, 2011.
194. 2882706.ged, Date of Import: Apr 8, 2011.
195. 2847174.ged, Date of Import: Apr 8, 2011.
196. 2882706.ged, Date of Import: Apr 8, 2011.
197. 2847174.ged, Date of Import: Apr 8, 2011.
198. 2882706.ged, Date of Import: Apr 8, 2011.
199. 2847174.ged, Date of Import: Apr 8, 2011
200. 2882706.ged, Date of Import: Apr 8, 2011.
201. 2847174.ged, Date of Import: Apr 8, 2011.
202. 2882706.ged, Date of Import: Apr 8, 2011.
203. 2847174.ged, Date of Import: Apr 8, 2011.
204. 2882706.ged, Date of Import: Apr 8, 2011.
205. 2847174.ged, Date of Import: Apr 8, 2011.
206. 2882706.ged, Date of Import: Apr 8, 2011.
207. 2847174.ged, Date of Import: Apr 8, 2011.
208. 2882706.ged, Date of Import: Apr 8, 2011.
209. 2847174.ged, Date of Import: Apr 8, 2011.
210. 2882706.ged, Date of Import: Apr 8, 2011
211. 2847174.ged, Date of Import: Apr 8, 2011
212. 2882706.ged, Date of Import: Apr 8, 2011.
213. 2847174.ged, Date of Import: Apr 8, 2011.
214. 2882706.ged, Date of Import: Apr 8, 2011

215. 2847174.ged, Date of Import: Apr 8, 2011.
216. 2882706.ged, Date of Import: Apr 8, 2011.
217. 2847174.ged, Date of Import: Apr 8, 2011.
218. 2882706.ged, Date of Import: Apr 8, 2011.
219. 2847174.ged, Date of Import: Apr 8, 2011.
220. 2882706.ged, Date of Import: Apr 8, 2011.
221. 2847174.ged, Date of Import: Apr 8, 2011.
222. 2882706.ged, Date of Import: Apr 8, 2011.
223. 2847174.ged, Date of Import: Apr 8, 2011.
224. 2882706.ged, Date of Import: Apr 8, 2011.
225. 2847174.ged, Date of Import: Apr 8, 2011.
226. 2882706.ged, Date of Import: Apr 8, 2011.
227. 2847174.ged, Date of Import: Apr 8, 2011.
228. 2882706.ged, Date of Import: Apr 8, 2011.
229. 2847174.ged, Date of Import: Apr 8, 2011.
230. 2882706.ged, Date of Import: Apr 8, 2011.
231. 2847174.ged, Date of Import: Apr 8, 2011.
232. v92t0207.ged, Date of Import: Apr 9, 2011.
233. 2847174.ged, Date of Import: Apr 8, 2011.
234. v92t0207.ged, Date of Import: Apr 9, 2011.
235. 2847174.ged, Date of Import: Apr 8, 2011.
236. v92t0207.ged, Date of Import: Apr 9, 2011.
237. 2847174.ged, Date of Import: Apr 8, 2011.
238. v92t0207.ged, Date of Import: Apr 9, 2011.
239. 2847174.ged, Date of Import: Apr 8, 2011.
240. v92t0207.ged, Date of Import: Apr 9, 2011.
241. 2847174.ged, Date of Import: Apr 8, 2011.
242. v92t0207.ged, Date of Import: Apr 9, 2011.
243. 2847174.ged, Date of Import: Apr 8, 2011.
244. Doug Land.
245. 2847174.ged, Date of Import: Apr 8, 2011.
246. Doug Land.
247. 2847174.ged, Date of Import: Apr 8, 2011.
248. v53t0914.ged, Date of Import: Apr 9, 2011.
249. v65t0520.ged, Date of Import: Apr 9, 2011.
250. v53t0914.ged, Date of Import: Apr 9, 2011.
251. v65t0520.ged, Date of Import: Apr 9, 2011.
252. v53t0914.ged, Date of Import: Apr 9, 2011.
253. v65t0520.ged, Date of Import: Apr 9, 2011.
254. 2847174.ged, Date of Import: Apr 8, 2011.
255. v53t0914.ged, Date of Import: Apr 9, 2011.
256. v65t0520.ged, Date of Import: Apr 9, 2011.
257. v53t0914.ged, Date of Import: Apr 9, 2011.
258. v65t0520.ged, Date of Import: Apr 9, 2011.
259. v53t0914.ged, Date of Import: Apr 9, 2011.
260. v65t0520.ged, Date of Import: Apr 9, 2011.
261. v53t0914.ged, Date of Import: Apr 9, 2011.
262. v65t0520.ged, Date of Import: Apr 9, 2011.
263. 2847174.ged, Date of Import: Apr 8, 2011.
264. 2882706.ged, Date of Import: Apr 8, 2011.
265. 2847174.ged, Date of Import: Apr 8, 2011.
266. 2882706.ged, Date of Import: Apr 8, 2011.
267. 2847174.ged, Date of Import: Apr 8, 2011.
268. 2882706.ged, Date of Import: Apr 8, 2011.
269. 2847174.ged, Date of Import: Apr 8, 2011.
270. 2882706.ged, Date of Import: Apr 8, 2011.
271. 2847174.ged, Date of Import: Apr 8, 2011.
272. 2882706.ged, Date of Import: Apr 8, 2011.
273. 2847174.ged, Date of Import: Apr 8, 2011.
274. 2882706.ged, Date of Import: Apr 8, 2011.
275. 2847174.ged, Date of Import: Apr 8, 2011.
276. 2882706.ged, Date of Import: Apr 8, 2011.

277. 2847174.ged, Date of Import: Apr 8, 2011.
278. 2882706.ged, Date of Import: Apr 8, 2011.
279. 2847174.ged, Date of Import: Apr 8, 2011.
280. 2882706.ged, Date of Import: Apr 8, 2011.
281. 2847174.ged, Date of Import: Apr 8, 2011.
282. 2882706.ged, Date of Import: Apr 8, 2011.
283. 2847174.ged, Date of Import: Apr 8, 2011.
284. 2882706.ged, Date of Import: Apr 8, 2011.
285. 2847174.ged, Date of Import: Apr 8, 2011.
286. 2882706.ged, Date of Import: Apr 8, 2011.
287. 2847174.ged, Date of Import: Apr 8, 2011.
288. 2882706.ged, Date of Import: Apr 8, 2011.
289. 2847174.ged, Date of Import: Apr 8, 2011.
290. 2882706.ged, Date of Import: Apr 8, 2011.
291. 2847174.ged, Date of Import: Apr 8, 2011.
292. 2882706.ged, Date of Import: Apr 8, 2011.
293. 2847174.ged, Date of Import: Apr 8, 2011.
294. 2882706.ged, Date of Import: Apr 8, 2011.
295. 2847174.ged, Date of Import: Apr 8, 2011.
296. 2882706.ged, Date of Import: Apr 8, 2011.
297. 2847174.ged, Date of Import: Apr 8, 2011.
298. 2882706.ged, Date of Import: Apr 8, 2011.
299. 2847174.ged, Date of Import: Apr 8, 2011.
300. 2882706.ged, Date of Import: Apr 8, 2011.
301. 2847174.ged, Date of Import: Apr 8, 2011.
302. 2882706.ged, Date of Import: Apr 8, 2011.
303. 2847174.ged, Date of Import: Apr 8, 2011.
304. 2882706.ged, Date of Import: Apr 8, 2011.
305. 2847174.ged, Date of Import: Apr 8, 2011.
306. 2882706.ged, Date of Import: Apr 8, 2011.
307. 2847174.ged, Date of Import: Apr 8, 2011.
308. 2882706.ged, Date of Import: Apr 8, 2011.
309. 2847174.ged, Date of Import: Apr 8, 2011.
310. 2882706.ged, Date of Import: Apr 8, 2011.
311. 2847174.ged, Date of Import: Apr 8, 2011.
312. 2882706.ged, Date of Import: Apr 8, 2011.
313. 2847174.ged, Date of Import: Apr 8, 2011.
314. 2882706.ged, Date of Import: Apr 8, 2011.
315. 2847174.ged, Date of Import: Apr 8, 2011.
316. 2882706.ged, Date of Import: Apr 8, 2011.
317. 2847174.ged, Date of Import: Apr 8, 2011.
318. 2882706.ged, Date of Import: Apr 8, 2011.
319. 2847174.ged, Date of Import: Apr 8, 2011.
320. v92t0207.ged, Date of Import: Apr 9, 2011.
321. 2847174.ged, Date of Import: Apr 8, 2011.
322. v92t0207.ged, Date of Import: Apr 9, 2011.
323. 2847174.ged, Date of Import: Apr 8, 2011.
324. Doug Land.
325. 2847174.ged, Date of Import: Apr 8, 2011
326. v53t0914.ged, Date of Import: Apr 9, 2011.
327. v65t0520.ged, Date of Import: Apr 9, 2011.
328. 2847174.ged, Date of Import: Apr 8, 2011.
329. v53t0914.ged, Date of Import: Apr 9, 2011.
330. v65t0520.ged, Date of Import: Apr 9, 2011.
331. v53t0914.ged, Date of Import: Apr 9, 2011.
332. v65t0520.ged, Date of Import: Apr 9, 2011.
333. v53t0914.ged, Date of Import: Apr 9, 2011.
334. v65t0520.ged, Date of Import: Apr 9, 2011.
335. Broderbund Family Archive #110, Vol. 1, Ed. 6, Social Security Death Index: U.S., Date of Import: Jan 1, 2000, Internal Ref. #1.111.6.142771.61
336. v65t0520.ged, Date of Import: Apr 9, 2011.

337. Broderbund Family Archive #110, Vol. 1, Ed. 6, Social Security Death Index: U.S., Date of Import: Jan 1, 2000, Internal Ref. #1.111.6.142771.61
338. v65t0520.ged, Date of Import: Apr 9, 2011.
339. 2847174.ged, Date of Import: Apr 8, 2011.
340. 2882706.ged, Date of Import: Apr 8, 2011.
341. 2847174.ged, Date of Import: Apr 8, 2011.
342. Wanda Sue Daniel.
343. 2847174.ged, Date of Import: Apr 8, 2011.
344. v92t0207.ged, Date of Import: Apr 9, 2011.
345. 2847174.ged, Date of Import: Apr 8, 2011.
346. Anna Gipson.
347. 2847174.ged, Date of Import: Apr 8, 2011.
348. v92t0207.ged, Date of Import: Apr 9, 2011.
349. 2847174.ged, Date of Import: Apr 8, 2011.
350. Doug Land.
351. 2847174.ged, Date of Import: Apr 8, 2011.
352. v53t0914.ged, Date of Import: Apr 9, 2011.
353. v65t0520.ged, Date of Import: Apr 9, 2011.
354. v53t0914.ged, Date of Import: Apr 9, 2011.
355. v65t0520.ged, Date of Import: Apr 9, 2011.
356. v53t0914.ged, Date of Import: Apr 9, 2011.
357. v65t0520.ged, Date of Import: Apr 9, 2011.
358. v53t0914.ged, Date of Import: Apr 9, 2011.
359. v65t0520.ged, Date of Import: Apr 9, 2011.
360. v53t0914.ged, Date of Import: Apr 9, 2011.
361. v65t0520.ged, Date of Import: Apr 9, 2011.
362. v53t0914.ged, Date of Import: Apr 9, 2011.
363. v65t0520.ged, Date of Import: Apr 9, 2011.
364. v53t0914.ged, Date of Import: Apr 9, 2011.
365. v65t0520.ged, Date of Import: Apr 9, 2011.
366. 2847174.ged, Date of Import: Apr 8, 2011.
367. 2882706.ged, Date of Import: Apr 8, 2011.
368. 2847174.ged, Date of Import: Apr 8, 2011.
369. Wanda Sue Daniel.
370. 2847174.ged, Date of Import: Apr 8, 2011.
371. v92t0207.ged, Date of Import: Apr 9, 2011.
372. 2847174.ged, Date of Import: Apr 8, 2011.
373. Anna Gipson.
374. 2847174.ged, Date of Import: Apr 8, 2011.
375. Anna Gipson.
376. 2847174.ged, Date of Import: Apr 8, 2011.
377. Anna Gipson.
378. 2847174.ged, Date of Import: Apr 8, 2011.
379. v92t0207.ged, Date of Import: Apr 9, 2011.
380. 2847174.ged, Date of Import: Apr 8, 2011.
381. Doug Land.
382. 2847174.ged, Date of Import: Apr 8, 2011.
383. Doug Land.
384. 2847174.ged, Date of Import: Apr 8, 2011.
385. Doug Land.
386. 2847174.ged, Date of Import: Apr 8, 2011.
387. v53t0914.ged, Date of Import: Apr 9, 2011.
388. v65t0520.ged, Date of Import: Apr 9, 2011.
389. v53t0914.ged, Date of Import: Apr 9, 2011.
390. v65t0520.ged, Date of Import: Apr 9, 2011.
391. v53t0914.ged, Date of Import: Apr 9, 2011.
392. v65t0520.ged, Date of Import: Apr 9, 2011.
393. 2882706.ged, Date of Import: Apr 8, 2011.
394. 2847174.ged, Date of Import: Apr 8, 2011.
395. Wanda Sue Daniel.
396. 2847174.ged, Date of Import: Apr 8, 2011.
397. v92t0207.ged, Date of Import: Apr 9, 2011.

398. 2847174.ged, Date of Import: Apr 8, 2011.
399. v92t0207.ged, Date of Import: Apr 9, 2011.
400. 2847174.ged, Date of Import: Apr 8, 2011.
401. Doug Land.
402. 2847174.ged, Date of Import: Apr 8, 2011.
403. v53t0914.ged, Date of Import: Apr 9, 2011.
404. v65t0520.ged, Date of Import: Apr 9, 2011.
405. 2847174.ged, Date of Import: Apr 8, 2011.
406. v92t0207.ged, Date of Import: Apr 9, 2011.

Kinship of Curtis Land

(Civil & Canon Numbers refer to the Generation)

Name	Relationship with Curtis Land	Civil	Canon
(Bailey), Kate	Wife of the 5th great-grandson		
??, Rebekah	Wife of the great-grandson		
???, Elizabeth Martha	Wife of the 2nd great-grandson		
Adams, Living	Wife of the 8th great-grandson		
Adams, Marie Gladis	Wife of the 7th great-grandson		
Agee, Alice	6th great-granddaughter	VIII	8
Agee, Amanda	6th great-granddaughter	VIII	8
Agee, Callie	6th great-granddaughter	VIII	8
Agee, Charles	6th great-granddaughter	VIII	8
Agee, Eliza	6th great-granddaughter	VIII	8
Agee, George Walford	6th great-grandson	VIII	8
Agee, Harriett	6th great-granddaughter	VIII	8
Agee, Howard	6th great-grandson	VIII	8
Agee, Martha	6th great-granddaughter	VIII	8
Agee, Mary Jane	6th great-granddaughter	VIII	8
Agee, Ruben	Husband of the 5th great-granddaughter		
Agee, Squire	6th great-grandson	VIII	8
Agee, William	6th great-grandson	VIII	8
Allison, Cornielia Jane	5th great-granddaughter	VII	7
Allison, Drury	5th great-grandson	VII	7
Allison, Eliza Amanda	5th great-granddaughter	VII	7
Allison, James H.	5th great-grandson	VII	7
Allison, James Lowrey	Husband of the 4th great-granddaughter		
Allison, John H.	5th great-grandson	VII	7
Allison, Lowrey Gillespie	5th great-grandson	VII	7
Allison, Malinda Lucinda	5th great-granddaughter	VII	7
Allison, Mary Ann	5th great-granddaughter	VII	7
Allison, Mary Evalina	5th great-granddaughter	VII	7
Allison, Matilda	Wife of the 5th great-grandson		
Allison, Nancy	Wife of the 4th great-grandson		
Wife of the 5th great-grandson			
Allison, Nancy C.	5th great-granddaughter	VII	7
Allison, Thomas N.	5th great-grandson	VII	7
Allison, William	5th great-grandson	VII	7
Andrews, Clarissa Seralda	Wife of the 6th great-grandson		
Andrews, Columbus	7th great-grandson	IX	9
Andrews, Estelle Pearl	7th great-granddaughter	IX	9
Andrews, Jane B.	7th great-granddaughter	IX	9
Andrews, McGruder	7th great-grandson	IX	9
Andrews, Rebecca Ann	7th great-granddaughter	IX	9
Andrews, Sarah E.	7th great-granddaughter	IX	9
Andrews, Thomas Alva	Husband of the 6th great-granddaughter		
Andrews, Thomas Carl	7th great-grandson	IX	9
Annas, Odus Finley	Husband of the 7th great-granddaughter		
Armstrong, Elizabeth	Wife of the great-grandson		
Armstrong, Lewis A.	Husband of the 5th great-granddaughter		
	Husband of the 6th great-granddaughter		
Armstrong, Living	Husband of the 8th great-granddaughter		
Armstrong, Living	9th great-grandson	XI	11
Arnett, Mary Ann	Wife of the 4th great-grandson		
Austin, Addie Theodosa	Wife of the 5th great-grandson		

Austin, John	Husband of the 7th great-granddaughter		
Auton, Emma Elizabeth	Wife of the 7th great-grandson		
Auton, Living	Husband of the 8th great-granddaughter		
Auton, Living	9th great-grandson	XI	11
Auton, Living	9th great-granddaughter	XI	11
Auton, Living	9th great-grandson	XI	11
Bailey, Albert Donald	6th great-grandson	VIII	8
Bailey, Aldean	7th great-granddaughter	IX	9
Bailey, Allen A.	5th great-grandson	VII	7
Bailey, Anna	8th great-granddaughter	X	10
Bailey, Arlene	7th great-granddaughter	IX	9
Bailey, Bertha	6th great-granddaughter	VIII	8
Bailey, Bettie Marie	8th great-granddaughter	X	10
Bailey, Bill	8th great-grandson	X	10
Bailey, Birdie	7th great-granddaughter	IX	9
Bailey, Brenda	8th great-granddaughter	X	10
Bailey, Carl	8th great-grandson	X	10
Bailey, Carol	8th great-granddaughter	X	10
Bailey, Carol	8th great-granddaughter	X	10
Bailey, Clarence	6th great-grandson	VIII	8
Bailey, Cleo	7th great-granddaughter	IX	9
Bailey, Clifford	6th great-grandson	VIII	8
Bailey, Dailey	8th great-grandson	X	10
Bailey, Danny	9th great-grandson	XI	11
Bailey, Diannah	Wife of the 3rd great-grandson		
Bailey, Donald	7th great-grandson	IX	9
Bailey, Donald	8th great-grandson	X	10
Bailey, Doris	Wife of the 7th great-grandson		
Bailey, Ella	6th great-granddaughter	VIII	8
Bailey, Elmer	6th great-grandson	VIII	8
Bailey, Eugene	7th great-grandson	IX	9
Bailey, Evalena	7th great-granddaughter	IX	9
Bailey, Evelyn	Wife of the 8th great-grandson		
Bailey, Fannie Lula	6th great-granddaughter	VIII	8
Bailey, Frankie Zula	6th great-granddaughter	VIII	8
Bailey, Frederick	6th great-grandson	VIII	8
Bailey, Gail	8th great-granddaughter	X	10
Bailey, Gary	9th great-grandson	XI	11
Bailey, George Washington	5th great-grandson	VII	7
Bailey, Gerald	9th great-grandson	XI	11
Bailey, Gertie	6th great-granddaughter	VIII	8
Bailey, Glenn	8th great-grandson	X	10
Bailey, Gordon	8th great-grandson	X	10
Bailey, Guy	7th great-grandson	IX	9
Bailey, Harold	8th great-grandson	X	10
Bailey, Herbert Theodore	Husband of the 7th great-granddaughter		
Bailey, Irene	6th great-granddaughter	VIII	8
Bailey, James	8th great-grandson	X	10
Bailey, James Burley	7th great-grandson	IX	9
Bailey, James Theadore	6th great-grandson	VIII	8
Bailey, Janey	5th great-granddaughter	VII	7
Bailey, Jewel	7th great-granddaughter	IX	9
Bailey, Jeweletta	8th great-granddaughter	X	10
Bailey, John	Husband of the 3rd great-granddaughter		
Bailey, John	4th great-grandson	VI	6
Bailey, John W. B.	5th great-grandson	VII	7

Bailey, Living	8th great-grandson	X	10
Bailey, Living	8th great-grandson	X	10
Bailey, Living	8th great-grandson	X	10
Bailey, Living	8th great-granddaughter	X	10
Bailey, Living	8th great-grandson	X	10
Bailey, Living	8th great-grandson	X	10
Bailey, Living	8th great-grandson	X	10
Bailey, Living	8th great-granddaughter	X	10
Bailey, Lucille	8th great-granddaughter	X	10
Bailey, Manda	6th great-granddaughter	VIII	8
Bailey, Manley	7th great-grandson	IX	9
Bailey, Martha C.	5th great-granddaughter	VII	7
Bailey, Mary Elizabeth "Matilda"	5th great-granddaughter	VII	7
Bailey, Maude	6th great-granddaughter	VIII	8
Bailey, Mayborn	6th great-grandson	VIII	8
Bailey, Mazie	6th great-granddaughter	VIII	8
Bailey, Mildred	7th great-granddaughter	IX	9
Bailey, Moses	5th great-grandson	VII	7
Bailey, Mrytle	6th great-granddaughter	VIII	8
Bailey, Noble	7th great-grandson	IX	9
Bailey, Olen	6th great-grandson	VIII	8
Bailey, Patricia	8th great-granddaughter	X	10
Bailey, Rhodes	5th great-grandson	VII	7
Bailey, Richard	9th great-grandson	XI	11
Bailey, Roger	8th great-grandson	X	10
Bailey, Ruby	7th great-granddaughter	IX	9
Bailey, Sarah	4th great-granddaughter	VI	6
Bailey, Sarah	5th great-granddaughter	VII	7
Bailey, Sherril	8th great-grandchild	X	10
Bailey, Sibyl	7th great-granddaughter	IX	9
Bailey, Susan "Susie"	5th great-granddaughter	VII	7
Bailey, Tilda Pearl	6th great-granddaughter	VIII	8
Bailey, Tola	6th great-granddaughter	VIII	8
Bailey, Virgil	6th great-grandson	VIII	8
Bailey, William Millard	7th great-grandson	IX	9
Bailey, William Millard "Bill"	8th great-grandson	X	10
Bailey, William Solomon	6th great-grandson	VIII	8
Bailey, William W.	4th great-grandson	VI	6
Baker, Louise	Wife of the 7th great-grandson		
Baker, Nathan	Husband of the 4th great-granddaughter		
Baldridge, Corey	8th great-grandson	X	10
Baldridge, Felicia	8th great-granddaughter	X	10
Baldridge, Noland	Husband of the 7th great-granddaughter		
Bankester, Living	Wife of the 5th great-grandson		
Bankester, Warrene Avis	Wife of the 5th great-grandson		
Barham, Sarah Parker	Wife of the 6th great-grandson		
Barlow, Charlotte	5th great-granddaughter	VII	7
Barlow, Dicey	5th great-granddaughter	VII	7
Barlow, Elizabeth	Wife of the 3rd great-grandson		
Wife of the 4th great-grandson			
Barlow, Emily	5th great-granddaughter	VII	7
Barlow, Georgia Grace	Wife of the 8th great-grandson		
Barlow, Hamilton	5th great-grandson	VII	7
Barlow, Horton	5th great-grandson	VII	7
Barlow, Julia	5th great-granddaughter	VII	7
Barlow, Minnie	Wife of the 7th great-grandson		

Barlow, Parish	Husband of the 4th great-granddaughter		
Barnes, Fred Eli	8th great-grandson	X	10
Barnes, Living	8th great-granddaughter	X	10
Barnes, Living	8th great-granddaughter	X	10
Barnes, Living	8th great-granddaughter	X	10
Barnes, Living	8th great-grandson	X	10
Barnes, Nathan	Husband of the 7th great-granddaughter		
Barnes, Osie A.	8th great-grandson	X	10
Barnes, Peter	8th great-grandson	X	10
Barnes, Smith J.	8th great-grandson	X	10
Barnett, Living	Husband of the 8th great-granddaughter		
Barnett, Living	9th great-grandson	XI	11
Barnhill	Husband of the 4th great-granddaughter		
Barnhill, Caroline Virginia	5th great-granddaughter	VII	7
Barnhill, Carrie D.	5th great-granddaughter	VII	7
Barnhill, David W.	5th great-grandson	VII	7
Barnhill, Edgar J.	5th great-grandson	VII	7
Barnhill, Irene	6th great-granddaughter	VIII	8
Barnhill, John R.	Husband of the 4th great-granddaughter		
Barnhill, Logan Jasper	5th great-grandson	VII	7
Barnhill, Lulu	5th great-granddaughter	VII	7
Barnhill, Lyculus "Lucius"	5th great-grandson	VII	7
Barnhill, Robert Edwin	6th great-grandson	VIII	8
Barnhill, Walter	5th great-grandson	VII	7
Barton, Laura	Wife of the 7th great-grandson		
Bartus, Living	Husband of the 8th great-granddaughter		
Batchelor, Nancy B.	Wife of the 4th great-grandson		
Batts, Burrell Thomas	6th great-grandson	VIII	8
Batts, John F.	6th great-grandson	VIII	8
Batts, John Farmer	Husband of the 5th great-granddaughter		
Batts, Sally Ann Elizabeth	6th great-granddaughter	VIII	8
Batts, Susan J.	6th great-granddaughter	VIII	8
Bean, Living	Husband of the 8th great-granddaughter		
Bean, Living	9th great-grandson	XI	11
Bean, Living	9th great-granddaughter	XI	11
Bean, Living	9th great-grandson	XI	11
Bennett, Nettie Evaline	Wife of the 5th great-grandson		
Benson, William S.	Husband of the 7th great-granddaughter		
Beshears, Gaither	Husband of the 7th great-granddaughter		
Best, Dee	Wife of the 6th great-grandson		
Bigbee, Frank	Husband of the 6th great-granddaughter		
Birchfield, John	Husband of the 5th great-granddaughter		
Bird, Priscilla	Wife of the grandson		
Bird, Priscilla	Wife of the grandson		
Bird, Priscilla	Wife of the grandson		
Bird, Priscilla	Wife of the grandson		
Bird, Priscilla	Wife of the grandson		
Bishop, Living	Husband of the 7th great-granddaughter		
Bishop, Living	8th great-grandson	X	10
Bishop, Living	8th great-grandson	X	10
Bishop, Living	8th great-granddaughter	X	10
Bishop, Living	8th great-granddaughter	X	10
Black, Virginia	Wife of the 7th great-grandson		
Blakley, Annie	Wife of the 7th great-grandson		
Blansett, Leon	8th great-grandson	X	10
Blansett, Mildred Arlene	8th great-granddaughter	X	10

Blansett, Millard	Husband of the 7th great-granddaughter		
Blow, Alice Leigh	Wife of the 7th great-grandson		
Bohanon, Living	Husband of the 8th great-granddaughter		
Bohanon, Living	9th great-granddaughter	XI	11
Bollin, Polly	Wife of the 2nd great-grandson		
Bowen, Julia Faye	Wife of the 6th great-grandson		
Bowers, Britton	Husband of the 2nd great-granddaughter		
Boyd, Joe	Husband of the 8th great-granddaughter		
Boyd, Living	9th great-granddaughter	XI	11
Bradburn, Amanda	7th great-granddaughter	IX	9
Bradburn, Elizabeth	7th great-granddaughter	IX	9
Bradburn, Etta	7th great-granddaughter	IX	9
Bradburn, Gertrude	7th great-granddaughter	IX	9
Bradburn, Jefferson D.	Husband of the 6th great-granddaughter		
Bradburn, Marjorie Josie	7th great-granddaughter	IX	9
Bradburn, Sarah	7th great-granddaughter	IX	9
Bradburn, Walter S.	Husband of the 6th great-granddaughter		
Bradford, Carol	8th great-granddaughter	X	10
Bradford, Elbert	8th great-grandson	X	10
Bradford, Michael	8th great-grandson	X	10
Bradford, Shirley	8th great-granddaughter	X	10
Bradford, Sol	Husband of the 7th great-granddaughter		
Bragg, Living	Wife of the 7th great-grandson		
Brannon, Lindsy	Wife of the 6th great-grandson		
Braswell, Benjamin Guilford	Husband of the 4th great-granddaughter		
Braswell, Benjamin S.	Husband of the 4th great-granddaughter		
Braswell, Callie Berry	5th great-grandson	VII	7
Braswell, Isaac	Husband of the 2nd great-granddaughter		
Braswell, Robert Stringer	Husband of the 4th great-granddaughter		
Braswell, Sarah Martha	5th great-granddaughter	VII	7
Braswell, Sophronia	3rd great-granddaughter	V	5
Brewer, Leola	Wife of the 6th great-grandson		
Brice, Lois Rebecca	Wife of the 5th great-grandson		
Brittain, Living	Wife of the 7th great-grandson		
Brookshire, Prudence	Wife of the 4th great-grandson		
Brown, Houston	Husband of the 6th great-granddaughter		
Brown, Hubbard	Husband of the 6th great-granddaughter		
Brown, Jean	Wife of the 7th great-grandson		
Brown, Living	Husband of the 8th great-granddaughter		
Broyhill, William Andrew	Husband of the 5th great-granddaughter		
Bryant, Jacob	Husband of the 4th great-granddaughter		
Bulloch, Martha	Wife of the 3rd great-grandson		
Bulloch, Mary	Wife of the 3rd great-grandson		
Bumgardner, Eula	Wife of the 7th great-grandson		
Burch, Ruth	Wife of the 4th great-grandson		
Burt, Aaron	Husband of the 4th great-granddaughter		
Butler, G. W.	Husband of the 7th great-granddaughter		
Butler, Ruth Anne	8th great-granddaughter	X	10
Caldwell, Mary Jane	Wife of the 5th great-grandson		
Wife of the 6th great-grandson			
Calvin, Hattie	Wife of the 5th great-grandson		
Campbell, Bersheba	Husband of the great-granddaughter		
Campbell, Bersheba	2nd great-granddaughter	IV	4
Cantey, Carolyn	Wife of the 5th great-grandson		
Cantey, Virginia Olive	Wife of the 4th great-grandson		
Carla	Wife of the 7th great-grandson		

Carlton, Albert C.	5th great-grandson	VII	7
Carlton, Allen	5th great-grandson	VII	7
Carlton, Allen Burton	5th great-grandson	VII	7
Carlton, Amanda	5th great-granddaughter	VII	7
	6th great-granddaughter	VIII	8
Carlton, Ambrose M.	5th great-grandson	VII	7
	6th great-grandson	VIII	8
Carlton, Celia	4th great-granddaughter	VI	6
Carlton, Charles R.	5th great-grandson	VII	7
Carlton, Cynthia	4th great-granddaughter	VI	6
Carlton, Daniel Milton	5th great-grandson	VII	7
Carlton, Daughter	5th great-granddaughter	VII	7
Carlton, Daughter	5th great-granddaughter	VII	7
Carlton, Elizabeth	Wife of the 7th great-grandson		
Carlton, Elizabeth	5th great-granddaughter	VII	7
	6th great-granddaughter	VIII	8
Carlton, Emma	Wife of the 7th great-grandson		
Carlton, Eunice Nicey	5th great-granddaughter	VII	7
	6th great-granddaughter	VIII	8
Carlton, Evaline	5th great-granddaughter	VII	7
Carlton, Henry	4th great-grandson	VI	6
Carlton, Henry	5th great-grandson	VII	7
Carlton, Henry	5th great-grandson	VII	7
Carlton, Henry E.	5th great-grandson	VII	7
Carlton, James D.	5th great-grandson	VII	7
	6th great-grandson	VIII	8
Carlton, Jane	4th great-granddaughter	VI	6
	Wife of the 4th great-grandson		
Carlton, Joel Anderson	5th great-grandson	VII	7
Carlton, John	4th great-grandson	VI	6
Carlton, John	5th great-grandson	VII	7
Carlton, John Jasper	5th great-grandson	VII	7
	6th great-grandson	VIII	8
Carlton, John Smith	5th great-grandson	VII	7
Carlton, John Winston	5th great-grandson	VII	7
	6th great-grandson	VIII	8
Carlton, John Wood	5th great-grandson	VII	7
Carlton, Larkin	5th great-grandson	VII	7
Carlton, Lewis	4th great-grandson	VI	6
Carlton, Lewis	5th great-grandson	VII	7
	Husband of the 4th great-granddaughter		
Carlton, Lewis M.	5th great-grandson	VII	7
	6th great-grandson	VIII	8
Carlton, Lewis P.	5th great-grandson	VII	7
	6th great-grandson	VIII	8
Carlton, Living	Husband of the 8th great-granddaughter		
Carlton, Martha Eads	5th great-granddaughter	VII	7
Carlton, Mary	5th great-granddaughter	VII	7
	6th great-granddaughter	VIII	8
Carlton, Mary	4th great-granddaughter	VI	6
Carlton, Mary	5th great-granddaughter	VII	7
Carlton, Mary Ann	5th great-granddaughter	VII	7
Carlton, Matilda	Wife of the 5th great-grandson		
Carlton, Nancy	4th great-granddaughter	VI	6
Carlton, Nancy	5th great-granddaughter	VII	7
	6th great-granddaughter	VIII	8

Carlton, Rebecca M	5th great-granddaughter	VII	7
Carlton, Thomas	Husband of the 3rd great-granddaughter		
Carlton, Thomas	4th great-grandson	VI	6
Carlton, Thomas	5th great-grandson	VII	7
	Husband of the 4th great-granddaughter		
Carlton, Thomas	5th great-grandson	VII	7
Carlton, Thomas B.	5th great-grandson	VII	7
6th great-grandson	VIII		8
Carlton, Thomas Chedle	5th great-grandson	VII	7
Carlton, William Elias	5th great-grandson	VII	7
Carre, Living	Wife of the 8th great-grandson		
Carre-Land, Living	9th great-grandson	XI	11
Carroll, Living	Spouse of the 7th great-granddaughter		
	Wife of the 8th great-grandson		
Carter, Mary Anne Webb	Wife of the great-grandson		
Cashaw, Living	Wife of the 8th great-grandson		
Cathy	Wife of the 6th great-grandson		
Chappell, Martha	Wife of the 2nd great-grandson		
Church, Living	Wife of the 8th great-grandson		
Clark, Henry Aubrey	Husband of the 5th great-granddaughter		
Clark, Living	Wife of the 8th great-grandson		
Clemmons, Lucinda Hedrltra	Wife of the 6th great-grandson		
Cleta	Wife of the 5th great-grandson		
Coble, David	9th great-grandson	XI	11
Coble, Laurie	9th great-granddaughter	XI	11
Coble, Lisa	9th great-granddaughter	XI	11
Coble, Ray	Husband of the 8th great-granddaughter		
Coble, Ronald	9th great-grandson	XI	11
Coker, Eulard Gertrude	7th great-granddaughter	IX	9
Coker, Helen Jane	7th great-granddaughter	IX	9
Coker, James Walter	7th great-grandson	IX	9
Coker, Living	7th great-grandson	IX	9
Coker, Living	7th great-grandson	IX	9
Coker, Living	7th great-granddaughter	IX	9
Coker, Living	7th great-granddaughter	IX	9
Coker, Living	8th great-granddaughter	X	10
Coker, Living	8th great-granddaughter	X	10
Coker, Living	8th great-granddaughter	X	10
Coker, Living	8th great-granddaughter	X	10
Coker, Living	8th great-granddaughter	X	10
Coker, Living	8th great-grandson	X	10
Coker, Living	8th great-grandson	X	10
Coker, Living	8th great-granddaughter	X	10
Coker, Living	8th great-granddaughter	X	10
Coker, Living	8th great-granddaughter	X	10
Coker, Walter Jackson	Husband of the 6th great-granddaughter		
Collins, Living	Husband of the 7th great-granddaughter		
Collins, Living	8th great-granddaughter	X	10
Collins, Living	8th great-grandson	X	10
Collins, Living	8th great-grandson	X	10
Collins, Living	8th great-grandson	X	10
Collins, Living	8th great-grandson	X	10
Collins, Living	8th great-granddaughter	X	10
Collins, Living	8th great-granddaughter	X	10
Collins, Living	8th great-grandson	X	10
Collins, Living	8th great-granddaughter	X	10

Cooper, Mary Ann	Wife of the great-grandson		
Cooper, Mary Ann	Wife of the great-grandson		
Cooper, Mary Ann	Wife of the great-grandson		
Cooper, Mary Ann	Wife of the great-grandson		
Cox, Cynthia Elizabeth	Wife of the 6th great-grandson		
Cox, Living	Wife of the 7th great-grandson		
Cox, Living	Husband of the 8th great-granddaughter		
Cox, Living	Wife of the 8th great-grandson		
Crabtree, John	Husband of the 6th great-granddaughter		
Crabtree, Living	7th great-granddaughter	IX	9
Crawford, Virgil	Husband of the 6th great-granddaughter		
Crisp, Faye Land	7th great-granddaughter	IX	9
Crisp, Living	7th great-granddaughter	IX	9
Crisp, William Cornelius	Husband of the 6th great-granddaughter		
Cromwell, Lewis	Husband of the 4th great-granddaughter		
Crosby, Rebecca W.	Wife of the 4th great-grandson		
Crotts, J.W.	Husband of the 6th great-granddaughter		
Crouch, Caroline	5th great-granddaughter	VII	7
Crouch, George	Husband of the 4th great-granddaughter		
Crouch, Living	Husband of the 8th great-granddaughter		
Crouch, Living	9th great-grandson	XI	11
Crouch, Living	9th great-granddaughter	XI	11
Crouch, Living	9th great-granddaughter	XI	11
Crouch, Rebecca	5th great-granddaughter	VII	7
Crouch, Rutha	5th great-granddaughter	VII	7
Crouse, Living	Husband of the 8th great-granddaughter		
Crowder, Living	Husband of the 7th great-granddaughter		
Crowder, Living	8th great-granddaughter	X	10
Crowder, Living	8th great-grandson	X	10
Crowder, Living	Husband of the 7th great-granddaughter		
Crowder, Living	8th great-granddaughter	X	10
Crowder, Living	8th great-grandson	X	10
Crowson, Living	Wife of the 8th great-grandson		
Crumpley, Henry	Husband of the 3rd great-granddaughter		
Cullen, Living	Wife of the 8th great-grandson		
Cummings, Oliver Chromwell	Husband of the 6th great-granddaughter		
Curtis, Living	Husband of the 6th great-granddaughter		
Curtis, Living	7th great-granddaughter	IX	9
Dail, Dennis	8th great-grandson	X	10
Dail, J. R. "Bob"	Husband of the 7th great-granddaughter		
Dail, Jane Lynn	8th great-granddaughter	X	10
Dail, Johnnie	8th great-grandson	X	10
Dail, Robin	8th great-granddaughter	X	10
Darby, Tabitha	Wife of the 2nd great-grandson		
Davidson, G.E.	Husband of the 7th great-granddaughter		
Davis, "Bill" W. A.	Husband of the 5th great-granddaughter		
Davis, Cade	Husband of the 4th great-granddaughter		
Davis, Elizabeth	Wife of the 5th great-grandson		
Davis, Lelia	6th great-granddaughter	VIII	8
Davis, Living	Husband of the 8th great-granddaughter		
Davis, Living	9th great-granddaughter	XI	11
Davis, Living	9th great-grandson	XI	11
Davis, Living	Husband of the 8th great-granddaughter		
Davis, Living	9th great-granddaughter	XI	11
Davis, Molly	6th great-granddaughter	VIII	8
Davis, Myrtle Bailey	Wife of the 6th great-grandson		

Davis, Thelma Nel	7th great-granddaughter	IX	9
Davis, William Clark	6th great-grandson	VIII	8
Davis, Zona	6th great-granddaughter	VIII	8
Daws, Patsy	Wife of the 2nd great-grandson		
Day, Allen	5th great-grandson	VII	7
Day, Calvin	5th great-grandson	VII	7
Day, Clarissa	5th great-granddaughter	VII	7
Day, Hastings	5th great-grandson	VII	7
Day, John	Husband of the 4th great-granddaughter		
Day, Larkin	5th great-grandson	VII	7
Day, Lot	5th great-grandson	VII	7
Day, Milus	5th great-grandson	VII	7
Day, Wiley	5th great-grandson	VII	7
Day, Wyatt	5th great-grandson	VII	7
Decker, Abraham	Husband of the 4th great-granddaughter		
Decker, Corbett	5th great-grandson	VII	7
Decker, Evaline	5th great-granddaughter	VII	7
Decker, Frank Culam	5th great-grandson	VII	7
Decker, Homer	5th great-grandson	VII	7
Decker, Joe Shelby	5th great-grandson	VII	7
Decker, Walter	5th great-grandson	VII	7
Degana, Living	Wife of the 8th great-grandson		
Dela Land, Katy	8th great-granddaughter	X	10
Della	Wife of the 5th great-grandson		
Dellman, Juanita Belle	Wife of the 6th great-grandson		
Depew, Living	Wife of the 7th great-grandson		
Dickson, Charles Newton	Husband of the 5th great-granddaughter		
Divine, Lona Mae	Wife of the 5th great-grandson		
Dock	Husband of the 4th great-granddaughter		
Dodson, Elisha	Husband of the 4th great-granddaughter		
Doutridge, Charity	4th great-granddaughter	VI	6
Doutridge, Susan	4th great-granddaughter	VI	6
Doutridge, Willie	Husband of the 3rd great-granddaughter		
Dove, Nancy	Wife of the 6th great-grandson		
Dozier, Louisana Caroline	Wife of the 5th great-grandson		
Wife of the 6th great-grandson			
Dula, Jane Sophena	Wife of the 6th great-grandson		
Duncan, James	Husband of the 5th great-granddaughter		
Duncan, Living	Wife of the 8th great-grandson		
Dunnehoo, Mid	Husband of the 5th great-granddaughter		
Dye, Mary	Wife of the 3rd great-grandson		
Dyson, Living	Wife of the 7th great-grandson		
Eadon, Vivian	Wife of the 5th great-grandson		
Eads, Mary Thomas	Wife of the 5th great-grandson		
Earp, Andrew	5th great-grandson	VII	7
Earp, Annie	5th great-granddaughter	VII	7
Earp, Elizabeth	5th great-granddaughter	VII	7
Earp, Nancy	Wife of the 4th great-grandson		
Earp, Thomas	Husband of the 4th great-granddaughter		
Earp, Thomas S.	5th great-grandson	VII	7
Earp, William Martin	5th great-grandson	VII	7
Edmondson, Della	Wife of the 5th great-grandson		
Edwards, Helen Marie	6th great-granddaughter	VIII	8
Wife of the 6th great-grandson			
Edwards, Opie Gray	6th great-grandson	VIII	8
Edwards, Opie Gray	7th great-grandson	IX	9

Edwards, William	Husband of the 5th great-granddaughter		
Edwards, William	7th great-grandson	IX	9
Elane, Rebecca	Wife of the 5th great-grandson		
Eller, James	Husband of the 5th great-granddaughter		
Ellidge, Elizabeth	Wife of the great-grandson		
Ellidge, Elizabeth	Wife of the great-grandson		
Elliott, Henderson	Husband of the 7th great-granddaughter		
Elliott, Mary	Wife of the 5th great-grandson		
Ellis, Elizabeth H.	Wife of the 4th great-grandson		
Elms, Willie	Wife of the 6th great-grandson		
Elrod, Lauris	Wife of the 6th great-grandson		
Elumbaugh, Living	Wife of the 8th great-grandson		
Elvyn	Wife of the 5th great-grandson		
English, Mazie	Wife of the 7th great-grandson		
Enoch, William	Husband of the 4th great-granddaughter		
Evans, Elizabeth "Betty"	Wife of the 4th great-grandson		
Eveland, Living	Husband of the 8th great-granddaughter		
Featherstone, Obedience	Wife of the 3rd great-grandson		
Ferguson, Cynthia	Wife of the 5th great-grandson		
Ferguson, Living	Wife of the 7th great-grandson		
Ferguson, Williard Winfred	Husband of the 7th great-granddaughter		
Fleming, Living	Wife of the 8th great-grandson		
Floyd, Living	Wife of the 7th great-grandson		
Fortner, Elizabeth	Wife of the 6th great-grandson		
Foster, Elizabeth	Wife of the 5th great-grandson		
Foster, F. Fountain	Husband of the 5th great-granddaughter Husband of the 6th great-granddaughter		
Foster, John P.	Husband of the 5th great-granddaughter Husband of the 6th great-granddaughter		
Fox, Charlie Lee	8th great-grandson	X	10
Fox, George W.	8th great-grandson	X	10
Fox, Harvey Alexander	8th great-grandson	X	10
Fox, James Jefferson	Husband of the 7th great-granddaughter		
Fox, Levina Luna	8th great-granddaughter	X	10
Fox, Living	8th great-granddaughter	X	10
Fox, Living	8th great-granddaughter	X	10
Fox, Living	8th great-grandson	X	10
Fox, Living	8th great-grandson	X	10
Fox, Robert Doughton	8th great-grandson	X	10
Foxhall, Martha Ann	Wife of the 4th great-grandson		
France, William	Husband of the 3rd great-granddaughter		
Freeman, Jeremiah	Husband of the 4th great-granddaughter		
Freeman, Oma	Wife of the 7th great-grandson		
Fudge, Living	Husband of the 8th great-granddaughter		
Fudge, Living	9th great-grandson	XI	11
Fudge, Living	9th great-granddaughter	XI	11
Fudge, Living	9th great-granddaughter	XI	11
Gann, Delmer	6th great-grandson	VIII	8
Gann, Earl	6th great-grandson	VIII	8
Gann, Helen	6th great-granddaughter	VIII	8
Gann, Marion Author	Husband of the 5th great-granddaughter		
Gann, Muriam	6th great-granddaughter	VIII	8
Gann, Russell	6th great-grandson	VIII	8
Gardner, Martha Ann Foxhall	Wife of the 4th great-grandson		
Gardner, William Ann	5th great-granddaughter	VII 7	
Garrott, Stephen	Husband of the 4th great-granddaughter		

Garver, Sarah Vada	Wife of the 6th great-grandson		
Gates, Living	Wife of the 8th great-grandson		
Geiger, Edith Virginia	Wife of the 5th great-grandson		
Gilbert, Velma	Wife of the 5th great-grandson		
Giles, Elizabeth A.	Wife of the 4th great-grandson		
Gillium, Frances	Wife of the 4th great-grandson		
Gipson, Living	Husband of the 7th great-granddaughter		
Gisinger, Living	Wife of the 8th great-grandson		
Gladden, Silas	Husband of the 3rd great-granddaughter		
Goble, Living	Wife of the 8th great-grandson		
Godfrey, Living	Wife of the 8th great-grandson		
Gray, Amanda	5th great-granddaughter	VII	7
Gray, Anna	5th great-granddaughter	VII	7
Gray, Cinthia	5th great-granddaughter	VII	7
Gray, Frances Louise	5th great-granddaughter	VII	7
Gray, John	Husband of the 4th great-granddaughter		
Gray, Mary Adaliane	5th great-granddaughter	VII	7
Gray, Mira	5th great-granddaughter	VII	7
Gray, Nancy	5th great-granddaughter	VII	7
Gray, Ruth	5th great-granddaughter	VII	7
Gray, Thomas	5th great-grandson	VII	7
Gray, Warren	5th great-grandson	VII	7
Gray, William	Husband of the 4th great-granddaughter		
Gray, William	5th great-grandson	VII	7
Gray, Wilson	5th great-grandson	VII	7
Green, Simon	Husband of the 3rd great-granddaughter		
Greer, Living	Wife of the 8th great-grandson		
Spouse of the 8th great-granddaughter			
Gressley, Living	Husband of the 8th great-granddaughter		
Gressley, Living	9th great-granddaughter	X	11
Gressley, Living	9th great-granddaughter	I	11
Gressley, Living	9th great-granddaughter	X	11
Gressley, Living	9th great-granddaughter	I	11
Griffin, Richard Taswell	Husband of the 5th great-granddaughter		
Griffin, Sarah Anita	Wife of the 6th great-grandson		
Griffith, Margaret	Wife of the 4th great-grandson		
Gulley, Amanda	5th great-granddaughter	VII	7
Gulley, Thomas	5th great-grandson	VII	7
Gulley, Willis	Husband of the 4th great-granddaughter		
Guynes, Living	Husband of the 8th great-granddaughter		
Guynes, Living	9th great-granddaughter	XI	11
Guynes, Living	9th great-grandson	XI	11
Guynes, Living	Wife of the 8th great-grandson		
Hackworth, Almon	6th great-grandson	VIII	8
Hackworth, Elmer	6th great-grandson	VIII	8
Hackworth, Irene	6th great-granddaughter	VIII	8
Hackworth, James Calvin	Husband of the 5th great-granddaughter		
Hackworth, Jerry	6th great-grandson	VIII	8
Hackworth, John	6th great-grandson	VIII	8
Hackworth, Mary	6th great-granddaughter	VIII	8
Hackworth, Ruby	6th great-granddaughter	VIII	8
Hackworth, Thelma	6th great-granddaughter	VIII	8
Hale, Leira	Wife of the 7th great-grandson		
Hall, Ann	Wife of the 5th great-grandson		
Hall, William	Husband of the 5th great-granddaughter		
Hamill, Lillian	Wife of the 6th great-grandson		

Hammond, Living	Husband of the 8th great-granddaughter		
Hampton, Anne	Wife of the 5th great-grandson		
Hargrove, Alphons "Alva" Gray	5th great-grandson	VII	7
Hargrove, Annie	4th great-granddaughter	VI	6
Hargrove, Charles Bardwood	5th great-grandson	VII	7
Hargrove, Delta	4th great-granddaughter	VI	6
Hargrove, Duncan	Husband of the 3rd great-granddaughter		
Hargrove, Duncan	Husband of the 3rd great-granddaughter		
Hargrove, Edward L	4th great-grandson	VI	6
Hargrove, Edward L.	4th great-grandson	VI	6
Hargrove, Edwin Thomas	5th great-grandson	VII	7
Hargrove, Elizabeth "Lizzie" Geraldine	5th great-granddaughter	VII	7
Hargrove, Florence Anna	4th great-granddaughter	V	6
Hargrove, Florence Anna	4th great-granddaughter	I	6
Hargrove, Frances Deller "Della"	4th great-granddaughter	V	6
Hargrove, Frank Lesley	6th great-grandson	I	8
Hargrove, George S.	5th great-grandson	V	7
Hargrove, Gray Lemon	4th great-grandson	I	6
Hargrove, Hattie Idora	5th great-granddaughter	VIII	7
Hargrove, Ina Elizabeth	4th great-granddaughter	VII	6
Hargrove, James Burrel (Burwell)	4th great-grandson	VI	6
Hargrove, James Busnell	4th great-grandson	VII	6
Hargrove, John David	5th great-grandson	VI	7
Hargrove, Joseph Marion	5th great-grandson	VI	7
Hargrove, Lee David	6th great-grandson	VI	8
Hargrove, Lena Bruce	6th great-grandson	VII	8
Hargrove, Living	8th great-grandson	VII	10
Hargrove, Living	8th great-grandson	VIII	10
Hargrove, Living	8th great-grandson	VIII	10
Hargrove, Living	8th great-grandson	X	10
Hargrove, Living	8th great-grandson	X	10
Hargrove, Living	8th great-grandson	X	10
Hargrove, Lossie Jane	6th great-granddaughter	X	8
Hargrove, Louisana Jane	4th great-granddaughter	X	6
Hargrove, Louisiana	4th great-granddaughter	X	6
Hargrove, Lucinda	5th great-granddaughter	VIII	7
Hargrove, Lucy	5th great-granddaughter	VI	7
Hargrove, Lucy Ella	5th great-granddaughter	VI	7
Hargrove, Mae Krider	6th great-granddaughter	VII	8
Hargrove, Malvina	4th great-granddaughter	VII	6
Hargrove, Malvina Catherine	4th great-granddaughter	VII	6
Hargrove, Manse Leroy	6th great-grandson	VIII	8
Hargrove, Martha Ann Charity	4th great-granddaughter	VI	6
Hargrove, Martha Ann Charity	4th great-granddaughter	VI	6
Hargrove, Martha Ann Charity	4th great-granddaughter	VIII	6
Hargrove, Martha Gray	5th great-granddaughter	VI	7
Hargrove, Mary	5th great-granddaughter	VI	7
Hargrove, Mary Elizabeth	4th great-granddaughter	VI	6
Hargrove, Melonia	4th great-granddaughter	VII	6
Hargrove, Musa Dora	6th great-granddaughter	VII	8
Hargrove, Nellie Gray	6th great-granddaughter	VI	8
Hargrove, Peyton Clifford	5th great-grandson	VI	7
Hargrove, Prudence	5th great-granddaughter	VIII	7
Hargrove, Robert Gray	5th great-grandson	VIII	7
Hargrove, Robert Henry	5th great-grandson	VII	7
Hargrove, Robert Henry	6th great-grandson	VII	8

Hargrove, Sallie	5th great-granddaughter	VII	7
Hargrove, Sallie Capitola	5th great-granddaughter	VII	7
Hargrove, Sally Gray	7th great-granddaughter	IX	9
Hargrove, Samuel H.	6th great-grandson	VIII	8
Hargrove, Samuel Henry	4th great-grandson	VI	6
Hargrove, Sara Nina	4th great-granddaughter	VI	6
Hargrove, Sarah	4th great-granddaughter	VI	6
Hargrove, Susan N.	4th great-granddaughter	VI	6
Hargrove, Thomas Daniel	4th great-grandson	VI	6
Hargrove, Walter Clark	6th great-grandson	VIII	8
Husband of the 6th great-granddaughter			
Hargrove, Walter Clark	7th great-grandson	IX	9
Hargrove, William H.	5th great-grandson	VII	7
Hargrove, Willie Franklin	5th great-grandson	VII	7
Harper, Emma Louise	Wife of the 5th great-grandson		
Harris, Ray	Husband of the 7th great-granddaughter		
Harrison, Elgin	7th great-grandson	IX	9
Harrison, Lois Marie	7th great-granddaughter	IX	9
Harrison, Minzo	Husband of the 5th great-granddaughter		
Harrison, Otto	Husband of the 5th great-granddaughter		
Harrison, Stairett	Husband of the 6th great-granddaughter		
Harrison, Steve	8th great-grandson	X	10
Hart, Elizabeth	Wife of the 2nd great-grandson		
Hartley, Living	Wife of the 8th great-grandson		
Hatsfield, Helen	Wife of the 3rd great-grandson		
Hatsfield, Helen	Wife of the 4th great-grandson		
Hattan, Barbara Elois	Wife of the 7th great-grandson		
Hawkins, Franklin Nathaniel	Husband of the 7th great-granddaughter		
Hawkins, Living	8th great-grandson	X	10
Hawkins, Living	8th great-grandson	X	10
Hawkins, Living	8th great-grandson	X	10
Hawkins, Living	8th great-grandson	X	10
Hawkins, Living	8th great-grandson	X	10
Hawkins, Living	9th great-grandson	XI	11
Hawkins, Living	9th great-granddaughter	XI	11
Hawkins, Living	9th great-grandchild	XI	11
Hays, Living	Husband of the 7th great-granddaughter		
Heath, Living	Husband of the 8th great-granddaughter		
Heath, Living	9th great-grandson	XI	11
Hedrick	Husband of the 7th great-granddaughter		
Hefner, Opal	Wife of the 5th great-grandson		
Helms, Permelia	Wife of the 4th great-grandson		
Henderson, Nellie	Wife of the 5th great-grandson		
Hendrick, Cain V.	6th great-grandson	VIII	8
Hendrick, Calvin James	6th great-grandson	VIII	8
Hendrick, Carrie	6th great-granddaughter	VIII	8
Hendrick, Della	6th great-granddaughter	VIII	8
Hendrick, Edward	6th great-grandson	VIII	8
Hendrick, Leander J.	Husband of the 5th great-granddaughter		
Hendrick, Martha	6th great-granddaughter	VIII	8
Hendrick, Mary E.	6th great-granddaughter	VIII	8
Hendrick, Nola	Wife of the 7th great-grandson		
Hendrick, William T.	6th great-grandson	VIII	8
Hennessee, Living	Wife of the 8th great-grandson		
Hepler, Patricia	8th great-granddaughter	X	10
Hepler, Randal	8th great-grandson	X	10

Hepler, Sharon	8th great-granddaughter	X	10
Hepler, Wanda	Husband of the 7th great-granddaughter		
Hicks, Vivian Olive	Wife of the 6th great-grandson		
Hight, Edward Leonard	Husband of the 7th great-granddaughter		
Hillis, Robert	Husband of the 7th great-granddaughter		
Hix, Carol	Wife of the 7th great-grandson		
Hodges, Mary	Wife		
Hogan, Almus	Husband of the 7th great-granddaughter		
Hogan, Karen	8th great-granddaughter	X	10
Hogan, Melissa	8th great-granddaughter	X	10
Hogan, Paula	8th great-granddaughter	X	10
Hogan, Ronnie	8th great-grandson	X	10
Hogan, Sam Willie	Husband of the 5th great-granddaughter		
Hogue, Irene	Wife of the 5th great-grandson		
Hogue, L. J.	7th great-grandson	IX	9
Hogue, Levi Augustus	Husband of the 6th great-granddaughter		
Hogue, Shirley Evon	7th great-granddaughter	IX	9
Holder, Living	Wife of the 8th great-grandson		
Holder, Margaret	Wife of the 5th great-grandson		
Wife of the 6th great-grandson			
Holder, Sarah A.	Wife of the 5th great-grandson		
Holland, Richard	Husband of the 4th great-granddaughter		
Holland, Richard	Husband of the 4th great-granddaughter		
Holloway, Living	Husband of the 8th great-granddaughter		
Holloway, Living	9th great-grandson	XI	11
Holsclaw, John	Husband of the 5th great-granddaughter		
Holsclaw, Living	Husband of the 8th great-granddaughter		
Holsclaw, Living	9th great-grandson	XI	11
Holsclaw, Living	9th great-grandson	XI	11
Holsclaw, Living	9th great-granddaughter	XI	11
Holsclaw, Living	9th great-granddaughter	XI	11
Holsclaw, Living	9th great-grandson	XI	11
Holsclaw, Living	9th great-grandson	XI	11
Holsclaw, Living	9th great-granddaughter	XI	11
Hood, Living	Husband of the 8th great-granddaughter		
Hoover, Living	Wife of the 6th great-grandson		
Horseman, Lila	Wife of the 6th great-grandson		
Horsman, Allen	8th great-grandson	X	10
Horsman, Carma Jane	8th great-granddaughter	X	10
Horsman, Freddie Fry	8th great-grandson	X	10
Horsman, Wayne Fry	Husband of the 7th great-granddaughter		
Hossick, Eleanor	Wife of the 4th great-grandson		
Hudson, Elizabeth	Wife of the 5th great-grandson		
Hughes	Husband of the 4th great-granddaughter		
Hughes, Augustine Clark	6th great-grandson	VIII	8
Hughes, Augustine Clark	Husband of the 5th great-granddaughter		
Hughes, Betty Joyce	6th great-granddaughter	VIII	8
Hughes, Birdie	5th great-granddaughter	VII	7
Hughes, Bonnie Sue	7th great-granddaughter	IX	9
Hughes, Buddy Carson	6th great-grandson	VIII	8
Hughes, Cheryl Lynn	7th great-granddaughter	IX	9
Hughes, Crystal	7th great-granddaughter	IX	9
Hughes, Dillion	8th great-grandson	X	10
Hughes, Donna Carol	7th great-granddaughter	IX	9
Hughes, Eugene	6th great-grandson	VIII	8
Hughes, Gray	6th great-grandson	VIII	8

Hughes, Harold	6th great-grandson	VIII	8
Hughes, Henry F.	5th great-grandson	VII	7
Hughes, Imogene Evelyn	6th great-granddaughter	VIII	8
Hughes, James Edgar	5th great-grandson	VII	7
Hughes, James Henry	6th great-grandson	VIII	8
Hughes, James Henry, Jr.	7th great-grandson	IX	9
Hughes, Joseph Brian	7th great-grandson	IX	9
Hughes, Martha Anna	5th great-granddaughter	VII	7
Hughes, Mary	6th great-granddaughter	VIII	8
Hughes, Mary Emma	5th great-granddaughter	VII	7
Hughes, Michael	7th great-grandson	IX	9
Hughes, Patricia Dail	7th great-granddaughter	IX	9
Hughes, Ronnie	6th great-grandson	VIII	8
Hughes, Rosy	5th great-granddaughter	VII	7
Hughes, Shelia Renee	7th great-granddaughter	IX	9
Hughes, Thomas	7th great-grandson	IX	9
Hughes, Thomas Dail	6th great-grandson	VIII	8
Hughes, Thomas Jefferson	5th great-grandson	VII	7
Hughes, Virginia Denise	7th great-granddaughter	IX	9
Huskey, Edgar	Husband of the 7th great-granddaughter		
Huskey, Living	8th great-granddaughter	X	10
Huskey, Living	8th great-granddaughter	X	10
Huskey, Living	8th great-grandson	X	10
Huskey, Living	8th great-grandson	X	10
Huskey, Living	8th great-grandson	X	10
Huskey, Living	8th great-granddaughter	X	10
Huskey, Living	8th great-grandson	X	10
Huskey, Living	8th great-granddaughter	X	10
Huskey, Living	8th great-granddaughter	X	10
Huskey, Living	8th great-grandson	X	10
Hutchens, Betty	2nd great-granddaughter	IV	4
Hutchens, Lewis	Husband of the great-granddaughter		
Hutchens, Pressillian	2nd great-granddaughter	IV	4
Hutchens, Robert	2nd great-granddaughter	IV	4
Hutchinson, Amanda	5th great-granddaughter	VII	7
Hutchinson, Benjamin	Husband of the 4th great-granddaughter		
Hutchinson, Benjamin Perry	5th great-grandson	VII	7
Hutchinson, Child	5th great-granddaughter	VII	7
Hutchinson, Daughter	5th great-granddaughter	VII	7
Hutchinson, Eliza Ellen	5th great-granddaughter	VII	7
Hutchinson, John D.	5th great-grandson	VII	7
Hutchinson, Martha	5th great-granddaughter	VII	7
Hutchinson, Sarah M.	5th great-granddaughter	VII	7
Hutchinson, William	5th great-grandson	VII	7
Hutchison, Charles Henry	7th great-grandson	IX	9
Hutchison, Larkin H.	Husband of the 6th great-granddaughter		
Hutchison, Living	7th great-grandson	IX	9
Irick, Agatha Robinson	Wife of the 5th great-grandson		
Isbell, Daniel	Husband of the 3rd great-granddaughter		
Isbell, Elizabeth	Wife of the 3rd great-grandson		
Isenhour, Anna	Wife of the 5th great-grandson		
Jacobs, Living	Wife of the 8th great-grandson		
Jacobs, Nellie B.	Wife of the 6th great-grandson		
Janes, Blanche	Wife of the 6th great-grandson		
Jean, Living	Wife of the 8th great-grandson		
Jefferies, Ethel	6th great-granddaughter	VIII	8

Jefferies, Fred	Husband of the 5th great-granddaughter		
Johnson, Lita	Wife of the 7th great-grandson		
Johnson, Living	Husband of the 8th great-granddaughter		
Johnson, William	Husband of the 4th great-granddaughter		
Joiner, Curtis	2nd great-grandson	IV	4
Joiner, Elizabeth	2nd great-granddaughter	IV	4
Joiner, John	Husband of the great-granddaughter		
Joiner, John	2nd great-grandson	IV	4
Jones, Billy Joe	6th great-grandson	VIII	8
Jones, Carson	6th great-grandson	VIII	8
Jones, Frances Elizabeth	Wife of the 4th great-grandson		
Jones, Gene	6th great-grandson	VIII	8
Jones, James Gerald	6th great-grandson	VIII	8
Jones, Juanita	6th great-granddaughter	VIII	8
Jones, Lehman	6th great-grandson	VIII	8
Jones, Living	Husband of the 7th great-granddaughter		
Jones, Living	8th great-granddaughter	X	10
Jones, Living	8th great-granddaughter	X	10
Jones, Living	7th great-granddaughter	IX	9
Jones, Mary	Wife of the 2nd great-grandson		
Jones, Oneida	6th great-granddaughter	VIII	8
Jones, Vera	6th great-granddaughter	VIII	8
Jones, Virginia Estele	Wife of the 4th great-grandson		
Jones, Virginia Estelle	Wife of the 4th great-grandson		
Jones, William	Husband of the 5th great-granddaughter		
Jordon, Catherine	4th great-granddaughter	VI	6
Jordon, Charles	4th great-grandson	VI	6
Jordon, Ethelred	Husband of the 3rd great-granddaughter		
Jordon, Henry	4th great-grandson	VI	6
Jordon, John	4th great-grandson	VI	6
Jordon, Marion Strom	Husband of the 5th great-granddaughter		
Jordon, Martha	4th great-granddaughter	VI	6
Jordon, Smith	4th great-grandson	VI	6
Josephine, Sarah	Wife of the 4th great-grandson		
Joyner, Amos	5th great-grandson	VII	7
Joyner, Burrell Hildsman	4th great-grandson	VI	6
Joyner, David D.	4th great-grandson	VI	6
Joyner, Eliza	4th great-granddaughter	VI	6
Joyner, Eliza JOYNER	4th great-granddaughter	VI	6
Joyner, Ella	5th great-granddaughter	VII	7
Joyner, Florence	5th great-granddaughter	VII	7
Joyner, Francis M.	4th great-grandson	VI	6
Joyner, George	5th great-grandson	VII	7
Joyner, George W.	4th great-grandson	VI	6
Joyner, Ira E.	4th great-grandson	VI	6
Joyner, Ira Ellis	4th great-grandson	VI	6
Joyner, John A.	5th great-grandson	VII	7
Joyner, John David "DAVID"	4th great-grandson	VI	6
Joyner, John R.	5th great-grandson	VII	7
Joyner, Jonas A.	4th great-grandson	VI	6
Joyner, Josiah J.	5th great-grandson	VII	7
Joyner, Littleberry	4th great-grandson	VI	6
Joyner, Littleberry	4th great-grandson	VI	6
Joyner, Lucy	5th great-granddaughter	VII	7
Joyner, Madora	5th great-granddaughter	VII	7
Joyner, Mary Ann	5th great-granddaughter	VII	7

Joyner, Matthew H.	5th great-grandson	VII	7
Joyner, Nathan	4th great-grandson	VI	6
Joyner, Nathan T.	4th great-grandson	VI	6
Joyner, Nathan Thomas "THOMAS"	Husband of the 3rd great-granddaughter		
Joyner, Ora	5th great-granddaughter	VII	7
Joyner, S.	5th great-granddaughter	VII	7
Joyner, S. Anna	5th great-granddaughter	VII	7
Joyner, Susan A.	5th great-granddaughter	VII	7
Joyner, Thomas	Husband of the 3rd great-granddaughter		
Joyner, William N.	5th great-grandson	VII	7
Jr, Frances Land	3rd great-grandson	V	5
Jr, John Land	4th great-grandson	VI	6
Kaylor, Living	Husband of the 8th great-granddaughter		
Kaylor, Living	9th great-grandson	XI	11
Kaylor, Living	9th great-granddaughter	XI	11
Kaylor, Living	9th great-granddaughter	XI	11
Kays, Edward	Husband of the great-granddaughter		
Kellett, Jasper	Husband of the 6th great-granddaughter		
Kendrick, Living	Husband of the 8th great-granddaughter		
Kennedy, Joel Chandler	Husband of the 5th great-granddaughter		
Kerley, Hannah Marinda	Wife of the 5th great-grandson		
Kerley, Mary Carolyn	Wife of the 6th great-grandson		
Kerley, Sarah Minerva	Wife of the 5th great-grandson		
Killebrew, Lucinda	Wife of the 4th great-grandson		
Kimbley, Martha	Wife of the 5th great-grandson		
Wife of the 6th great-grandson			
King, John	Husband of the 7th great-granddaughter		
King, Laura	Wife of the 6th great-grandson		
King, Leon	8th great-grandson	X	10
King, Living	Husband of the 8th great-granddaughter		
King, Mamie	Wife of the 4th great-grandson		
King, Stanley	8th great-grandson	X	10
Kinlaw, J.M.	Husband of the 7th great-granddaughter		
Klein, Living	Husband of the 8th great-granddaughter		
Knight, Callie Estella	Wife of the 7th great-grandson		
Knight, Living	Husband of the 8th great-granddaughter		
Knight, Living	9th great-granddaughter	XI	11
Knight, Rebecca Frances	Wife of the 5th great-grandson		
Knight, Reuben	Husband of the 4th great-granddaughter		
Knight, William Rufus	Husband of the 5th great-granddaughter		
Husband of the 6th great-granddaughter			
Krider, Dora Mae	Wife of the 5th great-grandson		
Lancaster, Bird	4th great-grandson	VI	6
Lancaster, Joseph	Husband of the 3rd great-granddaughter		
Land, "Dona" Francis Caldonia	4th great-granddaughter	VI	6
Land, Aaron Carter	7th great-grandson	IX	9
Land, Alfred Homer	7th great-grandson	IX	9
Land, Alica Tabitha	7th great-granddaughter	IX	9
Land, Allison	5th great-grandson	VII	7
Land, Amanda Serilda	7th great-granddaughter	IX	9
Land, America	5th great-granddaughter	VII	7
Land, Amy	3rd great-granddaughter	V	5
Land, Ann	4th great-granddaughter	VI	6
Land, Ann	5th great-granddaughter	VII	7
Land, Anna	4th great-granddaughter	VI	6
Land, Annie	5th great-granddaughter	VII	7

Land, Annie M.	5th great-granddaughter	VII	7
Land, Augusta B.	7th great-granddaughter	IX	9
Land, Baby	8th great-grandchild	X	10
Land, Barbara	6th great-granddaughter	VIII	8
Land, Benjamin	2nd great-grandson	IV	4
Land, Benjamin Franklin	3rd great-grandson	V	5
Land, Benjamin Smith	6th great-grandson	VIII	8
Land, Benjamin Smith	5th great-grandson	VII	7
Land, Betty	8th great-granddaughter	X	10
Land, Betty	2nd great-granddaughter	IV	4
Land, Bird	Great-grandson	III	3
Land, Bird	Great-grandson	III	3
Land, Bird	Great-grandson	III	3
Land, Bird	Great-grandson	III	3
Land, Bird	3rd great-grandson	V	5
Land, Bonnie Charlene	7th great-granddaughter	IX	9
Land, Bryson Henderson	7th great-grandson	IX	9
Land, Burnett Guthrie	5th great-grandson	VII	7
Land, Calvin	6th great-grandson	VIII	8
Land, Calvin C.	7th great-grandson	IX	9
Land, Calvin Henderson	7th great-grandson	IX	9
Land, Carlos Eugene	5th great-grandson	VII	7
Land, Caroline	4th great-granddaughter	VI	6
Land, Catherine	3rd great-granddaughter	V	5
Land, Catherine Jane	6th great-granddaughter	VIII	8
Land, Cecila	4th great-granddaughter	VI	6
Land, Ceth Smith	3rd great-grandson	V	5
Land, Ceth Smith	4th great-grandson	VI	6
Land, Ceth Smith	5th great-grandson	VII	7
Land, Charles	Great-grandson	III	3
Land, Charles	Great-grandson	III	3
Land, Charles	Great-grandson	III	3
Land, Charles	Great-grandson	III	3
Land, Charles	4th great-grandson	VI	6
Land, Charles	2nd great-grandson	IV	4
Land, Charles	2nd great-grandson	IV	4
Land, Charles	2nd great-grandson	IV	4
Land, Charles	2nd great-grandson	IV	4
Land, Charles	2nd great-grandson	IV	4
Land, Charles	3rd great-grandson	V	5
Land, Charles Cleveland	7th great-grandson	IX	9
Land, Charles Edward	5th great-grandson	VII	7
Land, Charles Hugh	4th great-grandson	VI	6
Land, Charles Lester	5th great-grandson	VII	7
Land, Charlotte	2nd great-granddaughter	IV	4
Land, Charlotte	3rd great-granddaughter	V	5
Land, Charlotte	4th great-granddaughter	VI	6
Land, Clara Rebecca	8th great-granddaughter	X	10
Land, Clarence Ramon	7th great-grandson	IX	9
Land, Claude Earl	7th great-grandson	IX	9
Land, Clyde Err	7th great-grandson	IX	9
Land, Cora	7th great-granddaughter	IX	9
Land, Curtis	Self		0
Land, Curtis	Son	I	1
Land, Curtis	Grandson	II	2
Land, Curtis	Grandson	II	2

Land, Curtis	Grandson	II	2
Land, Curtis	Grandson Great-	II	2
Land, Curtis	grandson Great-grandson	III	3
Land, Curtis	Great-grandson	III	3
Land, Curtis	Grandson	III	3
Land, Curtis III	6th great-granddaughter	II	2
Land, Cynthia Ellen	5th great-granddaughter	VIII	8
Land, Daisy	3rd great-grandson	VII	7
Land, Daniel	4th great-granddaughter	V	5
Land, Daughter	3rd great-grandson	VI	6
Land, David	5th great-grandson	V	5
Land, David	4th great-grandson	VII	7
Land, David	7th great-grandson	VI	6
Land, David	8th great-grandson	IX	9
Land, David Albert	6th great-grandson	X	10
Land, David V.	3rd great-grandson	VIII	8
Land, David Yearty	4th great-granddaughter	V	5
Land, Delilah	4th great-granddaughter	VI	6
Land, Delilah Lucresa	4th great-granddaughter	VI	6
Land, Della	5th great-granddaughter	VI	6
Land, Della Mae	6th great-granddaughter	VII	7
Land, Dewanna W.	7th great-grandson	VIII	8
Land, Dewey	4th great-granddaughter	IX	9
Land, Dora Ada	5th great-granddaughter	VI	6
Land, Dora Annie	4th great-granddaughter	VII	7
Land, Dorcas	6th great-granddaughter	VI	6
Land, Doretha	3rd great-grandson	VIII	8
Land, Edwin	6th great-grandson	V	5
Land, Elcanah Brison	6th great-grandson	VIII	8
Land, Eldridge H.	3rd great-grandson	VIII	8
Land, Eldridge Hall	3rd great-granddaughter	V	5
Land, Eleanor	3rd great-grandson	V	5
Land, Eledge Hall	4th great-grandson	V	5
Land, Eledge Hall	6th great-grandson	VI	6
Land, Eli Jason	6th great-grandson	VIII	8
Land, Elias	4th great-grandson	VIII	8
Land, Elihu	4th great-grandson	VI	6
Land, Elijah R.	4th great-granddaughter	VI	6
Land, Elisia Evaline	4th great-granddaughter	VI	6
Land, Eliza	4th great-granddaughter	VI	6
Land, Eliza E.	5th great-granddaughter	VI	6
Land, Elizabeth	5th great-granddaughter	VII	7
Land, Elizabeth	Great-granddaughter	VII	7
Land, Elizabeth	4th great-granddaughter	III	3
Land, Elizabeth		VI	6
Wife of the 5th great-grandson			
Land, Elizabeth	4th great-granddaughter	VI	6
Land, Elizabeth	4th great-granddaughter	VI	6
Land, Elizabeth	3rd great-granddaughter	V	5
Land, Elizabeth	3rd great-granddaughter	V	5
Land, Elizabeth	5th great-granddaughter	VII	7
Land, Elizabeth	3rd great-granddaughter	V	5
Land, Elizabeth	6th great-granddaughter	VIII	8
Land, Elizabeth	6th great-granddaughter	VIII	8
Wife of the 6th great-grandson			
Land, Elizabeth	6th great-granddaughter	VIII	8

Land, Elizabeth	7th great-granddaughter	IX	9
Land, Elizabeth	7th great-granddaughter	IX	9
Land, Elizabeth	7th great-granddaughter	IX	9
Land, Elizabeth Jane	4th great-granddaughter	VI	6
Land, Ella Mae	7th great-granddaughter	IX	9
Land, Ellen Lou	6th great-granddaughter	VIII	8
Land, Ellison	5th great-grandson	VII	7
Land, Elmira Sherman	4th great-granddaughter	VI	6
Land, Elridge Hall	5th great-grandson	VII	7
Land, Emeline	3rd great-granddaughter	V	5
Land, Emily	5th great-granddaughter	VII	7
Land, Emily	5th great-granddaughter	VII	7
Land, Emma Jane	7th great-granddaughter	IX	9
Land, Enos	4th great-grandson	VI	6
Land, Ephraim	2nd great-grandson	IV	4
Land, Ethel	6th great-granddaughter	VIII	8
Land, Eula Mattie	7th great-granddaughter	IX	9
Land, Eveline	5th great-granddaughter	VII	7
Land, F.	6th great-grandson	VIII	8
Land, Fannie	2nd great-granddaughter	IV	4
Land, Florence	7th great-granddaughter	IX	9
Land, Florence Lee	5th great-granddaughter	VII	7
Land, Fountain	4th great-grandson	VI	6
Land, Fountain William	5th great-grandson	VII	7
Land, Frances	4th great-granddaughter	VI	6
Land, Frances Ellidge	2nd great-grandson	IV	4
Land, Frances H.	4th great-grandson	VI	6
Land, Frances Hatcher	4th great-granddaughter	VI	6
Land, Frances Isabell	4th great-granddaughter	VI	6
Land, Frances Louise	7th great-granddaughter	IX	9
Land, Frances, Jr.	2nd great-grandson	IV	4
Land, Frank Henry	7th great-grandson	IX	9
Land, Franka	3rd great-granddaughter	V	5
Land, Fred	8th great-grandson	X	10
Land, Fred	7th great-grandson	IX	9
Land, Fred Columbus	7th great-grandson	IX	9
Land, Fred R.	6th great-grandson	VIII	8
Land, George	3rd great-grandson	V	5
Land, George	6th great-grandson	VIII	8
Land, George	4th great-grandson	VI	6
Land, George Edward	7th great-grandson	IX	9
Land, George Edward	8th great-grandson	X	10
Land, George W.	5th great-grandson	VII	7
Land, George Washington	7th great-grandson	IX	9
Land, George Washington	7th great-grandson	IX	9
Land, Gertrude Nesbitt	5th great-granddaughter	VII	7
Land, Grace Leann	7th great-granddaughter	IX	9
Land, Grace Lee	5th great-granddaughter	VII	7
Land, Gracie Alice	7th great-granddaughter	IX	9
Land, Greene	5th great-grandson	VII	7
Land, Gussie Jane	7th great-granddaughter	IX	9
Land, Hannah Ninabelle	6th great-granddaughter	VIII	8
Land, Hasting	5th great-grandson	VII	7
Land, Havries Seleyn	6th great-grandson	VIII	8
Land, Hayden James	7th great-grandson	IX	9
Land, Henderson P.	5th great-grandson	VII	7

Land, Henrietta	4th great-granddaughter	VI	6
Land, Henrietta	3rd great-granddaughter	V	5
Land, Henry	2nd great-grandson	IV	4
Land, Henry	4th great-grandson	VI	6
Land, Henry	2nd great-grandson	IV	4
Land, Henry	4th great-grandson	VI	6
Land, Henry Fountain	6th great-grandson	VIII	8
Land, Howard Columbus	6th great-grandson	VIII	8
Land, Howard Douglas	8th great-grandson	X	10
Land, Ida	5th great-granddaughter	VII	7
Land, Ida	7th great-granddaughter	IX	9
Land, Inez	6th great-granddaughter	VIII	8
Land, Infant Daughter	6th great-granddaughter	VIII	8
Land, Isaiah	3rd great-grandson	V	5
Land, Isham	2nd great-grandson	IV	4
Land, Jack L.	8th great-grandson	X	10
Land, James	6th great-grandson	VIII	8
Land, James	4th great-grandson	VI	6
Land, James	4th great-grandson	VI	6
Land, James	5th great-grandson	VII	7
Land, James B.	4th great-grandson	VI	6
Land, James C.	6th great-grandson	VIII	8
Land, James Calvin	5th great-grandson	VII	7
Land, James Dewitt	5th great-grandson	VII	7
Land, James Dewitt	6th great-grandson	VIII	8
Land, James Edgar	7th great-grandson	IX	9
Land, James Eli	6th great-grandson	VIII	8
Land, James Herbert	8th great-grandson	X	10
Land, James Howard	8th great-grandson	X	10
Land, James Jefferson	6th great-grandson	VIII	8
Land, James L.	7th great-grandson	IX	9
Land, James Linville	6th great-grandson	VIII	8
Land, James McConnell	6th great-grandson	VIII	8
Land, James Monroe	6th great-grandson	VIII	8
Land, James Noah	4th great-grandson	VI	6
Land, James R.	4th great-granddaughter	VI	6
Land, James Smith	2nd great-grandson	IV	4
Land, James W.	7th great-grandson	IX	9
Land, James William	7th great-grandson	IX	9
Land, Jane	3rd great-granddaughter	V	5
Land, Jane K.	4th great-granddaughter	VI	6
Land, Janie	5th great-granddaughter	VII	7
Land, Jasper H.	7th great-grandson	IX	9
Land, Jemima	4th great-granddaughter	VI	6
Land, Jeremiah	4th great-grandson	VI	6
Land, Jesse	2nd great-grandson	IV	4
Land, Jesse	3rd great-grandson	V	5
Land, Jesse Tilden	7th great-grandson	IX	9
Land, Jessey	4th great-granddaughter	VI	6
Land, Jinnie	4th great-granddaughter	VI	6
Land, Joel Cameron	5th great-grandson	VII	7
Land, Joel Cameron	6th great-granddaughter	VIII	8
Land, John	6th great-grandson	VIII	8
Land, John	3rd great-grandson	V	5
Land, John	2nd great-grandson	IV	4
Land, John	Grandson	II	2

Land, John	Grandson	II	2
Land, John	Great-grandson	III	3
Land, John	Great-grandson	III	3
Land, John	2nd great-grandson	IV	4
Land, John	2nd great-grandson	IV	4
Land, John	3rd great-grandson	V	5
Land, John	2nd great-grandson	IV	4
Land, John	3rd great-grandson	V	5
Land, John	4th great-grandson	VI	6
Land, John	4th great-grandson	VI	6
Land, John	2nd great-grandson	IV	4
Land, John	4th great-grandson	VI	6
Land, John	3rd great-grandson	V	5
Land, John	6th great-grandson	VIII	8
Land, John	7th great-grandson	IX	9
Land, John	5th great-grandson	VII	7
Land, John Braxton	3rd great-grandson	V	5
Land, John Calhoun	4th great-grandson	VI	6
Land, John Calhoun	5th great-grandson	VII	7
Land, John Clyde	5th great-grandson	VII	7
Land, John David	7th great-grandson	IX	9
Land, John Fisher	4th great-grandson	VI	6
Land, John G.	4th great-grandson	VI	6
Land, John Henry	3rd great-grandson	V	5
Land, John T.	4th great-grandson	VI	6
Land, John Thomas	5th great-grandson	VII	7
Land, John Thomas	5th great-grandson	VII	7
Land, John Thomas	4th great-grandson	VI	6
Land, John Wesley	6th great-grandson	VIII	8
Land, Johnny Franklin	8th great-grandson	X	10
Land, Johnny Ross	7th great-grandson	IX	9
Land, Jonathan	3rd great-grandson	V	5
Land, Jonathan	7th great-grandson	IX	9
Land, Jonathon	4th great-grandson	VI	6
Land, Jordon	3rd great-granddaughter	V	5
Land, Jordon	4th great-grandson	VI	6
Land, Joseph	5th great-grandson	VII	7
Land, Joseph	3rd great-granddaughter	V	5
Land, Joseph Lindsey	6th great-grandson	VIII	8
Land, Joseph R.	5th great-grandson	VII	7
Land, Josiah Joseph B.	5th great-grandson	VII	7
Land, Judith	4th great-granddaughter	VI	6
Land, Judith Rosellen	7th great-granddaughter	IX	9
Land, Kinson	3rd great-grandson	V	5
Land, Leann	7th great-granddaughter	IX	9
Land, Lenora	7th great-granddaughter	IX	9
Land, Leroy M.	5th great-grandson	VII	7
Land, Lettice	4th great-granddaughter	VI	6
Wife of the 5th great-grandson			
Land, Levina	2nd great-granddaughter	IV	4
Land, Lewellen	2nd great-grandson	IV	4
Land, Lewellen	2nd great-grandson	IV	4
Land, Lewellen	2nd great-grandson	IV	4
Land, Lewis	2nd great-grandson	IV	4
Land, Lewis	4th great-grandson	VI	6
Land, Linny	5th great-granddaughter	VII	7

Land, Linville	5th great-grandson	VII	7
Land, Littleberry	2nd great-grandson	IV	4
Land, Littleberry	4th great-grandson	VI	6
Land, Littleton	4th great-grandson	VI	6
Land, Living	8th great-grandson	X	10
Land, Living	8th great-granddaughter	X	10
Land, Living	8th great-grandson	X	10
Land, Living	8th great-grandson	X	10
Land, Living	8th great-granddaughter	X	10
Land, Living	8th great-grandson	X	10
Land, Living	8th great-grandson	X	10
Land, Living	9th great-grandson	XI	11
Land, Living	9th great-grandson	XI	11
Land, Living	9th great-grandson	XI	11
Land, Living	8th great-grandchild	X	10
Land, Living	8th great-granddaughter	X	10
Land, Living	8th great-granddaughter	X	10
Land, Living	8th great-granddaughter	X	10
Land, Living	8th great-granddaughter	X	10
Land, Living	8th great-grandson	X	10
Land, Living	8th great-grandson	X	10
Land, Living	7th great-grandson	IX	9
Land, Living	8th great-granddaughter	X	10
Land, Living	8th great-granddaughter	X	10
Land, Living	8th great-grandson	X	10
Land, Living	9th great-grandson	XI	11
Land, Living	9th great-grandson	XI	11
Land, Living	9th great-granddaughter	XI	11
Land, Living	7th great-granddaughter	IX	9
Land, Living	7th great-grandson	IX	9
Land, Living	8th great-granddaughter	X	10
Land, Living	8th great-granddaughter	X	10
Land, Living	8th great-grandson	X	10
Land, Living	8th great-granddaughter	X	10
Land, Living	8th great-grandson	X	10
Land, Living	8th great-granddaughter	X	10
Land, Living	8th great-grandson	X	10
Land, Living	8th great-granddaughter	X	10
Land, Living	9th great-grandson	XI	11
Land, Living	9th great-grandson	XI	11
Land, Living	9th great-granddaughter	XI	11
Land, Living	9th great-granddaughter	XI	11
Land, Living	9th great-grandson	XI	11
Land, Living	9th great-grandson	XI	11
Land, Living	9th great-grandson	XI	11
Land, Living	9th great-granddaughter	XI	11
Land, Living	9th great-granddaughter	XI	11
Land, Living	8th great-granddaughter	X	10
Land, Living	8th great-granddaughter	X	10
Land, Living	8th great-grandson	X	10
Land, Living	8th great-granddaughter	X	10
Land, Living	9th great-granddaughter	XI	11
Land, Living	8th great-granddaughter	X	10
Land, Living	8th great-granddaughter	X	10
Land, Living	8th great-grandson	X	10
Land, Living	8th great-grandson	X	10

Land, Living	8th great-grandson	X	10
Land, Living	8th great-granddaughter	X	10
Land, Living	8th great-grandson	X	10
Land, Living	9th great-granddaughter	XI	11
Land, Living	9th great-granddaughter	XI	11
Land, Living	9th great-grandson	XI	11
Land, Living	9th great-grandson	XI	11
Land, Living	9th great-grandson	XI	11
Land, Living	9th great-grandson	XI	11
Land, Living	9th great-grandson	XI	11
Land, Living	9th great-grandson	XI	11
Land, Living	9th great-grandson	XI	11
Land, Living	8th great-grandson	X	10
Land, Living	8th great-granddaughter	X	10
Land, Living	9th great-grandson	XI	11
Land, Living	8th great-granddaughter	X	10
Land, Living	8th great-grandson	X	10
Land, Living	8th great-grandson	X	10
Land, Living	8th great-grandson	X	10
Land, Living	8th great-grandson	X	10
Land, Living	8th great-granddaughter	X	10
Land, Living	8th great-grandson	X	10
Land, Living	8th great-grandson	X	10
Land, Living	8th great-grandson	X	10
Land, Living	8th great-granddaughter	X	10
Land, Living	8th great-grandson	X	10
Land, Living	9th great-grandson	XI	11
Land, Living	9th great-grandson	XI	11
Land, Living	9th great-grandson	XI	11
Land, Living	9th great-grandson	XI	11
Land, Living	9th great-grandson	XI	11
Land, Living	9th great-granddaughter	XI	11
Land, Living	9th great-grandson	XI	11
Land, Living	9th great-grandson	XI	11
Land, Living	9th great-grandson	XI	11
Land, Living	9th great-grandson	XI	11
Land, Living	9th great-grandson	XI	11
Land, Living	9th great-grandson	XI	11
Land, Living	9th great-granddaughter	XI	11
Land, Living	9th great-granddaughter	XI	11
Land, Living	9th great-grandson	XI	11
Land, Living	9th great-grandson	XI	11
Land, Living	9th great-granddaughter	XI	11
Land, Living	9th great-grandson	XI	11
Land, Living	8th great-granddaughter	X	10
Land, Living	8th great-grandson	X	10
Land, Living	8th great-granddaughter	X	10
Land, Living	8th great-granddaughter	X	10
Land, Living	8th great-granddaughter	X	10
Land, Living	8th great-grandson	X	10
Land, Living	8th great-grandson	X	10
Land, Living	7th great-grandson	IX	9
Land, Living	9th great-grandson	XI	11
Land, Living	9th great-grandson	XI	11
Land, Living	8th great-granddaughter	X	10
Land, Living	8th great-granddaughter	X	10

Land, Living	5th great-grandson	VII	7
Land, Living	8th great-granddaughter	X	10
Land, Living	8th great-granddaughter	X	10
Land, Living	8th great-grandson	X	10
Land, Living	9th great-grandson	XI	11
Land, Living	7th great-grandson	IX	9
Land, Living	7th great-grandson	IX	9
Land, Living	7th great-granddaughter	IX	9
Land, Living	8th great-grandson	X	10
Land, Living	8th great-granddaughter	X	10
Land, Living	8th great-grandson	X	10
Land, Living	8th great-grandson	X	10
Land, Living	8th great-grandson	X	10
Land, Living	9th great-granddaughter	XI	11
Land, Living	9th great-grandson	XI	11
Land, Living	8th great-grandson	X	10
Land, Living	8th great-grandson	X	10
Land, Living	9th great-granddaughter	XI	11
Land, Lizzie Mae	7th great-granddaughter	IX	9
Land, Lottie	5th great-granddaughter	VII	7
Land, Lucas	2nd great-grandson	IV	4
Land, Lucas	2nd great-grandson	IV	4
Land, Lucas	2nd great-grandson	IV	4
Land, Lucetta Jane	5th great-granddaughter	VII	7
Land, Lucinda	5th great-granddaughter	VII	7
Land, Lucretia	2nd great-granddaughter	IV	4
Land, Lucretia	2nd great-granddaughter	IV	4
Land, Lucretia	2nd great-granddaughter	IV	4
Land, Lucretia (Lou Crecy) Jane	5th great-granddaughter	VII	7
Land, Lucy	5th great-granddaughter	VII	7
Land, Luter	7th great-granddaughter	IX	9
Land, Maggie	6th great-granddaughter	VIII	8
Land, Maggie Edna	7th great-granddaughter	IX	9
Land, Mahala	4th great-granddaughter	VI	6
Land, Male	4th great-grandson	VI	6
Land, Male	4th great-grandson	VI	6
Land, Margaret Elizabeth	5th great-granddaughter	VII	7
Land, Martha A.	7th great-granddaughter	IX	9
Land, Martha Ann	4th great-granddaughter	VI	6
Land, Martha Caroline	5th great-granddaughter	VII	7
Land, Martha E.	6th great-granddaughter	VIII	8
Land, Martha Emma	5th great-granddaughter	VII	7
Land, Martha J.	4th great-granddaughter	VI	6
Land, Martha Jane	6th great-granddaughter	VIII	8
Land, Martha Lowe	6th great-granddaughter	VIII	8
Land, Martha Matilda Rosetta	4th great-granddaughter	VI	6
Land, Mary	4th great-granddaughter	VI	6
Land, Mary	6th great-granddaughter	VIII	8
Land, Mary	2nd great-granddaughter	IV	4
Land, Mary	3rd great-granddaughter	V	5
Land, Mary	4th great-granddaughter	VI	6
Land, Mary	4th great-granddaughter	VI	6
Land, Mary	4th great-granddaughter	VI	6
Land, Mary	5th great-granddaughter	VII	7
Land, Mary	3rd great-granddaughter	V	5
Land, Mary	5th great-granddaughter	VII	7

Land, Mary	4th great-granddaughter	VI	6
Land, Mary	5th great-granddaughter	VII	7
Land, Mary	3rd great-granddaughter	V	5
Land, Mary	6th great-granddaughter	VIII	8
Land, Mary	4th great-granddaughter	VI	6
Land, Mary	6th great-granddaughter	VIII	8
Land, Mary	4th great-granddaughter	VI	6
Land, Mary "Polly"	3rd great-granddaughter	V	5
Land, Mary Ann	4th great-granddaughter	VI	6
Land, Mary Beatrice	6th great-granddaughter	VIII	8
Land, Mary E.	4th great-granddaughter	VI	6
Land, Mary Elizabeth	6th great-granddaughter	VIII	8
Land, Mary Elizabeth	6th great-granddaughter	VIII	8
Land, Mary Ellen	7th great-granddaughter	IX	9
Land, Mary Frances	5th great-granddaughter	VII	7
Land, Mary J.	6th great-granddaughter	VIII	8
Land, Mary Jane	4th great-granddaughter	VI	6
Land, Mary Jane	7th great-granddaughter	IX	9
Land, Mary Lee	7th great-granddaughter	IX	9
Land, Mary Louise	6th great-granddaughter	VIII	8
Land, Mary Louise	5th great-granddaughter	VII	7
Land, Mary M.	6th great-granddaughter	VIII	8
Land, Mary Polly	3rd great-granddaughter	V	5
Land, Mary Serelda	6th great-granddaughter	VIII	8
Land, Mattie Bell	5th great-granddaughter	VII	7
Land, Mattie Lee	5th great-granddaughter	VII	7
Land, Maude T.	6th great-granddaughter	VIII	8
Land, Meschack	3rd great-grandson	V	5
Land, Mildred	Great-granddaughter	III	3
Land, Mildred	4th great-granddaughter	VI	6
Land, Millie	4th great-granddaughter	VI	6
Land, Milton	8th great-grandson	X	10
Land, Minerva	5th great-granddaughter	VII	7
Land, Minnie Belle	7th great-granddaughter	IX	9
Land, Mollie	7th great-granddaughter	IX	9
Land, Nancy	4th great-granddaughter	VI	6
Land, Nancy	3rd great-granddaughter	V	5
Land, Nancy	4th great-granddaughter	VI	6
Land, Nancy	4th great-granddaughter	VI	6
Land, Nancy	3rd great-granddaughter	V	5
Land, Nancy	4th great-granddaughter	VI	6
Land, Nancy	5th great-granddaughter	VII	7
Land, Nancy	4th great-granddaughter	VI	6
Land, Nancy N.	6th great-granddaughter	VIII	8
Land, Narcissa	5th great-granddaughter	VII	7
Land, Nathaniel	2nd great-grandson	IV	4
Land, Nicholas Rufus	4th great-grandson	VI	6
Land, Nimrod	5th great-grandson	VII	7
Land, Nimrod	6th great-grandson	VIII	8
Land, Noah	6th great-grandson	VIII	8
Land, Nora	7th great-granddaughter	IX	9
Land, Nora Estelle	5th great-granddaughter	VII	7
Land, Partee Vance	7th great-grandson	IX	9
Land, Pearl	7th great-granddaughter	IX	9
Land, Peter	4th great-grandson	VI	6
Land, Phoebe S.	5th great-granddaughter	VII	7

Land, Pickens O.	7th great-grandson	IX	9
Land, Priscilla	Great-granddaughter	III	3
Land, Ralph Caldwell	7th great-grandson	IX	9
Land, Raymond Timothy	5th great-grandson	VII	7
Land, Rebecca	Great-granddaughter	III	3
Land, Rebecca	5th great-granddaughter	VII	7
Land, Rebecca	5th great-granddaughter	VII	7
Land, Rebecca	7th great-granddaughter	IX	9
Land, Rebecca A.	5th great-granddaughter	VII	7
Land, Rebecca G.	7th great-granddaughter	IX	9
Land, Rebeccah	Granddaughter	II	2
Land, Rhody A. T.	4th great-granddaughter	VI	6
Land, Richard	4th great-grandson	VI	6
Land, Robert	Grandson	II	2
Land, Robert	Grandson	II	2
Land, Robert	Grandson	II	2
Land, Robert	Great-grandson	III	3
Land, Robert	2nd great-grandson	IV	4
Land, Robert Brice	7th great-grandson	IX	9
Land, Robert Carter	3rd great-grandson	V	5
Land, Robert Carter	4th great-grandson	VI	6
Land, Robert Lee	7th great-grandson	IX	9
Land, Roby Crisp	7th great-grandson	IX	9
Land, Ross Vance	7th great-grandson	IX	9
Land, Roy C.	7th great-grandson	IX	9
Land, Ruth	Great-granddaughter	III	3
Land, Sally	3rd great-granddaughter	V	5
Land, Sally Caroline	6th great-granddaughter	VIII	8
Land, Samuel	7th great-grandson	IX	9
Land, Sarah	4th great-granddaughter	VI	6
Land, Sarah	6th great-granddaughter	VIII	8
Land, Sarah A.	5th great-granddaughter	VII	7
Land, Sarah A.	6th great-granddaughter	VIII	8
Land, Sarah E.	4th great-granddaughter	VI	6
Land, Sarah Elmira	7th great-granddaughter	IX	9
Land, Sarah G.	4th great-granddaughter	VI	6
Land, Sarah Jane	6th great-granddaughter	VIII	8
Land, Sarah Rebecca	7th great-granddaughter	IX	9
Land, Sarah Sophia	3rd great-granddaughter	V	5
Land, Solomon R.	5th great-grandson	VII	7
Land, Sophia W.	5th great-granddaughter	VII	7
Land, Stephen	3rd great-grandson	V	5
Land, Sumter	3rd great-grandson	V	5
Land, Susan	4th great-granddaughter	VI	6
Land, Susan (Sophy)	2nd great-granddaughter	IV	4
Land, Susan J.	6th great-granddaughter	VIII	8
Land, Susanna (Suckey)	2nd great-granddaughter	IV	4
Land, Susannah	4th great-granddaughter	VI	6
Land, Susannah	4th great-granddaughter	VI	6
Land, Susannah "Susan"	4th great-granddaughter	VI	6
Land, Synthia Caroline	4th great-granddaughter	VI	6
Land, Thomas	Grandson	II	2
Land, Thomas	Great-grandson	III	3
Land, Thomas	2nd great-grandson	IV	4
Land, Thomas	3rd great-grandson	V	5
Land, Thomas	4th great-grandson	VI	6

Land, Thomas	4th great-grandson	VI	6
Land, Thomas	5th great-grandson	VII	7
Land, Thomas	5th great-grandson	VII	7
Land, Thomas	5th great-grandson	VII	7
Land, Thomas	7th great-grandson	IX	9
Land, Thomas Byron	5th great-grandson	VII	7
Land, Thomas C.	4th great-grandson	VI	6
Land, Thomas Charles	5th great-grandson	VII	7
Land, Thomas Clingman	6th great-grandson	VIII	8
Land, Thomas David	6th great-grandson	VIII	8
Land, Thomas Linville	7th great-grandson	IX	9
Land, Thomas Merideth	7th great-grandson	IX	9
Land, Thomas William	7th great-grandson	IX	9
Land, Tillman Howard	5th great-grandson	VII	7
Land, Tully	5th great-granddaughter	VII	7
Land, Turner	5th great-grandson	VII	7
Land, Unity	3rd great-granddaughter	V	5
Land, Valecie	8th great-granddaughter	X	10
Land, Venzuella	7th great-granddaughter	IX	9
Land, Vera	7th great-granddaughter	IX	9
Land, Vera Alma	7th great-granddaughter	IX	9
Land, Virginia Gertrude	5th great-granddaughter	VII	7
Land, Vivian	5th great-granddaughter	VII	7
Land, Vivian Eadon	6th great-granddaughter	VIII	8
Land, Warrington Oliver	5th great-grandson	VII	7
Land, Webb	2nd great-grandson	IV	4
Land, William	4th great-grandson	VI	6
Land, William	5th great-grandson	VII	7
Land, William	Son	I	1
Land, William	Grandson Great-	II	2
Land, William	grandson Great-grandson	III	3
Land, William	4th great-grandson	III	3
Land, William	5th great-grandson	VI	6
Land, William	3rd great-grandson	VII	7
Land, William	5th great-grandson	V	5
Land, William	6th great-grandson	VII	7
Land, William	4th great-grandson	VIII	8
Land, William	8th great-grandson	VI	6
Land, William Adam	5th great-grandson	X	10
Land, William Ebert	5th great-grandson	VII	7
Land, William H.	2nd great-grandson	VII	7
Land, William Henry	4th great-grandson	IV	4
Land, William Jefferson	6th great-grandson	VI	6
Land, William Langley	7th great-grandson	VIII	8
Land, William Robert	7th great-grandson	IX	9
Land, William Rodrick	6th great-grandson	IX	9
Land, William Taylor	4th great-grandson	VIII	8
Land, William Thomas		VI	6
Husband of the 4th great-granddaughter			
Land, William Thomas	6th great-grandson	VIII	8
Land, William Tyler	4th great-grandson	VI	6
Land, Williamson	3rd great-grandson	V	5
Land, Willie	5th great-grandson	VII	7
Land, Willie C.	6th great-grandson	VIII	8
Land, Willie G.	4th great-grandson	VI	6
Land, Willis	5th great-grandson	VII	7

Land, Willowdean	8th great-granddaughter	X	10
Land, Wilson	5th great-grandson	VII	7
Land, Wilson	6th great-grandson	VIII	8
Land, Winifred	Great-granddaughter	III	3
Land, Zachariah	3rd great-grandson	V	5
Land, Zedekiah	4th great-grandson	VI	6
Land, Zilluh Edna	5th great-granddaughter	VII	7
Lane, Living	Wife of the 8th great-grandson		
Laney, Mary A.	Wife of the 6th great-grandson		
Langford, Living	Wife of the 8th great-grandson		
Langley, Unknown	Husband of the 2nd great-granddaughter		
LaRue, Joe	Husband of the 5th great-granddaughter		
Lassiter, Winnafred	Wife of the 5th great-grandson		
Laurement, Living	Husband of the 8th great-granddaughter		
Laurement, Living	9th great-grandson	XI	11
Lefevers, Living	Wife of the 8th great-grandson		
Leinhart, Living	Husband of the 8th great-granddaughter		
Lemmons	Husband of the 5th great-granddaughter		
Lemmons, Lucy	6th great-granddaughter	VIII	8
Lemmons, Ora	6th great-grandson	VIII	8
Lesk, Living	Husband of the 8th great-granddaughter		
Lesk, Living	9th great-granddaughter	XI	11
Lester, Theodocia	Wife of the 5th great-grandson		
Lewellin, Rebekah	Wife of the great-grandson		
Lewis, Elizabeth L.	Wife of the grandson		
Lewis, Lynn Merel	Husband of the 7th great-granddaughter		
Lewis, Nichole	8th great-granddaughter	X	10
Lindsey, Penny H.	Wife of the 4th great-grandson		
Lindsey, Zaney Ann	Wife of the 4th great-grandson		
Little, Feletia	Wife of the 4th great-grandson		
Little, Felicia	Wife of the 4th great-grandson		
Little, Living	Wife of the 8th great-grandson		
Littleton, Elizabeth	Wife of the 3rd great-grandson		
Living	Wife of the 8th great-grandson		
Livingston, Callie O.	Wife of the 7th great-grandson		
Livingston, Edith	Wife of the 4th great-grandson		
Livingston, Jordon	Husband of the 6th great-granddaughter		
Livingston, Mary Jane	7th great-granddaughter	IX	9
Lockhart, Emmaline	Wife of the 7th great-grandson		
Louisiana	Wife of the 5th great-grandson		
Love, Anna Gayle	Wife of the 7th great-grandson		
Magee, Cary	Husband of the great-granddaughter		
Maltba, Living	Wife of the 8th great-grandson		
Maltba, Nancy	Wife of the 5th great-grandson		
Maltba, William	Husband of the 4th great-granddaughter		
Marley, Benjamin	7th great-grandson	IX	9
Marley, Frances	7th great-grandson	IX	9
Marley, Isabell	7th great-granddaughter	IX	9
Marley, Jaden	7th great-granddaughter	IX	9
Marley, James Jefferson	Husband of the 6th great-granddaughter		
Marley, Living	7th great-grandson	IX	9
Marley, Lomas J.	7th great-grandson	IX	9
Marley, Minnie	7th great-granddaughter	IX	9
Marley, Misty	7th great-granddaughter	IX	9
Marley, William H.	7th great-grandson	IX	9
Martin, Arnold Stewart	Husband of the 7th great-granddaughter		

Martin, Living	Husband of the 8th great-granddaughter		
Martin, Living	9th great-granddaughter	XI	11
Martin, Living	9th great-granddaughter	XI	11
Martin, Living	9th great-grandson	XI	11
Martin, Living	9th great-grandson	XI	11
Martin, Living	8th great-granddaughter	X	10
Martin, Living	8th great-grandson	X	10
Martin, Living	8th great-granddaughter	X	10
Martin, Living	8th great-granddaughter	X	10
Martin, Living	8th great-grandson	X	10
Martin, Living	8th great-granddaughter	X	10
Martin, Living	8th great-grandson	X	10
Martin, Living	9th great-grandson	XI	11
Martin, Living	9th great-grandson	XI	11
Martin, Living	9th great-grandchild	XI	11
Martin, Living	9th great-grandson	XI	11
Martin, Living	9th great-granddaughter	XI	11
Martin, Living	9th great-grandson	XI	11
Mary	Wife of the 5th great-grandson		
Masters, John Sacra	Husband of the 5th great-granddaughter		
Mastin, Ellie Ann	5th great-granddaughter	VII	7
Mastin, John Gabriel	5th great-grandson	VII	7
Mastin, Sinesca	Wife of the 7th great-grandson		
Mastin, William A.	Husband of the 4th great-granddaughter		
Mastin, William Conway	5th great-grandson	VII	7
McBee, Joseph C.	Husband of the 4th great-granddaughter		
McClanahan, Eleanor	Wife of the great-grandson		
McCrury	Husband of the 4th great-granddaughter		
McCrury, Gibson	5th great-grandson	VII	7
McFarland, Living	Husband of the 8th great-granddaughter		
McFarland, Living	9th great-grandson	XI	11
McGee, Andrew Wilson	Husband of the 5th great-granddaughter		
McGee, Anna Nancy	Wife of the 3rd great-grandson		
McGee, Bartlett	6th great-grandson	VIII	8
McGee, Calvin Lee	6th great-grandson	VIII	8
McGee, J. Linville	6th great-grandson	VIII	8
McGee, Mary E.	6th great-granddaughter	VIII	8
McGee, William Bradford	6th great-grandson	VIII	8
McGill, Johnny	Wife of the 5th great-grandson		
McGuire, Bill	Husband of the 6th great-granddaughter		
McGuire, Jeff	7th great-grandson	IX	9
McGuire, Laura Lea	7th great-granddaughter	IX	9
McGuire, Peggy Sue	7th great-granddaughter	IX	9
McIlroy, Alma	6th great-granddaughter	VIII	8
McIlroy, Eva	6th great-granddaughter	VIII	8
McIlroy, Hite	6th great-grandson	VIII	8
McIlroy, Irene	6th great-granddaughter	VIII	8
McIlroy, Lee	Husband of the 5th great-granddaughter		
McIlroy, Lela	6th great-granddaughter	VIII	8
McIlroy, Pauline	6th great-granddaughter	VIII	8
McLemore, Mary	Wife of the 2nd great-grandson		
McLemore, Mary "Molly"	Wife of the 2nd great-grandson		
McLemore, Mary "Molly"	Wife of the 2nd great-grandson		
McPherson	Husband of the 4th great-granddaughter		
McPherson, Living	Wife of the 8th great-grandson		
Mead, Living	Husband of the 8th great-granddaughter		

Mead, Living	9th great-granddaughter	XI	11
Merriman, Jane	Wife of the 4th great-grandson		
Milam, Grovr	Husband of the 6th great-granddaughter		
Mildred	Wife of the 7th great-grandson		
Miles, Living	Husband of the 8th great-granddaughter		
Miles, Living	9th great-grandson	XI	11
Miles, Living	9th great-granddaughter	XI	11
Miles, Living	9th great-granddaughter	XI	11
Miller, Cora	6th great-granddaughter	VIII	8
Miller, Emmett	7th great-grandson	IX	9
Miller, Ethel Lottie	6th great-granddaughter	VIII	8
Miller, Eva	6th great-granddaughter	VIII	8
Miller, Frank	6th great-grandson	VIII	8
Miller, Glen	Husband of the 6th great-granddaughter		
Miller, Henry Harrison	Husband of the 5th great-granddaughter		
Miller, Henry Harrison	6th great-grandson	VIII	8
Miller, Ira	6th great-grandson	VIII	8
Miller, Junius	7th great-grandson	IX	9
Miller, Lawrence	7th great-grandson	IX	9
Miller, Living	Wife of the 7th great-grandson		
Miller, Rebecca	Wife of the 5th great-grandson		
Miller, Rebecca Ann	7th great-granddaughter	IX	9
Miller, Thomas C.	6th great-grandson	VIII	8
Husband of the 6th great-granddaughter			
Miller, Unknown	Husband of the 2nd great-granddaughter		
Miller, Virgil	6th great-grandson	VIII	8
Miller, Virginia Jane	Wife of the 4th great-grandson		
Miller, William	Husband of the 5th great-granddaughter		
Miller, William J.	6th great-grandson	VIII	8
Miller, Willie	6th great-grandson	VIII	8
Mills, Collin Timothy	8th great-grandson	X	10
Mills, Timothy	Husband of the 7th great-granddaughter		
Mitchell, James David	7th great-grandson	IX	9
Mitchell, John Wesley	Husband of the 6th great-granddaughter		
Mitchell, John Wilson	7th great-grandson	IX	9
Mitchell, Living	Wife of the 7th great-grandson		
Mitchell, Mary Glee	7th great-granddaughter	IX	9
Mitchell, Pauline	7th great-granddaughter	IX	9
Mitchell, Virginia	7th great-granddaughter	IX	9
Mitchum, Living	Wife of the 7th great-grandson		
Mitt, Louisa	Wife of the 3rd great-grandson		
Moak, Mozell S.	Wife of the 6th great-grandson		
Montgomery, Ena	Wife of the 5th great-grandson		
Montgomery, Living	Wife of the 8th great-grandson		
Mooney, Delphia	5th great-granddaughter	VII	7
Mooney, Franklin	5th great-granddaughter	VII	7
Mooney, Harrison	5th great-grandson	VII	7
Mooney, Harvey	Husband of the 4th great-granddaughter		
Mooney, Margaret	Wife of the 4th great-grandson		
Mooney, Martha	5th great-granddaughter	VII	7
Mooney, William	5th great-grandson	VII	7
Moore, Joseph	Husband of the 4th great-granddaughter		
Moore, Living	Wife of the 8th great-grandson		
Moore, Rebecca Tennessee	Wife of the 4th great-grandson		
Moore, Unknown	Wife of the 6th great-grandson		
Morgan, Elizabeth	Wife of the 3rd great-grandson		

Mortimer, Furman	Husband of the 4th great-granddaughter		
Moses, Sarah Ann	Wife of the 5th great-grandson		
Mullins, Living	9th great-granddaughter	XI	11
Muphey, George	Husband of the 6th great-granddaughter		
Murphey, Rettie Victoria	Wife of the 6th great-grandson		
Murphy, Jinney	Wife of the 5th great-grandson		
Murry, Mary Beth	Wife of the 3rd great-grandson		
Myers, Alice Marie	Wife of the 7th great-grandson		
Neal, Living	Wife of the 8th great-grandson		
Nell, Mary	Wife of the 7th great-grandson		
Nicholson, Frances B.	Wife of the 3rd great-grandson		
Nixon, Beulah Mae	Wife of the 6th great-grandson		
Nudo, Living	Husband of the 8th great-granddaughter		
Odom, Caroline Crumpley	Wife of the 3rd great-grandson		
Odom, Caroline Crumply	Wife of the 3rd great-grandson		
Oliver, Freeman	Husband of the 5th great-granddaughter		
Oliver, Mattie Lee	Wife of the 4th great-grandson		
Owens, Alice A.	Wife of the 6th great-grandson		
Oxford, Freddie Roston	7th great-grandson	IX	9
Oxford, Jenner Arguile	7th great-grandson	IX	9
Oxford, John McLeod	Husband of the 6th great-granddaughter		
Oxford, Linnie Bell	7th great-granddaughter	IX	9
Oxford, Mary Lou	7th great-granddaughter	IX	9
Oxford, Minnie Dora	7th great-granddaughter	IX	9
Oxford, Sarah Etta "Sallie"	Wife of the 6th great-grandson		
Padgett, ?	8th great-granddaughter	X	10
Padgett, Bryon Lamar	Husband of the 6th great-granddaughter		
Padgett, Chris Lamar	7th great-grandson	IX	9
Padgett, Kathy Cornelia	7th great-granddaughter	IX	9
Padgett, Mark John	7th great-grandson	IX	9
Padgett, Mindy Joy	8th great-granddaughter	X	10
Padgett, Tara Elaine	8th great-granddaughter	X	10
Palmer, Katie	Wife of the 5th great-grandson		
Parott, Living	Husband of the 8th great-granddaughter		
Parott, Living	9th great-grandson	XI	11
Parott, Living	9th great-grandson	XI	11
Parott, Living	9th great-granddaughter	XI	11
Parris, Albert Clarence	6th great-grandson	VIII	8
Parris, Amanda	5th great-granddaughter	VII	7
Parris, Anna Mae Bell	6th great-granddaughter	VIII	8
Parris, Austin Brook	8th great-grandson	X	10
Parris, Benson Lamar	7th great-grandson	IX	9
Parris, Caroline Anne	8th great-granddaughter	X	10
Parris, Cecil Leo	6th great-grandson	VIII	8
Parris, Chandler Christene	8th great-grandson	X	10
Parris, Cinthia	5th great-granddaughter	VII	7
Parris, Donald Lester	7th great-grandson	IX	9
Parris, Elbert Melton	5th great-grandson	VII	7
Parris, Elizabeth Elaine	7th great-granddaughter	IX	9
Parris, Gregory David	8th great-grandson	X	10
Parris, Harold Lester	6th great-grandson	VIII	8
Parris, Hazel Cornelia	6th great-granddaughter	VIII	8
Parris, Henry Dillard	5th great-grandson	VII	7
Parris, James Michael	8th great-grandson	X	10
Parris, Jim Warner	7th great-grandson	IX	9
Parris, Jubal Robert	8th great-grandson	X	10

Parris, Kathleen	8th great-granddaughter	X	10
Parris, Lois Theodosia	6th great-granddaughter	VIII	8
Parris, Lucas Martin	8th great-grandson	X	10
Parris, Martha Ann	5th great-granddaughter	VII	7
Parris, Mary Lou	5th great-granddaughter	VII	7
Parris, Max Warner	8th great-grandson	X	10
Parris, Nathan Calvin	Husband of the 4th great-granddaughter		
Parris, Nathaniel Benson	8th great-grandson	X	10
Parris, Nellie Octavia	6th great-granddaughter	VIII	8
Parris, Nimrod Wells	Husband of the 4th great-granddaughter		
Parris, Noah Jackson	8th great-grandson	X	10
Parris, Noten Dickerson	Husband of the 4th great-granddaughter		
Parris, Otis Clifton	6th great-grandson	VIII	8
Parris, Robert David	6th great-grandson	VIII	8
Parris, Robert David	7th great-grandson	IX	9
Parris, Roney Jefferson	5th great-grandson	VII	7
Parris, Sarah Elizabeth	8th great-granddaughter	X	10
Parris, Susan Virginia	7th great-granddaughter	IX	9
Parris, Travie	5th great-granddaughter	VII	7
Parris, Warner David	5th great-grandson	VII	7
Parris, William Benson	6th great-grandson	VIII	8
Parris, William Griffin	7th great-grandson	IX	9
Parris, William Stephen	5th great-grandson	VII	7
Parris, William Thomas	5th great-grandson	VII	7
Parrish, Garland	Husband of the 4th great-granddaughter		
Parrish, Oliver Posey	Husband of the 4th great-granddaughter		
Parsons, James Cicero	Husband of the 6th great-granddaughter		
Parsons, Living	7th great-granddaughter	IX	9
Parsons, Living	7th great-granddaughter	IX	9
Parsons, Living	7th great-granddaughter	IX	9
Parsons, Living	7th great-granddaughter	IX	9
Parsons, Mary Dorris	7th great-granddaughter	IX	9
Patterson, Living	Husband of the 8th great-granddaughter		
Pearson, Eleanor Nellie	Wife of the 5th great-grandson		
Pearson, James Blaine	Husband of the 7th great-granddaughter		
Pennell, Anna	Wife of the 5th great-grandson		
Pennell, Bertha Malissa	Wife of the 7th great-grandson		
Pennell, Julie Eva	Wife of the 7th great-grandson		
Pennington, Jane H. L.	Wife of the great-grandson		
Penry, Allene	6th great-granddaughter	VIII	8
Penry, Dorothy	6th great-granddaughter	VIII	8
Penry, J. Lee	5th great-grandson	VII	7
Penry, Jack E.	5th great-grandson	VII	7
Penry, Louis Curl	5th great-grandson	VII	7
Penry, Lucille	6th great-granddaughter	VIII	8
Penry, Mildred	6th great-granddaughter	VIII	8
Penry, Silas Browm	Husband of the 4th great-granddaughter		
Penry, W.H.	5th great-grandson	VII	7
Pettit, Rebie Elizabeth	Wife of the 5th great-grandson		
Pickett, Catherine Virginia	Wife of the 6th great-grandson		
Pickett, Vernadean	Wife of the 6th great-grandson		
Piercy, Living	Wife of the 8th great-grandson		
Piety, Living	Wife of the 8th great-grandson		
Pipes, Thomas	Husband of the 5th great-granddaughter		
Plemmons, Rhoda	Wife of the 4th great-grandson		
Plowden, Martha Cocksrey	Wife of the 5th great-grandson		

Plowden, Rosa Lee	Wife of the 5th great-grandson		
Poarch, Dolcie Irene	Wife of the 7th great-grandson		
Pollard, Denise	Wife of the 7th great-grandson		
Pope, Elizabeth	Wife of the 5th great-grandson		
Pope, Henry H.	Husband of the 6th great-granddaughter		
Pope, Living	7th great-granddaughter	IX	9
Pope, Living	7th great-grandson	IX	9
Pope, Living	7th great-grandson	IX	9
Pope, Living	Husband of the 8th great-granddaughter		
Pope, Living	9th great-granddaughter	XI	11
Pope, Living	7th great-granddaughter	IX	9
Pope, Living	7th great-grandson	IX	9
Pope, Living	7th great-grandson	IX	9
Posey, Unknown	Husband of the 6th great-granddaughter		
Prevett, Edna Laura	Wife of the 5th great-grandson		
Prickett, Living	Husband of the 8th great-granddaughter		
Proffit, Rhoda	Wife of the 5th great-grandson		
Puccini, Living	Husband of the 8th great-granddaughter		
Puccini, Living	9th great-granddaughter	XI	11
Puccini, Living	9th great-grandson	XI	11
Puccini, Living	9th great-grandson	XI	11
Quillman, Billy	Husband of the 7th great-granddaughter		
Quillman, Living	8th great-granddaughter	X	10
Quinton, Emma Sarah	Wife of the 4th great-grandson		
Wife of the 5th great-grandson			
Ragsdale, Mary	Wife of the 4th great-grandson		
Rains, Juanita	Wife of the 7th great-grandson		
Ramsay, Mahulda	Wife of the 4th great-grandson		
Ramsey, Living	Wife of the 7th great-grandson		
Randall, Sarah Ann	8th great-granddaughter	X	10
Randall, Tim	Husband of the 7th great-granddaughter		
Raper, James Franklin	Husband of the 7th great-granddaughter		
Raper, Living	8th great-granddaughter	X	10
Raper, Living	8th great-granddaughter	X	10
Raper, Living	8th great-grandson	X	10
Raper, Living	8th great-grandson	X	10
Rawlings, Sarah Holt	Wife of the great-grandson		
Rawlings, Susanna	Wife of the 2nd great-grandson		
Rector, Bessie	7th great-granddaughter	IX	9
Rector, David Richard	Husband of the 6th great-granddaughter		
Rector, Frances	7th great-granddaughter	IX	9
Rector, Living	Wife of the 8th great-grandson		
Rector, Robert	7th great-grandson	IX	9
Reed, Bessie Tennessee	6th great-granddaughter	VIII	8
Reed, Charles Jett	6th great-grandson	VIII	8
Reed, Charles Monroe	Husband of the 5th great-granddaughter		
Reed, Clyde	6th great-grandson	VIII	8
Reed, Frank Carter	6th great-grandson	VIII	8
Reed, Girl	7th great-granddaughter	IX	9
Reed, Glades Mae	6th great-granddaughter	VIII	8
Reed, Harry James	8th great-grandson	X	10
Reed, James Alvis	6th great-grandson	VIII	8
Reed, Jessie James	7th great-grandson	IX	9
Reed, Joe Luther	6th great-grandson	VIII	8
Reed, Living	7th great-granddaughter	IX	9
Reed, Living	7th great-grandson	IX	9

Reed, Living	7th great-granddaughter	IX	9
Reed, Living	7th great-granddaughter	IX	9
Reed, Living	7th great-grandson	IX	9
Reed, Living	7th great-grandson	IX	9
Reed, Living	7th great-grandson	IX	9
Reed, Living	7th great-grandson	IX	9
Reed, Living	7th great-granddaughter	IX	9
Reed, Living	7th great-granddaughter	IX	9
Reed, Living	7th great-granddaughter	IX	9
Reed, Living	8th great-grandson	X	10
Reed, Living	8th great-granddaughter	X	10
Reed, Living	8th great-granddaughter	X	10
Reed, Living	8th great-grandson	X	10
Reed, Living	8th great-grandson	X	10
Reed, Living	8th great-granddaughter	X	10
Reed, Living	8th great-granddaughter	X	10
Reed, Living	7th great-grandson	IX	9
Reed, Living	7th great-grandchild	IX	9
Reed, Living	7th great-granddaughter	IX	9
Reed, Living	8th great-granddaughter	X	10
Reed, Living	8th great-grandson	X	10
Reed, Living	8th great-granddaughter	X	10
Reed, Living	9th great-granddaughter	XI	11
Reed, Living	9th great-granddaughter	XI	11
Reed, Living	9th great-grandson	XI	11
Reed, Living	9th great-grandson	XI	11
Reed, Living	9th great-grandson	XI	11
Reed, Living	9th great-granddaughter	XI	11
Reed, Living	9th great-grandson	XI	11
Reed, Living	9th great-grandson	XI	11
Reed, Living	9th great-grandson	XI	11
Reed, Living	9th great-granddaughter	XI	11
Reed, Living	9th great-granddaughter	XI	11
Reed, Martin Luther	7th great-grandson	IX	9
Reed, Mattie Beatrice	6th great-granddaughter	VIII	8
Reed, Ora Dellar	6th great-granddaughter	VIII	8
Reed, Walter Collins	6th great-grandson	VIII	8
Reeves, Sue J.	Wife of the 4th great-grandson		
Register, Barbara	7th great-granddaughter	IX	9
Register, Fred Floyd	Husband of the 6th great-granddaughter		
Reid, Aelaide	Wife of the 5th great-grandson		
Reid, Living	Wife of the 8th great-grandson		
Renfroe, Amanda	5th great-granddaughter	VII	7
Renfroe, Emily Mildred	5th great-granddaughter	VII	7
Renfroe, James M.	5th great-grandson	VII	7
Renfroe, Jemina	5th great-granddaughter	VII	7
Renfroe, John	5th great-grandson	VII	7
Renfroe, Joseph	Husband of the 4th great-granddaughter		
Renfroe, Joseph	5th great-granddaughter	VII	7
Renfroe, Mary Ann	5th great-granddaughter	VII	7
Renfroe, Nancy	5th great-granddaughter	VII	7
Renfroe, Nathaniel	5th great-grandson	VII	7
Renfroe, Peter	Husband of the 4th great-granddaughter		
Renfroe, Polly Taylor	Wife of the 4th great-grandson		
Renfroe, Rebecca	5th great-granddaughter	VII	7
Renfroe, Rebecca Narcissus	Wife of the 3rd great-grandson		

Renfroe, Rhoda	5th great-granddaughter	VII	7
Renfroe, Thomas Jefferson	5th great-grandson	VII	7
Revelise, Ruth	Wife of the 7th great-grandson		
Reynolds, Rita Jean	Wife of the 8th great-grandson		
Rhyne, Living	Husband of the 7th great-granddaughter		
Rice, Ernest	Husband of the 7th great-granddaughter		
Rice, Gay	8th great-granddaughter	X	10
Rice, Novella	8th great-granddaughter	X	10
Rice, Ola	8th great-granddaughter	X	10
Richards, Sarah Maude	Wife of the 3rd great-grandson		
Richardson, Lindell	Husband of the 6th great-granddaughter		
Richardson, Living	Wife of the 8th great-grandson		
Richerson, Living	Wife of the 7th great-grandson		
Rickman, Miriam	Wife of the 7th great-grandson		
Riddle, Earl Monroe	6th great-grandson	VIII	8
Riddle, Ervin Lee	6th great-grandson	VIII	8
Riddle, Ervin Lee	7th great-grandson	IX	9
Riddle, Faye	6th great-granddaughter	VIII	8
Riddle, Jean	6th great-granddaughter	VIII	8
Riddle, Linda Oma	7th great-granddaughter	IX	9
Riddle, Louisa Luceille	6th great-granddaughter	VIII	8
Riddle, Mildred	6th great-granddaughter	VIII	8
Riddle, Plyllis Laverne	7th great-granddaughter	IX	9
Riddle, Ray	6th great-grandson	VIII	8
Riddle, Virginia	7th great-granddaughter	IX	9
Riddle, William Carrell	Husband of the 5th great-granddaughter		
Roberts, Bernice Oma	Wife of the 6th great-grandson		
Roberts, John	Husband of the 5th great-granddaughter		
Roberts, Living	Husband of the 8th great-granddaughter		
Roberts, Mahala	Wife of the 5th great-grandson		
Roberts, Mary	Wife of the 5th great-grandson		
Roberts, William F.	Husband of the 5th great-granddaughter		
Robinett, Living	7th great-granddaughter	IX	9
Robinett, Mira Suzanne	Wife of the 6th great-grandson		
Robinett, Romulus Zebulon	Husband of the 6th great-granddaughter		
Rodriguez, Ruth Dorothy	Wife of the 7th great-grandson		
Ronnie, Living	Husband of the 8th great-granddaughter		
Rorie, Living	Wife of the 7th great-grandson		
Ruffin, James L.	6th great-grandson	VIII	8
Ruffin, Robert G.	7th great-grandson	IX	9
Rusk, Unknown	Husband of the 6th great-granddaughter		
Rutherford, Virginia	Wife of the 6th great-grandson		
Ruyle, Celia Amy	Wife of the 6th great-grandson		
Ruyle, Emily	Wife of the 4th great-grandson		
Samples, Living	Husband of the 7th great-granddaughter		
Samples, Living	8th great-granddaughter	X	10
Sanders, Osborne	Husband of the 5th great-granddaughter		
Sands, Barbara	Wife of the 4th great-grandson		
Saner, Sarah Catherine	Wife of the 5th great-grandson		
Sapp, Living	Husband of the 7th great-granddaughter		
Sapp, Living	8th great-grandson	X	10
Sapp, Living	8th great-grandson	X	10
Sapp, Living	9th great-grandson	XI	11
Sapp, Living	9th great-grandson	XI	11
Sapp, Living	9th great-grandson	XI	11
Sapp, Living	9th great-grandson	XI	11

Sapp, Living	9th great-granddaughter	XI	11
Sapp, Living	9th great-grandson	XI	11
Sapp, Living	9th great-granddaughter	XI	11
Sapp, Living	9th great-granddaughter	XI	11
Sapp, Living	9th great-granddaughter	XI	11
Sapp, Living	9th great-grandson	XI	11
Sapp, Living	9th great-granddaughter	XI	11
Saunders, Judith	Wife of the 4th great-grandson		
Savage, Minnie	Wife of the 6th great-grandson		
Schraeder, Living	Husband of the 8th great-granddaughter		
Schraeder, Living	9th great-granddaughter	XI	11
Scott, James	Husband of the 4th great-granddaughter		
Scott, Mary Catherine	Wife of the 7th great-grandson		
Shanks, Living	Wife of the 6th great-grandson		
Sheffield, Virginia	Wife of the 6th great-grandson		
Shipley, Libon	Husband of the 7th great-granddaughter		
Shoemaker, Living	Husband of the 8th great-granddaughter		
Sims, Bess	Wife of the 5th great-grandson		
Sipe, Jacob	Husband of the 6th great-granddaughter		
Sipe, James Oscar	7th great-grandson	IX	9
Sipes, Charles Knox	Husband of the 7th great-granddaughter		
Sleeter, Unknown	Wife of the 3rd great-grandson		
Slonaker, Living	Husband of the 8th great-granddaughter		
Slonaker, Living	9th great-granddaughter	XI	11
Smart, Living	Husband of the 8th great-granddaughter		
Smart, Living	9th great-granddaughter	XI	11
Smart, Living	9th great-granddaughter	XI	11
Smart, Living	9th great-granddaughter	XI	11
Smyth, Susanna	Wife of the 4th great-grandson		
Snodgrass, Maud	Wife of the 7th great-grandson		
Soloman, Living	Husband of the 8th great-granddaughter		
Soloman, Living	9th great-grandson	XI	11
Spears, Sarah J	Wife of the 5th great-grandson		
Spicer, Emma	6th great-granddaughter	VIII	8
Spicer, Ernest	6th great-grandson	VIII	8
Spicer, Harriet	6th great-granddaughter	VIII	8
Spicer, Henry	6th great-grandson	VIII	8
Spicer, Lena	6th great-granddaughter	VIII	8
Spicer, Mary	6th great-granddaughter	VIII	8
Spicer, Prudy	6th great-granddaughter	VIII	8
Spicer, Rosa	6th great-granddaughter	VIII	8
Spicer, William Calvin	Husband of the 5th great-granddaughter		
Staggs, Living	8th great-grandson	X	10
Staggs, Living	9th great-grandson	XI	11
Staggs, Russell	Husband of the 7th great-granddaughter		
Stanley, Louise	Wife of the 5th great-grandson		
Statin, Jesse	Husband of the 7th great-granddaughter		
Storie, Eli	Husband of the 5th great-granddaughter		
Strange, Edmond	Husband of the 3rd great-granddaughter		
Strother, Living	Husband of the 6th great-granddaughter		
Strother, Living	7th great-grandson	IX	9
Strother, Living	8th great-granddaughter	X	10
Suddreth, Living	Wife of the 8th great-grandson		
Suggs, Sara	Wife of the 3rd great-grandson		
Sumter, Anne	Wife of the 2nd great-grandson		
Sumter, Mary	Wife of the 2nd great-grandson		

Susie	Wife of the 8th great-grandson		
Suzie	Wife of the 7th great-grandson		
Swanson, Eleanor	Wife of the 4th great-grandson		
Swanson, Living	Husband of the 8th great-granddaughter		
Swanson, Living	9th great-grandson	XI	11
Taylor, Amy	8th great-granddaughter	X	10
Taylor, Franklin	Husband of the 5th great-granddaughter		
Taylor, Rebecca	Wife of the 2nd great-grandson		
Taylor, Ronnie	Husband of the 7th great-granddaughter		
Teeters, Gustave	Wife of the 7th great-grandson		
Teeters, Luther	Husband of the 7th great-granddaughter		
Thacker, Rebecca	Wife of the 7th great-grandson		
Thigpen, Mary Jane	Wife of the 3rd great-grandson		
Thigpen, Susan Jane	Wife of the 5th great-grandson		
Thomas, Jane Dula	Wife of the 5th great-grandson		
Thomas, Nancy Jane	Wife of the 3rd great-grandson		
Thomas, Nancy Jane	Wife of the 4th great-grandson		
Wife of the 5th great-grandson			
Thomison, Living	Wife of the 8th great-grandson		
Thompson, Caroline	6th great-granddaughter	VIII	8
Thompson, Fountain	6th great-grandson	VIII	8
Thompson, Leonard Joshua	Husband of the 5th great-granddaughter		
Thompson, Living	Wife of the 8th great-grandson		
Thompson, Living	Wife of the 8th great-grandson		
Thompson, Rebecca J.	6th great-granddaughter	VIII	8
Thompson, Sarah Bass	Wife of the 4th great-grandson		
Thompson, Selina B.	6th great-granddaughter	VIII	8
Thompson, Shannon	Husband of the 3rd great-granddaughter		
Thompson, Unknown	Husband of the 6th great-granddaughter		
Tilley, Benjamin	Husband of the 3rd great-granddaughter		
Torbett, Mary Ann	Wife of the 6th great-grandson		
Tribble, Carolyn	8th great-granddaughter	X	10
Tribble, David	8th great-grandson	X	10
Tribble, Irene	8th great-granddaughter	X	10
Tribble, John	Husband of the 7th great-granddaughter		
Tribble, Novelene	8th great-granddaughter	X	10
Tribble, Paulette	8th great-granddaughter	X	10
Tribble, Wesley Allen	8th great-grandson	X	10
Triplett, Calvin Carter	7th great-grandson	IX	9
Triplett, Carlisle Columbus	7th great-grandson	IX	9
Triplett, Creed M.	7th great-grandson	IX	9
Triplett, Elizabeth	7th great-granddaughter	IX	9
Triplett, George Washington	Husband of the 6th great-granddaughter		
Triplett, James Wellington	Husband of the 6th great-granddaughter		
Triplett, Martha Alice	7th great-granddaughter	IX	9
Triplett, Milliard Taylor	7th great-grandson	IX	9
Triplett, Molten	7th great-grandson	IX	9
Triplett, Oney W.	7th great-grandson	IX	9
Triplett, Sarah Jane	7th great-granddaughter	IX	9
Triplett, Thomas Wilson	7th great-grandson	IX	9
Tucker, Living	Husband of the 8th great-granddaughter		
Turner, Onalee	8th great-granddaughter	X	10
Turner, Ronald	8th great-grandson	X	10
Turner, William	Husband of the 7th great-granddaughter		
Turnmire, Living	Husband of the 8th great-granddaughter		
Turnmire, Living	9th great-grandson	XI	11

Turnmire, Living	9th great-granddaughter	XI	11
Turnmire, Living	9th great-granddaughter	XI	11
Turnmire, Living	9th great-granddaughter	XI	11
Tyler, Agnes Faye	6th great-granddaughter	VIII	8
Tyler, Alice Rose	6th great-granddaughter	VIII	8
Tyler, Bertha Deliah	5th great-granddaughter	VII	7
Tyler, Betty Inez	5th great-granddaughter	VII	7
Tyler, Booker Beshear Shore "Doc"	Husband of the 4th great-granddaughter		
Tyler, Brenda Lea	7th great-granddaughter	IX	9
Tyler, Clyde Abe	6th great-grandson	VIII	8
Tyler, Edward Leo	6th great-grandson	VIII	8
Tyler, Ernest Levi	6th great-grandson	VIII	8
Tyler, Gerald Cloyce	6th great-grandson	VIII	8
Tyler, Glendon Ray	6th great-grandson	VIII	8
Tyler, Gomer Earnest	5th great-grandson	VII	7
Tyler, Harold Eugene	6th great-grandson	VIII	8
Tyler, Ida Arizona	5th great-granddaughter	VII	7
Tyler, James Curtis	5th great-grandson	VII	7
Tyler, John Lawson	6th great-grandson	VIII	8
Tyler, John Paris	5th great-grandson	VII	7
Tyler, Joseph James Rufus	5th great-grandson	VII	7
Tyler, Joseph James Rufus, Jr.	6th great-grandson	VIII	8
Tyler, Leslie Elvin	7th great-grandson	IX	9
Tyler, Leslie Wade	6th great-grandson	VIII	8
Tyler, Luther "Bea"	6th great-grandson	VIII	8
Tyler, Luther Edward	5th great-grandson	VII	7
Tyler, Mary	Wife of the 3rd great-grandson		
Tyler, Modene	6th great-granddaughter	VIII	8
Tyler, Noami Evelyn	6th great-granddaughter	VIII	8
Tyler, Pash Lynn	7th great-grandson	IX	9
Tyler, Twin	5th great-granddaughter	VII	7
Tyler, Veda Iretha	6th great-granddaughter	VIII	8
Tyler, William Seward "Bill"	5th great-grandson	VII	7
Tyler, William Woodrow	6th great-grandson	VIII	8
Tyler, Wilma	6th great-granddaughter	VIII	8
Unknown	Wife of the great-grandson		
Wife of the 2nd great-grandson			
Unknown, Agnes	Wife of the great-grandson		
Unknown, America	Wife of the 4th great-grandson		
Unknown, Anna	Wife of the 3rd great-grandson		
Unknown, Deliha	Wife of the 5th great-grandson		
unknown, Dollie	Wife of the 6th great-grandson		
Unknown, Eleanor	Wife of the 2nd great-grandson		
Unknown, Elizabeth	Wife of the 5th great-grandson		
Unknown, Elizabeth	Wife of the 3rd great-grandson		
Unknown, Elizabeth A.	Wife of the 6th great-grandson		
Unknown, Elizabeth Martha	Wife of the 2nd great-grandson		
unknown, Living	Wife of the 7th great-grandson		
Unknown, Living	Husband of the 8th great-granddaughter		
Unknown, Living	9th great-grandson	XI	11
Unknown, Living	9th great-grandson	XI	11
unknown, Living	Wife of the 7th great-grandson		
unknown, Living	Wife of the 8th great-grandson		
unknown, Living	Wife of the 8th great-grandson		
Unknown, Louisa L.	Wife of the 6th great-grandson		
Unknown, Mary	Wife of the 4th great-grandson		

Unknown, Mary	Wife of the 3rd great-grandson		
Unknown, Mary E.	Wife of the 4th great-grandson		
Unknown, Matilda	Wife of the 3rd great-grandson		
Unknown, Molly	Wife of the 3rd great-grandson		
Unknown, Mrs. Curtis Land	Wife of the great-grandson		
Unknown, Mrs. John Land	Wife of the grandson		
Unknown, Nancy	Wife of the 3rd great-grandson		
Unknown, Nettie G.	Wife of the 6th great-grandson		
unknown, Tressie	Wife of the 6th great-grandson		
Unknown, William Ann	Wife of the 5th great-grandson		
Uptmore, Living	Wife of the 7th great-grandson		
Uzzle, John H.	Husband of the 5th great-granddaughter		
Uzzle, Joseph A.	6th great-grandson	VIII	8
Vaughn, Elizabeth	Wife of the great-grandson		
Waddell, Wells	Husband of the 6th great-granddaughter		
Wagner, Nancy	Wife of the 5th great-grandson		
Walker, Marlone	Husband of the 7th great-granddaughter		
Walters, James	Husband of the 5th great-granddaughter		
Ward, John Robert	Husband of the 5th great-granddaughter		
Ward, Johnnie	Husband of the 5th great-granddaughter		
Warren, Amia "Annie"	Wife of the 4th great-grandson		
Watson, Clara Lee	Wife of the 6th great-grandson		
Watson, Living	Wife of the 8th great-grandson		
Weatherly, Living	Husband of the 8th great-granddaughter		
Weatherly, Living	9th great-granddaughter	XI	11
Weatherly, Living	9th great-granddaughter	XI	11
Weatherly, Living	9th great-granddaughter	XI	11
Weaver, Charles	4th great-grandson	VI	6
Weaver, Easter Morning	4th great-granddaughter	VI	6
Weaver, Isaac Soloman	4th great-grandson	VI	6
Weaver, Jeremiah B.	4th great-grandson	VI	6
Weaver, Jethro	Husband of the 3rd great-granddaughter		
Weaver, Piety	Wife of the 2nd great-grandson		
Weeks, Grace Malta	Wife of the 7th great-grandson		
Weill, Albert	5th great-grandson	VII	7
Weill, Charles	Husband of the 4th great-granddaughter		
Weill, Frank Lee	6th great-grandson	VIII	8
Weill, Isidore	5th great-granddaughter	VII	7
Weill, John	5th great-grandson	VII	7
Weill, Leopold	5th great-grandson	VII	7
Weir, Dee	Husband of the 5th great-granddaughter		
Wells, Bertie	Wife of the 6th great-grandson		
Wells, Clarence	Husband of the 6th great-granddaughter		
Wells, Preston	7th great-grandson	IX	9
Wessel, George Frasier	Husband of the 6th great-granddaughter		
West, Alexander B.	Husband of the 5th great-granddaughter		
West, Obedience Biddy	Wife of the 2nd great-grandson		
West, Thomas Harvey	6th great-grandson	VIII	8
Whatley, Ellie Gertrude	Wife of the 6th great-grandson		
Wherry, Margarete	Wife of the 4th great-grandson		
Wherry, Silas	Husband of the 4th great-granddaughter		
Whitaker, Melvin	Husband of the 7th great-granddaughter		
White, Adam	6th great-grandson	VIII	8
White, Carl	6th great-grandson	VIII	8
White, David	Husband of the 4th great-granddaughter		
White, Deborah	7th great-granddaughter	IX	9

White, John Monroe	Husband of the 5th great-granddaughter		
White, John Monroe, Jr.	6th great-grandson	VIII	8
White, Kenneth	Husband of the 7th great-granddaughter		
White, Living	Wife of the 8th great-grandson		
White, Living	8th great-granddaughter	X	10
White, Living	8th great-grandson	X	10
White, Living	8th great-granddaughter	X	10
White, Luke	6th great-grandson	VIII	8
White, Maylon	Husband of the 6th great-granddaughter		
White, Morgan	Husband of the 5th great-granddaughter		
White, Paul	7th great-grandson	IX	9
White, Pauline	6th great-granddaughter	VIII	8
White, Pearl	6th great-granddaughter	VIII	8
White, Ricky	7th great-grandson	IX	9
White, Russell	6th great-grandson	VIII	8
White, Willard	6th great-grandson	VIII	8
White, Zanuel	Husband of the 7th great-granddaughter		
Whitehead, Matthew	Husband of the 2nd great-granddaughter		
Whitlock, Oscar	Husband of the 7th great-granddaughter		
Whitlow, Mary Jane	Wife of the 7th great-grandson		
Wiesigert, Anna Abbot	Wife of the 5th great-grandson		
Wilburn, Evelyn	Wife of the 7th great-grandson		
Wiley, Emma Rebecca	6th great-granddaughter	VIII	8
Wiley, Henry C.	Husband of the 5th great-granddaughter		
Wiley, Nancy Addie	6th great-granddaughter	VIII	8
Wiley, Phebe	6th great-granddaughter	VIII	8
Wiley, Theodore F.	6th great-grandson	VIII	8
William, Jr. Turner	8th great-grandson	X	10
Williams, Harry	7th great-grandson	IX	9
Williams, Living	Husband of the 8th great-granddaughter		
Williams, Living	9th great-granddaughter	XI	11
Williams, Malach M.	Husband of the 5th great-granddaughter		
Williams, Oscar	Husband of the 6th great-granddaughter		
Williams, Roberta	7th great-granddaughter	IX	9
Williamson, Mary	Daughter-in-law		
Williamson, Mary	Daughter-in-law		
Williamson, Mary	Daughter-in-law		
Williamson, Mary	Daughter-in-law		
Williamson, Mary	Daughter-in-law		
Willis, Elizabeth H.	Wife of the 5th great-grandson		
Willis, Jane	Wife of the 4th great-grandson		
Willis, Martha Morton	Wife of the 5th great-grandson		
Wilson, Bill Thomas	Husband of the 7th great-granddaughter		
Wilson, Ira	Wife of the 6th great-grandson		
Wilson, Living	8th great-grandson	X	10
Wilson, Living	8th great-grandson	X	10
Wilson, Living	8th great-granddaughter	X	10
Wilson, Living	8th great-grandson	X	10
Wilson, Living	8th great-granddaughter	X	10
Wilson, Living	8th great-granddaughter	X	10
Wilson, Living	8th great-granddaughter	X	10
Wilson, Living	Wife of the 7th great-grandson		
Wilson, Living	9th great-grandson	XI	11
Wilson, Living	9th great-grandson	XI	11
Wilson, Living	9th great-granddaughter	XI	11
Wilson, Living	9th great-granddaughter	XI	11

Wilson, Living	9th great-granddaughter	XI	11
Wilson, Living	9th great-granddaughter	XI	11
Wilson, Living	9th great-grandson	XI	11
Wilson, Living	9th great-grandson	XI	11
Wilson, Living	9th great-grandson	XI	11
Wilson, Living	9th great-granddaughter	XI	11
Wilson, Living	Husband of the 8th great-granddaughter		
Wilson, Living	9th great-grandson	XI	11
Wilson, Living	9th great-granddaughter	XI	11
Wilson, Margaret A.	Wife of the 4th great-grandson		
Wilson, Thomas	Husband of the 4th great-granddaughter		
Wimbley, Pearl	Husband of the 6th great-granddaughter		
Wink, Living	9th great-granddaughter	XI	11
Wink, Mike	Husband of the 8th great-granddaughter		
Winstead, Denise	Wife of the 5th great-grandson		
Winstead, J. C.	Husband of the 4th great-granddaughter		
Wood, Living	Husband of the 8th great-granddaughter		
Wood, Living	9th great-granddaughter	XI	11
Wood, Living	9th great-granddaughter	XI	11
Wood, Living	9th great-grandson	XI	11
Wood, Susannah	Wife of the 4th great-grandson		
Woodruff, Living	Wife of the 7th great-grandson		
Worsley, Nancy L.	Wife of the 4th great-grandson		
Wortman, Living	Husband of the 8th great-granddaughter		
Wortman, Living	9th great-granddaughter	XI	11
Wright, Charles Calvin	Husband of the 6th great-granddaughter		
Wright, Clyde Robert	7th great-grandson	IX	9
Wright, David Ralph	7th great-grandson	IX	9
Wright, James Thomas Carr	7th great-grandson	IX	9
Wright, Living	7th great-grandson	IX	9
Wright, Living	8th great-granddaughter	X	10
Wright, Living	8th great-grandson	X	10
Wright, Living	8th great-granddaughter	X	10
Wright, Mary Doris	7th great-granddaughter	IX	9
Yates, Living	Wife of the 8th great-grandson		
Yearty, Frances	Wife of the 2nd great-grandson		
Yoho, Living	Husband of the 8th great-granddaughter		
Yopp, Living	Husband of the 8th great-granddaughter		
Yow, Living	Wife of the 8th great-grandson		

REVOLUTIONARY WAR
RECORDS OF THE
LAND FAMILIES

Thomas Land

Birth 1720 in Virginia

Death 17 Oct 1788 in Lands Ford.Rocky Creek, Chester Countv.South Carolina

Family Members

Parents

lames land
1700-1755

ElizabethJBetsevl

Spouse & Children

: Elinor (flUe) McCienachan
1727-1802

lamoLaod
1745- 1781

lohnland
1746- 1781

William Land
1748-1798

Benjpn land
1749- 1781

Jane land
1751-1809

1\gDCSland
1752-1830

Eleanor {Nellie) land
1759-

ThomasCloydLand
1760-1822

1720 **Birth**
Virginia

1744 **Marriage to Elinor (Ellie) McClenachan**
Augusta County, Virginia
Age: 24

Militruy
lands Ford, RockyCreek, Chester, North Carolina
Age:60 "captain", South carolina Mililia, Revolutionary War

1788 **Death**
I"Oct Lands Ford.Rocky Creek, Chester County.South Carolina
Age:68 Killed in the 'Battle of Rocky Creek' when Land's Ford was overrun by British.

South Carolina

Pursuant to a precept directed to me by [illegible] dated the 6th day [illegible] January A.D. 1787 I have admeasured and laid out unto Thomas Land a tract of land containing one hundred acres, situate lying and being in Lynes Branch, a branch of [illegible] Creek, in Craven County [illegible] &c. [illegible] land [illegible] John [illegible], and Isaac Montgomery and on all other sides on vacant land. And hath such shape form and marks as appears by the above delineated plat.

Certified for me the [illegible] day April 1787.

[illegible] Fawcock D.S.

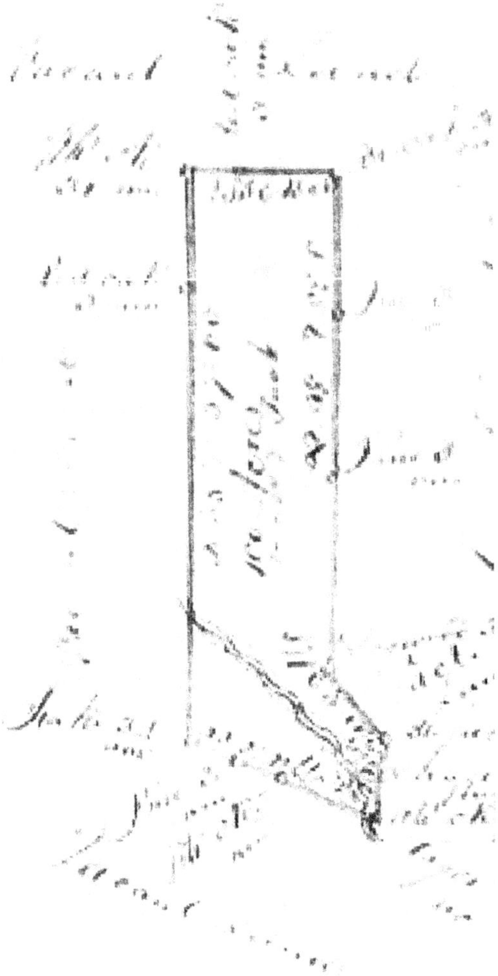

STUB ENTRIES

TO

INDENTS

ISSUED IN PAYMENT OF

Claiins A.gainst South Carolina

Growing Out of the Revolution

BOOKS R-T

Edited by
A. S. SALLEY, JR.
Secretary of the Historical Commission of South Carolina

Benjamin Land

Birth, **1749** in Augusta Countv. Virginia

Death **Mar 1781** in Lands Ford. RockyCreek. Chester. South Carohna

Family Members

Parents

Thomas land
1720-1788

Elinor !Ellie) McCienachan
1727- 1002

Spouse & Children

Mary Ann Smith
1748-

Patience land
1780-

***Marv* Ann CPollyHand**
1781-

1749 Birth
Augusta County. Virginia

1780 Jan Age:31 Marriage to Mary Ann Smith
Lands Ford. RockvCreek. Chester. South Carolina

1780 ;\Ge: 31 Revolutionary War
South Carolina Mititia
Se!ved aS a Private.

1781 Mar Age: 32 Death
Lands d. RockyCreek, Chester. South Carolina
Captured wring the British and Terie attack of lands Fort Later died in captiv.itY.

STUB ENTRIES

TO

INDENTS

ISSUED IN PAYMENT OF

Claitns Against South Carolina

Growing Out of the Revolution

BOOKS R-T

Edited by
A. S. SALLEY, JR.
Secretary of the Historical Commission of South Carolina

No 526 (
Book R S

Issued the 13 of June 1785 to Mr Isaac Lancy for Seven Pounds two Shillings and ten Pence Sterling for Sundries for Militia use as pr Account Audited-- Principal-£7-2-10 4- Annual Interest £0-9-D-

No 527 [
Book R)

Issued the 13 of June 1785. to Mr. "\Villiam Lewis for Sixteen Pounds ten Shillings Sterling for Sundries for Militia use in 1780. and 1781 as pr. Account Audited--
--Principal-£11>-10- - Annual Interest £1,.3-1-

No 528 I
Book R)

Issued the 13 of June 1785 to Mr John Leard for Nine Pounds two Shillings and ten Pence Sterling for Sundries for Militia use in 1780 as pr. Account Audited.
--Principal-£9-2-101;4- Annual Interest £0-12-9-

N°. 529
Book R. J

Issnccl to J\Ir. Robert Lerper the 13th. Jnne 1785 for Fifty nine pounds 19/3 Sterling for Sundries for l\filitia use as per Account Audited, say part of Accot-
Principal £59,19, 3- Annual Interest £4,3.11

No 530 I
Book R J

Issued the 13 of *tT*une 1785 to Messrs Robert & Arihnr Lattimore for Twenty Nine Ponnds fourteen Shillings and three Pence Sterling for Sundries for J\filitia use as pr. Account Audited-
Principal-£2D.14.31j1- Annual Interest._£2,1,7-

No 531 /
Book R 5

Issned the 13 of June 1785 *to* For Estate of J\fr .John Land for Three Pounds Eleven Shillings and five Pence Sterling for Sundries for l\filitia use as pr. Account Audited----
Principal £3),11,5- Annual Interest £0,,4,)1-

No 532 (
Book R 5

Issued the 13 of Jnne 1785 to For Estate of JVIr. Benjamin Land for Three Ponnds Eleven Shillings nnd five Pence Sterling for Snndries fcr use of the Militia. pr. Account Audited---
Principal £3-11-5 Annual Inter,est £0,4,11

Received the 13 June 1785 full Satisfaction for the
within Certificate Interest No. 532 Book L for
£17..17..1½ Sterling by an Order Moses Smith

Benj. Lam Jun.
No. 732

State of So. Carolina } Personally appeared Littleton [illegible]
Camden District } [illegible] & Elisha [illegible] & being sworn app[raised]
[illegible] mare [illegible] the Property of
→ To Benj. Land dec'd. } Benjamin Land Lost in the Public
(Capt. Hay's) Service he being taken Prisoner then
25 Days @ 20/ £25 — they appraise said Mare to one hundred
To a Mare — 100 — Pounds Sworn before me 17th June 1785
125
17-17-1½

[illegible] J.P.

22

No. 11.

Jentlemen — Please Deliver the Indent Due My Husband
→ Deceas'd (Benjamin Land) to Moses Smith & his Rect.
Shall be your Sufficiant Discharge — from Jentlemen
your Humbl. & Very Hbl. Servt. —

To the Commrs. of the Treasurey of } Mary her X mark Land
the State Of S. Carolina. —

Taken & Acknowlidg'd before
Edwd. Lacey J.P. 5th May 1785 —

32

Isaac Land

Birtfu 1750 in Poss Anson Co or Augusta Co. Virginia. South carolina. United States

Death 26 Sep 1821 in Richland. Haywood. North Carolina. United States

Family Members

Parents

Thomas land
1712-1788

Eleanor McClanahan
1715- 1784

Spouse &: Children

No Spouse or Children

1750 **Birth**

Pass Anson Co or Augusta Co. Virginia. South carolina. United States

1821 26Sep Age:71 **Death**

Richland. Haywood. North Carolina. United States

ISAAC LAND

STUB ENTRIES

INDENTS

iSSUED IN PAYMENT

Clairns Against South Carolina

Growing Out of the Revolutionary

BOOK X--PART II

Ed ted by

A. S. SALLEY. Jfi..,

Secretary of the Historical Commission of South Car...

Printed for

THE HISTORICAL COMMISSION OF SOUTH CAR...

fi)'rhe :::tat:.:: ,.:::or;gpsoy, Coluroblo,

!9"...5

1°. Kelso £4..5..8%
iegt. 'lfl a/auditecl-
L terest. £0..5..11-

Jno Kelso J1.mr.
melons regt <tfl a/

Iut £1..2..11

Achiles Kenneday
'n Brandons Rig1.mt

nterest £0.6.7.

William Kenneday
in Bl.'andous Regi-

I. Interest £5..H..10

[\:enncdy £51..7..11½
1 a/audited'
Int. £3.11.10

Pahner Kindrick
il1g 'lflr. afaudited
cnn·l. 111terest £0.6.2

Bt-nja.min Kill for
s Jleg:iment '[?r. a/.

il Interest £i.S.4--

James Killpatriek
ir: Branclons Tit\g:i··

aiJI Interest £1.18.2

"William Knave for-
1s1\.t>.giment. qf.r. a/.

An[l] Intrest 7/.

n above is: £82..1.5

N°- 2958 {
Book . X) Isued 12' June 1786 to I.\1r. Thomas Kirk fol' £35..7.11½ Sterling duty in Brandons Regiment r. A/. audited

Ant Intrest £ -9 5

N°. 2959 }
Book X { Isued 12 June 1786 to M[r] Leonard Keilon for £21.11.5 Sterling duty m Brandons Hegimt>nt r a/ audited

Ann[l]. Interest £1.10.:W2

No 2960 (
Book X) Isued 12h .June 1786.to Mr. Francis Lattimore for £157 :10, Sterling duty in Brandons Regiment r. aj.andited

Anl Interest £1LO.\i

No. 29tH {
Lib X issued 12 June 86 to Geo: Linam (Serjt.) £33..19..7_7.4 Stz duty in Branclons regt. ¥J ajandited
Principal £.33..19..7% Interest £2..7..G

N°- 2962 /
Book X Isued 12' June 1786 to Mr. Moses Lipham fut £2.18.6% Sterbng ciuty in Brandons Regjm::'d —— . A/.auditecl

£0 4.1 an[l]. Interest

N°- '2963 (
Book X Isued 1-2. June l'iSti to Mr. Abraham -.l:, ,, St.eding d11(Y w Bran(h,n:, Hc·;·im,·:.< audited

An[l]. Int...

N°- :2fltiol f
Book :S:: \ Isut•d 1::: .fun(' ESt tc, jJ•. t 'h.,-n,:..., Lii•· , ..., £12.11.] ½ Sterling duty in Brandons Regiment [r] a/. audited

An[l]. Interest ...

N°- 2965 f
Book X) Isued 12' 3uue 178G to llir. .fsaac L:::nd :f:n.· £14.8.6 Sterling duty in Brandons Regiment r. a;. audited £14.8.6% annl. Int.rcs £LO 3)f·-

LAND #

4419

Wilson, Jas. (D.A.R. Lin. Bks. & Magazines.)

SOUTH CAROLINA--ILLINOIS

Gaston, Wm••Olll, TbcUI••Wood8,]Do• .Meana, Wm••McClurklD; Tboa••)k!MJUian, lDaal. • Lusk,)'as••GWlbam, Isaac••l.«Dd, Moeea••Wal'DOCil, Joa••(From: D. A. a. LtD.. BU. "Mapzlnes.)

SOUTH CAR.OIJNA SOLDIERS BUR.IED 1M 0810

Barr, Christopher••BerrJhlll, Ala••Campbell,)DO••Caldwell. Wm••CUmd....,)la.. l)tckey, Robt••Farl.,, O.ncl. .Bale, Wm. N••Mortoa, }Do• .McGaw, Wm••Stephtuoa, }Do••Stewart, Wm. Sr••StaDe, Seal••Straia, DaY••WU1t•m'"Ol, Rn. Wm••(J'J:Om: ••omc. Roster Sold. Amer. Rno. Bar. Olllot'; D.A.R. LIL BU. 6 KqulDea.)

SOUTH CAROIJNA SOLDIERS TO TENNESSEE

/1rmstroii(C, Robt. .Barnett, --•.Bo.Uc,]DO••Blair,]Do••.BurDs, Laird, .Carter, lDanl.. DaYis, ADCIJ'nr, Abaolom, .Fredlt. .Dtal, jeremf&Jl. .J'rlerSOD, Wm••J'ruka, MarlsJal. •

James Land

S;rth **1745** in Staunton, Augusta, Virg1n1a

Death 23 **Mar 1781** ilands Ford, Chester. South Carolina

Family tlembers

Parents

Thomas Land
1720 - 1788

Elinor (Ellie) McCl _nachan
!727- 1802

Spouse & Children

Sabrina (Sabra) Hemphlll
1753- 1839

fi.iill.ard larK!
1770- 1837

John l l!4
1772 -

r ahl.and
1774- 1850

Be.niam in Land
1776- 1207

llisl[1_Q
1778- 1840

l'iaatJ.su!!l
1780- 1342

SJ.S41Ui!lJQ
1781 - 182

1745 Birth

Staunton, Augusta, Virginia

Marriage to Sabrina (S:1brill Icmphilt

Rocky Creek, Chester, South Carolina

Age: 24

1780 Milita ry

Col Wm. Henderson's, SC Regiment

Age: 35 "Captain", Revolutionary War

Deatl1

Lands Fod, Chester, South Carolina

Age: 36 "Battle of Rocky Mountain", Revolutionary War

Burial

Lands Ford. Chester, South Carolina

Sabra buried his body under the roots of a tree so the British could not desacratehis body.

Family Members

Parents

Thomas land
1720-1788

Elinor {Ellie) McCienacban
1Tl7-1002

Spouse & Children

Mary Sumter
1745-

lobo land
1768-1830

Birth

Stauton; Augusta. Virginia

Marriage to Mary Sumter

Land's Ford, Chester. South Carolina

ge:19

Revolutionary War

South Carolina MiRtia

ge: 34 Served as a Ca in of Horsemen.

Death

1781
3 Mar
ge:35

Land's Ford, Chester. South Carolina

Killed in the 'Battle of Rocky Creek' when land's Ford was overrun by British.

Will

Camden District. Kershaw. South Carolina

ge: 35 James owens aRJiied for Administrator, in right of his wife, Mary Sumter Land Owens.

IJf

State of South Carolina Dr To John Sand[illegible]
Lacey[illegible] Capt Steel[illegible] in Col. Edward Laceys Regiment
[illegible] in the Horse Service 25 days at [illegible] per day [illegible]

From the Year 1780
25 [illegible]
10 0 0

To 1 Horse lost appraised to
(for his [illegible])
£ 125 0 9
£ 17-17-1¼

Recd the appr. [illegible] above Horse
X Wm Yate[illegible]

2bb

5th May 1785.—

Edwd Lacey J.P.

2-bb-1

Laid before the President & Council the 19th May 1778 for Waggon hire £55— which was on the 18 June following postponed because of its being not dated nor Certified and overcharged beside since which it is rectified as within..

3bb-1 9ll1 [illegible] 3bb-3.

4bb

Gentlemen Please Deliv[er]

→ Deceas'd — John Land

this Rec.t Shall be your

Ant.n your friend & H[umble]

To the Comm[issioner]s of the T[reasury]

Of the State of S.Carolina

Taken & Acknowledg'd

Edw.d Lacey Ass

266-1

Laid before the President & Council the 19th May 1778. for Waggon hire £55— which was on the 18 June following postponed because of its being not dated nor Certified and overcharged besides since which it is rectified as within..

29 Sept. 1779. 1 C

Widow Lane

Received the 13 June 1785 full satisfaction for the within account in Indent No 531 Book R

Sterling — [illegible]

TO

INDENTS

ISSUED IN PAYMENT OF

Claims Against South Carolina

Growing Out of the Revolution

BOOKS R-T

Edited by
A. S. SALLEY, JR.
Secretary of the Historical Commission of South Carolina

Printed for
THE HISTORICAL COMMISSION OF SOUTH CAROLINA
By The State Company, Columbia, S.C.
1917

hn Land
MILITIA

KPI

r
t

No. 31 K
Mr. John Land
the Estate of
his Account of Sund.
for Militia use,
Amo.g to £17. 17. 1½ Stg
Seventeen Pounds,
seventeen Shillings &
one Penny half Penny
Sterling.
only £25 Curr. for £3.
11. 5 Stg of which is
Certified.

Exd

17.17.1½
3.11.5
14.5.8½

4:17
20
4/97
n
11/9 9

1.66

Petition dj'IJ £;

John Lanes —

praying Compensation for a horse lost in the service the During ye War

Come Indents —

4

To the Honorable the Speaker of the House of Representatives and Members of the Same

The petition of John Land Humbly Sheweth, that your petitioners father was an officer in the late American War and had the Misfortune to loss his life in the Same, previous to his death he lost a Certain Horse, which was appraised by [illegible] and Returned Made to the proper officer, But By Some [illegible] or other the Statement Could Never be found by the [illegible] tors of the Said Estate, your petitioner being then a Minor [illegible] Had it Not in his power to petition the Legislature, But Having Now arrive to the Age of Maturity Lays his Case before your Honourable Body. And Hopes He May be allowed Some Compensation, Such as You in Your Wisdom may think proper, and your petitioner as in duty bound Will Ever pray — Nov. the 26th 1802 —

John Land —

56b

The Committee to whom

Lands was referred Report

That

necessary Vouchers, recommend the

to the Comptroller for investigation

thereon at the next meeting of

The petitioner should take nothing —

Report on petition of
John Lande —

No. 4 —

Decr. 1. 1802

tomorrow

Decr. 4 1802
Concurred in

referred to Comptroller
General

Examined, Minutes

20th March 1779

the publick of South Carolina to John Kent Dr.

for the use of Colo. ... Regiment in publick Service

To 401 lb of Bacon 32/6 pr pound £ 651 - 12 . 6

to 250 lb of flower @ £65 pr hundred 167 10 0

£ 819 2 . 6

Certified pr J. Johnston Lt Col.

the above account duly attested before me this 29th Day of ... 1779

Alexander Turner J.P.

651 . 12 . 6
167 . 10 .
819 . 2 . 6

The State of South Carolina

A Return of John Land Waggon Bill to the Publick

To A waggon & teem Eleven days

Richard Richardson's Regiment

the seventeenth day of July 1776

To Eleven days at £2/10 per day — £ 29=10

Camden District }

Personally came before me John Land and made Oath that the Above Account is just and true of the days he was in the Service with his Waggon. Sworn to the 2d day of January 1778

John Smith J.P.

John Land

[illegible]

in Col. Richardson's Regiment from the 17 July 1776 to the 27th following inclusive, eleven days at £4. 10s ℔ day

Forty nine pounds ten Shillings Currency

I have examined as far back as the date of this Account & do not find that it has ever been paid

3bb-2

B.D.

3bb-4

N. B. there was an Acco. of this person laid before the President & Council the 19th May 1778 for Waggon hire £55 — which was on the 18 June following postponed because of its being not dated nor Certified and overcharged beside since which it is rectified as within.

3bb-1

3bb-3.

4bb

Jentlemen Pleas Delive

→ Deceas'd — John Land

& his Rect Shall be your

Jentn your friend & the

To the Commrs of the Tr

Of the State of So Carolina

Taken & Acknowledg'd

Edwd Lacey J.P.

2bb-1

Laid before the President & Council the 14th May 1778 for Waggon hire £55 — which was on the 18 June following postponed because of its being not dated nor Certified and overcharged beside since which it is rectified as within.

3bb-1 29 Aprl 1779

4bb

State of South Carolina Dr. To John Land deceas'd
under Capt. Steel in Col. Edward Lacey's Regiment
in the Horse Service 25 days at 1/9 per day
From the Year 1780 .... £5.10.0
for a Horse lost appraised to 100 0 0
(for his Widow Land) £125 0 9
£17-17-1½

Rec'd the amt. of ye above stated
X Wm Tate

2bb

5th May 1785.—

3bb-1

3bb-3.

4bb

John Land

)vC, [illegible]

531 K

Mr John Land

the Estate of

his Account of Sund.^{s}

for Militia use,

Amo.^{tg} to £17.17.1½ St.^{g}

Seventeen Pounds,

seventeen Shillings &

one Penny half Penny

Sterling.

only £25 Curr. for £3.

11.5 St.^{g} of which is

Certified.

Ex.^{d}

12.17.1½
3.11.5
14.5.8½

J.G

J.Mc.A.

24.19"
20
4/99
2
11/99

1.Lb

N 471 } Issued the 27th.. June 1785 To John Lowrey for N
Lib: T } Thirteen Pound four Shillings and three pence Lib
1,4 sterling for Militia. Duty Per account audited
Principal £13..4..3 4 annual Interest £0..18..5..

N 472 Issued the 27th.. Jnne 1785 To William Leving-
Lib: T S ston for Six pound Eleven Shillings and five
pence Sterling for Militia Duty Per account audited Principal £6..11..5 annual Interest £0..9..2-

N 473 / Issued the 27th.. June 1785 To John Leach :for Six
tib: T: pound Eleven Shillg and five pence Sterling for N
Militia Duty Per account audited Lit
Principal £6..11..5 annual Interest £0..9..2..

N 474 } Issued The 27th.. June 1787 To James Lyon for
Lib: T: } Sixteent Pound Seven Shillings and ten p nce - K
Sterling for Militia Duty Per account Audited Lil
Principal £16..7..101,4 annual Interest £1..12..2..

N 475 Issued the 27th .. June 1785 To Thomas Lemire
tib: T: S for Twenty pound five Shillg; and Six pence Y2 N
Sterling for Militia Duty also for Provisions Li
Supply'd the Militia Per account audited
Principal £20..5..6y2 Ann1: Ins: £1..8..4

N 476 1 Issued the 27th.• June 1785 To George Lymbike N
L1b: T: for Twenty Six pound five Shillgs and Eight Li
pence % Sterling for Militia Duty Per account
audited
Principal £26..5..81f2 annual Interest £1..16..19..-

N 477 Issued the 27th.. June 1785 To James Letcher L
Lib: T: J for Seven Pound Sterling For Militia Duty Per
account audited Principal £7..0..0..
Annual Interest £0..9..n..

N 478 (Issued the 27th.. June 1785 To Thomas Land for L
Lib: T: Nine pound Eighteen Shillings and Six pence i
Sterling for Militia. Duty Per account audited
Principal £9..18..63A, annual Interest £()..13..10..-

Recd Sept 20th 1785. One years Interest on the within Indent
£0.13.10 John Orr [illegible]

Recd 21st Nov 1785, One Years Interest on the within Indent
£1.14.10 Thos Johnson

Recd Dec 22d 1786, One Years Interest on the within Indent
£0.13.10 Thos Johnson

Recd Aug 22d 1787 One Years Int
£1.13.10 Thos Johnson

Recd Sept 18th 1787 from Comrs Treasury £16 [illegible] in full satisfaction on the within Indent
Thos Johnson

Tho. Johnson
£ 17 . 1 . 5 [illegible]

W.A. Book [illegible]
Cancelled

SOUTH-CAROLINA;

PURSUANT to an ACT of the GENERAL ASSEMBLY passed the 16th of March, 1783, We, the COMMISSIONERS of the TREASURY, have this Day delivered to Mr. Thomas Sand this our INDENTED CERTIFICATE, for the Sum of Nine Pounds eighteen Shillgs six Pence three farthings Stg for Militia Duty in ...

the said Thos. Sand his Executors, Administrators, or Assigns, will be entitled to receive from this Office the Sum of Thirteen Shillings ... Pence, on the Demand, for one Year's Interest on the principal Sum of Nine Pounds eighteen Shillings, & six Pence, 3/4 and the like Interest annually.

The said Thos. Sand his Executors, Administrators or Assigns, will be entitled also to receive, and shall be paid, if demanded, the principal Sum of Nine Pounds, eighteen Shillings, & six Pence, three farthings on the twenty seventh of June 1787. And the said Thomas Sand his Executors, Administrators or Assigns, may make any Purchases at any Public Sales of Confiscated Property, (except such as shall be ordered by the Legislature for special Purposes;) and this INDENT shall be received in Payment.

For the true Performance of the several Payments in Manner above-mentioned, the PUBLIC TREASURY is made liable, and the FAITH of the STATE pledged by the aforesaid ACT.

GIVEN under our Hands at the TREASURY-OFFICE, in CHARLESTON, the twenty seventh Day of June One Thousand Seven Hundred and Eighty-five

Edward Blake } Commissioners of the Treasury.

£. 9.18.6 3/4 Principal.

£. 0.13.10 Annual Interest.

No. 478

Book. S

3dd

June 27th 1785 Paid satisfaction in the [illegible]
Indent 1142 [illegible] Book [illegible]
[illegible]

[illegible]

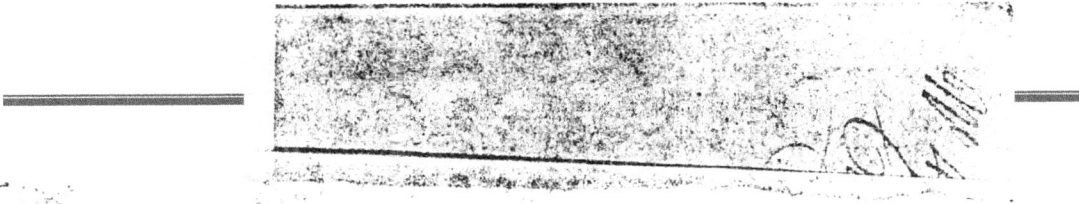

Pay to Mr. John Owen or order the sum Seventeen pounds One Shilling & 5d. Sterling in an Indent To which I am en=titled to for Services done the Public of the State South Carolina in the Millitia As per Account delivered into the Auditor Gen. Office — August 13th 1784

his
Thomas ⊣ Land
mark

To
The Commissioners of the Treasury
Charleston

State of So. Carolina }
Ninety Six district } Personally appeared Thos. Land and made oath that he gave and assigned the above Order to Mr. John Owen for the sum of Seventeen pounds One shilling And 5d. Sterling in an Indent and saith he has Recd. full satisfaction for the same by the Hands of James Lamar Junr.

Sworn to this 13th day August 1784
Before John Thomas J.P.

his
Thomas ⊣ Land
mark

2dd

GIVEN under our Hands at the TREASURY-OFFICE, in CHARLESTON, the twenty seventh Day of June One Thousand Seven Hundred and Eighty-four

Edward Blake } Commissioners of the Treasury.

£. 9..18..6¾ Principal.
£. 0..13..10 Annual Interest.

No. 478
Book, S

State of Carolina

Dr. to Thomas Land

for Duty pd Col. Anderson's Return — £ 09:10

Stg £ 9:18:6¾

THOMAS LAND

S.C. MILITIA

478
L.T.
No. 60
June 27th 1785

Mr. Thomas Land
his Account of
Duty as private
in the Militia
since the reduction
of Charlestown
Amtg to £6.9.10
Stg £9.18.6¾

Nine Pounds
Eighteen Shillings
& Sixpence, three
faths. 9d Sterlg

69.9.11
13.8.9
10

EN under our Hands at the TREASURY-OFFICE, in
CHARLESTON, the twenty seventh
Day of June One Thousand
Seven Hundred and Eighty-Four

Edward Blake } Commissioners of the Treasury.

6 3/4 Principal.
10 Annual Interest.

Thomas Cloyd Land

B1rth 1760 in Lands Ford. RockyCreek. Chester. South Carolina
Death 1822 in Chester County, South Carolina

Family Members

Parents

Thomas land
1720- 1788

Elinor <Ellie) McCJenachan
1727- 1802

Spouse & Children

Sallie Allen

Other Spouse & Children

Elizabeth

Other Spouse & Children

Mary Mullin

1760 — **Birth**
Lands Ford. RockyCreek. Chester. South Carolina

1781 — **Revolutioruuy War**
Aof: 21
South Carolina Miljtia
Served with his brothel's as a Private-

Marriage to Mruy Mullin
Age:23
Chester County. South Carolina

1789 — **Chester County Court Records**
Aoe: 29
Chester County. South Carolina
Returnt!d the Administration of his father, Thomas Land's Estate to him from his brother-in-law, .Arorew Hemphill.

1790 — **Residence**
Aoe: 30
Chester County, South Carolina

1799 20Feb — **Sold father's property. left in estate.**
Age:39
Rocky Creek. Chester. South Carolina
Sold to samuel 5andifur

1800 25Jun — **Dower property sold**
Aoe: 40
~~Chester Coun~~, South Carolina
Signed 17twife, Eizabeth.

1820 -;.\ug — **Residence**
Age: 60
Wilkinson County. MississiPpi

1822 — **Death**
Age: 62
Chester Coun , South Carolina

Notes for ROGER L'ESTHANEE:
Baronetcies of England, Ireland and Scotland, Lade-Lyde, Page 312
Nicholas L'Esthanee, Esq. of Huntington, who was oriented a Bahonet by King Charles I. 1st June 1629. Sir Nicholas married Anne, daughter of Sir Edward Lewkenor, knt of Denbans, in Suffolk and had issues.
I. Nicholas, his heir II, John, of Gressinball m- Dorothy, daughter of Hamon L'Estrange, Esq. of Barton Mero, in Suffolk, and left issues.
III. Roger, of Hoo, in Norfolk, who had three wives. He d in October 1706, aged sixty-three, and buried at Hoo, leaving issues only by his 2nd wife Susan daughter and co-heir of Francis Land, gent of Thaxton via Lewkenor.
Roger
John
Hellen

Janice or Janie Rudderford was a headright in Francis Land's (1604 - 1657) 1648 patent for 250 acres.She was the widow of Richard Rutherford.
Lower Norfolk County, Virginia Court Records Book Before 1691, Book B, p. 77 according to Alice Granbery Walter. See also Book C, p. 31 and 31 "Virginia Colonial Abstracts", p 11 by Beverly Fleetand and "Cavaliers and Pioneers", p. 18.

"the first mention of Francis Land in Virginia records was in 1647. . . ." p. 12
"Francis Land continued to be prominent in Princess Anne County. Captain Francis Land was a vestryman of Lynnhaven Parish in 1723 and . . . ." p. 12; "Francis Land House 122 - 123" p. 20
Old Virginia Houses: The Mobjack Bay Country
By Emmie Ferguson Farrar, Emilee Hines
Published by Bonanza, 1955
Original from the University of Virginia
Digitized Nov 30, 2007
175 pages

The property on which this house sits was patented a wealthy planter named Francis Land in 1654. When he died, it was part of a 1,000+ acre tract, which was subdivided among the next generation of the Land family.

The house was originally situated on the Pine Tree Branch of the Lynnhaven River, which is now little more than a dry creek bed. In the early 20th century, this house sat near the intersection of the "Kempsville Road to the village of London Bridge" and a road leading up Little Neck peninsula. Now, with one of the city's main thoroughfares in its front yard, we have to use our imagination to picture the house as it would have been when the affluent Land family lived there.

For some time, it was believed that the existing house was built in 1732 - as indicated by a brick in the cellar. Captain Francis Land III, an influential planter who played a major role in local law enforcement (he was a sheriff, a justice, a vestryman, and a member of the House of Burgesses), would have lived there at that time. Oral history also says that, during the Civil War, the house was inhabited by Union troops, who imprisoned Confederate Loyalists in the basement - but no solid proof of this has been found.

Dendrochronology placed the date of construction around 1804, indicating that the house was probably built by the sixth generation Francis Moseley Land. His daughters inherited his property in 1819, and the house passed out of the Land family in 1836.

In 1954, the Francis Land House was purchased by Mr. and Mrs. Colin Studds, who renovated and constructed additions to the house, and turned the first floor into an upscale dress shop called "Rose Hall." After twenty years in business, the family was forced to sell the house and all its contents at a public auction. The City of Virginia Beach bought the property, and opened the house to the public in 1986.

Page 73 of the book "Colonial Families of the United States" describes Francis Land as one of the earliest settlers of Lower Norfolk County, coming from England in 1630. The book states that he was elected Church Warden of Lynn Haven Parish on August 3, 1640 and that he was one of the largest land owners in the county. His will, dated April 15, 1654 split his 1020 acres of property between his two sons, Renatus and Francis.

"RENATRIS LAND of Linhaven pish, Lower Norlfolk County in Virg. . .
Book 4f. 96
dated 1 Oct 1680
proved 10 May 1681 by Geo. Walker
. . . to my eldest sonne Ronatus Land ye rest of my plantation, that Is now In the occupation of

David Whitford att ye age of Nineteene years . . . a gould ring with a signe of a deaths head upon it
. . . unto my second sone Edward Land and my third sone Robt Land, my plantation I now live upon
. . . a payre of silver Cod piste buttons, and a sett of Silver buttons for shirt collar & wrist . . .
. . . unto my sonne Robert Land . . . a Silver hatt band . . .
. . . unto my Eldest daughter Elizabeth Land . . . a Small diamond ring . . .
. . . unto my daughter Ann Land . . .
. . . unto my wife frances Land . . .
. . . my sonne Renatris Land, and my brother francis Land my Execuetors . . .
witnesses Wm Webb
Geo. Walker

Renatres Land and Seale

Abstract of the will of Renatus Land to his wife Frances and children Renatus, Edward, Robert, Elizabeth, and Ann as it appears in the book: Brief Abstract of Lower Norfolk County.

[78b]

Ordered to be Recorded ye 22th day of March 165?

To all xpian people to Whome this p'sents Writinge shall come I JOHN / BAKER of Lynhaven p'ish in the County of Lower Norfolk in ye Country / of Virginia singleman, sonn & heire apparent of JOHN BAKER late of y^e / p'ish of St Martins in the fields in ye County of Middlesex nere London in / England late Deceased Send greetinge in our Lord God Everlastinge Knowe / yee that I the said JOHN BAKER for Diverse good causes and Valuable cons / ideracons me there unto movinge, whereof and Wherewith I acknowledge / my selfe fully satisfied and contented & paid Have granted bargained sould / Enfeoffed and Confirmed, and by these p'sents doe grant bargaine sell infeoffe and / confirme Unto FFRANCIS LAND of Lynhaven p'ish aforesaid in ye said County of / Lower Norffolke Planter All my right title interest and Estate Whatsoev^r of / right or in any manner of Waies belonginge or appertaininge to me ye said JOHN / BAKER W^th in ye Common Wealth of England, as well All such Messuages / Lands tenem^ts Edifices meadowes pastures Woods feedings, & all other hereditam^ts / Whatsoev^r beinge freehould or Chartehould scituate lyeinge and beinge W^th in / the p'ish of St Martins in ye fields in ye County of Middlesex alsoe in / Hedge Lane in ye p'ish aforesaid nere London in the Common wealth of / England aforesaid And likewise All such farmes Lands houses Meadowes / pastures tenem^ts & hereditam^ts Whatsoev^r scituate lyeinge & beinge in Seafeild / towards Wales in England aforesaid, or scituate lyeinge & beinge in any / other place W^th in ye said Common Wealth of England W^ch is my inheritance / or otherwise of right belonge Unto me, As alsoe all bills bonds Evidences / debts goods Chattels & all manner of moveables Whatsoev^r W^ch late Were in the / hands & possession of ELIZABETH BAKER widd. my mother, now Deceased, or any / other p'son or p'sons Whatsoev^r in ye aforesaid Common Wealth of England To / have and To hold All thaforesaid Messuages Lands tenem^ts Meadowes / pastures feedings and hereditam^ts Whatsoev^r together W^th all thaforesaid bills / bonds Evidences debts & moveables To him thaforesaid FFRANCIS LAND / and his heires for ever, And I ye aforesaid JOHN BAKER doe for me my / heires Executo^rs administrato^rs and Assignes Covenant & grant to & W^th the said / FFRANCIS LAND, his heires Executo^rs Administrato^rs and assignes y^t he ye said FFRANCIS / LAND his heires & assignes shall quietly & peaceably have hold occupie / possesse and enjoy All thaforesaid p'mises W^th out the Lett trubblance or / molestacon of me ye said JOHN BAKER or any other claiminge Under mee. / And further I ye said JOHN BAKER doth Covenant & grant to & W^th ye said / FFRANCIS LAND heires Executo^rs and Administrato^rs that I ye said / JOHN BAKER / have not made any other or former sale of my aforesd rights or p'mises / bargained conveyed to any p'son or p'sons whatsoev^r But that I the said JOHN / BAKER shall and Will at all tymes hereafter Duringe the space of three / yeeres at the Cost and charges of the said FFRANCIS LAND doe and suffer / all such act and acts things and things, Device and devices in the Law / for the full settlinge and confirminge of all thaforesaid p'mises Unto the / said FFRANCIS LAND and his heyres, and by him the said FFRANCIS LAND, / (the)

[79]

heires Executors, Administrators & assignes or his or their Councell / Learned in the law shallbe reasonably advised devised and required / In Witnesse: Whereof I have hereunto set my hand and seale this / fifteenth day of November Ao dni. One thousand Six hundred fifty / and three.

Read sealed & deliv'ed in the p'sence
of Us: EDWARD CANNON — JOHN BAKER
JOHN JOHNSONs mrke [sic] — wth seale
SIMON BARROWES

Ordered to be Recorded this 22th: of March 1653

These p'sents Witnesse that I GREGORY PARRETT doe assigne over to THOMAS / DAYNES A Cowe & two Calves, Wch Cowe is about five yeres of age marked / Wth a halfe Moone under the right Eare Wth a hot [sic] downe & a peece cutt of ye / topp of ye same Eare, the other Eare Whole One Cowe calve colored Redd wth / White belly of the same marke, of the same Cowe & thother Calve of the same / marke for the Wch: I doe bind freely to THOMAS DAYNES for the paymt. of One / Thousand forty & nyne pounds of good sound mrchandizable tobacco, & caske for / ye Wch. some of tobacco uppon due paymt. uppon the fower & twentieth day of / December next Ensewinge the date, that then ye sd DAYNES shall Enjoy these / Cattle specified in this note forever freely, or if these cattle should miscarry & / Dye before this Date, yet ye sd PARRETT shallbe lyable to pay ye Debte to / THOMAS DAYNES or his assignes, as Witnes my hand this 16th of ffebruary / Ao: 1652 GREGORY PARRETT

Test WILL: DAYNES

signe
JOHN ✦ MARSHALL. More to this bill to pay twenty / seaven pounds of tobacco
Pr: scripe: Received more to this bill ye some of Eighty Eight pounds of tobacco & caske
p me GREGORY PARRETT

As a Quarter Cte, held at James / City the 14th: of March 1653

Present RICHD: BENNETT Esqr: Governor

Coll: WILLIAM CLAYBOURN	Coll: HUDSON
Coll: THOMAS PETTUS	Coll: HIGINSON
Leift Coll: FFREEMAN	Coll: Wm TAYLOR

Mr FFRANCIS EMPEROR is by the Governor & Councell Elected & Chosen / High Sheriffe for Lower Norfolke County and to be sworne next / County Court there held.

Test ROBT: HUBERD Cler. Concils

[79b]

she the said Else with all her increase should be equally divided amongst all her children, agreeable to the intent of her first husband's will, and further declared that she left the said Else with the said John Whitehurst for her Victuals & clothes as she the said Else was a fast breeder. Your orator & oratrix further shew that the said John Knowis & Mary his wife by a deed of gift dated 25 May 1753, gave unto the children that the said John Smyth had begot on the body of the aforenamed Mary, to wit, James Smyth, Mary Whitehurst your now oratrix, Amy Smyth, Elizabeth, Keziah Smyth and Frances Smyth, one Negro woman called Else & her children, to wit, Sarah, Sabina, China, Jemima and Courtney with all her future increase, after the decease of the said Mary. Your orator & oratrix further shew that the said Wench Else has greatly increased and that these defendants, Elizabeth Whitehurst, widow of William Whitehurst, son of Charles, John Whitehurst, Gentleman, Richard Dosier, George Cox, and John Fentress have in their hands & possession these following slaves increase of the said Else, to wit, Elizabeth Whitehurst five slaves, named Sabina, Willoughby, Else, Abraham & Lettice. John Whitehurst three slaves, Else and two whose names are not known. Richard Dosier three slaves, to wit, China, Tony, and one whose name is not known. George Cox four slaves, to wit, Jemima, Simon, and two slaves whose names are not known. John Fentress one slave named Courtney.

30 May 1772. Summons for Sarah Lyon, Mary Ann Hancock, Frances Hancock, Margaret Smith and Margaret Dudley to answer a bill in Chancery exhibited against them by Walter Lyon. Discontinued July 1772.

1 June 1770. Capias for William Cox to answer Robert Steel and Sarah his wife of a plea of debt for £20:4:9½, damage £5. Dism'd July 1772.

2 July 1772. Mary Dudley made oath that she is afraid James Lovett will beat, wound, maim or kill her. Warrant issued for James Lovett to give bond to keep the peace.

10 June 1772. Sheriff of Narsemond County is commanded to summon John Moore, heir at law to Hillary Moore dec'd, to appear in Pr. Anne court to contest the validity of the will of the said Hillary Moore if any reason he hath.

"In Obedience to an Order of the said Princess Anne County Court to us directed, & hereby annexed we the Subscribers have met, & being first Sworn viewed the Lands mentioned in the said annexed Order Wherein a Public Road is proposed to be cleared by William Moseley

Gentn., & others, & think that a Road runing in manner & form following to wit begining at the Road at Jeremiah Lands near along the Road now in use by Richd & Edwd Lands to the Land of Henry Dudley, from the Corner of the said Dudleys Land through the Land of the said Moseley to the southern of a deaded Piece of Ground belonging to the said Moseley called Gotherds to the Line between the said Moseley & Capt. Wm. Woodhouse Junr. & from thence near a strait Course, or where the Road now in use goes to Mesrs Hutchings's Land, & from thence to a Beech Tree marked A. W. standing on Mr. Walkes Land, & from thence to the Line between the said Walke & Hutchings's to a Corner Tree of the said line, & from thence through the said Walkes Land near his Woods Pasture Fence out to the main Road at the Corner of the said Walkes Plantation called Pools that leads to Cates Bridge will be of no inconvenience or prejudice to the Proprietors of the above mentioned Lands, & of great conveniency to the said Moseley, & others who hold Land near where the said Road is proposed to be cleared. An this is our Report. Given under our Hands this 9th Day of July 1772. James Kempe, Tully Robinson, Andrew Stewart."

8 Sept 1772. Summons for Thurmer Hoggard, Sam: Holmes & Mary Thelaball to testify for Samuel Nicholas vs. John Chapman. Also summoned by the plaintiff on the same day were Lemuel Roberts & Elizabeth Cooke, both of Norfolk County, and James Moore, Frances Chapman, Sharwood Lee, Thomas Cully & his wife; Amy Simmons, Eleanor Galler and Francis Thorowgood, all of Pr. Anne County.

27 Jan. 1770. Capias for Charles Nicholson to answer William Keeling (son of John), assignee of Thomas Carraway of a plea of Debt for thirty pounds, damage forty shillings, due by bond dated 4 March 1769. In this bond Chas Nicholson of Pr. Anne bound himself to pay £30 to Thos Carraway "of the County Dobbs in North Carolina." The bond was signed in the presence of David (his mark) Etheredge and James Carraway. Judgment Aug. 1772.

Decree Oct. 1772. Your oratrices Jaquet, Amy and Mary Hunter by Samuel Boush their next friend, shew that John Hunter died intestate leaving Mary his widow and four children, to wit, your oratrices and John Hunter, his only son and heir at law (who is now an infant). The said John Hunter the elder died possessed of these slaves, to wit, Nan, Peter, James, Bob, Lewis, Ned, Violet, Rachel, Caesar, Dinah & Berry, being the remaining slaves after the dower of the said Mary his widow was set apart. Administration of the intestate's estate was granted to one James Hunter, who by his long absence from this

Descendants of Francis Land I

Generation No. 1

1. I FRANCIS[1] LAND I was born Unknown in Tiverton Devon, England/Devon, England, and died Unknown in Tiverton, Devon, England. He was said to be the son of Sir Francis Land. Burke's American Families with British Ancestry gives his birth date as 1604 -1611 in Kent, England. He married UNKNOWN NICE ENGLISH LADY Cir. 1600 in England. She was born Unknown in England, and died Unknown in England.

More About FRANCIS LAND and UNKNOWN NICE ENGLISH LADY:
Marriage: Cir. 1600, England

Child of FRANCIS LAND and UNKNOWN NICE ENGLISH LADY is:
2. i. II FRANCIS[2] LAND II, b. Cir. 1604, DEVONSHIRE, ENGLAND; d. 1659, LOWER NORFOLK CO.VA.

---

2. II FRANCIS[2] LAND II *(FRANCIS[1])* was born Cir. 1604 in DEVONSHIRE, ENGLAND, and died 1659 in LOWER NORFOLK CO.VA. He married (1) FRANCES UNKNOWN Cir. 1638 in unknown. He married (2) JANICE RUDDERFORD Cir. 1649 in Virginia. He married (3) ANNE PHILLIPS 26 April 1655.

More About FRANCIS LAND and FRANCES UNKNOWN:
Marriage: Cir. 1638, unknown

More About FRANCIS LAND and JANICE RUDDERFORD:
Marriage: Cir. 1649, Virginia

Notes for ANNE PHILLIPS:
Anne Phillips was the widow of Matthew Phillips not Lawrence Phillips as stated in the Land Family group sheet prepared and researched by Alice Granbery Walter in Princess Anne Co. Va.

More About FRANCIS LAND and ANNE PHILLIPS:
Marriage: 26 April 1655

Children of FRANCIS LAND and FRANCES UNKNOWN are:
3. i. RENATUS[3] LAND, b. Cir. 1641, LOWER NORFOLK TW.VA; d. 1 May 1681, PRINCESS ANNE CO., VA.
ii. III FRANCIS LAND, b. Cir. 1643, PRINCESS ANNE CO., VA; m. KATHERINE UNKNOWN, Princess Anne co. VA.
More About FRANCIS LAND and KATHERINE UNKNOWN:
Marriage: Princess Anne co. VA

3. RENATUS[3] LAND *(FRANCIS[2], FRANCIS[1])* was born Cir. 1641 in LOWER NORFOLK TW.VA, and died 1 May 1681 in PRINCESS ANNE CO., VA. He married FRANCES KEELING Cir. 1659 in VA, daughter of ENS. KEELING and ANNE THOROWGOOD. She was born Cir. 1647 in Lower Norfolk Co. , Lynnhaven Pr VA, and died Cir. 1694 in Princess Anne Co., VA.

More About RENATUS LAND and FRANCES KEELING:
Marriage: Cir. 1659, VA

Children of RENATUS LAND and FRANCES KEELING are:

4. i. SR. EDWARD[4] LAND SR., b. Bet. 1657 - 1667, PRINCESS ANNE CO., VA; d. 27 November 1722, PRINCESS ANNE CO., VA.

ii. ELIZABETH LAND, b. Cir. 1660, PRINCESS ANNE CO., VA; m. DANIEL FRIZZELL.

iii. JR. RENATUS LAND, b. Cir. 1661, PRINCESS ANNE CO., VA; d. 1684, Princess Anne Co. Va.

iv. ROBERT LAND, b. Cir. 1665, Princess Anne Co. VA; m. PHEBE BONNY ca 1700. He died 20 May 1727, Lynn Haven, Prince William Co., VA.
Children of ROBERT LAND and PHEBE BONNY (BONNEY):
(a) SARAH ANN LAND d. 1770
(b) FRANCIS LAND (1702-1742)
(c) EDWARD LAND (1710-1785)
(d) SARAH LAND (1713-1813)
(e) JOHN ROBERT BATSON LAND (1714-1740)
(f) MARY LAND (1723-1728)
(g) RICHARD LAND (1723-1778)
(h) RENATUS LAND (1724-1724)

v. ANN LAND, b. Cir. 1669, PRINCESS ANNE CO., VA; m. ROBERT FOUNTAIN.

4. SR. EDWARD[4] LAND SR. *(RENATUS[3], FRANCIS[2], FRANCIS[1])* was born Bet. 1657 - 1667 in PRINCESS ANNE CO., VA, and died 27 November 1722 in PRINCESS ANNE CO., VA. He married (1) ELIZABETH EDWARDS SALMONS 1690 in Princess Anne Co. VA, daughter of JOHN EDWARDS. She was born 1675 in Princess Anne County, Va., and died Cir. 1697. He married (2) MARY KEMP Aft. 1697 in Princess Anne co. VA, daughter of GEORGE KEMP and MARY LOVETT. She was born Cir. 1656.

More About EDWARD LAND and ELIZABETH SALMONS:
Marriage: 1690, Princess Anne Co. VA

More About EDWARD LAND and MARY KEMP:
Marriage: Aft. 1697, Princess Anne co. VA

Child of EDWARD LAND and ELIZABETH SALMONS is:

i. III RENATUS[5] LAND, b. Cir. 1692, PRINCESS ANNE CO., VA; m. SARAH UNKNOWN, Cir. 1717, Princess Anne Co. VA.
More About RENATUS LAND and SARAH UNKNOWN:
Marriage: Cir. 1717, Princess Anne Co. VA

Children of EDWARD LAND and MARY KEMP are:

5. ii. JR. EDWARD[5] LAND JR., b. PRINCESS ANN CO., VA/Virginia; d. 17 February, PRINCESS ANN CO., VA.

iii. MARY LAND, b. PRINCESS ANNE CO., VA; m. THOMAS BRINSON.

iv. PEGGY LAND.

v. ROBERT LAND.

vi. SARAH LAND.

vii. ELIZABETH LAND, b. 1712.

Edward Land was the youngest son of Renatus Land. He married Elizabeth Edwards in 1690, in Lower Norfolk Co. Va. She later died before 1697. He then married Mary Kemp about 1698. They had 6 children between them. They lived on his grandfather's original estate in Lower Norfolk Co. Va. In 1684, Edward and his brother Robert received 250 acres of land for the transport of 5 persons from England. They were : Ann Lewer, Edward Fallett, Eliza Copeland and Toby - a Negro. Upon Edward Land, Sr. death in 1722, he gave to his youngest son Edward Land, Jr. the Plantation that they lived upon in Princess Anne County, Virginia.

5. JR. EDWARD^5 LAND JR. *(EDWARD^4, RENATUS^3, FRANCIS^2, FRANCIS^1)* was born in PRINCESS ANN CO., VA/Virginia, and died 17 February in PRINCESS ANN CO., VA. He married (1) FRANCES WEST. He married (2) UNKNOWN WHITEHURST in Lynnhaven Par. VA, daughter of BATSON WHITEHURST and MARGARET SCOTT-SNAILE.

More About **EDWARD LAND and UNKNOWN WHITEHURST:**
Marriage: Lynnhaven Par. VA

Children **of EDWARD LAND and UNKNOWN WHITEHURST are:**

- i. **HORATIO^6 LAND, b. PRINCESS ANNE CO., VA.**
- ii. **MARTHA MAYE LAND, b. PRINCESS ANNE CO., VA.**
- iii. **MOSES LAND, b. PRINCESS ANNE CO., VA.**
- iv. **PEGGY LAND, b. PRINCESS ANNE CO., VA.**
- v. **SARAH LAND, b. PRINCESS ANNE CO., VA.**
- 6. vi. **SR. JEREMIAH B. LAND SR., b. Cir. 1747, PRINCESS ANNE CO., VA; d. 18 January 1799/00, PRINCESS ANNE CO., VA.**
- 7. vii. **REA LAND, b. 1749, Lower Norfolk Co. Lynnhaven Parish, VA.; d. Bet. 1802 - 1812, Princess Anne County, Va..**

6. SR. JEREMIAH B.^{6} LAND SR. *(EDWARD^5, EDWARD^4, RENATUS^3, FRANCIS^2, FRANCIS^1)* was born Cir. 1747 in PRINCESS ANNE CO., VA, and died 18 January 1799/00 in PRINCESS ANNE CO., VA. He married (1) ELIZABETH LANGLEY Cir. 1760 in Princess Anne Co. Va, daughter of THOMAS LANGLEY and BRIDGET WHITEHURST. She was born Cir. 1743. He married (2) ANNA WOODHOUSE MCCOY 12 August 1800 in Princess Ann Co. Va. She was born Cir. 1747.

More About **JEREMIAH LAND and ELIZABETH LANGLEY:**
Marriage: Cir. 1760, Princess Anne Co. Va

More About **JEREMIAH LAND and ANNA MCCOY:**
Marriage: 12 August 1800, Princess Ann Co. Va

Children **of JEREMIAH LAND and ELIZABETH LANGLEY are:**

- i. **AMY^7 LAND, b. PRINCESS ANNE CO., VA.**
- ii. **CAPT. CAPT. PETER LAND, b. PRINCESS ANNE CO., VA.**
- iii. **LANGLEY LAND, b. PRINCESS ANNE CO., VA.**
- iv. **SAMUEL BUTT LAND, b. PRINCESS ANNE CO., VA.**
- v. **WILLIS LAND.**
- 8. vi. **JR. JEREMIAH B. LAND JR., b. Cir. 1770, PRINCESS ANNE CO., VA; d. 1836, CURRITUCK CO., NC.**

7. REA[6] LAND *(EDWARD[5], EDWARD[4], RENATUS[3], FRANCIS[2], FRANCIS[1])* was born 1749 in Lower Norfolk Co. Lynnhaven Parish, VA., and died Bet. 1802 - 1812 in Princess Anne County, Va.. He married MARY ANNE SHIP Cir. 1792 in Princess Anne Co. VA.

More About REA LAND and MARY SHIP:
Marriage: Cir. 1792, Princess Anne Co. VA

Children of REA LAND and MARY SHIP are:

i. FRANCIS[7] LAND.
ii. EDWARD LAND, m. MARY OVERSTREET.
iii. HILLARY LAND.
iv. REE LAND, JR., m. (1) BETSY SMITH; m. (2) ELIZABETH UNKNOWN.
9. v. BENNETT LAND, b. 1800, Holland, Princess Anne Co. VA.; d. 15 July 1846, Holland, Princess Anne Co. VA..

8. JR. JEREMIAH B.[7] LAND JR. *(JEREMIAH B.[6], EDWARD[5], EDWARD[4], RENATUS[3], FRANCIS[2], FRANCIS[1])* was born Cir. 1770 in PRINCESS ANNE CO., VA, and died 1836 in CURRITUCK CO., NC. He married ELIZABETH SCURR 20 April 1793 in PRINCESS ANNE CO., VA, daughter of THOMAS SCURR and ELIZABETH APPLETON. She was born Cir. 1771 in Harlsey, YKSH. ENG, and died Bef. 1836 in CURRITUCK CO., NC.

Notes for JR. JEREMIAH B. LAND JR.:
Deed Book 7, p. 303-6] Pleasant Younghusband to Jeremiah Land. April 6, 1796. Four hundred pounds. Land in Currituck bounded by William Ferebee. /s/Pleasant Younghusband. Witnesses, Wm. Taylor and John Williams. May Term 1796. Registered, July 12, 1796. Second transaction with same parties and witnesses immediately follows, with the addition of Josiah Nicholson as a witness. Second one proved in open court on the oath of John Williams and Josiah Nicholson. Third transaction follows with same parties and same three witnesses of the second deed.

More About JEREMIAH LAND and ELIZABETH SCURR:
Marriage: 20 April 1793, PRINCESS ANNE CO., VA

Children of JEREMIAH LAND and ELIZABETH SCURR are:

10. i. THOMAS SCURR[8] LAND SR., b. Cir. 1800, CURRITUCK CO., NC; d. Cir. 1847, MISSISSIPPI.
11. ii. MELISSA LAND, b. Cir. 1803, Currituck Co. NC; d. Bef. 1836, CURRITUCK CO., NC.
12. iii. DR. DR. BENJAMIN C. LAND, b. 25 September 1806, Currituck Co. NC; d. 17 August 1868, Yalobusha Co. MISS.
13. iv. JAMES MADISON LAND, b. 23 April 1815, CURRITUCK CO., NC; d. 16 July 1871, CRAVEN/PAMLICO CO., NC.

9. BENNETT[7] LAND *(REA[6], EDWARD[5], EDWARD[4], RENATUS[3], FRANCIS[2], FRANCIS[1])* was born 1800 in Holland, Princess Anne Co. VA., and died 15 July 1846 in Holland, Princess Anne Co. VA.. He married SARAH SCOTT GASKINS 26 December 1820 in VA.

More About BENNETT LAND and SARAH GASKINS:
Marriage: 26 December 1820, VA

Children of BENNETT LAND and SARAH GASKINS are:

i. SARAH MARGARET[8] LAND, b. 1822, Princess Anne County, Va.; d. 1853, Princess Anne County, Va.; m. JOHNATHAN WOODHOUSE, 1841, Princess Anne Co. VA.

More About JOHNATHAN WOODHOUSE and SARAH LAND:
Marriage: 1841, Princess Anne Co. VA

ii. BENNET LAND JR., b. 1824.
iii. MARY ELIZABETH LAND, b. 1827, Princess Anne County, Va.; d. 1829, Princess Anne County, Va..
iv. SUSAN ANNE FRANCES LAND, b. 1831; d. 1921; m. JOHN CAMP SHEPHARD, 2 July 1856, Princess Anne Co. VA.
More About JOHN SHEPHARD and SUSAN LAND:
Marriage: 2 July 1856, Princess Anne Co. VA

v. GEORGE REE LAND, b. 5 May 1833, Princess Anne County, Va.; d. 23 September 1852, Norfolk, Virginia.
vi. JAMES EDWARD LAND, b. 1835.
vii. HENRY GASKINS LAND, b. 13 April 1839; d. 4 January 1888; m. JANE POYNER.

10. THOMAS SCURR[8] LAND SR. *(JEREMIAH B.[7], JEREMIAH B.[6], EDWARD[5], EDWARD[4], RENATUS[3], FRANCIS[2], FRANCIS[1])* was born Cir. 1800 in CURRITUCK CO., NC, and died Cir. 1847 in MISSISSIPPI. He married (1) MARIA SCURR in Currituck Co. NC, daughter of JOHN SCURR and ELIZABETH UNKNOWN. She was born 20 August 1806 in Currituck Co. NC, and died 25 February 1839 in Granada Co. Mississippi. He married (2) GRIZELLE BULL Aft. 1840 in MS. She was born 28 August 1813 in MS, and died 31 January 1863 in Granada Co MS..

More About MARIA SCURR:
Burial: Yellow Fever Cemetery, Granada Co. MS.

More About THOMAS LAND and MARIA SCURR:
Marriage: Currituck Co. NC

More About GRIZELLE BULL:
Burial: Yellow Fever Cemetery, Granada Co. MS.

Marriage Notes for THOMAS LAND and GRIZELLE BULL:
Yellow Fever Cemetery, Granada, MS

Land, Infants of T. S. & Grizzell Land no dates - stone broken

More About THOMAS LAND and GRIZELLE BULL:
Marriage: Aft. 1840, MS

Children of THOMAS LAND and MARIA SCURR are:
i. ELIZABETH[9] LAND.
ii. JEREMIAH LAND, b. 1825, MISS.; m. MARY JOSEPHINE SNIDER, 18 December 1850, Leflore Co. MS.
Notes for MARY JOSEPHINE SNIDER:
Have black and white photo of her.

More About JEREMIAH LAND and MARY SNIDER:
Marriage: 18 December 1850, Leflore Co. MS

iii. JR. DR. THOMAS S. LAND, JR., b. Cir. 1834, Miss?; d. Unknown, Virginia; m. AMANDA BRIGHT, 3 April 1855, Yalobusha County, MS; b. Unknown, MS; d. Unknown, VA?.
More About DR. LAND and AMANDA BRIGHT:

Marriage: 3 April 1855, Yalobusha County, MS

Children of THOMAS LAND and GRIZELLE BULL are:

iv. JOHN M.[9] LAND, b. October 1841, MS; d. Unknown, MS.
More About JOHN M. LAND:
Burial: Yellow Fever Cemetery, Granada Co. MS.

v. INFANTS? LAND.

11. MELISSA[8] LAND *(JEREMIAH B.[7], JEREMIAH B.[6], EDWARD[5], EDWARD[4], RENATUS[3], FRANCIS[2], FRANCIS[1])* was born Cir. 1803 in Currituck Co. NC, and died Bef. 1836 in CURRITUCK CO., NC. She married (1) EMERSON GOULD in CURRITUCK CO., NC. He was born Cir. 1794, and died 1 September 1823 in Currituck County, NC. She married (2) DR. WILLIAM F. DAVIS 5 May 1825 in Currituck Co. NC. He died 1837.

More About EMERSON GOULD:
Burial: Currituck, NC

More About EMERSON GOULD and MELISSA LAND:
Marriage: CURRITUCK CO., NC

More About WILLIAM DAVIS and MELISSA LAND:
Marriage: 5 May 1825, Currituck Co. NC

Child of MELISSA LAND and EMERSON GOULD is:

i. ELIZABETH[9] GOULD, b. February 1822.

Children of MELISSA LAND and WILLIAM DAVIS are:

ii. JEREMIAH LAND[9] DAVIS, b. CURRITUCK CO., NC; d. MISSISSIPPI ??.

iii. VIRGINIA ELIZABETH DAVIS, b. CURRITUCK CO., NC; d. MISSISSIPPI ??.

iv. MARIE SCURR DAVIS, b. 10 February 1828.

12. DR. DR. BENJAMIN C.[8] LAND *(JEREMIAH B.[7], JEREMIAH B.[6], EDWARD[5], EDWARD[4], RENATUS[3], FRANCIS[2], FRANCIS[1])* was born 25 September 1806 in Currituck Co. NC, and died 17 August 1868 in Yalobusha Co. MISS. He married (1) ANN W. WILSON 28 April 1830 in CURRITUCK CO., NC. She was born Cir. 1808 in Currituck Co. NC, and died Bef. 1845 in MS or NC? unknown d.s.p.?. He married (2) MARGARET A. E. GAGE 25 September 1845 in Madison Co. MS. She was born Unknown in MS, and died Unknown in MS.

Notes for DR. DR. BENJAMIN C. LAND:
Dr. Benjamin Land buried in Odd Fellows Cemetery, MS

Part 2 Vol III
Married in Currituck County, Mr. Benjamin Land to Miss Ann W. Wilson
RRsw Mon 19 Apr. 1830 3:4/RRw Thurs 22 Apr 1830 1:4/

More About DR. DR. BENJAMIN C. LAND:
Burial: Odd Fellows Cemetery, MS on Gage lot

More About DR. LAND and ANN WILSON:
Marriage: 28 April 1830, CURRITUCK CO., NC

More About MARGARET A. E. GAGE:

Burial: Unknown, MS

More About **DR. LAND and MARGARET GAGE:**
Marriage: 25 September 1845, Madison Co. MS

Child of **DR. LAND and ANN WILSON is:**

i. BENJAMIN C.[9] LAND DR., b. 1835, NC?; d. 1868, MS.

13. JAMES MADISON[8] LAND *(JEREMIAH B.[7], JEREMIAH B.[6], EDWARD[5], EDWARD[4], RENATUS[3], FRANCIS[2], FRANCIS[1])* was born 23 April 1815 in CURRITUCK CO., NC, and died 16 July 1871 in CRAVEN/PAMLICO CO., NC. He married ANNE ELIZABETH BAXTER Cir. 1843 in CURRITUCK CO., NC, daughter of THOMAS BAXTER and MARIE PHILLIPS. She was born Cir. 1818 in CURRITUCK CO., NC, and died 27 May 1854 in CURRITUCK CO., NC.

More About **JAMES MADISON LAND:**
Burial: Land Family Cemetery, Arapahoe, Pamlico Co. NC

More About **ANNE ELIZABETH BAXTER:**
Burial: Currituck County, NC

More About **JAMES LAND and ANNE BAXTER:**
Marriage: Cir. 1843, CURRITUCK CO., NC

Children of **JAMES LAND and ANNE BAXTER are:**

14. **i. JAMES KENNETH[9] LAND, b. 26 January 1841, CURRITUCK CO., NC; d. 13 November 1916, CRAVEN CO., NC.**

ii. THOMAS LAND, b. Cir. 1844, Currituck County, NC; d. Bef. 1854, Currituck County, NC d.s.p..

iii. JEREMIAH W. LAND, b. 6 June 1846, CURRITUCK CO., NC; d. 6 February 1872, PAMLICO CO., NC.

iv. SOPHRONIA GRACE LAND, b. 27 March 1849, CURRITUCK CO., NC; d. 13 April 1917, PAMLICO CO., NC; m. GEORGE WILSON BRINSON, 30 December 1875, CRAVEN CO., NC; b. 27 December 1852, PAMLICO CO., NC; d. 26 December 1923, PAMLICO CO., NC.
More About **GEORGE BRINSON and SOPHRONIA LAND:**
Marriage: 30 December 1875, CRAVEN CO., NC

15. **v. EDMUND BAXTER LAND, b. Cir. 1850, CURRITUCK CO., NC; d. Cir. 1880, VA.**

16. **vi. THOMAS ANN LAND, b. 17 May 1854, CURRITUCK CO., NC; d. 1 April 1932, NEW BERN, CRAVEN CO., NC.**

14. JAMES KENNETH[9] LAND *(JAMES MADISON[8], JEREMIAH B.[7], JEREMIAH B.[6], EDWARD[5], EDWARD[4], RENATUS[3], FRANCIS[2], FRANCIS[1])* was born 26 January 1841 in CURRITUCK CO., NC, and died 13 November 1916 in CRAVEN CO., NC. He married ALICE ELIZABETH BRINSON 7 December 1871 in CRAVEN CO., NC, daughter of *SIMON BRINSON and SARAH MCCOY. She was born 19 July 1856 in PAMLICO CO., NC, and died 12 April 1929 in CRAVEN CO., NC.

More About **JAMES LAND and ALICE BRINSON:**
Marriage: 7 December 1871, CRAVEN CO., NC

Children of **JAMES LAND and ALICE BRINSON are:**

i. LEON L.[10] LAND, b. NEW BERN, CRAVEN CO., NC; d. UNKNOWN;

m. LENA SANFORD.

ii. JAMES JEREMIAH LAND, b. 30 September 1872; d. 20 April 1938; m. LENA BOWDEN.

iii. ARTHUR THOMAS LAND, b. 17 September 1874; d. 5 March 1937; m. BEATRICE BOYD.

iv. MAUDE ELMA LAND, b. 2 September 1877, NEW BERN, CRAVEN CO., NC; d. 13 January 1958; m. JOSEPH WITTY WATSON.

17. v. EDMUND JOSEPHUS LAND SR., b. 1880, Pamlico CO., NC; d. Baton Rouge, LA.

18. vi. HERBERT KENNETH LAND, b. 30 October 1882, NEW BERN, CRAVEN CO., NC; d. 9 February 1970, NEW BERN, CRAVEN CO., NC.

vii. FREDERICK GUY LAND, b. 18 June 1889; d. 22 May 1906.

19. viii. ALICE GRACE LAND, b. 6 April 1893, New Bern, Craven Co., NC; d. 11 September 1985, New Bern, Craven Co., NC.

15. EDMUND BAXTER[9] LAND *(JAMES MADISON[8], JEREMIAH B.[7], JEREMIAH B.[6], EDWARD[5], EDWARD[4], RENATUS[3], FRANCIS[2], FRANCIS[1])* was born Cir. 1850 in CURRITUCK CO., NC, and died Cir. 1880 in VA. He married SARAH CAROLINE BRINSON 1 May 1872 in NC ?, daughter of *SIMON BRINSON and SARAH MCCOY. She was born 7 June 1855 in NC, and died 17 July 1930 in NORFOLK, VA.

More About EDMUND LAND and SARAH BRINSON:
Marriage: 1 May 1872, NC ?

Children of EDMUND LAND and SARAH BRINSON are:

20. i. WALTER SAMUEL[10] LAND, b. 1874, VA?; d. 16 April 1957, NORFOLK, VA.

ii. LELA ELFLETA LAND.

iii. JOHN S. LAND.

16. THOMAS ANN[9] LAND *(JAMES MADISON[8], JEREMIAH B.[7], JEREMIAH B.[6], EDWARD[5], EDWARD[4], RENATUS[3], FRANCIS[2], FRANCIS[1])* was born 17 May 1854 in CURRITUCK CO., NC, and died 1 April 1932 in NEW BERN, CRAVEN CO., NC. He married MARGARET ELLEN BRINSON 10 November 1875 in ARAPAHOE, NC, daughter of *SIMON BRINSON and SARAH MCCOY. She was born 29 June 1859 in CRAVEN/PAMLICO CO., NC, and died 28 November 1936 in WASHINGTON, D.C..

More About THOMAS ANN LAND:
Burial: Cedar Grove Cemetery, New Bern, NC

More About MARGARET ELLEN BRINSON:
Burial: Cedar Grove Cemetery, New Bern, NC

More About THOMAS LAND and MARGARET BRINSON:
Marriage: 10 November 1875, ARAPAHOE, NC

Children of THOMAS LAND and MARGARET BRINSON are:

21. i. KENNETH CLAUDE[10] LAND, b. 27 October 1876, Arapahoe, Pamlico Co. NC; d. 11 September 1956, PAMLICO CO., NC.

ii. FLORENCE IDESSA LAND, b. 11 October 1878, PAMLICO CO., NC; d. 11 April 1894, PAMLICO CO., NC (D.S.P.).
More About FLORENCE IDESSA LAND:
Burial: Land Family Cemetery, Arapahoe, Pamlico Co. NC

22. iii. THOMAS EUGENE LAND, b. 29 September 1880, PAMLICO CO., NC; d. 19 December 1965, NEW BERN, CRAVEN CO., NC.

23. iv. JAMES OSCAR LAND, b. 9 December 1882, PAMLICO CO., NC; d. 5 May 1963, FAIRFAX, VA.

24. v. CLARENCE EDISON LAND, b. 4 October 1884, PAMLICO CO., NC; d. 1 July 1945, NORFOLK, VA.

25. vi. HUGH HAMPTON LAND, b. 9 December 1886, PAMLICO CO., NC; d. 22 March 1937, WINSTON-SALEM, NC.

vii. WADE MADISON LAND, b. 18 July 1888, PAMLICO CO., NC; d. 6 April 1906, PAMLICO/CRAVEN CO., NC d.s.p..
More About WADE MADISON LAND:
Burial: Cedar Grove Cemetery, New Bern, NC

26. viii. EVA VIRGINIA LAND, b. 24 December 1892, ARAPAHOE, PAMLICO CO., NC; d. 6 February 1958, BETHESDA, MD.

27. ix. LELA GRACE LAND, b. 20 February 1895, PAMLICO CO., NC; d. 2 January 1970, Volusia Co. Fla...

28. x. ROY LAND, b. 29 September 1897, PAMLICO CO., NC; d. 19 September 1974, ALEXANDRIA, VA.

17. EDMUND JOSEPHUS[10] LAND SR. *(JAMES KENNETH[9], JAMES MADISON[8], JEREMIAH B.[7], JEREMIAH B.[6], EDWARD[5], EDWARD[4], RENATUS[3], FRANCIS[2], FRANCIS[1])* was born 1880 in Pamlico CO., NC, and died in Baton Rouge, LA. He married INEZ WHITTY.

Children of EDMUND LAND and INEZ WHITTY are:

i. EDMUND JOSEPHUS[11] LAND, JR., b. 1920.

ii. JAMES KENNETH LAND LAND II, b. 21 August 1922, Baton Rouge, LA.

18. HERBERT KENNETH[10] LAND *(JAMES KENNETH[9], JAMES MADISON[8], JEREMIAH B.[7], JEREMIAH B.[6], EDWARD[5], EDWARD[4], RENATUS[3], FRANCIS[2], FRANCIS[1])* was born 30 October 1882 in NEW BERN, CRAVEN CO., NC, and died 9 February 1970 in NEW BERN, CRAVEN CO., NC. He married ROBENA ELIZABETH BENNERS.

Child of HERBERT LAND and ROBENA BENNERS is:

i. JAMES BENNERS[11] LAND.

19. ALICE GRACE[10] LAND *(JAMES KENNETH[9], JAMES MADISON[8], JEREMIAH B.[7], JEREMIAH B.[6], EDWARD[5], EDWARD[4], RENATUS[3], FRANCIS[2], FRANCIS[1])* was born 6 April 1893 in New Bern, Craven Co., NC, and died 11 September 1985 in New Bern, Craven Co., NC. She married SR. JOHN R. TAYLOR. He was born 15 September 1889 in NC, and died 19 November in New Bern, Craven Co., NC.

Children of ALICE LAND and JOHN TAYLOR are:

i. ALICE[11] TAYLOR.

ii. ELIZABETH TAYLOR, b. New Bern, Craven Co., NC; m. JAMES HODGES.

iii. JR. JOHN R. TAYLOR JR., b. 24 October 1922, New Bern, Craven Co., NC; d. 3 March 1992, New Bern, Craven Co., NC; m. SUE.

20. WALTER SAMUEL[10] LAND *(EDMUND BAXTER[9], JAMES MADISON[8], JEREMIAH B.[7], JEREMIAH B.[6], EDWARD[5], EDWARD[4], RENATUS[3], FRANCIS[2], FRANCIS[1])* was born 1874 in VA?, and died 16 April 1957 in NORFOLK, VA. He married ELLA NORA WINTERS in VA. She was born Cir. 1892 in FALLSBURGH, NY, and died 21 July 1949 in VA.

More About WALTER LAND and ELLA WINTERS:
Marriage: VA

Children of WALTER LAND and ELLA WINTERS are:

- i. EDMUND BAXTER[11] LAND, b. 1908, New Bern, Craven Co. NC; d. Port Jarvis, NJ.
- ii. WALTER LEO LAND.
- iii. JAMES ARTHUR LAND.
- iv. KENNETH WILLIAM LAND.
- v. ELEANOR LAND, m. AL HAMLIN.

21. KENNETH CLAUDE[10] LAND *(THOMAS ANN[9], JAMES MADISON[8], JEREMIAH B.[7], JEREMIAH B.[6], EDWARD[5], EDWARD[4], RENATUS[3], FRANCIS[2], FRANCIS[1])* was born 27 October 1876 in Arapahoe, Pamlico Co. NC, and died 11 September 1956 in PAMLICO CO., NC. He married SARAH CALDONIA MIDYETTE 8 August 1897 in Pamlico CO., NC. She was born 1 March 1879 in Pamlico Co., NC, and died 25 January 1945 in PAMLICO CO., NC.

More About KENNETH CLAUDE LAND:
Burial: Oriental, NC

More About SARAH CALDONIA MIDYETTE:
Burial: Oriental, NC

More About KENNETH LAND and SARAH MIDYETTE:
Marriage: 8 August 1897, Pamlico CO., NC

Children of KENNETH LAND and SARAH MIDYETTE are:

- i. INA ELOISE[11] LAND, b. DC; d. November 1996, Florida; m. CLARENCE K. BUNN.
- ii. JACQUELINE IDESSA LAND.
- iii. DONALD O. LAND.
- iv. WILLIAM CLAUDE LAND.
- v. COLUMBUS LAND, b. 1897, Pamlico Co. NC; d. 1951, Pamlico Co. NC; m. MAHALIA GASKILL; b. 1897, NC; d. 22 July 1987, Pamlico Co. NC.
- vi. AROL THOMAS LAND, b. 23 September 1902, Oriental, Pamlico Co. NC; m. LUEVINE CARTER; b. Winston-Salem, NC; d. 25 September 1997, Oriental, Pamlico Co. NC.

22. THOMAS EUGENE[10] LAND *(THOMAS ANN[9], JAMES MADISON[8], JEREMIAH B.[7], JEREMIAH B.[6], EDWARD[5], EDWARD[4], RENATUS[3], FRANCIS[2], FRANCIS[1])* was born 29 September 1880 in PAMLICO CO., NC, and died 19 December 1965 in NEW BERN, CRAVEN CO., NC. He married (1) BESSIE FRENCH. She was born 13 March 1895 in New Bern, Craven Co. NC, and died 28 August 1977 in New Bern, Craven Co. NC. He married (2) ALLIE LETHA TYSON 9 November 1905 in CRAVEN CO., NC. She was born 25 February 1884 in New Bern, Craven Co. NC, and died 10 January 1916 in New Bern, Craven Co. NC.

More About THOMAS LAND and ALLIE TYSON:
Marriage: 9 November 1905, CRAVEN CO., NC

Children of THOMAS LAND and BESSIE FRENCH are:

i. BESSIE MAE[11] LAND, m. ROBERT THOMAS.
ii. JOYCE LAND, m. ALBERT MCCOTTER.
iii. SIDNEY RANDOLPH LAND, b. 15 May 1920, New Bern, Craven Co. NC; d. December 1985, New Bern, Craven Co. NC.

Children of THOMAS LAND and ALLIE TYSON are:

iv. EUGENE[11] LAND.
v. WADE LAND.
vi. THOMAS LAND.

23. JAMES OSCAR[10] LAND *(THOMAS ANN[9], JAMES MADISON[8], JEREMIAH B.[7], JEREMIAH B.[6], EDWARD[5], EDWARD[4], RENATUS[3], FRANCIS[2], FRANCIS[1])* was born 9 December 1882 in PAMLICO CO., NC, and died 5 May 1963 in FAIRFAX, VA. He married ELLA ROBERTS DAVIS. She was born 2 April 1891 in New Bern, Craven Co.NC, and died 19 October in Falls Church, VA.

Children of JAMES LAND and ELLA DAVIS are:

i. MARY MARGARET[11] LAND, b. 1 May 1905, WASHINGTON, DC; d. 1 August 1987, SPOTSYLVANIA, VA d.s.p.; m. RALPH AUGUSTUS LEISTER; b. 31 July 1904, PA; d. 19 March, VA.
ii. JAMES WILLIAM LAND, b. 31 July 1909; m. JULIA MAE SMITH, 25 February 1931.
More About JAMES LAND and JULIA SMITH:
Marriage: 25 February 1931

iii. GEORGE THOMAS LAND, b. 21 July 1911, Washington, DC; d. 24 January 1975, Washington, DC d.s.p..
iv. LIDA DAVIS LAND, b. 12 October 1913; m. (1) ARTHUR VERNON BATES; m. (2) WILLIAM NORMAN HERBERT.
v. ROBERT OSCAR LAND, b. 24 September 1915; d. HANCOCK, MD; m. DORIS ANNE AUMILLER.
vi. RUTH IDESSA LAND, b. 1 December 1919; d. August 1997; m. NORMAN FRANK ANNA.
vii. ANN ELIZABETH LAND, b. 25 January 1921, WASHINGTON, DC; m. (1) ROBERT AUGUST DOMENICK; b. 5 January 1914, New Jersey; d. 8 July 1972; m. (2) EDWARD ALBERT BRADFORD.

viii. DORIS LEE LAND, b. 18 July 1925, Washington, D. C.; d. 13 November 1975, VA d.s.p.; m. JOHN PAUL PERKINS; d. 1977, VA d.s.p..

24. CLARENCE EDISON^{10} LAND (*THOMAS ANN^{9}, JAMES MADISON^{8}, JEREMIAH B.^{7}, JEREMIAH B.^{6}, EDWARD^{5}, EDWARD^{4}, RENATUS^{3}, FRANCIS^{2}, FRANCIS^{1}*) was born 4 October 1884 in PAMLICO CO., NC, and died 1 July 1945 in NORFOLK, VA. He married FRANCES HARRIET BRAY, daughter of LEVI BRAY and SARAH BRINSON. She was born 19 March 1887, and died 24 September 1971 in VA.

Children of CLARENCE LAND and FRANCES BRAY are:

i. SARAH MARGARET^{11} LAND, b. 30 June 1913, NORFOLK, VA; d. 19 March, NORFOLK, VA; m. WARREN F. BEISNER.

ii. MARY CATHERINE LAND, b. 5 March 1919, Norfolk, VA; m. HOWELL T. BIGLAND.

iii. FRANCES AGNES LAND, b. 8 January 1922, Norfolk, VA; m. MORRIS AUSTIN.

25. HUGH HAMPTON^{10} LAND (*THOMAS ANN^{9}, JAMES MADISON^{8}, JEREMIAH B.^{7}, JEREMIAH B.^{6}, EDWARD^{5}, EDWARD^{4}, RENATUS^{3}, FRANCIS^{2}, FRANCIS^{1}*) was born 9 December 1886 in PAMLICO CO., NC, and died 22 March 1937 in WINSTON-SALEM, NC. He married SADIE LOUISE SHOUSE 23 July 1910 in FORSYTHE CO., NC. She was born in WINSTON-SALEM, NC, and died 19 January 1993 in WINSTON-SALEM, NC.

More About HUGH LAND and SADIE SHOUSE:
Marriage: 23 July 1910, FORSYTHE CO., NC

Children of HUGH LAND and SADIE SHOUSE are:

i. JR. HUGH HAMPTON^{11} LAND JR., b. 16 February 1912, Winston-Salem, NC; d. 31 January 1928, Winston-Salem, NC.

ii. LOUISE GRACE LAND, b. 7 November 1915, Winston-Salem, NC; d. 21 August 2000, Winston-Salem, NC; m. ROBERT LEE REID, 5 September 1936, Bassett, VA.
More About ROBERT REID and LOUISE LAND:
Marriage: 5 September 1936, Bassett, VA

iii. JACK ROBERT LAND, b. 12 October 1919, Winston-Salem, NC; d. 23 April 1994, Winston-Salem, NC; m. (1) NANNIE ALMA JONES; m. (2) HELEN HAYES SMOTHERS.

iv. BARBARA JEAN LAND, b. 8 November 1931, Winston-Salem NC; d. 3 February 1992, Winston-Salem, NC; m. RICHARD THEODORE OLIVER, 31 December 1949, High Point, NC.
More About RICHARD OLIVER and BARBARA LAND:
Marriage: 31 December 1949, High Point, NC

26. EVA VIRGINIA^{10} LAND (*THOMAS ANN^{9}, JAMES MADISON^{8}, JEREMIAH B.^{7},*

JEREMIAH B.[6], *EDWARD*[5], *EDWARD*[4], *RENATUS*[3], *FRANCIS*[2], *FRANCIS*[1]) was born 24 December 1892 in ARAPAHOE, PAMLICO CO., NC, and died 6 February 1958 in BETHESDA, MD. She married BENJAMIN HARRISON NELSON SR. 26 October 1910 in ELIZABETH CITY, NC, son of JOSEPH NELSON and PATTIE WILLIAMS. He was born 30 July 1888 in NEW BERN, CRAVEN CO., NC, and died 7 September 1951 in NEW BERN, CRAVEN CO., NC.

More About EVA VIRGINIA LAND:
Burial: 8 February 1958, Cedar Grove Cemetery, New Bern, NC

Notes for BENJAMIN HARRISON NELSON SR.:
Worked New Bern Sun for unknown number of years before going to Owen G. Dunn Printing Co.
Died from Uremic Poisoning after gall bladder surgery 1951, Sept 7.

More About BENJAMIN HARRISON NELSON SR.:
Burial: 9 September 1951, Cedar Grove Cemetery, New Bern, NC

Marriage Notes for EVA LAND and BENJAMIN NELSON:
They eloped by train to Elizabeth City to get married.

More About BENJAMIN NELSON and EVA LAND:
Death of one spouse: 7 September 1951, New Bern, Craven Co. NC
Marriage: 26 October 1910, ELIZABETH CITY, NC
Marriage Fact: 26 October 1910, Elizabeth City, Pasquotank Co. NC - eloped

Children of EVA LAND and BENJAMIN NELSON are:

i. ROSA DAIL[11] NELSON, b. 14 September 1911, NEW BERN, CRAVEN CO., NC; m. ORVILLE E. WILDES, 15 August 1936, WASHINGTON, DC; b. 27 January 1910, Wisconsin; d. Wisconsin.
More About ORVILLE WILDES and ROSA NELSON:
Marriage: 15 August 1936, WASHINGTON, DC

ii. JR. BENJAMIN H. NELSON JR., b. 19 November 1912, NEW BERN, CRAVEN CO., NC; d. 8 January 2000, New Bern, Craven Co. NC; m. EDITH LYLE BANKS, 1937, New Bern, Craven Co. NC; b. 8 January 1915, Craven Co. NC; d. 3 April 1997, New Bern, Craven Co. NC.
More About BENJAMIN NELSON and EDITH BANKS:
Marriage: 1937, New Bern, Craven Co. NC

iii. ELINOR VIRGINIA NELSON, b. 3 November 1913, NEW BERN, CRAVEN CO., NC; m. ROBERT W. BROWN, 9 June 1951, WASHINGTON, DC; b. 26 August 1913, BIRMINGHAM, ALA; d. 6 November 1984, ATLANTA, GA.
More About ROBERT BROWN and ELINOR NELSON:
Marriage: 9 June 1951, WASHINGTON, DC

iv. ALMA MAE NELSON, b. 31 May 1915, NEW BERN, CRAVEN CO., NC; d. 12 July 1989, NEW BERN, CRAVEN CO., NC; m. HARRY GORDON COUNCIL (LT. COL. US ARMY), 13 January 1943, NEW BERN, CRAVEN CO., NC; b. 4 September 1921, ALTOONA, BLAIR CO., PA; d. 20 December 1985, GREENSBORO, Guilford Co. NC.

More About ALMA MAE NELSON:
Burial: 15 July 1989, Cedar Grove Cemetery, New Bern, NC

Notes for HARRY GORDON COUNCIL (LT. COL. US ARMY):
Harry Gordon Council - stationed at Camp Battle in New Bern, N. C. 1942-43. Married in Jan 1943. Was Jump master at Ft. Bragg - year unknown. 1944-45 he was with OSS in Burma. This is a subject he kept to himself and would never talk about his service with OSS. Gail attended OSS Reunion of his DET-101 OSS group in September 27-29, 2001 in Atlanta, Ga and met with two men in photo of dad in Burma. Also received more information (classified but under the freedom of information act) and other photos of dad with these same two men - since they are still living their names will not be revealed.
Having watched a documentary on History Chanel it tells me he had to have been through jump school for OSS. 1945-46 he was Provost Marshall in Bamburg, Germany. Was with 101st Air Borne when they liberated prison camps in Germany, He was at Dachau. He was also at Nuremberg trials. His daughter Gail has possession of his Nuremberg scrapbook, military records from St. Louis and records from CIA and National Archives in College Pk, MD documenting his service during World War II. Some information still classified to protect the families and not available during daughter's lifetime. However, small details given and kept unrevealed in this genealogy.

More About HARRY GORDON COUNCIL (LT. COL. US ARMY):
Burial: 22 December 1985, Greensboro, NC

More About HARRY COUNCIL and ALMA NELSON:
Marriage: 13 January 1943, NEW BERN, CRAVEN CO., NC

v. SARAH ELLEN NELSON, b. 17 June 1918, NEW BERN, CRAVEN CO., NC; m. (1) JAMES ODELL BLEDSOE; b. 23 April 1915; d. 19 August 1962, New Bern, Craven Co., NC; m. (2) EDWARD ELLISON.

vi. EDMOND THOMAS NELSON, b. 29 July 1921, NEW BERN, CRAVEN CO., NC; d. 20 February 1992, GREENVILLE, PITT CO., NC; m. KATHERINE SEWELL, 7 March 1948, Carteret Co. NC; b. 1926, Carteret Co. NC.

More About EDMOND NELSON and KATHERINE SEWELL:
Marriage: 7 March 1948, Carteret Co. NC

27. LELA GRACE[10] LAND (*THOMAS ANN*[9], *JAMES MADISON*[8], *JEREMIAH B.*[7], *JEREMIAH*

B.[6], *EDWARD*[5], *EDWARD*[4], *RENATUS*[3], *FRANCIS*[2], *FRANCIS*[1]*)* **was born 20 February 1895 in PAMLICO CO., NC, and died 2 January 1970 in Volusia Co. Fla... She married SR. EMITT C. WITT. He was born Unknown, and died Unknown.**

Child of **LELA LAND and EMITT WITT is:**

- i. **EMITT CLEVELAND[11] WITT JR., b. 1 May 1917, Washington, DC; d. 19 May.**

28. ROY[10] LAND ***(THOMAS ANN[9], JAMES MADISON[8], JEREMIAH B.[7], JEREMIAH B.[6], EDWARD[5], EDWARD[4], RENATUS[3], FRANCIS[2], FRANCIS[1])*** **was born 29 September 1897 in PAMLICO CO., NC, and died 19 September 1974 in ALEXANDRIA, VA. He married GLADYS BRYANT Unknown in Unknown. She was born in D. C., and died 1939 in Unknown.**

Notes for **ROY LAND:**
buried Land Family Cemetery, Arapahoe, N. C.

More About **ROY LAND and GLADYS BRYANT:**
Marriage: Unknown, Unknown

Child of **ROY LAND and GLADYS BRYANT is:**

- i. **EILEEN MARGARET[11] LAND, b. 1934.**

www.ingramcontent.com/pod-product-compliance
Lightning Source LLC
Chambersburg PA
CBHW080414270326
41929CB00018B/3020
9780788455803